Wissenschaftliche Untersuchungen
zum Neuen Testament · 2. Reihe

Herausgegeben von
Martin Hengel und Otfried Hofius

85

Jesus and His ›Works‹

The Johannine Sayings in Historical Perspective

by

Peter W. Ensor

J.C.B. Mohr (Paul Siebeck) Tübingen

BS
2615.2
.E57
1996

Die Deutsche Bibliothek – CIP-Einheitsaufnahme

Ensor, Peter W.:
Jesus and his 'works': the johannine sayings in historical perspective / by Peter W.
Ensor. – Tübingen : Mohr, 1996
  (Wissenschaftliche Untersuchungen zum Neuen Testament : Reihe 2 ; 85)
  ISBN 3-16-146564-4
NE: Wissenschaftliche Untersuchungen zum Neuen Testament / 02

© 1996 by J.C.B. Mohr (Paul Siebeck), P.O. Box 2040, D-72010 Tübingen.

This book may not be reproduced, in whole or in part, in any form (beyond that permitted by copyright law) without the publisher's written permission. This applies particularly to reproductions, translations, microfilms and storage and processing in electronic systems.

The book was printed by Druck Partner Rübelmann GmbH in Hemsbach on non-aging paper from Papierfabrik Niefern and bound by Buchbinderei Schaumann in Darmstadt. Printed in Germany.

ISSN 0340-9570

Preface

This book first took shape as a PhD thesis submitted to the University of Aberdeen in 1993. The original text is reproduced here with only a few minor modifications.

I would like to take this opportunity to thank all those who have helped me in the production of this book: the Overseas Division of the Methodist Church in Great Britain, the Methodist Church in Kenya, and the Directors of St. Paul's United Theological College, Limuru, Kenya, for releasing me from my teaching duties at the college during the period 1991 to 1993 so that I might engage in doctoral research; the British Academy for providing the funding for this project; Rev. Dr. Ruth B. Edwards of the New Testament Department at Aberdeen for her work of supervision while the thesis was being written; Rev. Prof. I. Howard Marshall, head of the department, for his encouragement and perceptive comments on many points; Prof. Martin Hengel and the publishers for accepting the book for publication; and finally Mr. Andrew Warren of Wolfson College, Cambridge, for kindly agreeing to put the material into the correct camera-ready format required for publication.

It has been fashionable in biblical scholarship in recent years to yield to the current of postmodernism and engage in one of the newer forms of literary criticism of the biblical text. Nevertheless, it is my conviction that the older, historical questions will not go away, but will continue to tease the minds of scholars and ordinary laypeople for a good while to come. The Fourth Gospel provides a particularly challenging ground for such research. Despite the enormous amount of scholarly output on this Gospel over the past century and a half, there are still many important historical issues over which anything like a consensus is disconcertingly absent. The Gospel remains an enigma still.

This book deals with one corner of one issue - the 'works' sayings of Jesus as an aspect of the problem of the relationship between the Johannine presentation of the spoken ministry of Jesus and Jesus' own original speech. If its treatment of that corner is found convincing, and if it succeeds in shedding light on the wider issue, then it will not have been written in vain.

Limuru, September 1995   Peter Ensor

Table of Contents

Preface iii
Abbreviations xi

Chapter 1: Introduction 1

  1.1 The Aim and Plan of the Book 1
  1.2 A Survey of the Literature 2
  1.3 The Authorship of the Fourth Gospel 5
    1.3.1 The Internal Direct Evidence 5
    1.3.2 The Internal Indirect Evidence 10
    1.3.3 The External Evidence 11
    1.3.4 Conclusion 12
  1.4 The Fourth Gospel and the Synoptic Gospels 13
  1.5 The Fourth Gospel and Other Possible Sources 16
  1.6 Development Theories 21
  1.7 Conclusion 25

Chapter 2: The Question of Authenticity 27

  2.1 Introduction 27
  2.2 The Problem of Definition 27
  2.3 A Fresh Approach 32
  2.4 A Modern Analogy 34
    2.4.1 Type a: The Original Speech 34
    2.4.2 Type b: A Close Translation 35
    2.4.3 Type c: Looser Representations 36
      2.4.3.1 Paraphrases 36
      2.4.3.2 Summaries 37
      2.4.3.3 Interpretative Clarifications 37
    2.4.4 Conclusion 38
  2.5 The Burden of Proof 38
  2.6 The Criteria for Authenticity 40
    2.6.1 Introduction 40
    2.6.2 Multiple Attestation 40
    2.6.3 Language, Culture and Personal Idiom 41

2.6.4 Coherence	42
2.6.5 Dissimilarity	43
2.6.6 Anti-Redactional Features	45
2.6.7 Synthesis	45
2.6.8 Summary	46
2.7 Conclusion	47

Chapter 3: Authenticity and the Johannine Sayings ... 48

3.1 The Critical Problem	48
3.2 Some Negative Reactions	49
3.3 A More Positive Assessment	51
3.3.1 Introduction	51
3.3.2 Milieu	51
3.3.3 Points of Contact with the Synoptic Jesus	53
3.3.4 Style	56
3.4 The Critical Problem Again	57
3.5 The Fourth Evangelist's Handling of Old Testament Quotations as a Clue to his Handling of the Sayings of Jesus	58
3.5.1 Introduction	58
3.5.2 Category One	60
3.5.3 Category Two	69
3.5.4 Category Three	77
3.5.5 Conclusions	81
3.6 The Johannine Sayings of Jesus	83

Chapter 4: Jesus and His 'Works' 85

4.1 Introduction	85
4.2 Common Usage	86
4.3 Jewish Usage	87
4.4 Johannine Usage	89
4.5 Coherence with the Synoptic Evidence	91
4.5.1 Linguistic Coherence	91
4.5.2 Idiomatic Coherence	94
4.5.3 Theological Coherence	95
4.6 Conclusion	96

Chapter 5: The Divine Imperative.................. 98

5.1 Introduction	98
5.2 The Context of John 9.3b-4	98
5.2.1 The Johannine Context	98
5.2.2 John 9.1-10.21	100

5.2.3 John 9.1-7	101
5.2.4 John 9.2-5	103
5.3 The Authenticity of John 9.3b-4	108
5.3.1 Introduction	108
5.3.2 The Authenticity of τοῦ πέμψαντός με	108
5.3.3 The Textual Crux	110
5.3.4 General Maxim or Personal Statement?	113
5.3.5 The Authenticity of John 9.4: The Criteria Applied ...	114
5.3.6 The Authenticity of the ἔργα Motif in John 9.3b-4 ...	118
5.4 The Exegesis of John 9.3b-4	122
5.4.1 Introduction	122
5.4.2 John 9.4 as an Independent Saying	123
5.4.3 John 9.3b-4 in its Presumed Historical Context	124
5.4.4 John 9.3b-4 in its Total Johannine Context	125
5.5 The Exegesis of John 9.3b-4 in the Patristic Era	126
5.6 Conclusion	128

Chapter 6: Accomplishing God's Work 130

6.1 Introduction	130
6.2 The Context of John 4.34	130
6.2.1 John 4.1-42	130
6.2.2 John 4.31-34	134
6.3 The Authenticity of John 4.34	135
6.3.1 Introduction	135
6.3.2 The Criteria Applied	137
6.4 The Exegesis of John 4.34	149
6.4.1 Introduction	149
6.4.2 John 4.34 within the Context of John 4.31-34	149
6.4.3 John 4.34 within the Context of John 4.1-42	151
6.4.4 John 4.34 in its Total Johannine Context	152
6.5 The Context of John 17.4	154
6.5.1 John 13-17	154
6.5.2 John 17	155
6.5.3 John 17.1-5	156
6.6 The Authenticity of John 17.4	157
6.7 The Exegesis of John 17.4	159
6.8 The Exegesis of John 4.34 and 17.4 in the Patristic Era	161
6.9 Conclusion	162

Chapter 7: Doing What God Does (A) 164

| 7.1 Introduction .... | 164 |

7.2 The Context of John 5.17 164
   7.2.1 The Johannine Context 164
   7.2.2 John 5.1-9a 165
   7.2.3 John 5.9b-16 166
7.3 The Authenticity of John 5.17 184
7.4 The Exegesis of John 5.17 184
   7.4.1 Introduction 184
   7.4.2 John 5.17 in its Presumed Historical Context 184
   7.4.3 John 5.17 in its Total Johannine Context 191
7.5 The Exegesis of John 5.17 in the Patristic Era 191
7.6 Conclusion 193

Chapter 8: Doing What God Does (B) 195

8.1 Introduction 195
8.2 The Context of John 5.19-20 196
8.3 The Authenticity of John 5.19-20 201
   8.3.1 'Truly, truly, I say to you ...' 201
   8.3.2 '... the Son can do nothing of his own accord ...' 202
      8.3.2.1 The Possible Background to the Saying 202
      8.3.2.2 The Criteria Applied 205
   8.3.3 '... and greater works than these will he show him ...' . 215
8.4 The Exegesis of John 5.19-20 216
   8.4.1 'Truly, truly, I say to you ...' 216
   8.4.2 '... the Son can do nothing of his own accord ...' 217
      8.4.2.1 John 5.19-20a as a Saying of Jesus 217
      8.4.2.2 John 5.19-20a in its Total Johannine Context .. 221
   8.4.3 '... and greater works than these will he show him ...' . 221
8.5 The Exegesis of John 5.19-20 in the Patristic Era 222
8.6 Conclusion 225

Chapter 9: Indicators of Jesus' Identity 227

9.1 Introduction 227
9.2 The Exegesis of the Sayings 227
   9.2.1 John 5.36 227
      9.2.1.1 The Context of John 5.36 227
      9.2.1.2 The Scope of the ἔργα in John 5.36 229
      9.2.1.3 The Exegesis of John 5.36 230
      9.2.1.4 Conclusion 231
   9.2.2 John 10.25, 32, 37f. 232
      9.2.2.1 The Context of John 10.25, 32, 37f. 232
      9.2.2.2 The Scope of the ἔργα in John 10.25, 32, 37f. . 233

    9.2.2.3 The Exegesis of John 10.25............... 234
    9.2.2.4 The Exegesis of John 10.32............... 235
    9.2.2.5 The Exegesis of John 10.37f. 236
    9.2.2.6 Conclusion 238
   9.2.3 John 14.10f. 238
    9.2.3.1 The Context of John 14.10f. 238
    9.2.3.2 The Scope of the ἔργα in John 14.10f...... 239
    9.2.3.3 The Exegesis of John 14.10f. 240
    9.2.3.4 Conclusion 241
   9.2.4 John 15.24 241
    9.2.4.1 The Context of John 15.24 241
    9.2.4.2 The Scope of the ἔργα in John 15.24 242
    9.2.4.3 The Exegesis of John 15.24............. 242
    9.2.4.4 Conclusion 243
   9.2.5 Exegetical Conclusions 244
  9.3 Coherence with the Historical Jesus 245
   9.3.1 Introduction 245
   9.3.2 Matthew 11.2-6 par. Luke 7.18-23 246
   9.3.3 Matthew 11.20-24 par. Luke 10.12-15 251
   9.3.4 Conclusion to the Argument from Coherence 254
  9.4 The Johannine Redaction 256
  9.5 The Exegesis of the Texts in the Patristic Era........... 258
  9.6 Conclusion 261

Chapter 10: General Conclusions 263

  10.1 The Possibility of Finding 'Authentic' Sayings of Jesus in
   the Fourth Gospel 263
  10.2 The Nature of 'Authenticity' 264
  10.3 The Authenticity of the Works-Sayings of Jesus in the
   Fourth Gospel 265
  10.4 The Johannine Presentation of the Works-Sayings of Jesus . 268
  10.5 The Patristic Development of the Johannine Presentation of
   the Works-Sayings of Jesus 270

Appendix A: U.C. von Wahlde's Source Theory 272

Appendix B: Jesus' Claim to 'Do the Works of God' in
 John 10.37f. 278
  1 Introduction..................................... 278
  2 Doing the Works which God Commands................. 279
   2.1 Jewish Literature 279
   2.2 The New Testament 280

  2.3 The Fourth Gospel 281
  2.4 Conclusion 281
 3 Doing the Works which God Does in Imitation of Him 282
  3.1 Jewish Literature 282
  3.2 The New Testament 283
  3.3 The Fourth Gospel 283
  3.4 Conclusion 284
 4 Doing the Works which God Does by Being the Means by which
  He Does them 284
  4.1 Jewish Literature 285
  4.2 The New Testament 285
  4.3 The Fourth Gospel 286
  4.4 Conclusion 288
 5 General Conclusions 289

Bibliography 291
Index of Sources 305
Author Index 331
Subject Index 336

Abbreviations

BD	Blass, F., and Debrunner, A., *A Greek Grammar of the New Testament and Other Early Christian Literature*, ET 1961, CUP.
BJRL	*Bulletin of the John Rylands Library*
BZ	*Biblische Zeitschrift*
CBQ	*Catholic Biblical Quarterly*
CQR	*Church Quarterly Review*
EDNT	Balz, H., and Schneider, G., edd., *Exegetical Dictionary of the New Testament*, ET 1990, Edinburgh, T. & T. Clark.
ET	English Translation
ETL	*Ephemerides Theologicae Lovanienses*
Exp.T.	*Expository Times*
HJ	*Heythrop Journal*
JBL	*Journal of Biblical Literature*
JEH	*Journal of Ecclesiastical History*
JETS	*Journal of the Evangelical Theological Society*
JSNT	*Journal for the Study of the New Testament*
JTS	*Journal of Theological Studies* (n.s. new series)
MSR	*Mélanges de Science Religieuse*
NT	*Novum Testamentum*
NTS	*New Testament Studies*
RechBib	*Recherches Bibliques*
RHPR	*Revue d'Histoire et de Philosophie Religieuses*
RSR	*Recherches de Science Religieuse*
S.-B.	Strack, H.L., and Billerbeck, P., *Kommentar zum Neuen Testament aus Talmud und Midrasch*, 1924, München, C.H. Beck'sche Verlagbuchhandlung
SBL	*Society for Biblical Literature*
SJT	*Scottish Journal of Theology*
TB	*Tyndale Bulletin*
TDNT	Kittel, G., and Friedrich, G., edd., *Theological Dictionary of the New Testament*, ET 1964-1976, Grand Rapids, Eerdmans.
TLZ	*Theologische Literaturzeitung*
TZ	*Theologische Zeitschrift*
ZNW	*Zeitschrift für die Neutestamentliche Wissenschaft*
ZTK	*Zeitschrift für Theologie und Kirche*

Chapter 1

Introduction

1.1 The Aim and Plan of the Book

The aim of this book is to investigate the sayings attributed to Jesus in the Fourth Gospel in which he refers to his 'works', 'work' or 'working'. Within this general area special attention will be given to the linkage these sayings have with the ministry of the historical Jesus, and, to a lesser extent, to their use in the patristic era. This is how the phrase 'historical perspective' in the title of this book is to be understood. There will be no sustained attempt here to try to extract from the Gospel information about the history of the Johannine 'community' from which the Gospel is believed to have emerged, such as has been attempted in recent years by scholars such as J.L. Martyn, R.E. Brown and R.A. Whiteacre.[1] Such an attempt would in any case be very precarious, given the relatively few verses with which this book will be mostly occupied. Rather, an attempt will be made to trace, on the basis of the group of verses specified above, a trajectory of understanding concerning Jesus as a doer of the works of God, stemming from Jesus himself, through the author of the Fourth Gospel, to the writers of the patristic period.

Following a brief survey of the relevant literature available on these sayings, the rest of this chapter will be devoted to some important introductory questions which relate to the Fourth Gospel as a whole. In this part we will deal with the issues of the Gospel's authorship, its relationship with the Synoptic Gospels, its possible sources, and the stages of development through which it may have passed. In the second chapter the question of the 'authenticity' of the recorded sayings of Jesus will be addressed, and a new model will be offered for the understanding of this concept which hopefully will more fully satisfy the data which lies before us in the Gospels. In the third chapter, the particular historical problems associated with the sayings attributed to Jesus in the Fourth Gospel will be addressed, and a case will be made for the possibility of finding 'authentic' material of various kinds among the Johannine sayings, both on the grounds of some general considerations, and more particularly through a

---

[1] J.L. Martyn (1968), R.E. Brown (1979), R.A. Whiteacre (1982).

consideration of the manner in which the author appears to have handled Old Testament quotations in the Gospel.

In chapters 4 to 9 we will take a detailed look at the sayings themselves, examining their possible connection with the original teaching of Jesus, their meaning within the context of the Fourth Gospel, and their use in the patristic era. In these chapters, our attention will be directed to the relatively small group of sayings which speak in terms of Jesus' 'works', 'work' or 'working': Jn.4.34, 5.17, 19f., 36, 9.3f., 10.25, 32, 37f., 14.10f., 15.24, and 17.4. Thus no attempt will be made to give detailed consideration to all the sayings of Jesus and others in the Gospel which refer to 'work' or 'works' of other kinds (as in 3.19-21, 6.27-30, 7.3, 7, 8.39, 41, 14.12), though most of these texts will be mentioned at various points in the book. Rather our plan will be to concentrate mainly on those sayings in which Jesus himself is represented as speaking explicitly about his own activities.

Finally, in chapter 10 we will conclude with a summary of the major findings obtained from the research conducted in the main body of the book.

1.2 A Survey of the Literature

A survey of literature on the issues of the authenticity of the sayings of Jesus in general and the authenticity of the sayings of Jesus in the Fourth Gospel in particular will be incorporated in chapters 2 and 3 respectively, when those subjects will be dealt with. Here, we will look specifically at the literature written in recent years on the use of the 'works' concept in the Fourth Gospel.

The main impression is one of the paucity of the literature available, which is one reason why this book is being written. So far as I am aware, only two major books have appeared specifically on this theme in recent years, those of J. Riedl[2] and F. Grob,[3] written in German and French respectively. Riedl's treatment is exegetically very thorough, but he virtually ignores the question of the possible linkage between the 'works' sayings and the historical Jesus, and his exegesis is open to the criticism of importing post-Nicene understandings into the mind of the author. Grob's treatment is less thorough, contains questionable exegesis in a number of places, and again ignores the question of 'authenticity'. Neither of these authors delves in any kind of formal way into the post-Johannine use of the texts he handles.

---

[2] J. Riedl (1973).
[3] F. Grob (1986).

Apart from these books, and the notes on the relevant verses in the commentaries, there are only articles and passages from larger works to be consulted. Five categories of material may be distinguished:

(1) Firstly, there are the special sections in the commentaries devoted to the subject of 'miracles' or 'signs' or 'signs and works'. C.K. Barrett,[4] R.E. Brown,[5] R. Schnackenburg,[6] and L. Morris[7] have sections of this kind. Since these sections are mostly taken up with a discussion of the word σημεῖον, comparatively little space is devoted to a discussion of the use of the word ἔργον, with the result that these sections are of only limited value as far as our research is concerned.

(2) Secondly, there are sections in books on larger topics. Noteworthy here are the works of W. Wilkens,[8] S. Pancaro,[9] E. Albrecht[10] and R. Heiligenthal.[11] The section in Wilkens' book is again relatively brief, as against the very much larger proportion he devotes to the subject of σημεῖα in the Fourth Gospel, and his Bultmannian understanding of 'works' as another way of referring to 'words' is in any case highly questionable. Pancaro's treatment is angled in certain specific directions, such as the question whether Jesus broke the sabbath commandment or was guilty of blasphemy. A comprehensive analysis of the relevant texts is not attempted, though Pancaro's material on the Jewish background of the phrase 'doing the work (works) of God' is especially useful. Meanwhile Albrecht and Heiligenthal have short sections on some of the relevant texts, but both are concerned about the specific issue of behaviour as a form of 'witness', and both seek to cover the whole of the New Testament in their treatments, so the space they devote to the Fourth Gospel is understandably rather limited.

(3) Thirdly, there are articles in dictionaries and journals on the theme of 'works' or 'signs and works' in the Fourth Gospel. Among the various biblical and theological dictionaries, the article of G. Bertram in *TDNT* on the word ἔργον and its cognates is especially valuable,[12] but, as with all such articles which seek to give an overall picture of the biblical or New Testament view of the word, the amount of space devoted to the Fourth Gospel's distinctive usage is inevitably very brief. Otherwise, the articles of

---

[4] C.K. Barrett (1978[2]) 75-78.
[5] R.E. Brown (1966) 1.525-532.
[6] R. Schnackenburg (ET 1968) 1.515-528.
[7] L. Morris (1971) 684-691.
[8] W. Wilkens (1969) 83-86.
[9] S. Pancaro (1975) 9-22, 54-56, 63-76, 379-402.
[10] E. Albrecht (1977) 133-157.
[11] R. Heiligenthal (1983) 72-92, 135-142.
[12] G. Bertram (1964) *TDNT* 2.635-650.

L. Cerfaux[13] and M. de Jonge[14] are noteworthy, but, as in case of the material noted under (1) and (2) above, the attempt to deal with both the word 'signs' and the word 'works' in one article means that both can only be given a relatively cursory treatment.

(4) Fourthly, there are the articles on specific verses among those to be examined in this book, and on passages in which they appear. Thus, for example, in the former class O. Cullmann[15] and C. Maurer[16] have written on Jn. 5.17, C.H. Dodd[17] on Jn. 5.19f., and A. Vanhoye[18] on Jn. 5.36 and 17.4. In the latter class we have useful articles from J. Giblet,[19] J. Bligh,[20] A.C. Sundberg,[21] J. Bernard,[22] F. Gryglewicz,[23] and L.Th. Witkamp.[24] All these will be referred to in the course of the book. They are clearly helpful in clarifying individual points, but naturally fail to present an overall picture of the 'works' sayings in the Fourth Gospel, which is what will be attempted here.

(5) Finally, the 'works' sayings of the Fourth Gospel are sometimes discussed in connection with different theories concerning the sources the author may have used in the compilation of his Gospel, in view of the fact that the word usually occurs in discourses (always, if 3.19-21 is regarded as part of Jesus' speech), whereas the word 'sign' usually occurs in narrative sections of the Gospel. H.H. Wendt[25] and S. Temple[26] used this phenomenon to argue that the 'works' sayings belonged to a more primitive layer of the Gospel, whereas W. Nicol[27] and U.C. von Wahlde[28] argued that they belonged to a later layer. Both pairs of scholars may be wrong, as we shall see later in this chapter, but in both cases the treatment of the theological significance of these verses is very slight, and the question of ultimate 'authenticity', as opposed to 'a more primitive layer', is barely touched upon, except by Wendt, whose work is now very dated.

---

[13] L. Cerfaux (1958) 131-138.
[14] M. de Jonge (1978) 107-125.
[15] O. Cullmann (1951) 187-191.
[16] C. Maurer (1957) 130-140.
[17] C.H. Dodd (1962) 107-115.
[18] A. Vanhoye (1960) 377-419.
[19] J. Giblet (1955) 49-59, (1965) 17-25.
[20] J. Bligh (1962) 329-346, (1963) 115-134, (1966) 129-144.
[21] A.C. Sundberg (1970) 19-31.
[22] J. Bernard (1977) 13-44, (1979) 3-55.
[23] F. Gryglewicz (1980) 5-17.
[24] L.Th. Witkamp (1985) 19-47.
[25] H.H. Wendt (1902) 60-66.
[26] S. Temple (1975) 44-50.
[27] W. Nicol (1972) 113-123.
[28] U.C. von Wahlde (1989) 36-41, 184-186.

In conclusion, we find a gap in scholarship which this book is designed to fill.[29] Scholars who discuss 'authenticity' questions do not discuss the 'works' sayings of the Fourth Gospel in that connection. Those who discuss the 'works' sayings of the Fourth Gospel do not pay enough attention to their 'authenticity', and none pays any attention to their post-Johannine use in the patristic era. Moreover, this book will advance a new understanding of the whole concept of 'authenticity', and reasons why this understanding is particularly appropriate to the Fourth Gospel. First, however, we must have a brief look at some important introductory questions.

1.3 The Authorship of the Fourth Gospel

As in the case of many issues to do with the Fourth Gospel today, there is no consensus on the question of the identity of its author. Nevertheless, there is a fairly widespread belief that the Gospel was written either by one who had eyewitness experience of the ministry of Jesus or by one who was associated with such an eyewitness. That this position is not only credible but likely may now be shown by a brief summary of the evidence.

1.3.1 The Internal Direct Evidence

There are three verses in the Gospel where some form of eyewitness testimony is claimed:

Firstly, there is Jn. 1.14. Scholars are agreed that the fact that the object of the verb ἐθεασάμεθα here is δόξαν implies that the kind of 'seeing' in mind at least includes a 'seeing' with faith, but does it also include a literal seeing? This issue cannot be decided on the basis of an appeal to the usage of the verb θεῶμαι itself,[30] but the context definitely suggests the latter: the

---

[29] Two further works not mentioned above are those of G. Delling (1966) and H. Schlier (1968, a collection of essays which includes one on 'Le Révélateur et son oeuvre dans l'évangile de Saint Jean'). In both cases, however, the word 'work' used in their titles refers to the entire revealing, saving and judging work of Christ in the Fourth Gospel as a whole and not specifically to those verses in which a word for 'work' occurs. The amount of space devoted to these verses is therefore very small, and once again there is no attempt to link these verses with the historical Jesus.

[30] The secular usage of the verb included both seeing with the eyes and contemplating with the mind (cf. H.G. Liddell and R. Scott (1940[9]) 786), and, while in the New Testament the word seems to be always used in a literal sense (cf. G. Abbott-Smith (1981[3]) 203), we cannot be absolutely sure that the author of the Fourth Gospel is using the verb here in a different sense from those of his other verbs of seeing, e.g. ὁρῶ, βλέπω, and θεωρῶ, which can bear a purely spiritual meaning (cf. R. Bultmann (ET

two previous clauses, both using aorist tenses, refer to the historical event of the incarnation of the Word of God, so the clause which follows them, also using an aorist tense, most naturally refers to the contemporaneous historical event of the seeing of the glory of the incarnate Word of God. Such is also the most natural meaning of the language used in 1 Jn. 1.1-3. To say this, however, does not necessarily mean that the one who penned Jn. 1.14 had himself been an eyewitness (though this remains a possible interpretation), since the plural 'we' may refer to a Johannine community which included those who had participated only vicariously in the original eyewitness experience.[31]

Secondly, there is Jn. 19.35. Most scholars are agreed that the witness referred to here is the same person as the one elsewhere described as 'the disciple whom Jesus loved' (hereafter called the 'beloved disciple' according to current scholarly convention),[32] and that he is also the ἐκεῖνος of this verse, who is said to know that he tells the truth.[33] It is less clear

---

1971) 69). As is commonly recognised, the author is fond of using synonyms and these verbs may provide another example of this phenomenon (cf. C.C. Tarrelli (1946) 175-177).

[31] As R.E. Brown (1982) 160 comments on 1 Jn. 1.1-3. Some scholars believe that Jn. 1.14 implies that the writer includes himself among those who actually saw Jesus in the flesh. So B.F. Westcott (1908) 1.22, J.H. Bernard (1928) 1.21, R.C.H. Lenski (1943) 76f., R.H. Lightfoot (1956) 84f., D. Guthrie (1965) 217, J.Marsh (1968) 109-110, L. Morris (1971) 104, R. Schnackenburg (ET 1980) 1.270, M. Hengel (1989) 63, D.A. Carson (1991) 128. Others doubt this implication. So R. Bultmann (ET 1971) 69-70, W.G. Kümmel (ET 1975) 233, C.H.Dodd (1953 *Interpretation*) 167, C.K.Barrett (1978[2]) 143f., 166, B. Lindars (1972) 95, *TDNT* 5.345, G.R. Beasley-Murray (1987) 14. All are agreed, however, that the writer is associating himself in some sense with the original eyewitness experience.

[32] The only other alternative suggested is the soldier mentioned in 19.34, whom J.R. Michaels (1967) 102-109 identified with the centurion who is referred to in Mk. 15.39 (B. Lindars (1972) 589 also considers this possible). While this is conceivable, it seems less likely in view of the close correspondence in thought between 19.35 and 21.24 where the beloved disciple is definitely in mind. The fact that he is described as taking Jesus' mother to his own home in 19.27 is not an insuperable barrier to this interpretation, since he may have done so after Jesus' death.

[33] R. Bultmann (ET 1971) 679 agrees to this also, though he regards the text as corrupt and believes that it originally ran καὶ ἐκεῖνον οἴδαμεν ὅτι, though he can only claim Nonnos in support. A few commentators have suggested that it may refer to Christ in view of the fact that the same pronoun is used for him elsewhere in the Johannine writings (e.g. Jn. 3.28, 30, 7.11, 9.28, 1 Jn. 2.6, 3.3, 5, 7, 16). So E.C. Hoskyns (1947[2]) 2.638 and R.C.H. Lenski (1943) 1317. But there is nothing in the context of Jn. 19.35 to suggest that this is how the word should be taken here. The most natural understanding is therefore to take it to refer to the witness of Jesus' death. See C.K.Barrett (1978[2]) 557f. for other, even less probable, suggestions.

whether the same person wrote the verse itself,[34] but, whoever its author, the verse claims eyewitness testimony for at least one event in the Gospel's narrative, namely the manner of Jesus' death, and great stress is placed on the belief that this witness is true.

Thirdly, there is Jn. 21.24, where we have the clearest internal indication of all concerning the authorship of the Gospel. The verse states that the 'disciple who is bearing witness to these things' (i.e. the beloved disciple, as 21.20-23 makes clear) also 'wrote these things'. Whatever is meant by 'these things', it is unlikely that they include 21.24 itself, since the verse continues 'and we know that his testimony is true', which is most naturally taken to refer to another person or persons.[35] However it *is* likely that ταῦτα refers to the bulk of the Gospel, rather than to just part or all of ch.21,[36] and while the words ὁ γράψας ταῦτα *may* not necessarily imply that the subject of the verb actually penned the Gospel himself, as the cases

---

[34] Some regard it to be the work of the beloved disciple himself, whom they regard to be the author of virtually the whole Gospel. So B.F. Westcott (1908) liv-lvi, D. Guthrie (1965) 218, L. Morris (1971) 820, D.A. Carson (1991) 625f. Others regard it to be the work of the 'evangelist', i.e. the author of virtually the whole Gospel who is considered to be distinct from the beloved disciple. So J.H.Bernard (1928) 2.649f., C.K. Barrett (1978[2]) 118, G.R. Beasley-Murray (1987) 354. Others again regard it to be the work of a redactor who also added 21.24 and possibly other verses to the Gospel. So R. Bultmann (ET 1971) 678f., B. Lindars (1972) 589, J. Becker (1979) 2.600, R. Schnackenburg (ET 1982) 3.290, F.F. Bruce (1983) 376.

[35] *Pace* e.g. D. Guthrie (1965) 219, L. Morris (1971) 879, D.A. Carson (1991) 684. Scholars differ on exactly who the 'we' might refer to. It could be fellow Johannine disciples (so R.E. Brown (1966) 2.1124, F.F. Bruce (1983) 410), or members of the church in which the Gospel originated (so B. Lindars (1972) 641), or, more specifically, the church at Ephesus (so C.K. Barrett (1978[2]) 588), or the elders of the church at Ephesus (so J.H. Bernard (1928) 2.713, R.C.H. Lenski (1943) 1442), or, more generally, the phrase 'we know' could be the equivalent of saying 'as is well known' (so C.H. Dodd (1953 *JTS*)).

[36] *Pace* C.H. Dodd (1953 *JTS*), who thought it could apply to 21.22, 21.20-22, 21.15-22 or 21.1-22. While this is conceivable, it has been regarded as unacceptable by the vast majority of scholars, e.g. R.E. Brown (1966) 2.1124, L. Morris (1971) 880, B. Lindars (1972) 641, W.G. Kümmel (ET 1975) 236, E. Haenchen (1980) 602, R. Schnackenburg (ET 1982) 3.373, F.F. Bruce (1983) 409, J.A.T. Robinson (1985) 104, G.R. Beasley-Murray (1987) 414f., D.A. Carson (1991) 683. The verse recalls 20.30f. which clearly speaks about the main body of the Gospel (chs. 1-20); the beloved disciple appears in the main body of the Gospel as well as in ch. 21, so if he 'witnessed' and 'wrote' about the events of ch. 21 there is no reason for denying that the same applied to chs. 1-20; and anyway, if the person who wrote 21.24 wanted to inform his readers about the origin of stories contained in ch. 21, would he not have wanted to do the same for the rest of the Gospel? (Considerations from the style of ch. 21 in comparison with that of chs. 1-20 do not help us here. We cannot know for sure whether or not ch. 21 came from the same author as the one who wrote chs. 1-20 on stylistic grounds alone).

of Pilate and his agents (Jn. 19.19, 22) and Paul and Tertius (Rom. 15.15) make clear, the use of this word here is hardly compatible with the view that the actual penman was only remotely connected with the beloved disciple, or never knew him personally.[37] At the very least it would seem that the beloved disciple was the direct source of the testimony recorded in the Gospel and, if, as the present tense of μαρτυρῶν suggests, he was alive at the time of the writing of 21.24,[38] probably gave his 'imprimatur', so to speak, to what had been written.

The identity of the beloved disciple is, of course, a highly controverted question. An examination of the texts in which he appears in the Gospel (13.23-26, 19.26f., 20.2-10, 21.7, and 21.20-23) make unlikely the view that he is a purely symbolic figure.[39] He seems rather to have been a disciple

---

[37] Opinions differ as to how close such a person might have stood to the beloved disciple. For some he would have written at dictation. So J. Marsh (1968) 678, L. Morris (1971) 880, B. Lindars (1972) 641, O. Cullmann (ET 1976) 84, J.A.T. Robinson (1985) 105, D.A. Carson (1991) 685. For others a looser relationship is envisaged. Thus J.H. Bernard (1928) 2.713: the writer 'put into shape' the material he received. G. Schrenk, *TDNT* 1.743, suggests that 'the beloved disciple and his recollections stand behind this Gospel and are the occasion for its writing'. R.E. Brown (1966) 2.1123: the beloved disciple 'was the source of the historical tradition that has come into the gospel'; ibid. 1127: 'he has borne the witness echoed in the written gospel'. R. Schnackenburg (ET 1982) 3.373: the beloved disciple is 'a guarantor of the content of the written work'. G.R. Beasley-Murray (1987) 415: γράψας implies only 'spiritual responsibility'.

[38] J.H. Bernard (1928) 2.713, R.C.H. Lenski (1943) 1440, L. Morris (1971) 880, and J.A.T. Robinson (1985) 104f. believe that the word μαρτυρῶν implies this, whereas B.F. Westcott (1908) lvii, R.E. Brown (1966) 2.1123, R. Bultmann (ET 1971) 717, R. Schnackenburg (ET 1982) 3.372, and R. Kysar (1986) 321 think that the beloved disciple had died. The main argument for the latter view is that 21.20-23 seems to suggest that the beloved disciple had already died, but these verses are equally compatible with the view that he was approaching death or had outlived other contemporaries of Jesus. If this argument is set aside, we are left with the fact that the present participle μαρτυρῶν naturally points towards the supposition that he was still alive. We do not find μαρτυρήσας or μεμαρτυρηκώς here, and if the writer had meant to say that the disciple was witnessing even after his death *through* the written Gospel, why is ὁ μαρτυρῶν περὶ τούτων not placed after ὁ γράψας ταῦτα rather than before? Cf. R.C.H. Lenski (1943) 1440.

[39] E.g. the ideal disciple, or the ideal bearer of the apostolic witness, or of Gentile christianity, or, as in the case of A. Kragerud (1959), of Johannine prophetism. Cf. W.G. Kümmel (ET 1975) 238 n. 187 and the literature cited there. Also R. Schnackenburg (ET 1982) 3.376-380 for a critique of these views. These theories have not gained general consent. The details surrounding this figure are too specific. In particular, as J.J. Gunther (1981) 135 noted, misunderstandings do not normally surround the death of merely symbolic figures, and it is unlikely that the editor(s) would have appealed to the witness of one whom they intended to be understood as an imaginary person. This is not to say that the beloved disciple does not have 'paradigmatic significance', as K. Quast (1989)

who stood in a very close relationship to Jesus. The traditional view, of course, is that he was John the apostle.[40] Other suggestions in recent times have been John Mark,[41] Lazarus,[42] Jude,[43] Nathanael, Matthias, the rich young ruler,[44] and some unknown contemporary disciple of Jesus.[45] No judgment on this question will be offered here. The relevant point for our purposes is that, whoever he was, the beloved disciple was an *eyewitness* of the ministry of Jesus and is said in 21.24 to have 'written' (at least most of) the Gospel.

---

has argued, but it is to say that he is intended to be understood as being as real as any other character who appears in the Gospel's narratives.

[40] Cf. H.P.V. Nunn (1952), D. Guthrie (1965) 216-246, E.K. Lee (1966) 300, L. Morris (1969) ch. 4, S.S. Smalley (1978) 68-82, J.A.T. Robinson (1985) 93-122, J. Painter (1991) 63-73 and D.A. Carson (1991) 68-81, G.M. Burge (1992) 44f. *Themelios* 18.1, 1992, 35 announces a forthcoming book by J. Wenham which will defend this position again. P. Parker's (1962) 35-43 objections to it do not represent the last words on the subject.

[41] This identification is supported by P. Parker (1960) 97-110, G.J. Paul (1965) 25-28, J. Marsh (1968) 24f. L. Johnson (1965-6) 157f. believes that John Mark was the host at the Last Supper (see D. Rogers (1965-6) 214 and L. Johnson (1965-6) 380 for the continuation of the debate). J.K. Thornecroft (1986-7) 135-139 believes that the beloved disciple was the host at the Last Supper and was a priest, but does not identify him with John Mark.

[42] This identification is supported by F.V. Filson (1949) 83-88, J.N. Sanders (1954-5) 29-41, and J.N. Sanders and B.A. Mastin (1968) 31f.

[43] This identification is supported by J.J. Gunther (1981). Gunther regards him as a late believer, hence his late appearance in the Gospel. Being a brother of Jesus he would naturally have been given a special place at the Last Supper (*if* more than the Twelve were present) and would naturally have been entrusted with Mary. Gunther's further proposals that in fact Jude *was* one of the Twelve and should be identified with Judas 'not Iscariot' (14.22) assumes that the Twelve were formed at late stage in Jesus' ministry - an assumption which runs up against Jn. 6.67, 70 as well as the Synoptic evidence.

[44] Cf. D. Guthrie (1965) 223 for these last three names.

[45] Thus, for example, B. Lindars (1972) 34 proposes an unnamed member of the Twelve; O. Cullmann (ET 1976) proposes a Judaean disciple of Jewish heterodox origins; and R.E. Brown (1979), R. Schnackenburg (ET 1982) 3.375-388 - both modifying their previously held view that the beloved disciple was probably to be regarded as John the apostle - E. Haenchen (1980) 603, and G.R. Beasley-Murray (1987) lxxiii propose a more indeterminate unknown disciple of Jesus during the time of his ministry. Mention should also be made of M. Hengel's (1989) distinctive view that the beloved disciple was for the editors John 'the Elder', while for John 'the Elder' himself, who, Hengel believes, was the real author, he was John the apostle. This view, apart from being rather speculative, rests, of course, on the uncertain supposition that Papias spoke about *two* Johns in the well-known passage from his 'Expositions' which Eusebius quotes (*H.E.* 3.39.3f.).

We must remember that this verse was part of the Gospel when it was originally published (?90-100 AD).[46] There is no manuscript evidence for it being a later addition. It is highly likely therefore that whoever wrote it knew the truth of the Gospel's origin. As a consequence what it says must be taken with the utmost seriousness.

1.3.2 The Internal Indirect Evidence

The case for the belief that the Fourth Gospel is substantially the work of an eyewitness of the ministry of Jesus on the basis of internal indirect evidence was classically presented in English-speaking scholarship by B.F. Westcott.[47] Westcott argued strongly that in view of the author's evident acquaintance with the Old Testament, Jewish opinions and observances, the semitic character of his language, his knowledge of Palestinian geography, the vivid detail of his narrative, and his apparent claim to have been within the circle of Jesus' closest followers, he must have been a Palestinian Jew who was an eyewitness of Jesus' ministry and was in fact the apostle John.

While not many today would agree with Westcott's belief in apostolic authorship, many are convinced that eyewitness testimony lies behind the Gospel on the basis of this internal indirect evidence.[48] Others are not so sure. C.K. Barrett, for example, while conceding that 'here and there behind the Johannine narrative there lies eyewitness material',[49] thinks that many of the details may either have come from a source, or have been known by a diaspora Jew, or may have been added at a later stage of the tradition after the manner of the apocryphal Gospels.[50] The first possibility presents no problem, so long as the 'source' in question itself contains eyewitness testimony. The difficulty here is determining what in the Fourth Gospel has

---

[46] This is the date assigned to the Gospel by the vast majority of scholars. For notable exceptions to this consensus, we may mention J.A.T. Robinson (1975) 254-284 and L. Morris (1978) 170-172 who assign it a date before 70 AD.

[47] B.F. Westcott (1908) 1.x-lii, though cf. the equally impressive case presented before Westcott's commentary was published by J.B. Lightfoot in his *Biblical Essays* (1893) 3-44, 125-198.

[48] Cf. e.g. W.C. van Unnik (1964) 61: 'Many things in this Gospel are suggestive of personal reminiscence'; W. Barclay (1956) 1.xx: 'apparently unimportant details ... are inexplicable unless they are the memories of a man who was there'; R.D. Potter (1959) 1.337: 'We have in this Gospel ... the narrative of a reliable witness, a Palestinian Jew'. So one might go on.

[49] C.K. Barrett (1978[2]) 123.

[50] Ibid. 119-123. For a yet more reserved judgement cf. R. Schnackenburg (ET 1980) 1.94: 'From the narrative passages of the gospel itself, no certain arguments can be drawn either for or against the author's being an eye-witness'.

come from a source, as we shall see later. The second possibility also presents no problem, provided it is acknowledged that this diaspora Jew also had a good acquaintance with Palestine. The third possibility, however, goes to the heart of the question: are the 'vivid details' actually to be attributed to an imaginative writer of fiction rather than to an eyewitness? The problem with this suggestion is that when the apocryphal Gospels add spurious details they usually give themselves away as being apocryphal. The Fourth Gospel, by contrast, rings true. Its details are, at least for the most part, natural, credible, coherent, and consistent. The author does not 'give himself away' as a writer of fiction.[51] In short, the argument from the internal indirect evidence may still stand. Along with the direct evidence, it points to an author who was either an eyewitness of Jesus' ministry or in direct touch with such an eyewitness.

1.3.3 The External Evidence

As is well known, by the end of the second century AD the Fourth Gospel was almost universally accepted as being the work of John the apostle.[52] Since it is not part of our purpose here to defend apostolic authorship, there is no need to examine the strength of this tradition, or deal with the objection to apostolic authorship which arises out of the failure of earlier sources to make this particular attribution. Suffice it to say that by the time in question the Gospel had almost unquestioned authority in the early church.

---

[51] Cf. L. Morris (1969) 238-242, who argues against the theory that the Fourth Gospel should be ranked with the apocryphal Gospels. N.B. also the judgment of M. Hengel (ET 1989) 110: the Gospel 'hands down astonishingly accurate geographical, historical and religious details'. It is worth adding that the Gospel lays great emphasis on telling the truth, bearing witness to the truth, knowing the truth and other similar ideas (cf. especially 5.31-33, 7.18, 8.13f., 26, 32, 40, 44-46, 10.41, 14.6, 16.7, 17.17, 19, 18.37, 19.35, 21.24). In view of this emphasis and of the generally high spiritual tone of the Gospel as a whole, we have to ask ourselves the question whether its author could at the same time have deliberately manufactured the kind of detailed information he provides and inserted it into his Gospel just in order to give it the air of verisimilitude.

[52] This tradition is most fully and clearly expressed by Irenaeus, but it also receives support from Polycrates, Theophilus of Antioch, the Muratorian Canon, Clement of Alexandria, the gnostic Ptolemaeus, and the title of the Gospel itself (which, as M. Hengel has argued (1985) 66-84, and (1989) 7, 74-76, may go back to the original manuscript). The only alternative attribution mentioned in antiquity of which we have any knowledge is the attribution to Cerinthus by a group whom Epiphanius calls the 'Alogi', but this attribution is clearly theologically motivated and is not taken seriously by modern scholars.

The only additional point which needs to be made here is that there is also plenty of evidence to suggest that even earlier in the second century christian writers looked upon the Fourth Gospel as a source of authority. For the period c. 150-180 AD, we have evidence from Athenagoras, Tatian, Claudius Apollinaris, the 'Epistola Apostolorum', the Epistle of Diognetus, Melito of Sardis, the Apocryphon of John, Heracleon, and the Martyrdom of Polycarp. For the period of c. 140-150 AD, we have evidence for the existence of the Gospel in Egypt in the form of the Rylands papyrus 457 and of its use in the Egerton papyrus 2, the 'Apology' of Justin Martyr (if it is to be dated during this decade), the Gospel of Thomas, the Gospel of Truth, the Gospel of Peter, the Shepherd of Hermas, and the christian apocalypse 'The Rest of the Words of Baruch'.[53] Can we go back further still? Perhaps so. In Ref. 7.22.4 Hippolytus seems to be quoting the words of Basilides (c. 130 AD?) when he quotes Jn. 1.9.[54] Early second century catacomb paintings in Rome, showing the raising of Lazarus and eucharistic pictures reminiscent of Jn.6, perhaps indicate the influence of the Fourth Gospel in Rome in the early second century AD.[55] And finally M. Hengel reminds us that the longer ending of Mark (c. 110-130 AD?) and some of the variant readings in the Synoptic Gospels seem to show the influence of the Fourth Gospel at a very early stage.[56]

Thus we find the Gospel being gradually but uniformly accepted and used by christian writers throughout the Mediterranean world during the course of the second century. There must have been a very firm belief in its reliability and authority to give such a strong impetus to its spread and use during this period.

1.3.4 Conclusion

The evidence adduced here, and especially that drawn from the internal evidence, has been pointing in one direction, namely towards the likelihood that the Fourth Gospel has its origin in the testimony of one who had first-hand knowledge of the ministry of Jesus. If so, then the likelihood also

---

[53] For the details see J.B. Lightfoot (1893) 45-122, B.F. Westcott (1908) 1.lix-lxvii, J.H. Bernard (1928) 1.lxxi-lxxviii, J.N. Sanders (1943), H.P.V. Nunn (1952), J.J. Gunther (1980) 407-427, M. Hengel (1989) 1-23. These authors do not agree in every particular, and in any case it is difficult always to be sure whether an author is alluding to the Fourth Gospel or merely echoing its language by coincidence, but these uncertainties are not sufficient to overthrow the general point being made here.

[54] D.A. Carson (1991) 24.

[55] L. Morris (1971) 28, quoting the work of H.P.V. Nunn.

[56] M. Hengel (1989) 11.

exists that the Gospel contains 'authentic' traditions concerning Jesus which have no parallel in the Synoptic Gospels,[57] and that where it differs from the Synoptic Gospels we are not for this reason automatically to assume that the Fourth Gospel has got it wrong. It may in fact occasionally provide a fuller and more faithful picture than they. This factor will need to be kept in mind as we pursue our enquiry.

1.4 The Fourth Gospel and the Synoptic Gospels

In this and the next section we will be looking at the question whether the author of the Fourth Gospel may have used any written sources in the compilation of his Gospel. Perhaps one preliminary point should be made before we begin, which concerns the relationship between this question and the conclusions just reached concerned with the authorship of the Gospel: to affirm that the Fourth Gospel rests directly upon the testimony of an eyewitness is not necessarily to preclude the possibility that the author may have used sources in one way or another, even sources not written by eyewitnesses. To use a modern analogy: if someone today wanted to write a paper on the premiership of Edward Heath during the period 1970-4, in addition to personal reminiscences he or she might still want to consult sources of information written even by people who had no personal recollection of the events of that time, but who nevertheless had access to reliable sources. Similarly, the author of the Fourth Gospel, though probably an eyewitness of Jesus' ministry himself or dependent on one such eyewitness, may not have been averse to using sources composed by those who were not eyewitnesses. This is not to say that he did so, but only to say that the question is an open one, and not foreclosed by the view about authorship taken in the previous section.

That said, we can now approach the first question, namely whether the author used one or more of the Synoptic Gospels as a source for his own Gospel.

Ever since the time of Clement of Alexandria[58] it was commonly held that the author of the Fourth Gospel, as the last evangelist, must have known the Synoptic Gospels when he came to write his own. Even during the modern period of critical biblical research up until the earlier part of the present century this was the prevailing assumption.[59] It was P.

---

[57] In the light of this conclusion we may question B. Lindars' (1990) 26 assertion that 'John did not have a private pipeline of authentic tradition'.

[58] In Eus. *H.E.* 6.14.7.

[59] See J. Blinzler (1965) 16-49 for a helpful summary of views on this question in the modern period.

Gardner-Smith more than any other who broke this mould in 1938, in a book which has had an influence in Johannine scholarship out of all proportion to its size.[60] Going through the Gospel in order, Gardner-Smith argued that at point after point the most natural explanation for the divergences between the Fourth Gospel and the Synoptics is that the author did not know the Synoptics. He concluded that the Fourth Gospel could have been written early and should be regarded as an independent authority for the life of Jesus and one whose historical value may be very great indeed.[61]

Gradually the tide turned in favour of Johannine independence. In Britain, C.H. Dodd gave fuller substance to Gardner-Smith's thesis in his book *Historical Tradition in the Fourth Gospel*,[62] while on the continent B. Noack and E. Haenchen led the way in supporting the same position.[63] In the 1960s D.M. Smith was talking about a new 'consensus',[64] and a 'perceptible shift in the tide of critical opinion', and declared that 'the burden of the proof may be said to lie upon the scholar who wishes to maintain that John knew and used' the Synoptic Gospels.[65]

Certainly an impressive array of scholars have fallen into line behind Gardner-Smith's basic thesis,[66] though most acknowledge that there was probably some kind of interaction between the Synoptic and Johannine traditions at the pre-literary stage. More recently, however, a reaction has set in. C.K. Barrett, who had never accepted the idea of Johannine independence in the first place,[67] still maintained, in the second edition of his commentary on the Gospel in 1978, his belief that the author had seen at least the Gospels of Mark and Luke, though Barrett was aware that he was standing against the current of opinion.[68] Others also have recently upheld the traditional position in varying forms. Some, such as J. Blinzler and W. Kümmel, maintain that the author probably knew Mark and Luke but quoted

---

[60] P. Gardner-Smith (1938).
[61] Ibid. ch. 7.
[62] C.H. Dodd (1963).
[63] B. Noack (1954), E. Haenchen (1959).
[64] D.M. Smith (1964) 349.
[65] Ibid. (1963) 58 and 64 respectively.
[66] Including H. Riesenfeld (1957) 28, P. Borgen (1959) 247, A.J.B. Higgins (1960) chs. 1-2, P. Parker (1963) 317-336, R.E. Brown (1966) 1.xliv-xlvii, J.N. Sanders and B.A. Mastin (1968) 12, L. Morris (1969) 15-63, R.T. Fortna (1970) 10, R.P. Martin (1975) 208, S. Temple (1975) 9-14, S.S. Smalley (1978) ch. 1, J. Becker (1979) 1.36-38, R. Schnackenburg (ET 1980) 1.41f., J.A.T. Robinson (1985) 11f., J. Painter (1991) 74-80, and G.M. Burge (1992) 24f.
[67] C.K. Barrett (1955) 34-37.
[68] Idem (1978^2) 42-46.

them from memory.[69] Others, such as F. Neirynck, have argued for a much more thoroughgoing use of the Synoptics on the part of the author,[70] while G. Reim has argued that the author used a fourth 'Synoptic' Gospel, now lost, which was earlier than the other three.[71] All of these scholars have helped to weaken the earlier consensus, though they probably still represent a minority position. Generally speaking, the case for Johannine dependence on one or more of the Synoptic Gospels rests on the instances where there is agreement between them over the order of incidents,[72] the instances of identical wording in parallel passages,[73] and the use of the gospel form as a genre of literature, which is assumed to have begun with Mark.[74] On the other hand, it can be argued that the differences in order and wording between the Fourth Gospel and the Synoptics vastly outweigh the similarities; that the order at some points is inevitable in any case and at other points may rest on connected pieces of oral tradition or even a memory of the events themselves; that the instances of verbal identity do not require *literary* dependence; and that we need not imagine that the gospel genre could not have been 'invented' by two different people working independently on the basis of a common early oral tradition. All in all a strong case may still be made for Johannine independence at a literary level, even though, as noted above, there could well have been some interaction between the Johannine and Synoptic traditions at the pre-literary stage.

One further point may be made. Even proponents of Johannine dependence agree that the author of the Fourth Gospel did not use the Synoptics *in the same way* as Matthew and Luke are thought to have used Mark (according to the most widespread solution to the Synoptic problem). There is so much material in the Fourth Gospel which has no parallel in the Synoptics, and even 'parallel' passages are presented sometimes quite differently. How are we to account for this phenomenon? The most obvious conclusion is that, unless the Fourth Gospel is mostly a work of fiction - a position argued against in the previous section - the author must have had access to, or himself carried, a tradition about Jesus which to a large extent finds no place in the Synoptic Gospels, whether or not he also had access to one or more of the Synoptic Gospels as well. If so, it is just as possible that we may find 'authentic' sayings of Jesus in the Fourth Gospel, unparalleled

---

[69] J. Blinzler (1965) 57-59, W.G. Kümmel (ET 1975) 204.
[70] F. Neirynck (1977 and 1979).
[71] G. Reim (1974).
[72] See especially C.K. Barrett (1978²) 43.
[73] See especially ibid. 44f.
[74] See especially W.G. Kümmel (ET 1975) 204.

in the Synoptic Gospels, as it is that we may find them in the Synoptic Gospels themselves.

1.5 The Fourth Gospel and Other Possible Sources

Throughout the modern period of critical biblical research, numerous attempts have been made to discern sources which the author of the Fourth Gospel may have used other than the Synoptic Gospels.[75] Most now litter the graveyards of Johannine scholarship, succumbing to the fate (to use the words of W. Nicol) of being 'so hypothetical that no one but the critic himself believes it'.[76]

R. Bultmann in a sense summed up one phase of this research in his well-known commentary, in which he proposed an exceedingly complicated theory of three major sources (a signs-source, a discourse-source, and a passion narrative-source) welded together by the evangelist, whose work was then subjected to extensive redaction and re-arrangement.[77] Though Bultmann's view found a few supporters in the immediate aftermath of the publication of his commentary, probably no one gives it unqualified assent today. The major blow was struck through the researches of E. Ruckstuhl,[78] who, building on the work of E. Schweizer,[79] demonstrated that the Fourth Gospel has a greater degree of stylistic unity than Bultmann had allowed for, making it impossible for us to discover any sources the author may have used from the text as we have it today. As R. Kysar comments, under the impact of this blow, no further serious source criticism was undertaken for nearly two decades.[80]

The period 1970-1980 witnessed something of a revival of Johannine source criticism with the emergence of publications by J. Becker, R.T. Fortna, W. Nicol, H.M. Teeple, S. Temple, and R. Schnackenburg.[81] These theories will now be briefly surveyed and evaluated. That of U.C. von

---

[75] See H.M. Teeple (1974) ch. 4 for a helpful summary of these attempts.

[76] W. Nicol (1972) 4.

[77] R. Bultmann (ET 1971). For a detailed analysis of his theory see D.M. Smith (1965).

[78] E. Ruckstuhl (1951).

[79] E. Schweizer (1939) 82-112.

[80] R. Kysar (1975) 16. Cf. R.T. Fortna (1970) 13: 'the stylistic unity of John ... has probably served more than anything to bring about the decline in Johannine source criticism since the time of Bultmann'.

[81] J. Becker (1969/70, 1979), R.T. Fortna (1970), W. Nicol (1972), H.M. Teeple (1974), S. Temple (1975), R. Schnackenburg (ET 1980).

Wahlde,[82] which uses the 'works' terminology as a major criterion in separating out the Gospel's 'signs material' will be given more detailed attention in appendix A at the end of this book.

J. Becker argues for the existence of a signs source, which contained the seven miracle stories recorded in the Gospel plus a few narrative passages. He concedes that the stylistic unity of the Gospel is insufficient to indicate the extent of the source, but believes that its existence is established by aporias such as those in 20.31f. (which does not in his view fit as a conclusion to the present Gospel) and 4.54 (which seems to clash with 2.23 and 4.45) and by its content (presenting Jesus in the colours of a Hellenistic θεῖος ἀνήρ, whose spectacular miracles were recorded in the source to evoke faith). Becker believes that the author used the source in the Gospel but at the same time polemicised against its christology and modified its view of the importance of Jesus' miracles.

R.T. Fortna claims to be able to reconstruct a 'Gospel of Signs', which the author used, with a fair degree of exactness. It is made up of seven miracle stories (Fortna counts in 21.1-14 and regards 6.1-21 as one story), a passion narrative, and a few other narratives, but none of the teaching of Jesus. Fortna's main criterion is the existence of aporias in the Gospel, though he believes that ideological and stylistic criteria can play a supporting role. For him the source emerged from a Jewish-christian milieu and had contact with the Synoptic tradition. Like Becker, Fortna also believes that its christology has been tinged with the θεῖος ἀνήρ concept, which the evangelist sought to correct.

W. Nicol's proposed source is virtually confined to the miracles themselves, with the possible additions of the call of the disciples in 1.35-50 and parts of the Samaritan episode in ch. 4, though he is not confident about the possibility of reconstructing the source in the exact manner of Fortna. His foundational criterion is the form of the miracle stories, which basically follows the Synoptic pattern, but he also accepts a role for style, aporias and ideological tensions. In his view the source did *not* present Jesus in the colours of a θεῖος ἀνήρ, but rather in those of the eschatological messianic prophet of Jewish expectation. It was originally a missionary tract for Jews, but has been turned by the author into a Gospel for the edification of believers in the wake of the Jewish rejection of the gospel.

H.M. Teeple confidently sets forth what he believes to be the solution to the Johannine source problem. Apart from the prologue and chs. 20-1, which he believes had their own special sources, and occasional scribal glosses, four strands can be detected with some precision in the Gospel: S - a signs source; G - a semi-gnostic collection of documents expounding a

---

[82] U.C.von Wahlde (1989).

christian theology of Hellenistic mysticism; E - an editor; and R - a later redactor. Teeple chiefly relies on stylistic criteria, though literary structure, vocabulary and thought content also play a part. Regarding Ruckstuhl's stylistic characteristics as being too general, he feels free to use even the smallest marks of style - e.g. the presence or absence of the definite article with proper names - as signs of separate sources. In this way the whole Gospel is broken up into hundreds of fragments according to their sources.

S. Temple proposes a narrative-discourse source which contains miracle stories, discourses and a passion story and which, he believes, formed the original 'core' of the Gospel. To this source has been added material from at least ten further sources and numerous redactional comments and explanations. Temple relies principally on content criticism, but he also sometimes uses arguments from style and aporias. He believes the 'core' was written by an original Judaean disciple, possibly Nicodemus, and the additions made possibly by John the apostle, who sought to 'heighten' the effect of the original 'core' with his 'embellishments'.

Finally, R. Schnackenburg does not work out an elaborate source theory of his own in his commentary, but rather tentatively accepts the hypothesis of a signs source which contained the miracle stories recorded in the Fourth Gospel, minus what he regards as secondary additions, with possibly 20.30 as the conclusion. Apart from looking for redactional additions to the source, he also uses stylistic and ideological criteria in seeking to define its extent. He believes the source was relatively colourless theologically.

Apart from criticisms which may be levelled against details of the above theories individually,[83] the following general comments are appropriate here as reasons for not accepting any of them too hastily:

a. We must not forget that there is no external evidence for the existence of the kind of sources which are proposed above. None has survived or is quoted or referred to in extant literature. This is not to say that none of them could have existed, but it is to say that the burden of proof lies with those who wish to affirm their existence, not with those who deny it, and the greater the precision with which the proposed source is delineated, the greater the proof required. In the minds of a number of leading Johannine scholars, such proof is lacking.[84]

---

[83] See especially B. Lindars (1971) ch. 2 and D.A. Carson (1978) for particularly incisive criticisms of Fortna's theory, which is perhaps the strongest of those being considered.

[84] See section 1.6 below for alternative views of the literary origin of the Fourth Gospel. C.K. Barrett (1978[2]) 19 has said concerning the availability of a miracle source to the author: 'I see no evidence that proves, or indeed could prove, that it was so, or even that the hypothesis has such a weight of probability as to make it a valuable

b. As can easily be seen from the above survey, the theories proposed differ greatly from each other. The extent of the source varies from Schnackenburg's acceptance of the seven miracle stories themselves (minus redactional additions) and 20.30 to Temple's acceptance of the larger part of the Gospel. There are differences of opinion regarding the right criteria to be used in identifying the source, and the weight which should be attached to each one, and there are differences over the character and purpose of the proposed source. The only agreement seems to be over the existence of a source which included at least some of the material found in the miracle stories in the Gospel as we have it today. It is interesting to note at this point R. Kysar's decreasing optimism concerning the possibility of discovering a lost signs source which the author of the Fourth Gospel may have used. In 1973 he spoke of 'a growing consensus' among the source theorists.[85] In 1975 he had to admit that 'the method of source criticism of the Fourth Gospel is somewhat in shambles'.[86] By 1985, however, he is forced to say that 'none of these theories approaches the status of widespread acceptance ... there are still serious methodological problems eroding the competence of Fourth Gospel source criticism ... nothing like a consensus has emerged from among the source critics themselves'.[87]

c. Certain cautionary remarks need to be made concerning the use of stylistic criteria, on which all but Becker from the above scholars place some reliance. It has to be said that the major impression given by the Gospel is still one of stylistic unity,[88] and that what variety can be detected between passages may be due to the author's own tendency to vary his own style,[89] and to differences between type of material (e.g. story as against discourse) or subject matter.[90] Once all these factors have been taken into account it is highly dubious whether whatever differences remain unaccounted for are of sufficient weight to require the theory of a separate

---

exegetical tool'. R.E. Brown (1989) 147 speaks of 'a strong current movement rejecting a proposed pre-Johannine signs-source or gospel'.

[85] R. Kysar (1973).
[86] Idem (1975) 24.
[87] Idem (1985) 2402.
[88] P. Parker (1956) 304 remarked on this issue: 'It looks as though, if the author of the Fourth Gospel used documentary sources, he wrote them all himself'. E. Ruckstuhl (1977) has re-affirmed his 1951 thesis with only minor modifications in reaction to the attempts of Fortna and Nicol to use stylistic criteria to discern the existence of a signs source behind the Fourth Gospel.
[89] Cf. L. Morris (1969) 293-319, R. Kysar (1974) 310, D.A. Carson (1978) 425.
[90] Cf. H.M. Teeple (1962) 281-283, D.A. Carson (1978) 425f. It is to be regretted that Teeple did not take his own advice seriously enough when he came to write his own book on the literary origin of the Fourth Gospel 12 years later.

source with a separate author. In addition, as E. Ruckstuhl has pointed out,[91] there is a considerable danger of circular reasoning in the application of stylistic criteria. Once a critic has decided in his own mind what counts as marks of a non-Johannine style, the temptation is for him to excise from a passage he thinks is non-Johannine in origin whatever does not fit that style and then to use the same criteria to confirm his results. It is imperative that stylistic criteria be confirmed by other criteria if they are to have any weight.

d. Similarly, cautionary remarks need to be made concerning the use of aporias and differences in content as criteria in separating out a source which the author may have used from its context in the Gospel. It cannot be denied that aporias exist, but at the same time it has to be acknowledged that the use of a source is not the only way to explain them. We have to reckon with the possibility that the author himself composed the Gospel over a period of time and failed for some reason to give it a final editing which would have ironed out some of the poor connections between passages;[92] or that a later redactor made insertions or re-arrangements which disturbed what had previously been a smoothly flowing passage;[93] or that our standards of logical consistency and literary art were not necessarily shared by the original author.[94] It seems that the author himself had a tendency to express truth in a paradoxical way, or to let two complementary truths stand side by side in tension with each other without resolution (as a comparison of 5.31 and 8.14, or 8.15 and 8.16 illustrates), so apparent contradictions do not necessarily need different sources to explain them. Source critics therefore need to consider whether many of the aporias and content differences in the Gospel cannot be explained in one of these ways before they use them as indicators of a source.[95]

---

[91] E. Ruckstuhl (1977) 130f.

[92] Cf. W.F. Howard (1955⁴) 101, J.A.T. Robinson (1985) 18. D.A. Carson (1978) 423 further comments that 'an aporia may develop because of a mental lapse; or because the mind races ahead of the pen; or because of a less than logical step, taken quite unwittingly; or because the writer is disturbed at his work. We should not suppose that first century writers were exempt from such contingencies'.

[93] H.M. Teeple (1962) 281.

[94] B. Lindars (1971) 17 speaks of 'an over-subtle criticism discovering distinctions where none exist'. Cf. H.M. Teeple (1962) 284, W.G. Kümmel (ET 1975) 213, C.K. Barrett (1978²) 19.

[95] C.K. Barrett (1971) 572, reviewing Fortna's book, well sums up the thrust of these last two points when he says that Fortna assumes that 'an author writing independently of sources always presents his material from the same ideological point of view and never attempts to set out both sides of a question or belief, maintains a uniform style to such an extent that he never uses an idiom once only, and never allows a lack of connection or an inconsistency to escape him. The number of authors who satisfy these

Caution is therefore required as we consider the validity of these source theories. The most that can be said at the present stage of scholarship is that the author *may* have used a special written source in writing his account of some or all of the miracle stories in his Gospel, but, if so, its exact extent cannot be certainly delineated. As far as the question of the 'authenticity' of the words of Jesus in the Gospel is concerned, it can of course be argued from an acceptance of some form of source theory that the discourses which are attached to the source material are purely Johannine constructions, or drawn from a source which had nothing to do with the original Jesus tradition.[96] On the other hand, it is equally possible that they contain sayings which are in some sense 'authentic', but which originally belonged in another context within the Jesus tradition, or that the author was using different sources of information (whether written or oral) about the same event and combining them in his own way.

1.6 Development Theories

A different approach to the question of the literary origin of the Fourth Gospel is that which sees the Gospel as we have it today as a product of a long literary process whereby a basic stratum was added to and modified in various ways before reaching its final form. The main difference between these theories and the source theories reviewed above is that whereas the source theories view the literary origin of the Gospel in terms of a 'non-Johannine' source, which the evangelist then took and employed for his purpose, the development theories view the literary origin of the Gospel in terms of a 'Johannine' Gospel which was then supplemented and redacted by either the original evangelist himself or someone else or both.

H.M. Teeple has given a helpful summary of the multitude of theories of this nature from 1839 to 1970.[97] Here we may give a brief survey of four of the main theories which have held the attention of scholars in recent years, together with some evaluative comments. The theories to be surveyed are those of W. Wilkens, R.E. Brown, B. Lindars, and M.-É. Boismard.[98]

W. Wilkens proposes basically a three-stage development in the process of the formation of the Gospel. The first stage, comprised of a 'Grundevangelium', included the signs material and a passion narrative, all

---

conditions is perhaps not large'. Barrett even claims to find an aporia in Fortna's own work, which he does not attribute to the use of a source!

[96] As in the case of R. Bultmann's theory of a gnostic discourse source (ET 1971) 7-9.
[97] H.M. Teeple (1974) ch. 7.
[98] W. Wilkens (1958), R.E. Brown (1966), B. Lindars (1972), M.-É. Boismard and A. Lamouille (1977).

composed by the 'beloved disciple'. At the second stage discourse material was added by the same disciple, depending on his own mind and memory rather than on any written source. At the third stage, the same disciple rearranged the existing Gospel and added further material, including material with a strong passover theme so that the Gospel as a whole took on the form of a passover Gospel. Finally a redactor added the last two verses and a few other passages. Wilkens believes that the Gospel contains some accurate information about Jesus and has an anti-docetic bias in all the three main stages.

R.E. Brown proposes a five-stage development in the evolution of the Gospel. In the first stage there was a body of material consisting of a tradition concerning the words and deeds of Jesus which was independent of the Synoptic tradition. This body of material may have originated with an original disciple of Jesus.[99] In the second stage, this material was developed orally in Johannine ways by more than one person over several decades. The sayings of Jesus were woven into lengthy discourses of a solemn and poetic character. In the third stage, some of this material was organised and put down in writing, probably in Greek, by a disciple of the original disciple whom we may call 'the evangelist'. The basic shape of the Gospel as we now have it thus came into being. In the fourth stage, the evangelist edited his own material and made some additions reflecting the situation of the church at his time, e.g. the material concerning the expulsion of disciples from the synagogue. In the fifth and final stage, a friend or disciple of the evangelist made further alterations and additions after the evangelist's death, using material from the second stage of the Johannine tradition. In this way Brown seeks to account both for the stylistic unity of the Gospel and for the presence of its aporias.

B. Lindars differs from the views of Wilkens and Brown in that he denies any direct link between the evangelist and an original disciple. The evangelist for Lindars was a christian preacher and writer who gathered together Synoptic-like traditions from a wide variety of sources, developed them homiletically in his preaching ministry and then put them thus developed into writing. Further additions were made later in the wake of Jewish persecution in the 90s AD, and still more after the evangelist had passed from the scene. For Lindars, while the Gospel may contain traditional material, it also opens the door to a docetic christology in view of the evangelist's tendency to superimpose on Jesus the apologetic interests of the early church.

---

[99] In his commentary R.E. Brown suggested that this disciple was John the apostle, but in his later book *The Community of the Beloved Disciple* (1979) he suggested that the disciple was the unnamed disciple of 1.35-40 and not John the apostle.

Finally, M.-É. Boismard has proposed what R.E. Brown has called possibly 'the most ambitious literary construction of John ever attempted'.[100] For Boismard, the basic Gospel was written c. 50 AD in Aramaic possibly by the 'beloved disciple' (who was probably John the apostle or Lazarus). It expressed a primitive prophet-like-Moses christology and a futuristic eschatology, and had no pejorative attitude to the Jews or the world. Then c. 60-5 AD a second writer, who was probably John the elder, a Palestinian Jew who also wrote the epistles, added fresh narratives and discourses, carrying with them a Word/ Wisdom chistology, a realised eschatology, and a pejorative attitude to the Jews and the world. Later, c. 95 AD, the same writer, who by now knew all three Synoptic Gospels, changed the order of the first edition of his Gospel, omitted some of it and added fresh material, some with Synoptic affinities, stressing Christ's pre-existence and sonship, the importance of faith based on his words as opposed to his miracles, and the place of the sacraments. Finally, early in the second century, an otherwise unknown Jewish christian of the Johannine school in Ephesus inserted back in the Gospel some material which had been omitted by the second writer in his second edition, made fresh additions and altered the order of chs. 5 and 6. This final redaction stressed the final judgment and modified the anti-Jewish, anti-world tendencies of the second writer.

The overriding impression which a survey of these theories leave is that of their speculative nature. They are ingenious and yet unprovable. They set out a possible scenario for the development of the Gospel to its present form and yet fail to compel assent.[101] Nevertheless they have two points in their

---

[100] R.E. Brown (1978) 624.

[101] Cf. the judgments of: C.K. Barrett (1959) 829 on Wilkens: 'It (his theory) is incapable of verification'; D.M. Smith (1964) 347 on Wilkens: 'One can scarcely believe that an author's successive revisions of his work could be successfully reconstructed in the detail which Wilkens attempts'; R. Kysar (1975) 53 on Brown and Lindars: their theories 'are provocative and imaginative but essentially unprovable ... no amount of analysis of the gospel materials will ever produce convincing grounds for them'; C.K. Barrett (1978²) 25 on Brown: 'The gospel may have passed through as many as five stages of composition, though if this is so it seems to me no longer possible to distinguish them'; R.E. Brown (1978) 627 on Boismard: 'The theory of Johannine composition, like the earlier theory of the Synoptic inter-relationships, is so detailed, so complicated and so idiosyncratic that I suspect it will have little influence ... it cannot be proved wrong, nor can it be proved right'; J. Ashton (1991) 281 on Boismard: (his theory is) 'about as solid as a soap bubble', and ibid. 298 on Brown: (his theory involves) 'a whole ocean of speculation'. One is reminded B.H. Streeter's comment on the 'partition theories' of his day (1924) 377: 'Some of them are so intricate that merely to state is to refute them. For if the sources have undergone anything like the amount of amplification, excision, rearrangement, and adaptation which the theory postulates, then

favour, which would probably command general agreement, and which should be borne in mind in any analysis of the literary origin of the Fourth Gospel:

a. They recognise the likelihood that the Fourth Gospel was edited after it left the original evangelist's hands. Even the most conservative critic is prepared to acknowledge that 21.24, for example, was probably added by a later writer, and if this verse was, other verses may have been added also. The fact of a post-Johannine redaction may be said to have been established even though its precise extent is hard to determine, and has to be argued for verse by verse and passage by passage.

b. They recognise also the likelihood that the same person probably edited, or at least added to, his own material. Few would be so bold as to assert that the evangelist wrote the whole Gospel at one sitting. The likelihood is that he came back to it again and again, making alterations and fresh additions as he went along.[102] Such is the procedure normally adopted in the writing of any work, and such may well account for a large number of the aporias which occur in the Gospel. Source critics tend to jump too quickly from the recognition of an aporia to the supposition of a separate source with a separate author. Development theorists rightly dispute this tendency and at the same time give a more plausible account of the Gospel's unity of style.

As far as the question of the 'authenticity' of Jesus' words in the Fourth Gospel is concerned, there is nothing in the above theories to prevent a belief in the possibility that the Gospel may contain sayings attributed to Jesus which stand in a close relation to what he actually said. Moreover, we are not to imagine that such material must necessary be confined to the first edition of the Gospel only. One point to emerge from the above survey is that some of the critics are prepared to acknowledge that traditional material could have been introduced to the Gospel at the second or a later stage of its formation. Thus Wilkens believes that the discourse material added in the second edition depended on the mind and memory of the 'beloved disciple' himself; Brown believes that the friend or disciple of the evangelist at the fifth stage added in material from the second stage which had been omitted in previous editions; and Boismard believes that Synoptic materials could have been added at the third stage of his proposed scheme and that at the fourth stage early material which had been excised from the third stage was re-inserted. Thus even if a passage can be identified as belonging to a late stage in the process of the Gospel's formation, we are not thereby entitled to regard it as being wholly the creation of the one who inserted it. It may yet

---

the critic's pretence that he can unravel the process is grotesque. As well hope to start with a string of sausages and reconstruct the pig'.

[102] M. Hengel, (1989) 93f. has recently added his weight to this view.

contain traditional material which goes back to the ministry of the historical Jesus.

1.7 Conclusion

In sections 1.3 to 1.6 above we have been looking at four key issues in Johannine scholarship today which impinge on the question of the 'authenticity' of the sayings attributed to Jesus in the Fourth Gospel. Unfortunately, we have discovered that, as D.M. Smith once put it, Johannine scholarship is in these areas 'plagued with a mass of conflicting views'.[103] These views, moreover, partly because of their very variety, invite a guarded agnosticism rather than a confident acceptance. Nevertheless it has been argued that the likelihood exists that the author of the Gospel was either an eyewitness of the ministry of Jesus or a close associate of one such eyewitness; that the author was probably writing independently of the Synoptic Gospels (though the tradition he passes on may have had some contact with the Synoptic tradition at a pre-literary stage), and was probably using traditional material which is not represented in the Synoptic Gospels; that this extra traditional material *may* in part have taken the form of a written document such as the 'signs source' proposed by the scholars mentioned in section 1.5 above, but that if it did the author has so incorporated it into his Gospel that its exact original extent can no longer be definitely recovered; that the author probably worked on the Gospel over a period of time and made his own alterations and additions as he went along, and that the Gospel was subject to further redaction after it had left his hands.

Alongside these tentative results, however, it has also been argued that there is nothing in the theories which have been examined which necessarily damages the case that the Fourth Gospel may contain some sayings of Jesus which stand in a close relation to what he actually said and others which faithfully summarise the general thrust of his teaching. Material which has no parallel in the Synoptic Gospels need not be pure Johannine creation, but may derive from an equally 'authentic' alternative tradition; acceptance of some sort of signs source theory does not entail the elimination from the realm of 'authenticity' of all that does not occur in the source, even if this material may be detached from its original historical context; and belief in a series of editions to the Gospel does not mean that only the first edition need be taken seriously as far as 'authenticity' is concerned, since later additions may also have included early traditions. C.H. Dodd was sometimes

---

[103] D.M. Smith (1964) 348.

criticised for jumping over literary critical questions in order to get to grips with the historical tradition contained in the Fourth Gospel, but in view of what has been said in this introductory chapter his procedure may have been right after all.

Before we proceed further, however, in our evaluation of the 'authenticity' of the 'works' sayings of Jesus in the Fourth Gospel, it will be necessary to study the concept of 'authenticity' itself and the special problems the Fourth Gospel presents to those who would seek for 'authentic' Jesus material within it.

Chapter 2

The Question of Authenticity

2.1 Introduction

It will have been noticed that whenever the words 'authentic' or 'authenticity' were used in chapter 1, they were enclosed in inverted commas. The reason for this is that the words were being used in a rough and ready way without being precisely defined. The time has now come to examine the concept of authenticity in more detail.

We will begin by reviewing the way in which some scholars have been using these terms in recent years, thus illustrating the confusion which presently exists in this area. A fresh approach to the phenomenon of authenticity will then be proposed and illustrated with the help of a modern analogy. Finally, the issues of the burden of proof for authenticity and the criteria for authenticity will be addressed.

The *terminus post quem* for our review of the discussion of these issues will be E. Käsemann's lecture on the problem of the historical Jesus delivered on 20th Oct. 1953,[1] which, in the eyes of many New Testament scholars, re-opened the question of finding 'The Historical Jesus' following the years of radical scepticism concerning the historicity of the gospel records generated by classical form criticism.[2]

2.2 The Problem of Definition

Käsemann himself, in the lecture referred to above, gave no clear idea of what he understood by the word 'authentic', and a surprising number of

---

[1] Published first in *ZTK*, 51, 1954, 125-152, later as ch. 1 in *Essays on New Testament Themes* (1964). In the lecture Käsemann affirmed (1964) 22: 'It can hardly be doubted that the Synoptists intended in all good faith to give their readers authentic tradition about Jesus', and he went on to lay down a basis for discovering authentic material within the Synoptic Tradition.

[2] For a description of the rise of this new quest see J.M. Robinson (1959).

scholars subsequently have similarly found themselves able to write about the subject without actually defining what they mean by the word.[3]

Other scholars who have written on the subject have given simplistic definitions which fail to recognise the complexity of the matter. D.G.A. Calvert, for example, defines 'authentic' simply as 'words which Jesus actually spoke',[4] a definition with which R.N. Longenecker concurs.[5] Neither, however, addresses the question of the original language Jesus was using. Do they assume that Jesus regularly spoke in Greek and that some of his sayings are recorded 'verbatim' in the Gospels? Or should we assume rather, as most New Testament scholars now believe, that Jesus regularly spoke in Aramaic,[6] and that, apart from the rare instances where actual Aramaic words have been transliterated into the text of the Greek Gospels, what we have before us is at best a translation of the words he 'actually spoke'? If this second option is to be followed, then the question arises: what counts as 'authentic' words of Jesus? Are they the closest possible translation in Greek of the original Aramaic words Jesus used, or the original Aramaic words themselves which we are to search for behind the Greek text which we have today? These are questions which Calvert and Longenecker fail to deal with in the articles cited. R. Garrison, by contrast, is an example of a scholar who recognises the relevance of this question,[7] but, having begun by defining authentic words of Jesus as being 'words which Jesus actually spoke', he goes on to redefine them, in the light of the linguistic factor, as 'sayings which faithfully represent the *ipsissima verba Christi*', without apparently recognising that this a quite different definition.

Other scholars similarly give a blanket definition of a vaguer kind which also fails to recognise the complexity of the question. E.P. Sanders, for example, defines an 'authentic' saying as 'one which we have good reason to believe is as close to something that Jesus said as we can hope for'.[8] This leaves the door open, however, to a whole range of types of authenticity,

---

[3] Examples are: N. Perrin (1967) 15-49, M.D. Hooker (1971) 480-487, (1972) 570-581, and M. Borg (1984) 20-25.

[4] D.G.A. Calvert (1971-2) 209-219.

[5] R.N. Longenecker (1975) 217-229.

[6] Cf. G. Dalman (1902) 1-12, B. Fletcher (1967), J. Jeremias (ET 1971) 3-8, J.A. Fitzmyer (1975) 83f. It needs to be borne in mind, of course, that Jesus could probably have spoken Greek as well, as J.N. Sevenster (1968) 25-28, G.R. Selby (1989), and M. Hengel (ET 1989), e.g., have argued, but we may doubt N. Turner's (1965) 183 assertion that 'Biblical Greek ... was the normal language of Jesus in Galilee'. If Aramaic was Jesus' mother-tongue, as it almost certainly was, we may safely assume that he would have normally used it at least when speaking to those for whom Aramaic was their mother-tongue also.

[7] R. Garrison (1979) 17.

[8] E.P. Sanders (1985) 357 n. 30.

and covers anything from the actual Aramaic words Jesus used to the loosest form of interpretative paraphrase. As long as it is 'as close to something that Jesus said as we can hope for' - and in some cases we cannot hope to get very close - then for Sanders it counts as 'authentic'. Another blanket definition of a similar kind is that given by S. Westerholm, who defines 'authentic' as 'a reproduction, at least in essentials, of Jesus' words, and hence reliable evidence for his views'.[9] What counts as the 'essentials' of Jesus' words is left unclear, and once again we have the impression that the author is seeking for an all-embracing formula which will cover a wide variety of phenomena, and that in doing so he tends to blur necessary distinctions.

Other scholars have a more nuanced approach. Quite a few make a distinction between the *ipsissima verba* of Jesus and his *ipsissima vox*.[10] The *ipsissima verba* for these authors apparently mean the original Aramaic words of Jesus, but the phrase *ipsissima vox* has been variously explained. For J. Jeremias it means 'a way of speaking preferred by Jesus',[11] and he gives a number of examples of what he means by this in the first chapter of his book *New Testament Theology*: the use of the 'divine passive', antithetical parallelism, rhythm, alliteration, assonance and paronomasia, the use of parables and riddles, teaching about the Kingdom of God, using 'Amen' at the beginning of authoritative pronouncements and 'Abba' as a form of address to God. Jeremias is not claiming that where these phenomena occur we can be sure that Jesus used these stylistic devices precisely in those contexts, but rather that these were typical ways of speaking that Jesus regularly used in his ministry. It seems that these are the phenomena that J.H. Charlesworth also has in mind when he defines the *ipsissima vox* of Jesus as 'the sound of his own voice'.[12]

C. Blomberg and R.H. Stein, however, have a broader definition of the *ipsissima vox*. For Blomberg the *ipsissima vox* includes 'translations, summaries, paraphrases, and the use of indirect instead of direct speech'.[13] He recognises that these translations may be 'free',[14] and that this kind of authenticity includes the evangelists' 'editorial activity' in 'modifying the exact wording of Jesus' original speech'.[15] Similarly for Stein the *ipsissima*

---

[9] S. Westerholm (1978) 6.
[10] E.g. J. Jeremias (ET 1971) 1-37, R.H. Stein (1980) 229, C. Blomberg (1987) 183, (1990) 79, 166, J.H. Charlesworth (1989) 166, 198.
[11] J. Jeremias (ET 1971) 37.
[12] J.H. Charlesworth (1989) 166.
[13] C. Blomberg (1990) 79.
[14] Ibid. 80.
[15] Ibid. 166.

vox includes words which 'accurately express his intention and meaning'.[16] It will be clear that this kind of 'authenticity' need not reflect the kind of Aramaisms which Jeremias had in mind when he thought of the *ipsissima vox* and can extend to expressions which can be quite distant not only from the actual words Jesus originally used in Aramaic but even from a close Greek translation of those words.

Perhaps because of the breadth of meaning which can be attached to the *ipsissima vox* if so conceived, Charlesworth adds a third type of authenticity, that of the *ipsissimus sensus*.[17] Whereas the *ipsissma vox* for him must carry the 'sound of his own voice', the *ipsissimus sensus* need only carry 'the authentic intention of Jesus',[18] which he elsewhere defines as 'the meaning he poured forth through the words that appeared when he intended to communicate something to someone'.[19] A similar idea is found in a work by P.-G. Müller, in which he speaks of Q as conveying 'höchstens die authentische Sprachintention Jesu ... Sinnidentität mit dem geschichtlichen Sprechen Jesu', which he calls the *ipsissima intentio Jesu*.[20]

Other scholars make further distinctions still. R. Riesner, for example, speaks of a '"substanzieller" Echtheit ... wenn die formale Beständigkeit bei einer Wortüberlieferung ausreichend war, um die von Jesus intendierte inhaltliche Aussage zu bewahren', but he also recognises a category of 'die gedanklich- theologische Übereinstimmung von synoptischen Logienüberlieferungen mit der Verkündigung Jesu'.[21] The difference between the two is that in the former case there is the implication that the saying in question actually goes back to something specific which the earthly Jesus said, whereas in the latter case only a general agreement with his teaching is required. Here, then, we seem to have a further distinction between two types of material to be found in the Gospels, and Riesner assigns the word 'Echtheit' only to the former type. Similarly, R.T. France, while agreeing that the word 'authenticity' can cover a wide variety of phenomena including interpretative paraphrases, nevertheless draws the line at sayings such as Mt.28.19b which may 'represent what was implicit' in

---

[16] R.H. Stein (1980) 229. Cf. also N.J. McEleney (1972) 447 who makes a similar distinction between the '*ipsissima verba* and words substantially his' (i.e. Christ's).

[17] J.H. Charlesworth (1989) 198.

[18] Ibid. N. Anderson is being quoted with approval.

[19] Ibid. 166.

[20] P.-G. Müller (1982) 143f. F. Hahn (1974) 37 n. 67 also uses the phrase '*ipsissima intentio Jesu*', but defines it quite differently as containing 'nicht nur einen "allgemeinen" Eindruck von seinem Verkundigen und Wirken vermitteln, sondern sehr spezielle Eigenarten seines Redens und Handelns hervortreten lassen', a considerably stricter definition than the others we have been considering.

[21] R. Riesner (1988³) 87.

Jesus' teaching, but does not go back in its present form to Jesus.[22] This type of saying France would presumably, on the basis of his own terminology, count as 'credible' (i.e. 'consonant with what we know of the life and teaching of Jesus'), rather than as 'genuine' and therefore 'authentic'.[23] Again, the so-called 'Jesus Seminar' in America regards as 'authentic' both what 'Jesus undoubtedly said' and material probably 'like' what he said, but regards as 'inauthentic' material which only contains 'ideas ... close to his own'.[24]

On the other hand, it would appear that even this type of material can be counted 'authentic' by a scholar such as L. Cerfaux who speaks of three types of authentic sayings: 'les ipsissima verba, puis ce qui est authentique substantiellement, pour la doctrine transmise dans la tradition, et enfin ce qui reste fidèle, dans une adaptation plus accentuée, à l'essence de la révélation du Christ'.[25] The third category here declared as authentic could arguably cover cases like Mt.28.19b even on France's assessment of its historical pedigree. Another example of a scholar who is prepared to use the word 'authentic' to cover sayings which have no direct connection with what the earthly Jesus said is J. Knox. 'If Christ still lives', he writes, 'we have no right to limit his authentic utterances to words actually spoken by human lips in Galilee'.[26]

Finally mention may be made of F.C. Grant's view on the question.[27] He begins by saying that there are two kinds of authenticity: 'historical authenticity, and ... a veracious representation of the Great Event or Creative Idea which fashioned the gospel into ... Christianity', but then he goes on to name five types of 'validity':

   a. veracious, 'tape-recorded' utterances;

   b. sayings which are like a. in style and content;

   c. sayings which represent further extensions or applications of Jesus' utterances in view of new situations and problems faced by the early church;

   d. fresh 'words of the Lord' spoken by inspired prophets in the christian community;

   e. the dramatizations, in liturgy and in homily, of the messages of the exalted Christ, addressed to his church. Clearly, Grant is using the word 'authenticity' in a far more elastic sense here than would be thought admissible by most New Testament scholars today.

---

[22] R.T. France (1976) 131.
[23] Ibid. 101-2 n.
[24] R.W. Funk, B.B. Scott, and J.R. Butts (1988) 21f.
[25] L. Cerfaux (1968) 269.
[26] J. Knox (1953) 52; cf. (1962) 53-56.
[27] F.C. Grant (1954) 137-143.

From the foregoing it is easy to understand why J.M. Robinson speaks of the 'hopeless ambiguity' of the authentic/ inauthentic distinction,[28] and why G. Bornkamm asks whether the terms 'authentic' and 'inauthentic' really suit the material we are seeking to evaluate.[29] At least it is clear that anyone who seeks to use the term in any discussion of the historical or other worth of the sayings attributed to Jesus in the Gospels needs to define his use of the term before he proceeds. This point is particularly relevant to the search for the criteria for authenticity, since if there is a variety of types of authenticity then what may count as a criterion for one type of authenticity may not be a criterion for another.[30]

Having said this, it is now time to set out the understanding of authenticity which will be presupposed in the remainder of this book.

2.3 A Fresh Approach

Three basic types, or levels, of authenticity, may be distinguished, as follows:

Type a: The authenticity of the actual original words of Jesus. The well-worn phrase 'the *ipsissima verba* of Jesus' should strictly be reserved for this type of authenticity. On the assumption that Jesus normally spoke in Aramaic, these words will normally be Aramaic words. In the Gospels there are a number of Aramaic words which have been transliterated into Greek,[31] and in all such cases there is an immediate presumption in favour of the view that these words record the actual words of Jesus. It is highly unlikely that they would have come into the Gospels unless there had been a particularly strong and vivid memory that they had actually been used by Jesus himself and needed to be preserved as such. Apart from these rare cases, and cases where there are good grounds for believing that some words Jesus spoke in Greek have been preserved in the Gospel tradition, the *ipsissima verba* can only be found by postulating possible translations of words of Jesus believed to be especially close to something he said back

---

[28] J.M. Robinson (1959) 99 n. 3.
[29] G. Bornkamm (ET 1973) 21.
[30] Cf. D.L. Bock, for example, who, in an unpublished paper, accuses R.H. Stein of 'failing to distinguish when a criterion authenticates the exact wording of a saying versus only the conceptual thrust of the saying'.
[31] For a full list see J. Jeremias (ET 1971) 4-8. Some of the words he mentions are in fact of Hebrew origin, but in most cases they had been taken over into Aramaic, a common linguistic phenomenon.

into Aramaic. A number of scholars have engaged in this work,[32] but it has to be acknowledged that all such attempts remain tentative.[33]

Type b: The authenticity of close Greek translations of the original words of Jesus. Assuming that Jesus originally normally spoke in Aramaic, and that most of the sayings attributed to him in the Gospels are at best Greek translations of his original words, this type of authenticity stands for those translations which we have good reason to believe stand in a close relationship with something Jesus actually said, and bear the marks of his original style. When authors speak of 'authenticity' without differentiating the different types of authenticity, and apply the standard criteria for authenticity in assessing the authenticity of a particular saying, it seems to be this type of authenticity that they actually have in mind.

Type c: The authenticity of words which convey the general content of the original words of Jesus. The difference between types b and c, as here defined, is that whereas type b requires the reported words of Jesus to retain the style as well as the content of his original words, c requires that they need only reflect their content. This type may include paraphrases and summaries of Jesus' sayings, and even elaborations whereby what is implicit in Jesus' teaching is made explicit, so long as they are consonant with the meaning of his original words. Clearly, this is a very loose category, but needs to be recognised as one form in which the teaching of the historical Jesus has been reliably preserved, as will be argued in this book in the case of some of his Johannine sayings.

Two further points may be made at this stage:

Firstly, we need to recognise that the boundaries between these types of authenticity are not hard and fast, but rather that they merge into one another. The distinction between types a and b disappears altogether, of course, in the case of Greek words which have been preserved in the Gospels and which can be reliably attributed to Jesus (if there are such), and the distinction between types b and c is blurred in view of the fact that all translation necessarily involves a certain amount of creative interpretation. It is virtually impossible for any translation to be 100% exact, since words in one language rarely carry exactly the same range of connotations as even their closest counterparts in another, so the difference between types b and c is one of degree rather than one of kind, and there are clearly a multitude of intermediary steps or gradations between the two.

---

[32] Cf. e.g. G. Dalman (ET 1902), C.F. Burney (1925), M. Black (1946).

[33] See especially the articles by J.A. Fitzmyer (1975) 73-102 and M.O. Wise (1992), who stress how little we know of the precise form of Aramaic which Jesus spoke. It is difficult to be sure, therefore, as to the correctness of any attempted retroversions of Greek sayings in the Gospels into Jesus' Aramaic.

Secondly, we need to remember that the authors of the Gospels, along with other authors of their period, did not seem to have quite such a strong sense of the difference between direct speech and indirect speech as we have today. This is suggested by the facts that:

a. No punctuation marks were used, as far as we know, in the original manuscripts of the Gospels.

b. The Greek word ὅτι could be used to introduce *either* direct *or* indirect speech, which occasionally opens up the possibility of ambiguity. And

c. If the earliest surviving manuscripts are any guide, uncial script was consistently used in their writings, which eliminates one common way of distinguishing between direct and indirect speech.

The upshot of these considerations is that it is quite possible that the Gospel writers felt free to attribute to Jesus in direct speech rough representations of his original teaching which we today would more naturally express by means of indirect speech, as well as words which stood in a closer relationship with what he actually said. In other words, they themselves would have regarded types b and c, as defined above, as merging into one another, and would not have been greatly concerned with the difference between them. This possible flexibility in handling the Jesus tradition must be borne in mind as we approach the Gospel material.

This understanding of the nature of authenticity will now be clarified further through the use of a modern analogy.

2.4 A Modern Analogy

In this section we will take a small passage from the writings of J. Jeremias in German, and then give various reports of what he said in English. This will illustrate the various types of authenticity mentioned above. Jeremias' German in the analogy will correspond with Jesus' Aramaic and will therefore stand for type a authenticity, and the English reports will correspond with the reports of Jesus' words which we find in our Greek New Testaments and will therefore stand for authenticity of types b and c.

In what follows the English reports of Jeremias' words will be given in the form of direct speech, following what appears to be the convention of the New Testament writers, even though we might hesitate to do so in some cases if we were to follow the modern convention.

2.4.1 Type a: The Original Speech

The passage chosen runs as follows:

'Die Bergpredigt ist also nicht, das ist unser bisheriges Ergebnis, die Wiedergabe einer zusammenhängenden Predigt Jesu, so wenig wie die Gleichnisrede Mt. 13, sondern ist eine Sammlung von Jesusworten. Zu welchem Zweck wurde diese Sammlung veranstaltet? Wie kam man darauf? Hier ist es hilfreich, wenn wir uns an ein Resultat der Arbeiten des bekannten englischen Neutestamentlers C.H. Dodd erinnern, der die grundliegende Beobachtung gemacht hat, dass es in der ältesten Zeit überall in der Christenheit eine zweifache Form der Predigt gegeben hat, nämlich Verkündigung und Lehre, Kerygma und Didache. Diese beiden Begriffe werden unglücklicherweise ständig durcheinandergeworfen, obwohl jeder von ihnen, jedenfalls nach paulinischem Sprachgebrauch, etwas ganz Verschiedenes bezeichnet'.[34]

These are Jeremias' actual words in German. All that follows will be my words in English which will be seen to stand in differing relationships with this German text.

2.4.2 Type b: A Close Translation

Consider the following:

Jeremias says: 'Our conclusion so far is that the Sermon on the Mount is not the report of a continuous sermon of Jesus, any more than the series of parables in Mt. 13, but is a collection of sayings of Jesus. For what purpose was this collection organised? How was it arrived at? Here it is helpful if we remind ourselves of a result of the work of the well-known English New Testament scholar C.H. Dodd, who has made the basic observation that in the earliest period everywhere in christendom there was a twofold type of sermon, namely preaching and teaching, Kerygma and Didache. These two concepts are unfortunately constantly confused, although each of them, at any rate according to Pauline linguistic usage, is quite differently characterised'.

This is an attempt to translate Jeremias' words, as closely as possible, into good idiomatic English. It will be noticed that the German grammatical structure has not been slavishly followed in every instance. A more literal translation *could* be made, but only at the cost of spoiling a natural English style. Even at this point, however, it is worth making the obvious point that there is no *one* 'correct' translation, but many possible translations, all of which might be 'correct' in their own way. Similarly, when Jesus' Aramaic words were translated into Greek, we may safely assume that they were translated in different ways, yet many of the different translations may still

---

[34] The passage is taken from J. Jeremias (1966) 180-181.

have been 'correct' in their own way, even as close translations of what was originally said.

Another possible variation at this level is the inclusion of some of the original German words in the English translation. For example, instead of saying 'New Testament scholar' I might have kept the simpler German word 'Neutestamentler', putting it in inverted commas, as often happens to the German phrase 'Sitz im Leben' whenever it is found in a German text which is being translated into English (and even when it is not). The same phenomenon occurs in Jeremias' own text above in the case of the words 'Kerygma' and 'Didache', where original Greek words have been preserved through transliteration in his German text. As is well known, the phenomenon occurs also in the New Testament, where some of Jesus' original Aramaic words (such as 'Amen' and 'Abba') have found their way into the Greek reports of his speech. As mentioned above, when this happens we may be fairly sure that we have moved from a type b authenticity to type a, i.e. that we are actually hearing Jesus' original words.

2.4.3 Type c: Looser Representations

Under this heading we may consider three general categories: paraphrases, summaries (which may themselves closely reflect the original text or be more paraphrastic in nature), and interpretative clarifications.

2.4.3.1 Paraphrases
Consider the following rendering of Jeremias' text:

Jeremias says: 'If the foregoing argument can be accepted, we are not to imagine that Mt. 5-7 or Mt. 13 give straightforward accounts of what Jesus said on any one particular occasion, but we are rather to think of them as collections of utterances originally made on different occasions. We can best understand why and how this came about if we consider the point made by the English New Testament scholar C.H. Dodd when he distinguished between the preaching and teaching activities of the early church. People often mix them up, but they are in fact quite distinct, as Paul's way of using these words makes clear'.

It will be noticed that very few of the words used in this translation were used in the first translation given above. It is written in a slightly less formal style, sits more loosely to the text, and for the most part gives a 'dynamic equivalent', rather than a direct translation, of Jeremias' original words. Nevertheless, it still conveys accurately what Jeremias wanted to say. It remains faithful to his thought, even if it departs somewhat from his mode of expression. It may still be called an 'authentic' representation of the content of his thought as given in the text.

In addition, it is obvious that there is no hard and fast distinction between what we have called a 'direct translation' and a 'paraphrase'. There is a whole spectrum of possibilities in between, a 'sliding scale' of possible translations which may stand at a greater or lesser distance from the original text, and correspondingly give it a stricter or looser rendering.

2.4.3.2 Summaries
Consider the following summary of Jeremias' words:

Jeremias says: 'The Sermon on the Mount is a collection of sayings of Jesus which can best be understood when we remember C.H. Dodd's observation that in the earliest period in christendom there was a twofold type of sermon, namely preaching and teaching'.

What we have here is basically a shortened form of the direct translation given above under section 2.4.2. It mostly uses the words of the direct translation and accurately sums up the message of the passage. Once again there is a 'sliding scale' between full translations and the shortest of possible summaries, and we must remember that there can still be accurate, reliable, 'authentic' short summaries of very long passages.

Now let us consider the following summary:

Jeremias says: 'Mt. 5-7 and 13 should be regarded as collections of utterances originally made on different occasions. The origin of these chapters is best understood if we consider C.H. Dodd's distinction between the preaching and teaching activities of the early church.'

The difference between this summary and the previous one is that the previous one was based on the direct translation given above in section 2.4.2, whereas this one is based on the paraphrase given in section 2.4.3.1. Being a summary of a paraphrase, it is fairly distant in wording from the full, direct translation, but it still presents a reasonably accurate representation of the thrust of the original German passage. Such loose summaries may also be expected to exist in the Gospels.

We have now considered two possible types of variation from a close translation of words from one language into another, both of which may operate together as well as singly, thus producing a multitude of possibilities. We now consider a third type of variation, which increases yet further the complexity of the matter.

2.4.3.3 Interpretative Clarifications
This third type of variation from a close translation consists of loose representations in which an element of imaginative or creative interpretation enters in. Once again there is a 'sliding scale' of possibilities, since, as has

already been mentioned, even 'direct' translations involve an element of interpretation, however small. Here, however, the element becomes more pronounced, as the following example will make clear:

Jeremias says: 'The Sermon on the Mount is a collection of sayings of Jesus which can best be understood when we remember C.H. Dodd's observation that in the earliest period of christendom there was a twofold type of sermon, namely preaching and teaching. By determining which category the Sermon falls into, we shall understand better the processes which led to its present form.'

The first sentence is the same as the summary of the direct translation given in section 2.4.3.2, though, for the purpose of the point being made here, the full translation itself could equally well have been given. The interest here is in the second sentence, which does not correspond directly with anything in the original passage, but rather draws out one of its implications. In the light of the question concerning the purpose and origin of the present form of the Sermon on the Mount, and C.H. Dodd's distinction between preaching and teaching, the above presentation of Jeremias' words states explicitly what is implicit in the passage. This kind of explanatory elaboration cannot be regarded as 'authentic' in a strictly verbal sense, but it may yet accurately state the underlying implications of the passage and so authentically express the author's intended meaning. We need to be open to the possibility of material of this kind being present in the Gospels also.

2.4.4 Conclusion

The purpose of this section has been purely to illustrate at a theoretical level the variety of ways in which a person's speech can be represented at second hand, especially when that speech crosses a linguistic frontier. Whether these different types of representation in their manifold variety actually occur in any of the sayings attributed to Jesus in the Gospels, and in particular in the Fourth Gospel, has yet to be demonstrated, but at least the different types themselves have by now been adequately clarified.

2.5 The Burden of Proof

What has been said above about the various types of authenticity has relevance for the recent debate concerning the question of assigning the burden of proof for authenticity or inauthenticity. Are we to assume that the sayings of Jesus recorded in the Gospels are basically 'authentic' and require those who deny it to prove their case? Or are we, on the other hand, to assume that the sayings of Jesus are basically 'inauthentic' and require those who affirm their 'authenticity' to prove their case? The heirs of R. Bultmann and of the radical scepticism associated with classical form criticism have tended to hold the latter assumption,[35] while an increasing number of more conservative scholars have argued the former case.[36] Others again have tried to maintain a mediating position.[37] Yet the arguments become a little sterile when there is no prior clarity concerning the nature of the authenticity presupposed. Those who place the burden of proof on those who wish to deny the authenticity of the sayings of Jesus in the Gospels tend to operate with a fairly loose definition of authenticity, whereas those who place the burden of proof on those who wish to affirm their authenticity tend to operate with a fairly strict definition. To some extent, then, they are talking about different things.

To go into a detailed critique of the positions adopted by the early form critics which led to such scepticism towards the historicity of the gospel traditions would take us too far from the main subject of this book.[38] Suffice it to say for now that a strong case can be made for a kind of basic historicity which would at least give a strong presumption in favour of the authenticity of the sayings of Jesus in sense c as defined above, though even here we need to look for corroboration as will be explained in the next section. To say that a saying is authentic in sense b, however, or that an attempted reconstruction of Jesus' Aramaic words actually represents his *ipsissima verba*, does seem to require further evidence. In the light of the general character of the Gospels, with all their variety and evidence of redactional activity, we would be rash to assume that any one particular saying attributed to Jesus is a direct translation of something he actually said

---

[35] For R. Bultmann's position cf. (ET 1958) 14: 'I do indeed think that we can now know almost nothing concerning the life and personality of Jesus'. For the others cf. E. Käsemann (ET 1964) 34, 37, J.M. Robinson (1959) 38 n. 1, N. Perrin (1967) 39, E.P. Sanders (1985) 13.

[36] E.g. H.E.W. Turner (1963), J. Jeremias (ET 1971) 37, N.J. McEleney (1972) 447, R.T. France (1976) 107, I.H. Marshall (1977) 199, R. Latourelle (1978) 239, R.H. Stein (1980) 225-8, C. Blomberg (1987) 240-246, R. Riesner (1988³) 85.

[37] Cf. F.G. Downing (1968) 55, the articles of M.D. Hooker as in n. 3 above, B. Meyer (1979) 81-87, all of whom argue that the burden of proof lies on both sides, i.e. on anyone who wants to make an affirmation one way or the other. H.K. McArthur (1970-1) 116-119 argues that the burden of proof rests with those who claim the authenticity of any saying unless 3 or 4 separate sources contain it, in which case the burden of proof shifts on to the other side. This suggestion does not, however, seem to have won much support from other scholars.

[38] See, however, A.S. Dunstone (1964) 57-64 for a spirited riposte to this kind of scepticism.

unless we have good grounds for so believing. It is at this point that the criteria for authenticity come into play.

2.6 The Criteria for Authenticity

2.6.1 Introduction

Discussion of the criteria for authenticity in the period under review began with Käsemann himself and others of the same radical critical school. Since for them the sayings attributed to Jesus in the Gospels were 'inauthentic' until proved 'authentic', only those sayings which passed the various critical tests could be regarded as authentic.

They were followed by more conservative critics, for whom the sayings attributed to Jesus in the Gospels were 'authentic' (once all perceptible secondary redactional accretions had been removed) until proved 'inauthentic'. For them, therefore, the criteria were used more positively to confirm the 'authenticity' of sayings which were already regarded as 'authentic' on more general grounds, and the negative use of the criteria was eschewed.

In view of what has been said so far in this chapter, however, a third way is possible. We may start from a neutral position regarding whether a particular saying shares in one of the stricter types of authenticity and see the criteria, when they can be applied, as pointing towards the authenticity of Jesus' sayings in one of those senses of the term (once all perceptible secondary redactional accretions have been removed). At the same time we may be open to the possibility that certain sayings, which do not fare well under these tests, may yet possess a looser, type c, type of authenticity. How they may be judged to share in this degree of authenticity will emerge as we look at the criteria themselves.

2.6.2 Multiple Attestation

This criterion, which is regarded as important by a large number of scholars,[39] actually comes in two forms. Firstly, it is said that when a saying

---

[39] R.H. Fuller (1966) 97-98, N. Perrin (1967) 45-47, H.K. McArthur (1969) ch. 15, (1970-1) 116-119, M.D. Hooker as in n. 3, D.G.A. Calvert (1971-2) 209-219, R.S. Barbour (1972) 3f., C.L. Mitton (1975) 80-83, R.N. Longenecker (1975) 219ff., R.T. France (1976) 108ff., D. Catchpole (1977) 176, I.H. Marshall (1977) 203f., R. Latourelle (1978) 221-223, D.L. Mealand (1978) 42, B. Meyer (1979) 87, R.H. Stein (1980)

is found in a number of different and independent sources (e.g. Mark, Q, M, L, and John, depending on one's source-critical position), then the case for its 'authenticity' is thereby strengthened.[40] Secondly, it is said that when a saying is found in a number of different form-critical classifications (e.g. parables, pronouncement stories, or collections of unattached sayings) then again the likelihood of its 'authenticity' is thereby increased. Most scholars speak warmly in favour of this criterion. The verdict of McArthur is typical when he says that this is 'the most objective of the proposed criteria and one which will undoubtedly have a permanent place in the task of Gospel research'.[41]

Nevertheless, a few cautionary notes have been sounded. To begin with, we are reminded[42] that the usefulness of this criterion is limited by the fact that the Synoptic problem has not yet been finally resolved. No one theory commands universal consent, and it is not always clear from which source a saying may have come. A second cautionary note is that the criterion, in both its forms, can only take us back to an earlier stage in the transmission of the traditions about Jesus, without necessarily taking us back all the way to Jesus himself.[43] Thirdly we are reminded not to use the criterion negatively, i.e. to exclude from the realm of authenticity what only appears in one source or form-critical classification. It is perfectly possible for a tradition to be genuine even if it occurs only once in our present Gospels.[44]

2.6.3 Language, Culture and Personal Idiom

This criterion is also used by many scholars.[45] If a saying includes Aramaic words or can be easily and naturally translated back into Aramaic, the

---

229-233, R. Riesner (1988³) 87-89, M. Borg (1984) 24, E.P. Sanders (1985) 17, C. Blomberg (1987) 247, B. Witherington (1990) 28.

[40] R.H. Stein (1980) 231 makes the additional point that even when the same saying has been copied from one Gospel to another, the copier is thereby affirming and corroborating the authenticity of what he is copying.

[41] H.K. McArthur (1969) 140. Cf. also E. Trocmé (ET 1973) 34-39 who was generally sceptical about the possibility of retrieving certainly authentic individual sayings from the Gospels, but who placed great store by the multiple attestation of Gospel motifs which gave a stable, consistent and reliable portrait of the historical Jesus.

[42] E.g. by D.G.A. Calvert, I.H. Marshall and R.H. Stein.

[43] A point made, e.g., by R.H. Fuller, N. Perrin, H.K. McArthur, and I.H. Marshall.

[44] A point made by H.K. McArthur, M.D. Hooker, D.G.A. Calvert, D. Catchpole, I.H. Marshall, R.H. Stein, and R. Riesner.

[45] Cf. R.H. Fuller (1966) 97, F.G. Downing (1968) ch. 5, N. Perrin (1970) 71, M.D. Hooker as in n. 3, D.G.A. Calvert (1971-2), J. Jeremias (ET 1971) ch. 1, N.J. McEleney (1972) 438-440, 444f., R.S. Barbour (1972) 4, W.G. Kümmel (1974) 26, R.N.

likelihood of its authenticity in some sense is increased. The same is true when a saying reflects Jesus' Palestinian environment, the kind of social, domestic, agricultural and religious customs prevalent at his time, and when a saying contains marks of Jesus' personal style such as those mentioned above under Jeremias' description of Jesus' *ipsissima vox*.

This criterion has its limitations. We need to bear in mind that a semitic style and evidence of a Palestinian background may only take us back to the early Aramaic-speaking christian community rather than to Jesus himself.[46] The semitisms may simply bear witness to the fact that, at the time when the tradition of Jesus' sayings was being translated into Greek, it was being translated by people who thought semitically or who were under the influence of Septuagintal Greek.[47] On the other hand, the criterion cannot categorically be used negatively either in view of the way in which Hellenism had permeated Palestine in the three centuries preceding the time of Christ, bringing many foreign customs in its wake,[48] and in view of the fact that an original saying of Jesus may have lost its semitic colouring in the course of being translated and transmitted in the church. Finally we need to be reminded that Jesus himself may have spoken in Greek from time to time.[49]

Despite these reservations, this criterion may yet be of some help in strengthening an argument that a saying shares in a strict form of authenticity.

2.6.4 Coherence

This is another criterion accepted by a large number of scholars.[50] By means of it, material is judged authentic if it coheres well, or hangs well together, with other material which is judged to be authentic on other grounds.

Longenecker (1975) 220ff., R.T. France (1976) 109ff., D. Catchpole (1977) 173f., S. Westerholm (1978) 6, R. Latourelle (1978) 232-234, D.L. Mealand (1978) 41f., B. Meyer (1979) 86f., R.H. Stein (1980) 233-238, M. Borg (1984) 24, C. Blomberg (1987) 247, R. Riesner (1988³) 92-94, B. Witherington (1990) 28.

[46] A point made, e.g., by R.H. Fuller, N. Perrin, M.D. Hooker, D.G.A. Calvert, D. Catchpole, D.L. Mealand, and R.H. Stein.

[47] R.H. Stein (1980) 235.

[48] As amply documented by M. Hengel (ET 1974 and ET 1989) *passim*.

[49] See n. 6 above. H.K. McArthur, M.D. Hooker, D.G.A. Calvert, D. Catchpole, I.H. Marshall, R.H. Stein and R. Riesner warn against the negative use of this criterion.

[50] Cf. R.H. Fuller (1966) 98, N. Perrin (1967) 43-45, F.G. Downing (1968) 117, M.D. Hooker as in n. 3, D.G.A. Calvert (1971-2), N.J. McEleney (1972) 443f., R.S. Barbour (1972) 9ff., C.L. Mitton (1975) 85f., R.N. Longenecker (1975) 221ff., R.T. France (1976) 108ff., D. Catchpole (1977) 176, I.H. Marshall (1977) 204f., S. Westerholm

One problem with this criterion is that the concept of coherence itself is not clearly defined. It can range in the minds of those who use it anywhere from the idea of consistency, i.e. non-contradictoriness, to that of identity of content, which are quite distinct concepts. The degree to which this criterion is useful, therefore, depends in part on the stringency with which the term is used.

Another obvious criticism of this criterion is that since it is made dependent on other criteria, any mistakes made through the operation of those criteria will inevitably be magnified through the operation of this one.[51]

Further, it is a blunt instrument if we are looking for material which shares in a strict form of authenticity, since two sayings may cohere perfectly well together in terms of their content and yet be couched in a different style. It is in fact much more suitable for discovering material which shares in what has been described above as type c authenticity.

A final cautionary comment concerns the negative use of the criterion. We need to bear in mind the possibility that on occasion Jesus may have used paradox, irony, and hyperbole, and may have said apparently contradictory things in different circumstances which yet have an inner consistency.[52] Nevertheless, of all the criteria, this probably has the strongest negative use, since it may be used to pinpoint what may be regarded as anachronistic or incongruous in sayings attributed to Jesus.

2.6.5 Dissimilarity

E. Käsemann expressed his estimate of this criterion as follows: 'In only one case do we have more or less safe ground under our feet; when there are no grounds either for deriving a tradition from Judaism or for ascribing it to primitive Christianity ...'[53] This criterion has been much discussed since and has, on the whole, found acceptance with other scholars, though often with major qualifications.[54]

(1978) 7, R. Latourelle (1978) 226-229, D.L. Mealand (1978) 42, 44, R.H. Stein (1980) 249-251, A.E. Harvey (1982) 8, M. Borg (1984) 24, C. Blomberg (1987) 247, R. Riesner (1988³) 92, B. Witherington (1990) 28.

[51] This point is made, e.g., by M.D. Hooker, R.S. Barbour, and I.H. Marshall.

[52] Cf. the comments of F.G. Downing, M.D. Hooker, D.G.A. Calvert, R.S. Barbour, D. Catchpole, S. Westerholm, D.L. Mealand, R.H. Stein, and R. Riesner.

[53] E. Käsemann (ET 1964) 37.

[54] E.g. R.H.Fuller (1966) 94-97, N. Perrin (1967) 39-43, F.G. Downing (1968) 111-116, M.D. Hooker articles as in n. 3 above, D.G.A. Calvert (1971-2), R.T. France (1971) 18-22, (1976) 108ff., J. Jeremias (ET 1971) 2, R.S. Barbour (1972) 5-13, C.L. Mitton (1973) 84f., W.G. Kümmel (1974) 26, R. Longenecker (1975) 221-225, D.

One of the main problems with the criterion is that it assumes that we know enough about the Judaism of Jesus' day and about early christianity to enable us to use the criterion with confidence.[55] Since our knowledge is in fact so limited, we can never be sure that a particular tradition could not have come either from Judaism or from early christianity, and any conclusion runs the risk of falsification on the discovery of new evidence (e.g. from Qumran). M.D. Hooker adds the point that even supposing our knowledge were much greater than it is, we would not be able to prove that a particular saying had not been created by the early church and then no longer used, i.e. even the church could have created 'dissimilar' sayings.

A further major criticism is that this criterion at best can reveal only what was idiosyncratic about Jesus rather than what was characteristic of him.[56] It will reveal what distinguished Jesus from his environment and the ideas of his contemporaries, but not what he had in common with them. Used alone, it is bound to produce a distorted picture of him, since he is bound to have shared in many of the basic beliefs both of his Jewish contemporaries and of his later followers.

This leads to a third major criticism. Käsemann and others[57] used the criterion negatively, to exclude material which did not conform to it from the realm of authenticity. The majority of scholars have, however, rightly objected to this procedure, because of the 'overlap' which must have existed between Jesus and his contemporaries. Room must therefore be given for other criteria to uncover other authentic material which fails to pass this particular test.

The criterion of dissimilarity, therefore, should not be used negatively, but, with all due regard to our present relative ignorance, it can be quite powerful when used positively, especially in pinpointing material which may be credibly attributed to Jesus, which is both un-Jewish and at the same time unlikely to have been created by the early church.

Catchpole (1977) 174-176, I.H. Marshall (1977) 201-203, S. Westerholm (1978) 6, R. Latourelle (1978) 223-226, D.L. Mealand (1978) 41-50, B. Meyer (1979) 81-87, R.H. Stein (1980) 240-245, A.E. Harvey (1982) 8, M. Borg (1984) 20-24, E.P. Sanders (1985) 16f., C. Blomberg (1987) 247f., R. Riesner (1988³) 89-91, B. Witherington (1990) 28.

[55] This objection is raised by F.G. Downing, M.D. Hooker, D.G.A. Calvert, R.S. Barbour, I.H. Marshall, S. Westerholm, R.H. Stein, A.E. Harvey and M. Borg. D.L. Mealand argues that it should not be overstressed.

[56] This point is made by F.G. Downing, M.D. Hooker, R.T. France, D. Catchpole, I.H. Marshall, D.L. Mealand, R.H. Stein, A.E. Harvey, and M. Borg.

[57] E.g. R.H. Fuller, N. Perrin, and W.G. Kümmel.

2.6.6 Anti-Redactional Features

This criterion can be seen as a further refinement of the criterion of dissimilarity. Scholars who have advocated it draw attention to those elements in the Gospels which seem to stand in some contrast or tension with the purposes the Evangelists seem to have had when they wrote their Gospels.[58] These features seem to be present in the Gospels not because of the Evangelists' own creative activity but simply because they were in the Evangelists' sources.

This criterion has also met with some criticism. M.D. Hooker, for example, has argued that it can only take us back to an early stage in the transmission of the Gospel traditions, not necessarily to Jesus himself, and that, in any case, we do not know enough about the purposes of the Evangelists to be sure that purportedly 'anti-redactional' material is in fact anti-redactional.[59] Others[60] have made the by now familiar point that the criterion is not to be used negatively. What is, as far as we can tell, in accord with the Evangelists' particular purposes may also be authentic material, and even where they seem to have modified their sources, they may have done so under the influence of other reliable sources which are hidden from us today.

Given these caveats, this criterion is still of some use in adding strength to an argument in favour of the authenticity of a particular saying.

2.6.7 Synthesis

It may have been noticed that the above proposed criteria for authenticity seem to some extent to work against each other. Thus the first three criteria require that authentic sayings of Jesus should be seen to emerge naturally from their background and to belong to that background - the background of Palestinian Jewish culture, of Jesus' ministry, and of the Gospels themselves. The last two criteria by contrast require that authentic sayings should be seen to stand out *against* their background, or to stand in tension with it, by being 'dissimilar' from the Jewish culture from which Jesus came and from the thinking of his early followers, and by standing in tension with the purposes of the Evangelists. This observation, however, need not lead us to abandon either the one group of criteria or the other. A

---

[58] C.F.D. Moule (1967) 61-76, O. Cullmann (ET 1967) 189, D.G.A. Calvert (1971-2), C.L. Mitton (1975) 83f., R.N. Longenecker (1975) 225-229, I.H. Marshall (1977) 205-207, S. Westerholm (1978) 10f., R.H. Stein (198) 247f., R. Riesner (1988³) 91-94.

[59] M.D. Hooker (1972).

[60] E.g. O. Cullmann, S. Westerholm, R.H. Stein and R. Riesner.

synthesis may be found by recognising that whereas the first group on its own can only give a fairly weak support for an argument for authenticity of a strict kind, the second group in combination with the first can give very strong support indeed for such an argument.

Another analogy might help to clarify this point. Consider the following two statements which were once made by John Wesley, the founder of the Methodist Church, in the 18th century:

(1) 'Jesus died for me'; and
(2) 'I look upon the world as my parish'.

The first is not in any way out of the ordinary in Wesley's context and could have been said by thousands of people in his day. If the words did not come from his own pen but were merely attributed to him at second hand, we could well believe that the report that he had said them was true, but could equally well suspect that someone merely thought that he had said them simply because they are the kind of words a preacher of the gospel in the 18th century might have been expected to say. The second sentence, by contrast, is extraordinary and could only have been said sincerely by very few people in exceptional circumstances. It stands out against the background of Wesley's time, and even the normal content of his preaching and writing. Yet because it is at the same time credible on Wesley's lips and fits in plausibly with what we know of his career, if we did not know that he said these words but only heard them attributed to him at second hand, we would still have a strong inclination to accept them as his in view of their striking and memorable character.

2.6.8 Summary

It should be stressed that the criteria we have been looking at have been developed primarily with a view to uncovering sayings which stand in a close relationship with what Jesus originally said, i.e. sayings which have been described above as having a type b authenticity. To claim that a word or group of words are the *ipsissima verba* of Jesus, thus sharing in a 'type a' authenticity, one would have to argue additionally that a transliterated Aramaic word in the Greek Gospels, or an attempted retroversion of a saying from Greek into Aramaic, or a Greek word or words in the Gospels actually were words which the historical Jesus uttered.

As far as type c authenticity is concerned, all that is required is that a saying should be shown to cohere well, in the sense of sharing the same content, but not necessarily the same form or style, with material which can be said to possess a stricter type of authenticity. Summaries, paraphrases and elaborations may well be couched in the style of the Evangelist rather than that of Jesus himself, but it is quite possible for them nevertheless to express accurately, though in a modified form, the original content of Jesus' teaching, and an application of the criterion of coherence, taken in this strict sense, can demonstrate this to be the case.

2.7 Conclusion

This chapter has deliberately avoided mentioning the Fourth Gospel, because the intention has been to clarify some basic ideas as a necessary preliminary to approaching the text itself.

We began by indicating the ambiguous way in which the terms 'authentic' and 'authenticity' have been used in recent scholarship, and suggested that clarity on this issue is necessary before meaningful discussion can take place. We went on to propose three types or levels of authenticity: that of the actual words of Jesus; that of a close translation of his original words; and that of a loose representation of his original words whether in the form of a summary, a paraphrase or an interpretative clarification in which what is implicit in the original saying is made explicit. It was moreover stressed that there are no hard and fast boundaries between these types of authenticity, but rather a spectrum of possibilities, or a multitude of intermediary steps, between them, and that the various forms of looser representations can be used either singly or in different combinations, thus increasing still further the range of possible ways of reporting Jesus' original speech.

It was then suggested that we cannot simply assume that the sayings attributed to Jesus in the Gospels share in one of the first two types of authenticity. This has to be argued for on the basis of the use of the criteria for authenticity which have been developed in recent years as part of the new quests for the historical Jesus. Nevertheless, we are justified in making an initial presumption in favour of the view that the Gospels contain within themselves a roughly reliable guide to Jesus' original teaching, and confirmation that sayings attributed to him at least loosely represent his original thought may be sought by comparing their content with sayings which may reliably be assigned a stricter type of authenticity.

Having said this, we may now approach the Fourth Gospel itself and see what particular problems it presents to those who search for Jesus' teaching in it, and how those problems may best be understood.

Chapter 3

Authenticity and the Johannine Sayings

3.1 The Critical Problem

Even a cursory glance at Jesus' reported words in the Gospels reveals a decisive difference between the way he speaks in the Synoptic Gospels on the one hand and the way he speaks in the Fourth Gospel on the other. This difference manifests itself in various ways, such as the following:

(1) Vocabulary. Words commonly used by Jesus in the Fourth Gospel do not appear frequently, if at all, on the lips of Jesus in the Synoptic Gospels e.g. eternal life, light, darkness, love, truth, know, work, world, judge, abide, send, witness, believe in.

(2) Grammatical usages. There is a frequent use of parataxis and asyndeton. Certain usages occur regularly in the Greek, e.g. ἐκεῖνος used substantively, ἐμός rather than μου, ἀπ' ἐμαυτοῦ, ἐκ in place of the partitive genitive, ἵνα used epexegetically, and so on.[1] All these usages contribute to what is regarded as the distinctive Johannine style.

(3) Literary form. In the Synoptics, Jesus tends to use short, pithy sayings and parables. In the Fourth Gospel he engages in lengthy disputes and dialogues. As R.T. Fortna puts it, the 'poetry seems to float from heaven, giving an unearthly quality to the entire Gospel. Even when Jesus is ostensibly engaged in dialogue, he speaks with that same sonority, drowning out his interlocutors, confounding them with double meanings'.[2]

(4) Literary devices. Certain features regularly occur, e.g. the use of subsidiary characters as foils for Jesus' teaching, the use of their misunderstandings to further the conversation, the use of chiasm, and of a 'spiral' technique whereby basic points are repeated as stepping stones to a further development of a topic, leading up to a climax.[3]

(5) Theological emphases. It is a well known fact that in the Fourth Gospel Jesus speaks more explicitly of the present anticipation of future salvation and judgment than he does in the Synoptics, that he speaks more

---

[1] C.K. Barrett (1978²) 7f. The author's general style is reflected in Jesus' speech at these points.
[2] R.T. Fortna (1988) 2.
[3] Cf. S.S. Smalley (1978) 197-199.

in terms of a cosmic (above-below) than of a temporal (now-then) dualism, and that he seems more free to speak openly about himself than he does in the Synoptics, as the seven great 'I am ...' affirmations and other similar sayings illustrate.[4] For E. Käsemann, the author, in a quasi-docetic manner, 'changes the Galilean teacher into the God who goes about on earth'.[5]

This difference between the way in which Jesus speaks in the Synoptic Gospels and the way he speaks in the Fourth Gospel cannot be explained satisfactorily merely by saying that he was speaking to different kinds of people. It has been argued, for example, that in the Synoptics Jesus is speaking to the common people of Galilee whereas in the Fourth Gospel he speaks to the educated élite in Jerusalem.[6] This view founders on the discourse in ch. 6 where Jesus speaks in the same vein as elsewhere in the synagogue at Capernaum. Presumably the people in the synagogue were not totally other than the people Jesus was accustomed to speak to in the open air in Galilee, such as those he had fed in the story recorded in 6.1-14.

Another suggestion has been that the style of Jesus' speech in the Fourth Gospel was the style he used in private with his disciples, whereas the Synoptics tend rather to record Jesus' public preaching.[7] While there may be some truth in this suggestion, as will be affirmed later, it cannot serve as an all-embracing solution to the critical problem. The Fourth Gospel includes some of Jesus' public teaching as well as his private teaching to his disciples (e.g. in ch. 5), and likewise the Synoptics include private teaching as well as public (e.g. in Mt. 10), yet the style remains the same as for the rest of the teaching of Jesus in these Gospels. So the critical problem remains.

3.2 Some Negative Reactions

It is not surprising, in view of the above evidence, that a number of scholars have come to a fairly negative view of the historical trustworthiness of Jesus' words in the Fourth Gospel. In a survey of over a century of Gospel research, A. Schweitzer in his well-known book *The Quest of the Historical Jesus* stated the conclusion of many when he wrote: 'What matters for the historical study of the Life of Jesus is simply that the Fourth Gospel should be ruled out ... The speeches ... are unhistorical, and need not be taken into account in describing Jesus' system of thought'.[8] This kind of judgment has

---

[4] Cf. G.E. Ladd (1974) 216, C. Blomberg (1987) 154.
[5] E. Käsemann (1966) 27.
[6] D. Guthrie (1965) 266.
[7] C. Blomberg (1987) 184f.
[8] A. Schweitzer (ET 1954^3) 127.

been echoed by a string of scholars during the 20th century. R. Bultmann, for example, who believed that a gnostic source lay behind the discourses, was similarly dismissive: 'The Gospel of John cannot be taken into account at all as a source for the teaching of Jesus'.[9] For E. Käsemann the Fourth Gospel is 'completely unhistorical'.[10] For J. Ashton 'John has no interest in the historical Jesus as such ...'.[11] For A.T. Hanson 'those who believe in the Jesus of the Fourth Gospel as an actual account of the historical Jesus are putting their faith in a legendary figure'.[12] While for P.M. Casey the material in the Fourth Gospel is not only unhistorical but also represents a 'misleading' and 'deceptive' development in the story of the evolving christology of the early church.[13]

Even those who are prepared to see nuggets of 'authentic' material embedded within the Johannine reports of Jesus' speech still tend to assign the majority of the discourse material to the evangelist's creative activity. Thus, for example, J. Jeremias believed that 'The discourses of Jesus in the gospel of John ... to a considerable degree ... are homilies on sayings of Jesus composed in the first person'.[14] Similarly for B. Lindars the discourses in the Fourth Gospel function like speeches in a play, whereby the author expresses a considered understanding of the function and meaning of the characters.[15] Apart from individual sayings which the author has picked up from the Jesus tradition and has used as starting points for some of the discourses, 'the discourses must be the free composition of the evangelist, because they are concerned with aspects of christology which were simply not an issue previously'.[16] Similarly also for J.D.G. Dunn, 'the Johannine discourses are meditations or sermons on individual sayings or episodes from Jesus' life, but elaborated in the language and theology of subsequent Christian reflection'.[17] Even here, therefore, H. Strathmann's comment remains largely acceptable: 'the discourses uttered by the Johannine Christ are discourses of John about Christ'.[18]

Very often alongside such negative views of the historicity of the Johannine sayings material there has been a tendency to believe that the evangelist was decisively influenced by streams of thought in the Hellenistic

---

[9] R. Bultmann (ET 1935) 12.
[10] E. Käsemann (ET 1964) 60.
[11] J. Ashton (1991) 550; cf. 432, 514.
[12] A.T. Hanson (1991) 366f.; cf. 2f., 363f.
[13] P.M. Casey (1991) 20, 178.
[14] J. Jeremias (1971) 2; cf. idem (1967) 108.
[15] B. Lindars (1990) ch. 1.; cf. idem (1971, 1972, 1977, 1981 twice).
[16] B. Lindars (1990) 95.
[17] J.D.G. Dunn (1989^2) 30.
[18] Quoted with approval by R. Schnackenburg (ET 1980) 214; cf. 22.

world which have been regarded as alien to the kind of thought-world inhabited by the historical Jesus. Thus, there has been considerable effort to trace similarities of thought and expression between the Fourth Gospel on the one hand and various philosophies and religious movements known to have existed in the ancient world on the other, such as Platonism, Stoicism, the Mystery Religions, the Hermetic Literature, Gnosticism, the Mandean religion, and the kind of Hellenistic Judaism associated with Philo.[19] Obviously, the extent to which the author of the Fourth Gospel has been influenced by forces which were probably not operating in Jesus' own environment to any great degree will match the extent to which his account of Jesus' teaching must deviate from what was originally said.

3.3 A More Positive Assessment

3.3.1 Introduction

Part of the aim of this book is to argue that the kind of negative attitude towards the 'authenticity' of the Johannine sayings of Jesus which has just been presented is too extreme and categorical. In the first chapter it was argued that there is nothing in a plausible assessment of the authorship, sources and development of the Fourth Gospel to prevent us from believing that it may well contain sayings of Jesus which are in some sense 'authentic'. This argument will now be furthered by some general considerations concerning the Gospel's milieu, portrait of Jesus compared with that of the Synoptic Gospels, and style. Then a new model will be offered for understanding the 'authenticity' of the Johannine sayings on the basis of the author's use of Old Testament quotations, which will also take up the argument of chapter 2 and demonstrate its applicability to the Johannine material. Then we shall be ready to take a detailed look at the 'works' sayings in particular.

3.3.2 Milieu

We begin with the last argument presented in section 3.2 above. Is the Jesus of the Fourth Gospel authentically Jewish, or does he appear, so to speak, in an alien Greek dress? Several comments are relevant here:

---

[19] For a good summary see S. Smalley (1978) 41-59.

a. It is commonly recognised now that R. Bultmann[20] and C.H. Dodd[21] went too far in seeing a decisive influence on the author of the Fourth Gospel being exercised by the ideas contained in the Mandean literature and the Hermetic literature respectively. Both sets of literature post-date the Fourth Gospel (the Mandean literature is dated at c. 700 AD, and the Hermetic literature 2nd.- 4th. centuries AD), and the influence of the ideas they contain cannot be shown to go back into the 1st. century AD. Likewise the existence of a pre-christian form of gnosticism is now seriously in doubt,[22] though the basic ingredients which later went into gnosticism were probably already circulating in the 1st. century AD.

b. It is also commonly recognised now that it is wrong to regard 1st. century AD Palestine as a purely Jewish island in a Hellenistic sea.[23] Even to ask the question 'Is the Johannine Christ Jewish or Greek?' presents to some extent a false dichotomy, since even before the advent of Alexander the Great in Palestine in 333 BC, and much more afterwards, Hellenism was steadily infiltrating Jewish society. It has already been pointed out in chapter 2 that Jesus could well have spoken Greek as well as Aramaic,[24] and for the same reasons he may well have been influenced by other forms of Greek culture. We cannot simply assume that something cannot have been spoken by Jesus just because it bears a Hellenistic stamp.

c. As both C.K. Barrett[25] and D.A. Carson[26] have pointed out, the kind of language used by the Fourth Evangelist and by Jesus in the Fourth Gospel is in fact to a large extent of universal appeal and can be found in almost every religion. Words such as light, darkness, life, death, spirit, word, love, believing, water, bread, clean, birth, children of God are common religious words and we are not necessarily to search for the origin of their appearance in the Fourth Gospel outside the Palestinian milieu of Jesus himself.

d. The discovery of the Dead Sea Scrolls at Qumran made a big difference to the way the Fourth Gospel was viewed. Here was evidence for a Jewish sectarian group living in Palestine in the years before the destruction of the Temple and apparently using some very Johannine language in their religious writings. Particularly notable was their strong light-darkness dualism and their use of words such as truth, water and spirit,

---

[20] R. Bultmann (ET 1971). Cf. also the work of S. Schulz (1960) who leans heavily in Bultmann's direction in this area.
[21] C.H. Dodd (1953).
[22] See especially the work of E.M. Sidebottom (1961) and E. Yamauchi (1973).
[23] See especially M. Hengel (ET 1974 and ET 1989).
[24] See ch. 2 n. 6.
[25] C.K. Barrett (1975) 5.
[26] D.A. Carson (1991) 59.

all of which resembled Johannine usage at some points.[27] It is therefore not surprising that, in the light of these parallels and those between the Fourth Gospel and the Old Testament and rabbinic Judaism, a large number of scholars have come round to the opinion that the principal background for Johannine thought is the Palestinian Judaism of Jesus' time,[28] a view strengthened by the evangelist's evident understanding of Palestinian topography, ideas and traditions,[29] and the semitic character of his language.[30]

3.3.3 Points of Contact with the Synoptic Jesus

It was argued in chapter 1 that the Fourth Gospel was written probably in independence from the Synoptic Gospels. Here the point needs to be made that, despite this probable independence, there are yet considerable points of agreement between them and that the differences mentioned in section 3.1 above need to be counterbalanced by a consideration of their similarities.

C. Blomberg has helpfully gathered some of the evidence for sayings of Jesus in the Synoptics and the Fourth Gospel which bear a remarkable similarity with each other:

'One must be born again (or become like a little child) to enter the kingdom of God (Jn. 3.3; Mk. 10.15 pars.). An abundant harvest awaits the labourers (Jn. 4.35; Mt. 9.37-38 par.). A prophet is without honour in his homeland (Jn. 4.44; Mk. 6.4 pars.). Judgement of unbelievers will be according to their works (Jn. 5.29; Mt. 25.46) ... Jesus identifies himself metaphorically with the good shepherd who seeks to rescue the errant members of his flock (Jn. 10.1-16; Mt. 18.12-14; Lk. 15.3-7). True discipleship means servanthood as illustrated in the Last Supper (Jn. 13.4-5, 12-17; Lk. 22.24-27). Jesus faces and resists the temptation to abandon the way of the cross (Jn. 12.27; Mk. 14.35-36 pars.). Receiving Jesus means receiving the one who sent him (Jn. 12.44-45; Mk. 9.37; Mt. 10.40; Lk. 10.16). The disciple is not greater than his master (Jn. 13.16; Mt. 10.24;

---

[27] Cf. R.E. Brown (1966) xliii, lxii-lxiv, J.H. Charlesworth (1972), G.E. Ladd (1974) 219.

[28] E.g. A.J.B. Higgins (1960), D. Guthrie (1965), E.K. Lee (1966), R.E. Brown (1966), G. Delling (1966), A.M. Hunter (1968), G.E. Ladd (1974), S. Temple (1975), O. Cullmann (ET 1976), L. Morris (1978), S.S. Smalley (1978), D.M. Smith (1984), J.A.T. Robinson (1985), M. Hengel (ET 1989), J. Painter (1991), D.A. Carson (1991), G.M. Burge (1992).

[29] Cf. S.S. Smalley (1978) 34-38, 59f. and M. Hengel (ET 1989) 110: the Gospel 'hands down astonishingly accurate geographical, historical and religious details'.

[30] C.F. Burney (1922) and R.A. Martin (1989) have even argued that the Gospel was translated from an Aramaic document. While this goes too far for most scholars, the semitic character of the Gospel's language is undeniable, and strongly suggests either that the author is thinking in Aramaic as he writes in Greek, or that he is drawing on Aramaic sources.

Lk. 6.40). The Holy Spirit will tell the apostles what to say in the future (Jn. 14.26; 15.26; Mk. 13.11; Mt. 10.19-20 par.). The disciples will be expelled from the synagogues (Jn. 16.1-4; Mk. 13.9; Mt. 10.17-18 par.), scattered throughout various parts of the world (Jn. 16.32; Mk. 14.27 pars.), and given the authority to retain or forgive the sins of their brothers (Jn. 20.23; Mt. 18.18)'.[31]

So one might go on. In the Fourth Gospel, as in the Synoptics, Jesus has a fondness for metaphors and figurative or proverbial comparisons, even if narrative parables are missing. In the Fourth Gospel, as in the Synoptics, people marvel at the authority with which Jesus speaks. In the Fourth Gospel, as in the Synoptics, Jesus is misunderstood, as a result of which Jesus gives further teaching.[32] In the Fourth Gospel, as in the Synoptics, Jesus uses Old Testament quotations in his arguments, calls himself 'the Son of Man', addresses God as 'Father', and prefaces some of his sayings with the formula 'Truly, I say unto you' (though whereas in the Synoptics there is always only one 'Truly', in the Fourth Gospel it is always doubled). There are good grounds for believing that all the above features were marks of the ministry of the historical Jesus, and the arguments used for this position in relation to the Synoptic Gospels also hold good, of course, for the Fourth Gospel as well. As Higgins remarks, 'Perhaps ... the gap between Jesus' words in John and in the synoptics is not everywhere as wide as has been thought'.[33]

Three further observations are in place at this point:

a. There exists in the Fourth Gospel material which has no direct 'parallel' in the Synoptic Gospels as far as content is concerned, but yet which may be labelled 'Synoptic-type' material. Reference has already been made to the Fourth Gospel's parabolic forms, but other types of material exist, such as the dialogues which Dodd discusses in his book on historical tradition in the Fourth Gospel,[34] or the aphorisms, sixty of which Drummond sets out in his book on the Gospel.[35] This material has a Synoptic 'feel' to it, representing styles of speech which seem, on the basis of the Synoptics, to have been characteristic of the ministry of the historical

---

[31] C. Blomberg (1987) 157f. See also V.H. Stanton (1920) 264-276, and W.F. Howard (1955[4]) 306f. for a list of further parallels, and ibid. 219f. for the extent to which the ideas present in Mt. 11.25-27 par. are mirrored in the Fourth Gospel in different ways, a programme developed at some length in R. Garrison's Oxford D. Phil. thesis (1979). H.H. Wendt (1902) 187-206, after a review of the evidence, went so far as to say that 'With respect ... to all essentials ... the discourses of Jesus preserved in our source [i.e. Wendt's postulated discourse source] agree with the earlier Synoptic tradition', 206.

[32] For this particular point see E.E. Lemcio (1978).

[33] A.J.B. Higgins (1966-7) 384. For the paragraph as a whole see C. Blomberg (1987) 158f., and J.A.T. Robinson (1985) 308-311.

[34] C.H. Dodd (1963) 322-329.

[35] J. Drummond (1903) 18f.

Jesus. If this point is granted, then it needs to be taken into consideration in the process of weighing up the historicity of Jesus' sayings in the Fourth Gospel which, in terms of content, are unique to him.

b. There exists in the Fourth Gospel material which neither has any direct 'parallel' in the Synoptic Gospels nor conforms to Synoptic forms of speech, but which seems to express explicitly what is said implicitly in the Synoptic Gospels. For example the Fourth Gospel's 'I am the way' (Jn. 14.6) may be said to correspond with the Synoptic 'Follow me' (Mk. 1.17 par. etc.); the Fourth Gospel's 'I am the door' (Jn. 10.9) with the Synoptic 'Strive to enter by the narrow door' (Lk. 13.24); the Fourth Gospel's 'I am the resurrection and the life' (Jn. 11.25) with the Synoptic Jesus' promise that those who give everything up for his sake will, in the age to come, receive eternal life (Mk. 10.29f.).[36] Similarly, C.H. Dodd has shown that the main ideas of Jesus' discourse in Jn. 5.19-30, one of the most heavily christological passages in the whole Gospel, are all consistent with what is said in another way by Jesus in the Synoptic Gospels.[37] Speaking more broadly still, it can be argued that even the most exalted claims Jesus makes for himself in the Fourth Gospel can be seen as the natural corollaries of the claims he makes in the Synoptic Gospels, for example, to give a final adjudication on matters of the law, to forgive sin, to demand total loyalty from his disciples exceeding their obligations to their own families, to insist that no one knows God apart from himself and those to whom he chooses to reveal him and that a person's eternal destiny depends on the response made to himself.[38] As Robinson has put it, the Fouth Evangelist 'enables us ... to see the Synoptic Christ in depth',[39] and challenges us 'to penetrate behind and beyond the visible and superficial ... to enter at depth into the significance of Jesus' words and works and person'.[40]

c. It is true that the Johannine sayings usually form part of extensive discourses, whereas the Synoptic sayings tend to be apophthegmatic in character,[41] but we need to remember that Jesus probably did give extended addresses from time to time. In the words of Robinson, 'it is hardly to be

---

[36] These examples are take from A.C. Headlam (1948) 78. Cf. E.F. Harrison (1960) 29.

[37] C.H. Dodd (1967).

[38] See D.A. Carson (1991) 57f., C. Blomberg (1987) 166, J.A.T. Robinson (1985) 322-5, 343-52, R.A. Gruenler (1982) 111f.

[39] J.A.T. Robinson (1963) 68.

[40] J.A.T. Robinson (1985) 322.

[41] There are some long discourses in the Synoptics (see J. Drummond (1903) 17 for a detailed comparison between the Fourth Gospel and the Synoptic Gospels on this point), but scholars recognise that these discourses are for the most part collections of originally separate sayings. The same cannot be said, at least to the same extent, for the Johannine discourses.

supposed that Jesus went round peppering his auditors with pellets of disconnected apophthegms'.[42] Perhaps Jesus is portrayed giving these long discourses, whatever the origin of their content, as a memory of the kind of thing that actually took place during the course of his ministry.[43]

3.3.4 Style

We come back to the issue with which we began. Even if it is conceded that the Johannine Jesus fits a Palestinian milieu, that some of his sayings gain credibility as 'authentic' sayings in the light of a comparison with the Synoptic Gospels, and that Jesus may well have delivered long speeches on the occasions when he is described as so doing, what about that distinctive Johannine 'ring' to so much of what he says in the Gospel? Here, several comments are appropriate:

a. We have to be open to the possibility that Jesus' style of speech in the Fourth Gospel may be closer to reality than is often imagined. 'It is time to liberate ourselves', wrote R.E. Brown, 'from the assumption that Jesus' own thought and expression were always simple and always in one style, and that anything that smacks of theological sophistication must come from the (implicitly more intelligent) evangelists'.[44] In a perceptive article,[45] D.A. Carson warns against the dangers of what he calls 'histmatization', the process of working out an ideologically based, systematic understanding of history which is then used to 'filter out unacceptable elements in our texts'.[46] The reality, he reminds us, is far bigger than the relatively tiny amount of information the Gospels provide, and may be big enough to embrace them all.

b. Evidence that Jesus could have spoken occasionally in a 'Johannine' way comes not only from the Qumran literature, where, as Robinson has noted, 'mystical, pre-gnostic vocabulary' co-exists with 'the more militant and apocalyptic ... within the same stream of piety',[47] but also from the Synoptic Gospels themselves, which contain Johannine-type sayings such as Mt. 11.27 par. and Mk. 13.32 par., frequently acknowledged to be

---

[42] J.A.T. Robinson (1985) 304.

[43] As C.H. Dodd argued (1963) 317, there is an air of verisimilitude about the contexts the Fourth Evangelist gives to the discourses of Jesus in his Gospel. Cf. also E.F. Harrison (1960) 27.

[44] R.E. Brown (1966) lxiv.

[45] D.A. Carson (1981) 83-145. For subsequent discussion of the article see J.S. King (1983) and D.A. Carson (1985).

[46] D.A. Carson (1981) 116.

[47] J.A.T. Robinson (1985) 313.

'authentic' in a strict sense today. If Jesus really did speak in the manner these texts suggest, then quite a few sayings of Jesus in the Fourth Gospel enter the realm of historical possibilty again as 'authentic' in a similarly strict sense.

c. It is quite plausible to imagine that Jesus used this kind of language in informal settings, as unpremeditated 'table talk', so to speak, not geared for formal memorisation as much of the Synoptic material seems to have been,[48] and that this was the kind of speech that was cherished within the Johannine tradition. It could be that Jesus in fact sometimes used a different style that opened up the deeper truths of his person and mission to his disciples, and that the author of the Fourth Gospel has allowed this style to colour his treatment of other parts of Jesus' teaching. This could be the reason why Jesus in the Gospel seems to speak in the same way to everyone, even though, from an historical point of view, he probably only spoke in this way on certain occasions.

d. The statement that the Fourth Gospel is stylistically uniform needs to be qualified in the light of the fact that c. 148 words (c. 27.9% of a vocabulary of 530 words) are used in the speeches of Jesus in the Fourth Gospel which are not used in the rest of the Gospel, even though many of them would be as suitable for narrative as they are for discourse material. By contrast, only c. 97 words (c. 18.3% of the total) are not found in speeches attributed to Jesus in the Synoptic Gospels.[49] So a higher proportion of Jesus' Johannine words is found in his Synoptic words than in the remainder of the Fourth Gospel. The conformity of Jesus' style in the Fourth Gospel with the Fourth Gospel as a whole does not, then, seem to be complete, nor, once again, is the gap between the Fourth Gospel and the Synoptic Gospels in this area so great as has sometimes been imagined.

3.4 The Critical Problem Again

The case for the possibility of finding 'authentic' material of one kind or another in the Fourth Gospel, therefore, remains strong. Yet even after all these points have been taken into consideration, the fact of a general uniformity of style within the Fourth Gospel as a whole, which is also shared to a large extent by the Johannine letters, makes it highly likely that the Fourth Evangelist has moulded his material in his own way and put his

---

[48] The view of, e.g. H. Riesenfeld (1957) 28, and L. Morris (1969) 133ff.

[49] This piece of research was stimulated by the statistical evidence given by H.R. Reynolds (1888) cxxiii-cxxv, whose account, however, was found to contain a number of errors.

own stamp upon it, both as regards the structuring and as regards the content of the discourses.[50] At any rate, the sheer length and complexity of the discourses, assuming Jesus gave such lengthy discourses on occasion, would have made *verbatim* memorisation impossible, as even H. Riesenfeld admitted.[51] A certain amount of 'targumising' activity in the author's handling of his material is a much more plausible hypothesis.[52]

It is not our concern here to speculate on the factors which may have led the author to 'write up' the sayings of Jesus in the way he has, but only to try to understand their character as they stand in their relationship with the Jesus of history. To aid us in this task we will now take a look at the way in which the author handled the Old Testament quotations he included in his Gospel, as a possible clue to the way in which he also handled the tradition of Jesus' sayings which he had at his disposal.

3.5 The Fourth Evangelist's Handling of Old Testament Quotations as a Clue to his Handling of the Sayings of Jesus

3.5.1 Introduction

It should be made clear at the outset that the aim of this section is not primarily to discuss the Fourth Evangelist's theological use of the Old Testament,[53] nor to discuss how he obtained the Old Testament texts he quotes,[54] nor what evidence his use of the Old Testament may or may not

---

[50] Cf. G. Dalman (1902) 72, E. Schweizer (1939) 82-112, E. Ruckstuhl (1951), E.M. Sidebottom (1961) 20, 177, 187, F. Mussner (1967) *passim* but especially 81, R. Schnackenburg (ET 1968) 21, B. Lindars (1972) 47, W. Loader (1989) 197, D.A. Carson (1991) 23, G.M. Burge (1992) 82. For this reason it is sometimes difficult to know where a speech of Jesus ends and the comment of the evangelist begins, as, for example, in 3.1-21.

[51] H. Riesenfeld (1957) 18: for all the importance attached to memorisation in Jewish culture, 'an Oriental mind is not a tape-recorder'.

[52] This approach is favoured by, e.g., M. Black (1967³) 151, A.M. Hunter (1968) 101, M. McNamara (1972) 142-168, B. Lindars (1977) 115, and B. Gerhardsson (ET 1979) 84-8. The researches of P. Borgen (1983), especially part 1, have given it added weight.

[53] For which see, among others, C.H. Dodd (1952), B. Lindars (1961), and A.T. Hanson (1983) ch. 6 and (1991) *passim*.

[54] Whether directly, through reading the text, or indirectly through hearing the text read, or reading or hearing a collection of 'testimonia' or some other intermediary source. Nevertheless the point may be made here that the Gospel reveals an author who was thoroughly acquainted with the Old Testament, and who would therefore, very probably, at least at some point in his life, have had direct exposure to the texts he quotes

provide for source theories,[55] but rather to discuss his accuracy or otherwise in quoting the Old Testament text. For this reason also we are not concerned here with the many allusions to the Old Testament with which the Fourth Gospel abounds,[56] but only with explicit quotations, for only these can serve as a true parallel to quotations of the words of Jesus. Thus several of the texts which C. Goodwin, for example, examines in his article on this subject will not be scrutinised here since they fail to pass this test.[57]

What then is the evidence to be surveyed? We are left in effect with 19 passages in which the Old Testament is more or less explicitly quoted. I say 'more or less' because we may in fact detect certain gradations in the evidence which should be clarified at this point:

a. In the first category we may place those passages in which the author himself as narrator clearly quotes an Old Testament text. These are: 2.17, 12.15, 12.38, 12.40, 19.24, 19.36 and 19.37. These passages provide the strongest evidence for the way in which the author handled the words of the Old Testament.

b. In the second category we may place those passages in which the author reports *others* as clearly quoting an Old Testament text. These are: 1.23 (where John the Baptist is speaking), 6.31 (where 'the crowd' is speaking), and 6.45, 7.38, 10.34, and 13.18 (in all of which Jesus is speaking). While it is likely that the author quotes his characters quoting the Old Testament as he himself would quote it, it remains conceivable that in some cases he may be quoting them quoting it as they themselves quoted it, in which case these passages do not provide quite the same strength of evidence for the way in which the author himself handled the Old Testament text. Nevertheless, this possibility is so small that it need not be taken very seriously.

c. In the third category we may place those passages in which the author reports others as quoting an Old Testament text, but where either the speakers concerned are not themselves represented as explicitly quoting the Old Testament, or the author's use of ὅτι *could* introduce indirect rather than direct speech. The first phenomenon is found at 12.13 (where 'the crowd' is speaking) and at 19.28 (where Jesus is speaking) - but in both

---

from some version of the Old Testament itself. In the view of A.T. Hanson (1983) 113 the Gospel was written by 'someone who has spent long years studying scripture'.

[55] For which see, e.g., G. Reim (1974) 233-246, whose views have not, however, met with widesprerad acceptance. Cf. P. Borgen (1983) 81-91.

[56] As C.K. Barrett (1947), G. Reim (1974) ch. 2, A.T. Hanson (1983) ch. 6, (1991) *passim*, D.A. Carson (1988), and M. Hengel (1990), e.g., amply point out.

[57] C. Goodwin (1954). The texts he examines which are omitted from consideration here for this reason are: 1.1, 51, 2.4, 5, 3.14f., 9.39, 10.16, 12.27, 16.22. Similarly, 7.24, used by B. Noack (1954) 88, is omitted here for the same reason.

cases the author indicates (at 12.16 and 19.28 respectively) that there is a connection (to be examined later) between what they are saying and the text of the Old Testament. The second phenomenon is found at 7.42, 8.17, 12.34, and 15.25. The ambiguity of the use of the word ὅτι in these passages means that they can be used, if at all, only with caution as evidence for the way in which the author quotes the Old Testament, since here he may be only seeking to summarise its content in his own words.[58]

We may now proceed to examine the evidence and then draw the appropriate conclusions. An attempt will be made in each case firstly to determine the exact source or sources in the Old Testament which the author is using, both in terms of the verses he is quoting and in terms of the text he is using, and secondly to determine the ways, if any, in which he seems to have felt free to modify them.

3.5.2 Category One

(1) John 2.17

ὁ ζῆλος τοῦ οἴκου σου καταφάγεταί με

This quotation is found in the story of the cleansing of the temple in Jn. 2.13-22. Some commentators question whether the disciples' 'remembering' of this text from the Old Testament took place at the time of the temple-cleansing or (as in v. 22) after the resurrection,[59] but in the absence of any immediate indications to the contrary it would seem more natural to understand v. 17 to mean that for the author the disciples remembered this text of scripture at the time of the temple cleansing itself. Nevertheless the manner of its reproduction here is clearly entirely the author's work.

---

[58] At the same time this very ambiguity remains an important part of the evidence. ὅτι following a word for speaking, announcing, witnessing, prophesying, confessing, giving counsel or writing occurs approximately 66 times in the Fourth Gospel. Of these cases only 18 times does ὅτι clearly introduce direct speech (1.20, 32, 4.17, 39, 42, 6.42, 8.33, 8.54, 9.9, 11, 23, 41, 10.34, 36, 41, 13.11, 18.9, 20.18), and only 9 times does it clearly introduce indirect speech (1.34, 3.28, 4.51, 5.15, 36, 7.7, 9.19, 11.51, 18.37). In the remaining 39 cases (1.50, 3.11, 28 twice, 4.20, 35, 37, 4.44, 52, 5.24, 25, 6.14, 36, 65, 7.12, 42, 8.17, 24, 34, 48, 55, 9.9, 17, 10.7, 11.40, 12.43, 13.21, 33, 14.2, 15.25, 16.15, 16.20, 26, 18.8, 14, 19.21, 20.9, 21.23 twice) ὅτι could grammatically introduce either, even if the context usually inclines the translator in one direction or another. This surely shows that the author did not distinguish as sharply as we do between direct and indirect speech and that in quoting the words of others he may in fact in his own mind have been summarising the content of what they said in his own words.

[59] E.g. R.E. Brown (1966) 1.115, and D.A. Carson (1991) 180.

The text being quoted is without doubt Ps. 69.9a, which in the MT runs as follows: כִּי־קִנְאַת בֵּיתְךָ אֲכָלָתְנִי, and in the LXX (A text) as follows: ὅτι ὁ ζῆλος τοῦ οἴκου σου κατέφαγέν με. The LXX B and ℵ texts both read καταφάγεται instead of κατέφαγεν, but it is likely that they have been influenced by the Johannine text: the LXX usually translates Hebrew perfects by means of a Greek aorist and does so in the second half of the verse in question.[60] From this point of view, therefore, the author could have equally well been influenced by the Hebrew text as by the LXX.

Either way, we are faced with the fact that the author has changed a past tense into a future one. Whether this change was deliberate or, as C. Goodwin suggests, a result of a faulty memory,[61] it is difficult to say, but most commentators are agreed that the author has quoted the Old Testament text in such a way as to bring out its prophetic nature.[62] The author, in common with other New Testament writers, saw Ps. 69, which was traditionally thought to be about David, as a prophecy about Christ,[63] and this understanding has caused him to shape the quotation in this particular way. Moreover, it is likely that in its present context the word καταφάγεται includes an allusion to the coming death of Christ, an allusion which was of course absent from the original context.[64]

In conclusion, we may say that the author here followed the original text (whether the LXX or the Hebrew text) almost exactly, but introduced a slight variation which indicates the way in which he interpreted the original text as prophetic of Christ, and, by placing the quotation in its present context, gave a sharper definition to the manner in which the zeal of Christ would 'consume' him.

(2) John 12.15

μὴ φοβοῦ, θυγάτηρ Σιών·
ἰδοὺ ὁ βασιλεύς σου ἔρχεται,
καθήμενος ἐπὶ πῶλον ὄνου.

---

[60] E.D. Freed (1965) 9f., R. Schnackenburg (ET 1980) 1.347 n. 18. Similarly, a few MSS and early versions read κατέφαγε in Jn. 2.17, but this is almost certainly by assimilation to the LXX reading of Ps. 69. Cf. C.H. Toy (1884) 83, B. Noack (1954) 82, E.D. Freed (1965) 10.

[61] C. Goodwin (1954) 62.

[62] J.H. Bernard (1928) 1.92, E.D. Freed (1965) 10, R.E. Brown (1966) 1.124, R. Bultmann (ET 1971) 124 n. 3, C.K. Barrett (1978²) 198f., D.A. Carson (1991) 180.

[63] Cf. Mt. 27.34, 48, Acts 1.20, Rom. 11.9f., 15.3.

[64] Cf. R.E. Brown (1966) 1.124, R. Bultmann (ET 1971) 124 n. 3, G. Reim (1974) 10f., G.R. Beasley-Murray (1987) 38 who refers to Rev. 11.5, 12.4, and 20.9.

This quotation appears in the description of Jesus' final triumphal entry into Jerusalem. In the course of this description we are told that Jesus found a young ass and sat on it (v. 14), at which point the above quotation is given as an Old Testament prophecy of the event.

There can be no doubt that most of the quotation goes back to Zech. 9.9, but doubt surrounds the origin of the opening two words μὴ φοβοῦ, which contrast with the MT's גילי מאד and the LXX's Χαῖρε σφόδρα. It has been well observed that these words are very common in the Old Testament (cf. e.g. Isa. 35.4, 40.9, 41.10, 13, 43.1, 5, 44.2, 51.7, 54.4, Jer. 46.27f., Zeph. 3.16), and it could be that the author is paraphrasing the original opening phrase in Zech. 9.9 in other scriptural language.[65] As R. Schnackenburg notes, security in God, peace and joy are concomitant results of the messianic salvation.[66] Nevertheless, it is tempting to see here the specific influence of Zeph. 3.16 in particular in the light of the references to the 'daughter of Zion', 'shouting' and 'rejoicing', and the 'king' which occur in Zeph. 3.14f. as well as in Zech. 9.9.[67] If this influence is accepted then we have here an example of the conflation of two different Old Testament passages, a phenomenon which we will meet again in the author's handling of Old Testament quotations.

As far as the rest of the quotation is concerned, we need to look to the MT or LXX of Zech. 9.9.[68] These texts run as follows:

MT		LXX	
	גילי מאד בת־ציון		Χαῖρε σφόδρα, θύγατερ Σιών·
	הריעי בת ירושלם		κήρυσσε, θύγατερ Ἰερουσαλήμ·
	הנה מלכך יבוא לך		ἰδοὺ ὁ βασιλεύς σου ἔρχεταί σοι,
	צדיק ונושע הוא		δίκαιος καὶ σώζων αὐτός,
	עני ורכב על־חמור		πραῢς καὶ ἐπιβεβηκὼς ἐπὶ
	ועל־עיר בן־אתנות:		ὑποζύγιον καὶ πῶλον νέον.

---

[65] L. Morris (1971) 586 n. 46, e.g., doubts the need to find any specific OT passage behind the phrase.

[66] R. Schnackenburg (ET 1980) 2.376.

[67] The case for this connection is supported, among others, by. B. Lindars (1961) 114, E.D. Freed (1965) 78-80, and R.E. Brown (1966) 1.458.

[68] E.D. Freed's (1965) 80f. argument that the author is dependent on Matthew's form of the quotation in Mt. 21.5 is weak. It is true that they have ἰδοὺ ὁ βασιλεύς σου ἔρχεται in common, but these words are also in the LXX of Zech. 9.9 and are in any case a natural translation of the Hebrew הנה מלכך יבוא. The only other point of contact in the quotation itself is the occurrence of the words πῶλος and ὄνος, but Matthew does not link them together as the Fourth Evangelist does and this small similarity is in any case outweighed by the substantial differences between the two forms of the quotation. Moreover, Matthew clearly sees *two* animals involved in the action, an idea which is totally absent from the account in the Fourth Gospel. The Fourth Gospel's independence from Matthew at this point is affirmed by C.H. Dodd (1952) 48f., R.E. Brown (1966) 1.460f., G. Reim (1974) 31f., and J. Becker (1981) 2.378.

Of these two the MT is slightly the more likely source since the author's ἐπὶ πῶλον ὄνου resembles the MT's על־חמור ועל־עיר בן־אתנות more closely than it does the LXX's ἐπὶ ὑποζύγιον καὶ πῶλον νέον.[69] But in either case it is clear that the author has telescoped or summarised his source, omitting the parallelisms and the description of the king's qualities and replacing the word רכב/ἐπιβεβηκὼς with the simpler word καθήμενος. It seems quite likely, as C.K. Barrett suggests, that the author is quoting 'loosely from memory ... caring more for the sense than for verbal accuracy'.[70]

In conclusion, therefore, we may say that the author has here probably conflated two different passages and summarised his main text in a simple form. At the same time we may note that his summary in no way violates the sense of the original passage but rather faithfully reproduces its essential content.

(3) John 12.38

κύριε, τίς ἐπίστευσεν τῇ ἀκοῇ ἡμῶν;
καὶ ὁ βραχίων κυρίου τίνι ἀπεκαλύφθη;

This quotation is presented at the point at which the results of Jesus' public ministry (12.36b-50) are summed up before the passion narrative begins. It clearly goes back to Isa. 53.1 which describes the unbelief of the people when confronted with the prophet's message about the servant of the Lord.

The text used is clearly the LXX since the quotation agrees entirely with it and though the MT is also very close the latter lacks anything corresponding to the word κύριε. It may be that the author has the Old Testament, or another source containing the Old Testament quotation, before him as he writes, but the quotation is also short enough to be memorised perfectly and this possibility should not be ruled out.

Thus, while we have seen that the author sometimes modified his quotations, we now see that he was also capable of reproducing them *verbatim*.

(4) John 12.40

τετύφλωκεν αὐτῶν τοὺς ὀφθαλμοὺς καὶ ἐπώρωσεν αὐτῶν τὴν καρδίαν, ἵνα μὴ ἴδωσιν τοῖς ὀφθαλμοῖς καὶ νοήσωσιν τῇ καρδίᾳ καὶ στραφῶσιν, καὶ ἰάσομαι αὐτούς.

---

[69] J.H. Bernard (1928) 2.425, B. Lindars (1972) 424, and G. Reim (1974) 30 support the case for a Hebrew background for the quotation.

[70] C.K. Barrett (1978²) 418f. G. Reim (1974) 31 attributes the shortening of the quotation to the author's reliance on oral tradition.

This quotation closely follows the preceding one. It clearly goes back to Isa. 6.10, which describes the effects of Isaiah's ministry, but the exact text which has influenced the author most is less easy to determine. The MT and LXX versions run as follows:

MT	LXX
השמן לב־העם הזה	ἐπαχύνθη γὰρ ἡ καρδία τοῦ λαοῦ τούτου,
ואזניו הכבד	καὶ τοῖς ὠσὶν αὐτῶν βαρέως ἤκουσαν
ועיניו השע	καὶ τοὺς ὀφθαλμοὺς αὐτῶν ἐκάμμυσαν
פן־יראה בעיניו	μήποτε ἴδωσιν τοῖς ὀφθαλμοῖς
ובאזניו ישמע	καὶ τοῖς ὠσὶν ἀκούσωσιν
ולבבו יבין ושב	καὶ τῇ καρδίᾳ συνῶσιν καὶ ἐπιστρέψωσιν
ורפא לו:	καὶ ἰάσομαι αὐτούς.

On the one hand it is to be observed that the final phrase in the quotation, καὶ ἰάσομαι αὐτούς, agrees with the LXX against the MT text form, and that of the last 12 words in the quotation 10 are to be found in the LXX version; on the other hand the fact that *God* is the subject of the 'blinding' and 'hardening' process in the quotation makes it stand closer to the probable meaning of the Hebrew version, in which God commands the prophet to put the process into operation, than it does to the LXX version, in which the people bring the process upon themselves. In view of this fact most commentators see the Hebrew text as the major influence on the quotation's text-form.[71]

Whichever version was the primary source, it is clearly quoted very loosely. The author makes God the subject of the first two verbs, as has just been seen; he omits the clauses concerned with hearing God's word; he substitutes αὐτῶν for העם הזה / τοῦ λαοῦ τούτου; he changes the order of the first two clauses and changes the order of words within the first and fourth clauses; and, in comparison with the LXX, he uses words which differ from the LXX's words, even though they are rough equivalents (τετύφλωκεν for ἐκάμμυσαν, ἐπώρωσεν for ἐπαχύνθη, ἵνα μὴ for μήποτε, νοήσωσιν for συνῶσιν, and στραφῶσιν for ἐπιστρέψωσιν). The author, who seems to be quoting from memory,[72] seems to want to stress the place of sight (understandably in view of his reference to signs in v. 37, and his use of the theme of 'seeing' elsewhere in the Gospel), the role of God as judge, and through his use of the first person in the final verb the

---

[71] Cf. J.H. Bernard (1928) 2.450, R. Bultmann (ET 1971) 452 n. 2, 453 n. 2, B. Lindars (1972) 438, C.K. Barrett (1978[2]) 431, M.J.J. Menken (1988, *BZ*) 189-209, especially 202f., and D.A. Carson (1991) 448. E.C. Hoskyns (1940) 2.502 and C. Goodwin (1954) 71 prefer the LXX as the source. R.E. Brown (1966) 486 is unsure. G. Reim (1974) 38 believes that both versions had an influence on the oral tradition on which, in his view, the author drew.

[72] As C. Goodwin (1954) 71 and C.K. Barrett (1978[2]) 431 suggest.

role of Jesus as healer,[73] an interpretative nuance which would of course have been absent from both the Hebrew text and the LXX.

C. Goodwin accuses the author of 'seriously altering' and 'radically distorting' the meaning of his original text by making God the subject of the first two verbs.[74] Yet this is hardly a fair comment. Even if he was following the LXX, as Goodwin thinks he was, he may well have understood the opening word ἐπαχύνθη as an example of the 'divine passive',[75] and allowed this understanding to control the meaning of the passage. But we have already seen that the Hebrew text was probably the stronger influence and, at least by implication, attributes the initiative for the 'blinding' and 'hardening' process to God.[76] In addition we must not forget that, however much actions may be attributed to men, a biblically trained mind such as the author must have had will have seen everything as ultimately caused by God.[77]

We conclude therefore that the author was probably quoting Isa. 6.10 from memory, was influenced by the Hebrew version and possibly the LXX as well, and shaped his text freely according to his own style, theological emphases and christological understanding,[78] without, however, radically distorting its original thrust.

(5) John 19.24

διεμερίσαντο τὰ ἱμάτιά μου ἑαυτοῖς
καὶ ἐπὶ τὸν ἱματισμόν μου ἔβαλον κλῆρον.

This quotation comes at a point in the description of the crucifixion scene when the soldiers who had put Jesus on the cross shared his garments among them. At this point the author clearly quotes Ps. 22.18 (LXX Ps.

---

[73] As B.F. Westcott (1908) 2.135, L. Morris (1971) 604, R. Schnackenburg (ET 1980) 2.416, and M.J.J. Menken (1988, *BZ*) 206f. point out.

[74] C. Goodwin (1954) 70f.

[75] A legitimate understanding according to R. Schnackenburg (ET 1980) 2.416.

[76] This is implied by the imperatives. It is possible that the author may have read the unpointed verbs as examples of the infinitive absolute used for the perfect; or as straightforward perfects, as G. Reim (1974) 38, C.K. Barrett (1978[2]) 431 and M.J.J. Menken (1988, *BZ*) 199 suggest.

[77] Cf. R.E. Brown (1966) 1.484f., L. Morris (1971) 604, G.R. Beasley-Murray (1987) 216.

[78] Additionally M.J.J. Menken (1988, *BZ*) 189-209 argues that the position of αὐτῶν before its nouns and the use of ἵνα μή and στρέφω are marks of Johannine style; that λαός is avoided because of its positive uses at 11.50 and 18.14 and the fact that the author had particular groups (notably Pharisees and chief priests) in mind; and that νοήσωσιν is used instead of συνιῶσιν under the influence of Isa. 44.18 coupled with the author's desire to portray Jesus' enemies as idolaters.

21.19) by way of demonstrating that what the soldiers were doing was in his view part of the divine plan.

It is virtually certain that the author is here following the LXX rather than the Hebrew text, not just because his text form agrees exactly with the LXX, but also because his aorists are not a natural translation of the imperfects which the Hebrew text uses in this verse. Nevertheless we are not necessarily to assume that he had the text of Ps. 22 open before him as he wrote. The verse quoted is sufficiently short to have been quoted exactly from memory.

Once again, therefore, as with 12.38, we see that the author is capable of reproducing an Old Testament text *verbatim* as well as modifying it according to his needs.

(6) John 19.36

ὀστοῦν οὐ συντριβήσεται αὐτοῦ.

This quotation comes towards the end of the passion narrative when the soldiers came to remove the bodies from their crosses. Because Jesus had already died they did not break his legs but merely pierced his side (19.31-34). In these events the author sees the fulfilment of the scripture passages which he cites in 19.36f.

Scholars are not agreed concerning the origin of the quotation given in 19.36. The main candidates are as follows:

Ex. 12.10		
(Not in MT)		LXX καὶ ὀστοῦν οὐ συντρίψεται ἀπ'αὐτοῦ.
Ex. 12.46		
MT	ועצם לא תשברו־בו	LXX καὶ ὀστοῦν οὐ συντρίψετε ἀπ'αὐτοῦ.
Num. 9.12		
MT	ועצם לא ישברו־בו	LXX καὶ ὀστοῦν οὐ συντρίψουσιν ἀπ'αὐτοῦ.
Ps. 34.21		
MT	שמר כל־עצמותיו	LXX κύριος φυλάσσει πάντα τὰ ὀστᾶ αὐτῶν,
	אחת מהנה לא נשברה	ἓν ἐξ αὐτῶν οὐ συντριβήσεται.

The first three texts all refer to a regulation concerning the treatment of the passover lamb. This would suit the Gospel's passover typology well (cf. 1.29, 36, 18.28, 19.14, 29) and all these texts (especially Ex. 12.10 LXX) clearly stand closer to the wording of Jn. 19.36 than Ps. 34.21 does. In addition it can be pointed out that the Psalm is about *saving* someone from death whereas the passover victim actually died. Ps. 34.21, on the other hand, has the advantage of sharing the same verbal form συντριβήσεται with Jn. 19.36, and uses the possessive pronoun αὐτῶν with ὀστᾶ as Jn. 19.36 uses αὐτοῦ with ὀστοῦν. Moreover the theme of God's care for the righteous sufferer, which is a theme of the Psalm, is not unsuitable for the passion story, especially in view of the coming resurrection stories, and other Psalms have also just been used in the Johannine context at 19.24 and 28. In the light of these arguments we are probably right if we conclude that the author has been influenced *both* by the Pentateuchal texts *and* by Ps. 34 and that he has loosely conflated them from memory.[79] Either way, the LXX seems to be the predominant influence here, since Ex. 12.10, which stands closest to Jn. 19.36 linguistically, has no MT counterpart, and the MT of Ps. 34.21 has the Niph. perfect or participle נשברה which does not stand as close to the quotation as the LXX's συντριβήσεται.

(7) John 19.37

ὄψονται εἰς ὃν ἐξεκέντησαν.

This quotation follows the preceding one with only a short introductory formula separating the two. In the piercing of Jesus' side recorded in v. 34 the author sees a further fulfilment of scripture, and thereby a further confirmation that what happened to Jesus was part of the divine plan.

There can be no doubt that the quotation comes from Zech. 12.10, but it is less clear which text-form of that verse lies behind the quotation here. The LXX can be ruled out since it reads: καὶ ἐπιβλέψονται πρός με ἀνθ' ὧν κατωρχήσαντο, mistaking the Hebrew דקרו for רקדו (= skip about). The Hebrew text itself is a possibility,[80] but if so, in the light of its rather odd reading והביטו אלי את אשר־דקרו, we would have to assume either that our present MT is corrupt at this point and that it originally read אֶל־אֵת, אֱלַי־אֵת, or even אֵלָיו, instead of אֵלַי אֵת,[81] or that the author has simplified the Hebrew text he was using.

The alternative is to assume that the author was using a Greek translation of the Old Testament other than the LXX.[82] It is interesting to note that the later translations of Aquila, Symmachus, and Theodotion all understood the word דקרו to mean 'pierced' (Aquila and Theodotion using ἐξεκέντησαν, as in Jn. 19.37, and Symmachus using ἐπεξεκέντησαν), and this is the

---

[79] Broadly the conclusion of B. Noack (1954) 78, B. Lindars (1961) 96, (1972) 590, C.K. Barrett (1978²) 558, G.R. Beasley-Murray (1987) 355, and A.T.Hanson (1991) 222. R. Bultmann (ET 1971) 677 n. 1 believed that the evangelist's source had Ps. 34.21 in mind, but that the evangelist himself had Ex. 12.46 in mind.

[80] Favoured by E.D. Freed (1965) 114 and L. Morris (1971) 823 n. 105.

[81] אֶל־אֵת and אֱלַי־אֵת are proposed by the Biblia Hebraica Stuttgartensia, אֵלָיו by E.D. Freed (1965) 114 following C.C. Torrey.

[82] A possibility favoured by J.H. Bernard (1928) 2.652, B. Lindars (1961) 123, (1972) 590, R.E. Brown (1966) 2.938, R. Bultmann (ET 1971) 677 n. 2, and A.T. Hanson (1991) 223.

understanding also presupposed by the author of Rev. 1.7 (if other than the author of the Gospel) and by Theodoret in his commentary on a Greek version of the minor prophets.[83] It is possible that some Greek version other than the LXX as we now have it was available to the author and formed the basis of his quotation. Certainty in this area does not seem to be possible.[84]

Either way, there is no firm evidence that the author has modified his source in any way. What we have could be a direct translation of a Hebrew text or a direct transcription of a Greek text which was available to him.

So far we have looked at the seven quotations which occur in the narrative material of the Gospel and which give the best guide to the way in which the author handles his Old Testament sources when he wishes to quote them. Before proceeding to examine his other Old Testament quotations, it may be helpful to summarise our findings up to this point.

Perhaps the most important finding is the fact that the author quotes the Old Testament in a *variety* of ways. Sometimes he quotes with strict verbal accuracy, as in the case of 12.38, 19.24 and possibly 19.37. Sometimes he quotes with considerable freedom, as in the case of 12.40 where we find him altering the grammatical form of the Old Testament text, omitting words, changing the order of clauses and words within clauses, and shaping the quotation so as to bring out his own interpretation of it and his own theological emphases. Between these two extremes we find various degrees of freedom, from the case of 2.17, where the author merely changes the tense of a verb, to that of 19.36, where he maintains verbal accuracy but seems to weave two separate texts into one, to that of 12.15, where again he seems to conflate two separate texts and otherwise shortens and simplifies the content of his main text. In other words we find *gradations* of accuracy in his quotations from the Old Testament, and a *variety* of ways in which he exercises freedom with a text when he choses to do so.

Yet, secondly, for all the freedom the author felt with regard to the *wording* of his Old Testament quotations, we have found him to be reasonably accurate as far as the reproduction of their essential *content* is concerned. His alterations, when they occur, reveal his own christological interpretations of the passages he quotes and his own theological emphases, but they do not destroy or radically distort the fundamental content of the passages themselves. Or, to put the matter another way, there is still much that we could justifiably learn about the Old Testament itself from the author's quotations of it even if we were solely dependent on his quotations of it and were not in a position to consult it for ourselves.

---

[83] A. Sperber (1940) 281.
[84] As C.K. Barrett (1978^2) 559 observes.

Otherwise we have found that the author was influenced by the LXX, as the *verbatim* quotations of 12.38 and 19.24 show, and was probably also influenced by the Hebrew text, as 12.15, 12.40, and possibly 19.37 suggest. He may also have had access to another Greek translation of the Old Testament other then the LXX, as 19.37 may indicate. In most cases we have seen reason to believe that he quotes his source from memory.

How these findings relate to the author's handling of the sayings of Jesus is a question which will be left to the end of the chapter. For now we must see how far the remaining evidence confirms the conclusions reached so far.

3.5.3 Category Two

(1) John 1.23

ἐγὼ φωνὴ βοῶντος ἐν τῇ ἐρήμῳ· εὐθύνατε τὴν ὁδὸν κυρίου.

In the Johannine context this quotation appears on the lips of John the Baptist at the time when 'priests and Levites from Jerusalem' came to interrogate him concerning how he understood his role (1.19-28). The quotation clearly comes from Isa. 40.3.

The same quotation occurs in the Synoptic Gospels at Mt. 3.3, Mk. 1.2 and Lk. 3.4, but there the quotation (which is verbally identical in all three Gospels) is part of the narrative rather than part of John the Baptist's speech; it follows the LXX much more closely and preserves the original parallelism of Isa. 40.3; and its introductory formula occurs before rather than after the quotation. These factors, quite apart from others which may be drawn from the pericope as a whole, discourage us from believing that the author is using one of the Synoptic Gospels as his immediate source at this point.[85]

Similarly, though the text was quoted at Qumran, there is no firm evidence that the author was in any way influenced by the sect as far as the form of his quotation is concerned: the Qumran citations at 1 QS 8.14, 9.20 link the 'wilderness' with the 'preparation' rather than with the 'voice', as does the MT, against the Fourth Gospel and the LXX it seems; moreover in the scroll the quotation is used as an injunction or authorisation rather than as a prediction;[86] and in any case the sectarians regarded it as a command to

---

[85] As even C.K. Barrett (1947) 167 n. 1 admits. Cf. also C.H. Dodd (1952) 40, B. Noack (1954) 73, G. Reim (1974) 5-10.
[86] C.K. Barrett (1978[2]) 173 following C.F.D. Moule.

study the Torah more fervently within their own circle rather than to proclaim a message to the nation.[87]

We are left then, as usual, with a choice between the Hebrew text and the LXX as the major influence on the author's form of the quotation. They run as follows:

MT קול קורא במדבר   LXX φωνὴ βοῶντος ἐν τῇ ἐρήμῳ
    פנו דרך יהוה   Ἑτοιμάσατε τὴν ὁδὸν κυρίου,
    ישרו בערבה   εὐθείας ποιεῖτε
    מסלה לאלהינו   τὰς τρίβους τοῦ θεοῦ ἡμῶν.

Here the distinctive word εὐθύνατε in the evangelist's version of Isa. 40.3 cannot help us decide between the two, since it could equally well be his translation of פנו, or of ישרו, on the one hand, or a compressed form of εὐθείας ποιεῖτε on the other.[88] However, the balance tips slightly in the direction of the LXX by the fact noted above that both the LXX and the Gospel appear to understand the 'wilderness' to qualify the 'voice' rather than the 'preparation', and by the use of the verb βοῶ, which is a *hapax legomenon* in the Gospel.[89] If so, then the Gospel's εὐθύνατε is most naturally seen as a variant form of the phrase εὐθείας ποιεῖτε in the second half of the LXX's parallelism.

How then has the author modified his text? Apart from the insertion of the initial word ἐγώ, which was required to fit the quotation into its immediate context, the most likely explanation of the remaining data in view of what has just been said is that he has telescoped the two clauses of the LXX into one and has used the verbal expression of the second half of the parallelism with the objectival phrase of the first.[90] We have already seen the author telescoping other Old Testament texts (at 12.15 and 12.40), and he seems to be using the same technique here, perhaps out of a desire to concentrate attention on the idea of John the Baptist as a 'voice' rather than on the idea of the way he prepared.[91] Whatever his purpose, he has not in any serious way distorted the meaning of the original text.

---

[87] Cf. L. Morris (1971) 138, G. Reim (1974) 6.
[88] Cf. E.D. Freed (1965) 4-6, G. Reim (1974) 5, C.K. Barrett (1978²) 173.
[89] As M.J.J. Menken (1985) 193 points out, the author might have used κράζω or κραυγάζω which he uses elsewhere in the Gospel.
[90] Possibly also under the influence of Ecclus. 2.6, 37.15, 49.9 which link the verb εὐθύνειν with the noun ὁδός. Cf. E.D. Freed (1965) 5, C.K. Barrett (1978²) 173.
[91] Cf. R. Schnackenburg (ET 1980) 1.291. M.J.J. Menken (1985) argues that the use of the verb ἑτοιμάζω would have implied that Jesus would *follow* John the Baptist, whereas the evangelist wanted to depict their ministries as overlapping.

(2) John 6.31

ἄρτον ἐκ τοῦ οὐρανοῦ ἔδωκεν αὐτοῖς φαγεῖν

This quotation is put on the lips of the crowd in the course of a dialogue they have with Jesus on the day following the feeding of the five thousand. In saying it they are in effect challenging Jesus to repeat the miracle performed by Moses of providing manna for the Israelites to eat.

A number of verses have been been suggested as possible sources for this quotation, including Ex. 16.4, 15, Neh. 9.15, Ps. 78.24, 105.40, and Wis. 16.20, of which the three strongest candidates may be set out here:

Ex. 16.4
MT הנני ממטיר לכם   LXX ἰδοὺ ἐγὼ ὕω ὑμῖν
    לחם מן־השמים   ἄρτους ἐκ τοῦ οὐρανοῦ
Ex. 16.15
MT הוא הלחם   LXX οὗτος ὁ ἄρτος,
    אשר נתן יהוה לכם לאכלה   ὃν ἔδωκεν κύριος ὑμῖν φαγεῖν
Ps. 78.24
MT וימטר עליהם   LXX καὶ ἔβρεξεν αὐτοῖς
    מן לאכל   μάννα φαγεῖν,
    ודגן־שמים נתן למו: καὶ ἄρτον οὐρανοῦ ἔδωκεν αὐτοῖς

The Exodus texts fit the Johannine context well in that the reference to the 'murmuring' of the Jews in Jn. 6.41, 43 is reminiscent of the 'murmuring' of the people of Israel at Ex. 16.2, and in that according to a common Jewish homiletical tradition a text from the Law was often followed by one from the Prophets (here found at Jn. 6.45 where Isa. 54.13 is quoted).[92] In addition Ex. 16.4 provides the phrase מן־השמים / ἐκ τοῦ οὐρανοῦ which is not found in the other two and Ex. 16.15 provides the word לאכלה/φαγεῖν at the end of the sentence, where it is also placed in Jn. 6.31. The לכם/ὑμῖν can moreover be seen to be taken up in v. 32.[93] On the other hand, Ps. 78.24[94] has a word order closer to that of Jn. 6.31 than the other two verses, has למו /αὐτοῖς rather than לכם/ὑμῖν, again in agreement with Jn. 6.31, and also has the word φαγεῖν in the first clause. Lindars deals with the argument from homiletical tradition by saying that

---

[92] For this latter point cf. R. Schnackenburg (ET 1980) 2.41, following P. Borgen (1965).

[93] G. Reim (1974) 13f. additionally thinks the debate over the tense of 'give' in vv. 31f. reflects the ambiguity of the unpointed נתן in the Hebrew of Ex. 16.15, which could be understood either as a perfect or as a participle.

[94] Which is seen as the major influence on the author by B. Noack (1954) 73f., L. Morris (1971) 363, R. Bultmann (ET 1971) 228 n. 1, B. Lindars (1972) 256, E. Haenchen (1980) 321, and A.T. Hanson (1991) 84-86.

according to another theory the preacher began with a text which linked the Law and the Prophets together and by pointing out that Ps. 78.24 would qualify here since Ps. 78.1-8 is concerned with the teaching of the Law.[95]

It is very difficult to decide between these verses. The likeliest solution seems to be that the author was influenced by them all,[96] and has once again quoted loosely from memory. Given this fluidity, it is also difficult decide whether he was influenced more by the Hebrew text or the LXX. All we can say is that he was not influenced by the plural ἄρτους in the LXX of Ex. 16.4 or by the word ודגן in the MT of Ps. 78.24, which only here in the LXX is translated ἄρτον, making the LXX itself the more likely source as far as this verse is concerned.

We conclude therefore that the author has probably conflated a number of verses (and, if not, has quoted one rather loosely), but in no way has he distorted the meaning of the original texts themselves.

(3) John 6.45

καὶ ἔσονται πάντες διδακτοὶ θεοῦ

This quotation comes in the discourse on the bread of life and is used to emphasise the need for inward divine illumination as a condition for faith in Christ. The introductory formula, with its vague reference to 'the prophets', may mean that the author could not remember where the verse came from, or that he believed that the idea expressed in the quotation could be found in more than one place in the prophetic writings, or it could be a reference to the prophetic part of the Old Testament in accordance with the homiletic traditions referred to above.

However that may be, commentators are mostly agreed that Isa. 54.13 forms the major background to the quotation:

MT   וכל־בניך למודי יהוה
LXX   καὶ θήσω ... καὶ πάντας τοὺς υἱούς σου διδακτοὺς θεοῦ.

---

[95] B. Lindars (1972) 252f. Additionally, M.J.J. Menken (1988, *NT*) 43 reminds us that 6.31 is in any case spoken by the crowd and not Jesus, a fact which weakens both arguments from homiletical traditions. Menken himself supports the case for Ps. 78.24 being the major influence on Jn. 6.31 mainly on the grounds that it could more easily be twisted than the others to mean that *Moses* rather than God gave the manna, a view presupposed by Jesus' words in 6.32 and made credible by other evidence respecting Moses-veneration in the early centuries AD, but even he admits that Ex. 16.4 (or less probably Neh. 9.15) could have influenced the insertion of ἐκ τοῦ before οὐρανοῦ, ibid. 44.

[96] The decision of C.H. Toy (1884) 83, C. Goodwin (1954) 67f., and E.D. Freed (1965) 15. C.K. Barrett (1978²) 289 and G.R. Beasley-Murray (1987) 91 similarly think that the author was influenced by Ex. 16.15, Ps. 78.24 and Neh. 9.15.

The form of this Old Testament text resembles the Gospel's quotation most closely, and it is especially noteworthy that the word διδακτός only occurs here and at 1 Macc. 4.7 in the LXX. Of other possible background influences Jer. 31.34 is regarded as the most likely since it refers to 'all' (without 'your sons') in the nominative case, and its context uses ἑλκύω (31.3 LXX, cf. Jn. 6.44) and refers to the 'coming days' (31.31, 33, cf. Jn. 6.44 'the last day'). Nevertheless it is doubtful if we can put this text on an equal footing with Isa. 54.13.[97]

Regarding the precise text of Isa. 54.13 used, the use of the Hebrew text is favoured by the nominative case of πάντες and by the fact that the root of למוד, למד, may well stand behind the word μαθών later in Jn. 6.45. On the other hand, both the presence of the word διδακτός, noted above, and the fact that the author has θεοῦ and not κυρίου at the end of the quotation suggests LXX influence.[98] As so often, the exact original text is difficult to pin down with certainty and it seems likely that once again the author is quoting loosely from memory.

The only significant change the author has made to the quotation is the omission of the reference to the 'sons' of Israel. While this does not amount to a distortion of the original, it does leave the door open in the Johannine context to a universalistic application of the prophecy and this may have been the motive in omitting the phrase.[99]

(4) John 7.38

ἐάν τις διψᾷ ἐρχέσθω πρός με καὶ πινέτω. ὁ πιστεύων εἰς ἐμέ, καθὼς εἶπεν ἡ γραφή, ποταμοὶ ἐκ τῆς κοιλίας αὐτοῦ ῥεύσουσιν ὕδατος ζῶντος.

This quotation occurs in the report of what took place on the last day of the feast of Tabernacles in Jerusalem when Jesus is represented as saying the above words. The saying bristles with problems and, in view of the vast array of possible solutions which have been proposed, only tentative conclusions may be drawn.

---

[97] As E. Haenchen (1980) 324 does.
[98] *Pace* G. Reim (1974) 16f. In favour of the LXX text M.J.J. Menken (1988, *ETL*) further argues that the case of πάντες and the presence of ἔσονται are a natural consequence of omitting θήσω from the LXX and that the omission of 'your sons' is eased by the LXX reading of Isa. 54.15 which refers to proselytes finding protection in Israel. So also A.T. Hanson (1983) 119f., (1991) 90f.
[99] Cf. E.D. Freed (1965) 19, B. Lindars (1972) 264, though, as B.F. Westcott (1908) 1.235 reminds us, the emphasis of the quotation in its context lies not on the 'all' but on the phrase 'taught of God'.

The first problem we may raise here is the exact extent of the quotation itself. It is unlikely to refer to ὁ πιστεύων εἰς ἐμέ alone,[100] and even less likely to refer to ἐάν τις διψᾷ ἐρχέσθω πρός με καὶ πινέτω ὁ πιστεύων εἰς ἐμέ taken as a single sentence.[101] The live options seem to be either ὁ πιστεύων εἰς ἐμέ ... ποταμοὶ ἐκ τῆς κοιλίας αὐτοῦ ῥεύσουσιν ὕδατος ζῶντος (though this would be excluded if the initial phrase belongs to the prior sentence), or ποταμοὶ ... ζῶντος on its own.

Then the question arises as to who is referred to by the word αὐτοῦ. Commentators are roughly split between those who take ὁ πιστεύων εἰς ἐμέ with the prior sentence and see in αὐτοῦ a reference to Christ, and those who take it with what follows and see in αὐτοῦ a reference to the believer, for both of which positions good arguments can be advanced.[102] However it is taken, it is important to remember that the two interpretations are not actually very far apart: if αὐτοῦ refers to the believer, Jesus is still thought of as the ultimate source of the living water, as v. 37 itself makes clear; and if it refers to Jesus, then it is not necessarily implied that the believer is a source *for others*.[103]

The third main problem concerns the possible Old Testament text or texts which may lie behind the quotation, since there is no one obvious candidate for this role, however αὐτοῦ is understood. This problem is not resolved even if we take the phrase τῆς κοιλίας αὐτοῦ in an easier sense to mean 'his heart' or 'himself'.[104] If αὐτοῦ is seen to refer to Christ and the Tabernacles festival background is taken seriously, then it is tempting to see here allusions to those passages which speak about water issuing forth from the rock in the wilderness (e.g. Ex. 17.6, Num. 20.7-11, Neh. 9.15, 19f., Ps.

---

[100] The view of Chrysostom, recently revived by G. Reim (1974) 71-88, who sees Isa. 28.16 as the verse quoted. This solution seems to most commentators to be an unnatural reading of the Greek text and an easy evasion of the problems it poses. Cf. J.H.Bernard (1928) 1.281, E.C. Hoskyns (1940) 2.368, R. Schnackenburg (ET 1980) 2.477f. n. 69.

[101] A theoretical possibility, but one which no modern commentator adopts for similar reasons. Cf. B. Lindars (1972) 299.

[102] The former group includes R.E. Brown (1966) 1.320f., R. Bultmann (ET 1971) 303 n. 2, E. Haenchen (1980) 358, R. Schnackenburg (ET 1980) 2.153f., J. Becker (1981) 1.273f., G.R. Beasley-Murray (1987) 115, and A.T. Hanson (1991) 113. The latter group includes J.H. Bernard (1928) 1.281f., E.D. Freed (1965) 24, L. Morris (1971) 423f., B. Lindars (1972) 298-301, C.K. Barrett (1978²) 327 and D.A. Carson (1991) 323-325. The arguments mainly turn on the question of the correct punctuation of the passage.

[103] D.A. Carson (1991) 323, rightly, as against R.E. Brown (1966) 1.321.

[104] κοιλία is used occasionally in the LXX in the sense of 'heart'. It may also be a translation of the Aramaic words גו or גוה, which mean no more than 'midst' and 'self' respectively. Cf. R.E. Brown (1966) 1.323f., B. Lindars (1972) 300, R. Schnackenburg (ET 1980) 2.156, J. Becker (1981) 1.275, G.R. Beasley-Murray (1987) 116f. and D.A. Carson (1991) 324 for discussion of these possibilities.

78.16, 105.41, cf. 1.Cor. 10.4) and from the temple or from Jerusalem in the messianic age (e.g. Ezek. 47.1-12, Zech. 14.8, cf. Jn. 2.21), motifs which were recalled at the festival. If, on the other hand, αὐτοῦ is seen to refer to the believer then we may also take into account other passages which speak in a more general way about the blessings of God in terms of an abundance of water (e.g. Ps. 46.4, 114.8, Isa. 12.3, 35.6f., 41.18, 43.19f., 44.3, 49.10, 55.1, 58.11, Jer. 2.13, 17.13, Joel 3.18, Zech. 13.1, cf. Prov. 18.4, Song 4.15). It is also possible that the author is quoting a written source now lost, whether an alternative version of the Old Testament or an apocryphal work, or not a written source at all, but a tradition concerning what Jesus actually said on this occasion.

As said above, it is difficult to come to any firm conclusions about this difficult passage, and agnosticism is not a bad posture to take in this instance.[105] The most we can say is that the author seems to be giving a rough representation of the sense of a number of Old Testament passages rather than a clear cut quotation of any one in particular.[106]

(5) John 10.34

ἐγὼ εἶπα · θεοί ἐστε.

This quotation is used by Jesus in the course of defending himself against the attacks of 'the Jews'. The form of the quotation unambiguously indicates that ὅτι here introduces a direct quotation rather than an indirect allusion to the Old Testament text.

The source of the quotation is clearly Ps. 82.6 and the LXX is the most likely text used.[107] This is suggested by the facts that the quotation agrees *verbatim* with the LXX, excluding the personal pronoun אתם of the MT, and includes the rather rare form εἶπα (εἶπον being the regular form of the first person aorist indicative active of the verb λέγω in the Fourth Gospel). We may therefore rank this quotation alongside those in 12.38 and 19.24. It is also, like them, short enough to have been quoted exactly from memory.

(6) John 13.18

ὁ τρώγων μου τὸν ἄρτον ἐπῆρεν ἐπ' ἐμὲ τὴν πτέρναν αὐτοῦ

---

[105] C. Goodwin (1954) 72 calls this 'the great riddle' among all the Fourth Gospel's scripture texts. B. Lindars (1972) 298 calls it 'one of the most intractable problems of the whole gospel'.

[106] We may compare the way in which the phrase 'the Lamb of God' in Jn. 1.29,36 conjures up all kinds of Old Testament allusions rather than specifically referring to one.

[107] So G. Reim (1974) 23, B. Noack (1954) 82, E.D. Freed (1965) 61, D.A. Carson (1991) 397.

This quotation occurs during the account of the Last Supper sayings of Jesus and concerns the treachery of Judas. The textual variant μετ' ἐμοῦ for μου is worth mentioning here as being possibly correct since it is supported by some strong manuscript evidence (p66, א, A, D, W, Θ, Ψ, the Majority text etc. as against B, C, L etc. for μου). True, μετ' ἐμοῦ may have arisen through assimilation to Mk. 14.18, but then μου may have arisen by assimilation to the LXX.[108]

The source of the quotation is undoubtedly Ps. 41.9, and the text which seems to have most influenced the author's form of the quotation in this instance is that of the MT, as the following comparison will show:

MT   אוכל לחמי הגדיל עלי עקב
LXX   ὁ ἐσθίων ἄρτους μου, ἐμεγάλυνεν ἐπ' ἐμὲ πτερνισμόν.

The only differences from the MT are the use of ἐπῆρεν for הגדיל, and the addition of αὐτοῦ.[109] By comparison the author uses τρώγων instead of the ἐσθίων of the LXX, ἄρτον instead of ἄρτους, ἐπῆρεν instead of ἐμεγάλυνεν, and πτέρναν instead of πτερνισμόν, as well as having a different place for μου / μετ' ἐμοῦ, putting articles at different points and adding αὐτοῦ at the end. In view of these observations it is difficult to see how C. Goodwin can deny that the Gospel's wording is closer to the Hebrew.[110]

The only significant change introduced is the replacing of the rather obscure הגדיל with the more definite ἐπῆρεν, a change B. Lindars calls 'interpretative'.[111] Even so it is difficult to know precisely how the author understood the metaphor.[112]

All in all, therefore, we may say that the author has given here a generally accurate representation of the Hebrew of Ps. 41.9 with one small

---

[108] As E.D. Freed (1965) and C.K. Barrett (1978[2]) 444 point out.

[109] Even if μετ' ἐμοῦ is read, it may still be seen as a possible rendering of the suffix of לחמי according to R.E. Brown (1966) 2.554.

[110] C. Goodwin (1954) 66. Cf. C.H. Toy (1884) 89. The vast majority of commentators accept the nearer influence of the Hebrew text at this point, e.g. B.F. Westcott (1908) 2.153, J.H. Bernard (1928) 2.467, L. Morris (1971) 622 n. 42, G. Reim (1974) 40, C.K. Barrett (1978[2]) 444, J. Becker (1981) 2.430, R. Schnackenburg (ET 1982) 3.26, A.T. Hanson (1983) 130, (1991) 173, M.J.J. Menken (1990), and D.A. Carson (1991) 470.

[111] B. Lindars (1972) 454. M.J.J. Menken (1990) argues that the distinctive words ἐπῆρεν and αὐτοῦ have come in from 2 Sam. 18.28, which speaks of Absalom and those who joined him in his conspiracy 'raising their hand' against David, and that in particular the author is comparing Judas with Ahithophel.

[112] Suggestions range from shaking off the dust from one's feet, to kicking, to showing the sole of one's foot as a sign of contempt.

interpretative change in the interests of giving the word הגדיל a sharper definition.

3.5.4 Category Three

Of the six quotations mentioned above in section 3.5.1 as belonging to category 3, three (7.42, 8.17 and 12.34) probably use ὅτι to introduce indirect rather than direct speech and therefore cannot be relied upon to help us in our enquiry. In all three cases there are no single Old Testament texts which are obviously being quoted and we are left with the impression that the author is trying to reproduce the thrust of a number of different passages in these quotations.[113] Nevertheless the fact that he does so, coupled with the ambiguity of ὅτι itself, lends support to the view that this was sometimes his procedure when using ὅτι to introduce direct speech also.

This leaves us with the following three quotations:

(1) John 12.13

ὡσαννά · εὐλογημένος ὁ ἐρχόμενος ἐν ὀνόματι κυρίου, καὶ ὁ βασιλεὺς τοῦ Ἰσραήλ.

These words occur in the account of Jesus' final, triumphal, entry into Jerusalem at the climax of his public ministry. Their position in the third category of scripture quotations in the Gospel stems from the facts that the reported speakers, the crowd, not unnaturally do not claim to be quoting scripture and that the account of what they said may indeed have been influenced by an early tradition of what they said rather than simply, if at all, by the Old Testament.[114] Nevertheless 12.16 makes clear that the author

---

[113] In the case of 7.42 cf. 2 Sam. 7.12-16, Ps. 18.50, 89.3f., 35-37, 132.11, Isa. 11.1, 10, Jer. 23.5 etc. for Christ's Davidic origin, Mic. 5.2 for his birth at Bethlehem, and 1 Sam. 17.15 and 20.6 for Bethlehem as David's town. In the case of 8.17 cf. Deut. 17.7, 19.15 and Num. 35.30. In the case of 12.34 cf. 2 Sam. 7.16, Ps. 61.6f., 72.5, 89.36, 110.4, Isa. 9.6f., Ezek. 37.25, Dan. 7.14, cf. Ps.Sol. 17.4, Or. Sib. 3.49f., 767, 1 En. 49.1, 62.14.

[114] Similar acclamations are found in the other Gospels (at Mt. 21.9, Mk. 11.9f., and Lk. 19.38), and there are good reasons for believing that these accounts preserve an early historical tradition, though the differences between the Fourth Gospel's account and those of the other evangelists discourages us from accepting E.D. Freed's arguments (1965) 67-81 in favour of a dependence on the Synoptic Gospels themselves at this point.

believed that what they said was also 'written',[115] so we may tentatively treat the words in 12.13 as what the author himself believed to be an Old Testament quotation.

The ultimate source of the words ὡσαννά ... ἐν ὀνόματι κυρίου is clearly Ps. 118.25f., and the text being followed most closely is that of the MT as the transliterated ὡσαννά shows (the LXX has σῶσον δή at this point; for the rest the quotation agrees equally with the MT and the LXX). As far as the words καὶ ὁ βασιλεὺς τοῦ Ἰσραήλ are concerned, we may speculate that, if the evangelist saw them as part of the quotation from scripture at all rather than simply the words of the crowd, then he included them in conformity with Zech. 9.9, which is quoted more fully in Jn. 12.15, or with Zeph. 3.15, which is closely allied to Zech. 9.9[116] and actually contains the words βασιλεὺς Ἰσραήλ. This would certainly be in harmony with the author's technique, as seen in previous quotations, in which he conflates different loosely quoted texts in a mutually interpretative way.

The author's changes to the texts he handles are minimal. He merely omits a few words from Ps. 118.25 which lie between ὡσαννά and εὐλογημένος and (possibly) adds in καὶ ὁ before βασιλεὺς and τοῦ before Ἰσραήλ. He is also likely to have understood ἐν ὀνόματι κυρίου to go with ἐρχόμενος rather than with εὐλογημένος (which was the original connection),[117] but that would be an interpretative rather than a textual change.

In sum, therefore, the author produces a free but accurate representation of the texts quoted, revealing his messianic understanding of Ps. 118.26.

(2) John 15.25

ἐμίσησάν με δωρεάν.

These words occur in the farewell discourse at a point when Jesus is forewarning his disciples of the hatred of the world which they will encounter as they go about their mission. The world will hate them, Jesus says, even as it has hated him (15.18-25).

---

[115] The ταῦτα before the ἐποίησαν in 12.16 must include the actions reported in v. 13a, so the ταῦτα before the ἦν ... γεγραμμένα must include the quotation in v. 13b as well as that in v. 15.

[116] See on Jn. 12.15 above.

[117] So, e.g., R.E. Brown (1966) 1.457, R. Bultmann (ET 1971) 418 n. 1, L. Morris (1971) 585, C.K. Barrett (1978²) 418. This would cohere well with the Fourth Gospel's general theology, though B.F. Westcott (1908) 2.116 was of the opinion that the original understanding may also have been that of the author at this point.

As in the cases of 7.42, 8.17 and 12.34, it is theoretically possible that the word ὅτι introduces indirect speech here, which would invalidate the evidence of this verse for our purposes, but the closeness of the form of words used to some specific texts of the Old Testament make it more likely in this case that a direct quotation is intended, and that is how it will be tentatively treated here.

The texts most often cited by commentators in connection with this verse are Ps. 35.19, 69.4, 109.3, 119.161, Ps. Sol. 7.1. Of these Ps. 35.19 and 69.4 (which both have: MT שׂנאי חנם / LXX οἱ μισοῦντές με δωρεάν) are linguistically the closest, and out of these two Ps. 69.4 is normally favoured, since this Psalm is much used as a messianic Psalm in the New Testament and is the quarry from which two of the Gospel's other quotations seem to have been drawn (at 2.17 and 19.28).[118] Whether the MT or the LXX had the greater influence on the author it is impossible to say, since the LXX is an exact and natural translation of the Hebrew text.

If we are right in assuming that the author intends to quote Ps. 69.4 here, then the only change he has made is to turn the participial form of the verb into the aorist indicative form. This could have been done under the influence of Ps. Sol. 7.1 (which has οἳ ἐμίσησαν ὑμᾶς δωρεάν) - if this Psalm was known to the author[119]- but equally it could have been done just in order to fit the quotation more neatly into its Johannine grammatical context. Either way the change does nothing to distort the typological parallel drawn between the sufferings of David in the Psalm and those of Christ.

(3) John 19.28

διψῶ

This utterance on the part of Jesus comes towards the end of his passion shortly before his death. The use of the verbs τετέλεσται and τελειωθῇ in v. 28 and τετέλεσται in v. 30 drive home the point that the final completion of God's purposes for Jesus' earthly work is here being accomplished.

Verse 28 contains a number of uncertainties which cause it to fall into this third category of quotations. In particular, it is not clear whether the ἵνα clause refers back to τετέλεσται or forwards to λέγει; nor whether, assuming the second of these alternatives, Jesus himself is thought to be

---

[118] The solution of, e.g., J.H. Bernard (1928) 2.495, C.H. Dodd (1952) 58, B. Noack (1954) 75, B. Lindars (1972) 495, C.K. Barrett (1978[2]) 482, G.R. Beasley-Murray (1987) 276, D.A. Carson (1991) 527 and A.T. Hanson (1991) 187.

[119] An assumption which is questioned by R. Schnackenburg (ET 1982) 3.423 n. 87.

consciously fulfilling scripture or whether this is simply the author's comment on what was going on; nor is it clear whether the γραφή mentioned refers to the speaking of the word διψῶ itself, or the action it precipitated in v. 29. Most commentators, however, incline to the view that the ἵνα clause looks forwards to the speaking of the word διψῶ, whether or not Jesus himself is thought of as consciously fulfilling scripture, and this view may tentatively be assumed here.[120]

The next uncertainty concerns the text being referred to. Those suggested include Ps. 22.15, 42.2, 63.1, 69.3, 21. Of these Ps. 42.2 and 63.1 should probably be eliminated as being primary referents since they refer to a spiritual thirst, and Jesus' thirst in Jn. 19.28 is unquestionably physical. Of the remainder, Ps. 69.21 is the closest verbally (since it contains the words לצמאי / εἰς τὴν δίψαν μου) and should probably be seen as the primary referent.[121] The author has used Ps. 69 already for quotations at 2.17 and 15.25, and Ps. 69.21 is clearly alluded to in Jn. 19.29 with its reference to ὄξος. It is impossible to say, however, whether the author has been influenced more by the MT or the LXX. The quotation is too short for that.

As far as the form of the quotation is concerned, the author is clearly not concerned to give a *verbatim* Old Testament quotation. He is more concerned to report what Jesus said on the cross. The 'fulfilment' of scripture in this case takes place in the typological alignment of Jesus with the righteous sufferer of Ps. 69. Even so, the alignment is not complete in that in Ps. 69 the 'vinegar' is given with hostile intention whereas in Jn. 19.29 it is given as a final act of mercy to a dying man. Nevertheless the alignment was complete enough for the author to make him see Ps. 69.21 as a prophecy fulfilled in this word from the cross.

In conclusion we may see in this word διψῶ a free citation of Ps. 69.21, which is given fresh meaning in the light of the new context in which it has been placed.[122]

---

[120] This is the view adopted by, e.g., B.F. Westcott (1908) 2.315, J.H. Bernard (1928) 2.638, R. Bultmann (ET 1971) 674, C.K. Barrett (1978[2]) 553, R. Schnackenburg (ET 1982) 3.283, D.A. Carson (1988) 251.

[121] So B.F. Westcott (1908) 2.315, J.H. Bernard (1928) 2.638, C.H. Dodd (1952) 58, C. Goodwin (1954) 65, B. Lindars (1961) 100, 268, (1972) 580, R. Bultmann (ET 1971) 674 n. 1, G. Reim (1974) 49, C.K. Barrett (1978[2]) 553, R. Schnackenburg (ET 1982) 3.283, A.T. Hanson (1983) 28, 35, 115f., (1991) 212, G.R. Beasley-Murray (1987) 351, D.A. Carson (1988) 252, (1991) 619. E.D. Freed's (1965) 104-107 arguments for dependence on the Synoptic Gospels at this point fail to carry conviction. Cf. R.E. Brown (1966) 2.928, G. Reim (1974) 50.

[122] The fresh meaning will also include the symbolic overtones of this word in the context of the Fourth Gospel, e.g., a sense of dereliction in the light of 4.14 and 7.37-39, and of sin-bearing suffering in the light of 18.11.

3.5.5 Conclusions

We ended section 3.5.2 by asking the question to what extent the evidence to be surveyed in sections 3.5.3 and 3.5.4 confirmed the conclusions reached at the end of section 3.5.2. We may now reply that, even though the evidence surveyed in these sections is not as 'pure' as that surveyed in section 3.5.2, as explained in section 3.5.1, it nevertheless confirms the earlier conclusions to a considerable degree.

As before we have found that the author quotes the Old Testmament text in a *variety* of ways. We have found another example of a strictly accurate *verbatim* quotation of an Old Testament text in 10.34. We have also found examples of a very loose form of quotation in which several texts may have been in the author's mind, as in the case of 7.38 - a phenomenon not unlike those cases in which the author seems to be giving an *indirect* quotation or summary of Old Testament teaching (7.42, 8.17, 12.34). And in between these two extremes we have found varying degrees of freedom, ranging from the case of 15.25, where the author apparently merely changes a grammatical form (a participle into an aorist indicative) for the sake of the smoothness of the grammar in the context; to that of 13.18, where he appears to make just two small changes to the Hebrew text; to that of 12.13, where he seems accurately to conflate and contract two texts; to that of 1.23, where he seems to contract a text and make two small changes; to those of 19.28, 6.31 and 6.45 where a greater paraphrastic freedom is discernible, but where (unlike the case of 7.38) we can be fairly sure of the particular Old Testament texts which the author is handling. In other words the same phenomena occur here as occurred in section 3.5.2: the same variety in the degree to which a quotation will accurately represent its Old Testament counterpart(s), and the same variety of ways in which freedoms with the text are exercised.

At the same time we have found a basic loyalty to the thrust of the Old Testament texts used. Despite the freedoms the author felt to make small additions to and subtractions from his texts, to conflate two or more texts in a mutually interpretative way, and to rephrase his material, we have found time and again that he does not seriously distort the content of the original texts he handles. The only major question mark in this regard hangs over 7.38, but so many uncertainties hang over this verse anyway, as explained above, that it would be rash to draw any firm conclusions from it. The worst that can (tentatively) be said about it is that there does not appear to be any clear Old Testament basis for the phrase ἐκ τῆς κοιλίας αὐτοῦ.

As regards the other matters mentioned at the conclusion of section 3.5.2, we may again affirm that the author appears to have been familiar with both the MT (as 12.13 and 13.18 suggest) and with the LXX (as 1.23 and 10.34

suggest - all the other cases are ambiguous), and that the general looseness of his quotations together with the fact that at times he seems to lean towards the MT and at other times towards the LXX suggests that at least most of the time he is quoting from memory rather than from a written text which lies before him.

If we now ask what kind of freedoms the author used in quoting from the Old Testament, we find the following, exercised singly or in different combinations:

a. The freedom to make small additions to the text. This is not common, but is discernible in the addition of αὐτοῦ in 13.18 and arguably in the addition of ἐγώ in 1.23 and καὶ ὁ and τοῦ in 12.13.

b. The freedom to omit words from the text. Contractions, or simplifications, of the text are much more common and substantial, as has been seen in the case of 1.23 (probably), 6.45, 12.13, 12.15, and 12.40.

c. The freedom to conflate texts. This procedure seems to have taken place in the case of 6.31, 7.38, 12.15, and 19.36, and possibly also in the case of 12.13. In these instances more than one text seems to have been in mind at the same time and to have been woven together into one.

d. The freedom to paraphrase. This is not always easy to detect, especially when it is possible that the author is making his own translation of the Hebrew, but examples may be found, e.g., at 1.23 (where he seems to replace εὐθείας ποιεῖτε with εὐθύνατε, at 6.45 (where either the Hebrew or the Greek has obviously been rephrased), at 12.40 (where word order and clause order as well as grammatical structure has been changed), and at 19.28 (where a single word, διψῶ, seems to stand for the phrase 'for my thirst' in Ps. 69.21).

e. The freedom to interpret. Despite the author's general faithfulness to the content of the original texts, it is clear that occasionally he felt free to draw out their meaning in a particular direction, using any of the above freedoms in the process. This is, of course, in a general sense true of almost all the quotations we have been looking at, in the sense that almost all of them have interpreted the Old Testament *christologically*, seeing it as containing hidden references to the plan of God fulfilled in Christ, but it is also true in a more particular sense. For example, 6.45, as we saw, seems to open the door to a wider application of the promise of divine teaching than that originally intended by the writer of Isa. 54.13 (even if the author was using the LXX and saw a reference to proselytes in v. 15); 12.40 seems to place greater emphasis on God's role in the 'hardening' of unrepentant sinners and to see a reference to Christ's 'healing' ministry in the final phrase; and 13.18 seeks to clarify the original הגדיל/ἐμεγάλυνεν by the insertion of ἐπῆρεν (even though the precise significance of this word in this context still eludes modern scholars). In these small ways the author occasionally reveals his own understanding of the texts he handles and his own theological interests and emphases.[123]

3.6 The Johannine Sayings of Jesus

This has been a long digression, but it does seem to open up a potentially fruitful way of approaching a study of the Johannine sayings of Jesus. Simple deductions, of course, would not be appropriate, in view of the uncertainties surrounding the ways in which the author received his tradition of the Old Testament texts he quotes on the one hand and of Jesus' sayings on the other - uncertainties concerning whether he was relying on written documents or oral tradition in either case, and the number of 'removes' he was from the original source.[124] Nevertheless, the author's handling of his Old Testament quotations offers us a unique paradigm of the way he handled a source which he believed expressed the word of God, and as such it offers us a clue to the way he may well have handled the tradition of the sayings of Jesus which he possessed.[125] In particular we should note the following:

a. Just as the author was capable of transmitting verbally exact Old Testament quotations on occasion, we must be open to the possibility that he may also have transmitted verbally exact sayings of Jesus on occasion. It would be wrong to assume that everything he attributes to Jesus must necessarily be so imbued with his own style and theology that nothing can possibly be present which actually goes back to Jesus in roughly the form in which it is presented in the Gospel.

b. The concept of 'authenticity' as it relates to the sayings of Jesus should be understood in a much more flexible way than is common among contemporary New Testament scholars in the light of the way in which the author of the Gospel transmits his Old Testament quotations. It would hardly be possible to draw a line between two sets of Old Testament

---

[123] According to E.D. Freed (1965) 127 the author exercised probably greater freedoms in his quotations of the Old Testament texts than any other New Testament writer.

[124] Though, as was argued in chapter 1, there are good grounds for believing that the author was an eyewitness of the ministry of Jesus.

[125] In view of the uncertainties surrounding Johannine source criticism (as seen in chapter 1), the only source extant today which we can say the Fourth Evangelist *certainly* used was the Old Testament. Moreover he would have regarded both the words of the Old Testament and the words of Jesus to be the words of God (cf. Jn. 1.1, 7.16f., 8.28, 12.49f., 14.10, 24, 17.8, 20.28) and doubtless would have treated them with a similar respect.

quotations in the Gospel one of which could be labelled 'authentic' quotations and the other 'inauthentic'. The concept should be understood to indicate a range of possibilities, or degrees of closeness to the original text, rather than a simple, clear-cut, and easily applicable phenomenon. In other words the concept of 'authenticity' developed in chapter 2 of this book has been shown to be applicable to the Fourth Gospel's Old Testament quotations, and at least potentially to its reportage of Jesus' sayings.

c. In consequence, we may affirm that just as some Old Testament quotations in the Fourth Gospel which stand at some distance verbally from the original texts they quote may yet tell us something about their Old Testament originals, we should bear in mind the possibility that some of the sayings attributed to Jesus in the Gospel may also tell us something about what Jesus originally said, even though they may stand at some verbal distance from that original utterance. We are not to assume that a saying which is not a verbally exact reproduction of a saying of Jesus must therefore be a purely Johannine construction.

d. The types of freedom the author employs in his transmission of Old Testament texts may also guide us in our understanding of the way in which he has transmitted his tradition of the sayings of Jesus. We note especially his tendency to compress or simplify his material rather than to expand it, to conflate phrases or motifs from different passages and weave them into one, and to write up his material in his own way so as to bring out its meaning, especially as regards its christological meaning. We should not be surprised if we can detect the same tendencies at work in his presentation of Jesus' words also.

It is now time to turn to the specific sayings of Jesus in the Fourth Gospel which have been chosen for this book to see to what extent they can be shown to have a linkage with the historical Jesus through the application of the fresh understanding of authenticity which has been developed in these past two chapters, and also to see how they were understood in the patristic era.

Chapter 4

Jesus and His 'Works'

4.1 Introduction

The Fourth Gospel has been helpfully compared with a musical fugue in which various themes are introduced, developed, interwoven with other themes, dropped, resumed, interwoven with yet more themes, and so on.[1] It would take more than one book to examine in depth all the themes which appear in the words attributed to Jesus in the Fourth Gospel in the light of the ideas developed in chapters 1 to 3 above. Our more modest aim will be to apply these ideas to just one theme which occurs at various places in Jesus' teaching throughout the Gospel, namely the theme of his doing the 'work' or the 'works' of God.

In chapters 5 to 9 we will be taking a close look at the relevant texts themselves, but in this chapter we will consider the key words for 'work' which are used in them, namely ἔργον and ἐργάζομαι, and will argue that it is virtually certain that these words, or at least their Aramaic equivalents, must have formed part of the vocabulary of Jesus.

As we saw in chapter 2, it is usually assumed among Johannine scholars that the words which are attributed to Jesus in the Fourth Gospel bear little or no relation to what he actually said, even if they are translated, where possible, into the Aramaic language which Jesus is thought to have used for most, if not all, of his teaching ministry. This assumption is even shared to some extent by scholars such as J.A.T. Robinson and D.A. Carson, who otherwise hold a very high view of the general historicity of the Fourth Gospel, but who believe that the search for the *ipsissima verba* of Jesus in it is a hopeless task.[2]

It is this assumption which is to be questioned in this chapter in connection with the words ἔργον and ἐργάζομαι. L.Th. Witkamp called ἐργάζομαι 'Johannine coinage',[3] while C.H. Dodd called both words 'thoroughly Johannine',[4] the implication being in both cases that these

---

[1] C.H. Dodd (1953) 383. Dodd's image is also taken up by G.M. Burge (1992) 69.
[2] J.A.T. Robinson (1963) 64, D.A. Carson (1981) 127.
[3] L.Th. Witkamp (1985) 44 n. 108.
[4] C.H. Dodd (1963) 185 on Jn. 9.3f., cf. 325 on Jn. 4.34.

words have nothing to do with the historical Jesus. Likewise, those scholars who believe that the author used a 'signs source' tend to regard the words ἔργον and ἐργάζομαι as Johannine and secondary because they were, in their view, chosen by the author himself as better words to use for the miracles of Jesus rather than the word σημεῖον which he found in his source.[5] In a sense, of course, they clearly *are* 'Johannine', in that the author chose to include them in his Gospel and found them useful in expounding his understanding of the ministry and person of Christ, but whether in addition they were also used by the historical Jesus is another question, and the one to be investigated here.

It is not part of our purpose at this point to argue that every saying in which these words occur is a close approximation to the *ipsissima verba* of Jesus (though some of them may be), nor that Jesus uttered the words ἔργον and ἐργάζομαι (or one of their Aramaic equivalents) on every occasion in which he is reported as so doing in the Fourth Gospel (though he may well have done on at least some of those occasions). Rather, our concern is to argue that Jesus *did* occasionally describe his actions and his whole mission in words which are accurately translated by means of the Greek words ἔργον and ἐργάζομαι, and that this historical reality gave birth to the theological use to which they are put in the Fourth Gospel.

A certain degree of support for this contention will come from some of the chapters which follow, in which it will be argued that some of the sayings attributed to Jesus which include these key words actually do stand in a close relation to what he originally said, but here four more general lines of argument will be followed in support of this position, concerned with: common usage; Jewish usage; Johannine usage; and coherence with the Synoptic evidence.

4.2 Common Usage

It comes as no surprise to learn that the words ἔργον and ἐργάζομαι were very common words in the Greek language. Liddell and Scott include in their definition of ἔργον such words as: work, deed, action, contest, work of industry, tillage, tilled land, property, wealth, possessions, occupation, thing, matter, mischief, trouble, that which is made, machine, buildings, result of work, profit, and interest;[6] and in their definition of ἐργάζομαι such words as: work, labour, go on, make, do, perform, till, earn by

---

[5] Cf. e.g. W. Nicol (1972) 116-119, U.C. von Wahlde (1989) 36-41.
[6] H.G. Liddell and R. Scott (1940^9) 682f.

working, work at, practise, traffic, trade, and cause.⁷ Such concepts are so fundamental to everyday life that the main words used to convey them are bound to crop up frequently in any language, in both spoken and literary forms.

In the light of this fundamental fact, there is a strong antecedent probability that these words or their Aramaic equivalents would have featured in Jesus' vocabulary, quite apart from any direct evidence we may adduce from the records of his ministry.⁸

4.3 Jewish Usage

Septuagintal Greek confirms the impression already gained from Greek usage in general. Both ἔργον and ἐργάζομαι occur a large number of times in the LXX to translate a wide variety of terms. Thus the verb ἐργάζομαι was used to translate מלאכה, לקש pi., חטב, גמל, בגד, ארג, סחר, עבד qal, niph. and pu., עשה, פעל, שדד pi., and שת; while ἔργον was used to translate מלא pi., לקח, כלי, יגיע, חק, דרך, דבר, גמול, ארח, מלאכה, מס, משא, יד, משלח, מת, סבלה, עבד and cognates, עלילה and cognates, עצה, עשה, מעשה, פעל and cognates, פקדה, רעה, תועבה, and תזנות. Clearly, ἔργον and ἐργάζομαι were used as umbrella words to cover a wide range of activities, though their fundamental meanings, as in classical Greek, remained those of 'work/ do/ act' (in the case of the verb) and 'work/ deed/ act' (in the case of the noun). This is shown by the fact that of the 92 or so occurrences of the verb ἐργάζομαι, 41 times it is used for some part or derivative of עבד, 33 times for some part or derivative of פעל, and 7 times for some part or derivative of עשה; while of the 409 or so occurrences of the noun ἔργον, 161 times it is used for מעשה, 125 times for מלאכה, 37 times for עבדה, and 24 times for פעל.⁹

We need to remember that all our evidence suggests that Jesus was familiar with large parts of Old Testament scripture and frequently quoted it in his teaching. That he came across these common words in his reading of scripture (or in his hearing of it being read) can hardly be denied. Moreover, it is significant that the phrase 'the work (or works) of God (or of the Lord)' turns up fairly frequently both in canonical and extra-canonical literature, including the Qumran texts (1 QS 4.4, 1 QH 5.36, CD 1.1, 2.14, 13.7), and

---

⁷ Ibid. 681.

⁸ This argument is used by F. Gryglewicz (1980) 10 with reference to the word ἐργάζομαι in a defence of the authenticity (in a strict sense) of Jn. 5.17, but otherwise is not normally deployed by New Testament scholars.

⁹ Information derived from E. Hatch and H.A. Redpath (1897) 540f.

that occasionally *human beings* are said to 'do the works' of *God*.[10] Thus we can be fairly confident in saying that not only words for 'work' (both verb and noun), but also talk of the 'works of God' and more particularly 'doing the works of God' were part of Jesus' religious environment.

There can be no doubt that there were suitable Aramaic words which Jesus could have used in this connection. For the noun the main alternatives were עוֹבָדָא/עוּבְדָא/עֲבִידְתָּא/עֲבִידָא = labour, work, trade occupation,[11] עוּבְדָה = deed, work, occurrence, event, fact, case precedent,[12] מַעֲשֶׂה = deed, act, practice, fact, event,[13] and מְלָאכָה = work, trade, vocation, task;[14] while for the verb the main alternatives were עֲבַד = do, labour, make, act, fare, prosper, spend time,[15] and עֲשָׂה = do, work, prepare.[16] Though our knowledge of the kind of Aramaic Jesus spoke is uncertain owing to the paucity of evidence stemming from the first century and to uncertainty concerning which kind of Aramaic from later literature stands closest to the kind of Aramaic he spoke, we can be sure on the basis of the evidence which has survived that there were a number of words which Jesus could have used in Aramaic which would have had the same core meaning as the words ἔργον and ἐργάζομαι which are found in his speech in the Fourth Gospel.

That Jesus would have used these words in a religious context is highly likely, both in view of their very commonness as parts of everyday speech, and in view of their close correspondence with words which frequently occur in the Old Testament and other Jewish literature. Even apart from the evidence of the Fourth Gospel, therefore, it is very probable that he would have used these terms when referring to his individual actions, including those regarded as miraculous, and also when referring to his ministry as a whole.

---

[10] These cases will be dealt with more fully in appendix B. For the wider evidence see especially G. Bertram's article in *TDNT* 2.635-650 and S. Pancaro (1975) 380-384.

[11] M. Jastrow (1903) 2.1066.

[12] Ibid. 2.1046.

[13] Ibid. 2.819.

[14] Ibid. 2.786.

[15] Ibid. 2.1035.

[16] Ibid. 2.1124. Of these words, those derived from the עבד root became dominant in later Aramaic. The others do not even occur in the Targum of Onkelos according to E. Brederek (1906). However the other words were probably still common in Jesus' day.

4.4 Johannine Usage

As R.E. Brown has pointed out, the words ἔργον and ἐργάζομαι as used in the Fourth Gospel are almost always found on the lips of Jesus.[17]

If we look at the word ἔργον first, we discover that out of its 27 occurrences in the Gospel, it occurs at least 21 times in Jesus' speech (in 4.34, 5.20, 36 twice, 6.29, 7.7, 21, 8.39, 41, 9.3, 4, 10.25, 32 twice, 37, 38, 14.10, 11, 12, 15.24, and 17.4). If 3.16-21 may be added to the list of Jesus' speeches in the Gospel (a disputed question among scholars) then we have a further 3 occurrences of the word in the speeches of Jesus (3.19, 20, and 21). This leaves us with only 6.28, 7.3, and 10.33, but in two of these cases the word is used by other people in response to its use (or the use of ἐργάζομαι) by Jesus in the immediate context. The use of ἔργον in 6.28 by the people reflects the use of ἐργάζομαι in Jesus at 6.27, and its use in 10.33 by 'the Jews' reflects the use of the same word by Jesus in 10.32. Only therefore in 7.3 is the word used (by the brothers of Jesus) without any prompting by Jesus himself, but here the use of the other Johannine words for miracles (σημεῖον and τέρας) would have been much less appropriate in view of the fact that the brothers of Jesus are said in the immediate context to be unbelievers (7.5). Nowhere (if 3.16-21 is excluded) is the word ἔργον used in the narrative sections of the Gospel. In addition to this we may note that the word occurs only 3 times in 1 Jn. (in 3.8, 12, and 18) and only once each in 2 and 3 Jn. (in 2 Jn. 11, and 3 Jn. 10).

Turning now to the word ἐργάζομαι, we discover that out of its 8 occurrences in the Gospel, it occurs at least 5 times in Jesus' speeches (in 5.17 twice, 6.27, and 9.4 twice), possibly a sixth time if 3.21 is regarded as part of Jesus' speech, and that on the two other occasions when it is used (6.28 and 30), it is used immediately after Jesus has used the same verb (in 6.27). Nowhere is the word ἐργάζομαι used in narrative. Moreover the word does not occur in 1 Jn. and only once each in 2 and 3 Jn. (in 2 Jn. 8 and 3 Jn. 5).

To complete the picture it may also be noted that the author nowhere uses the cognate word ἐργασία, which occurs 5 times in Luke/ Acts, and nowhere the cognate word ἐργάτης, which occurs 6 times in Matthew and 5 times in Luke/ Acts.

Were it not for the speeches of Jesus in the Fourth Gospel the words from this word group could hardly be called 'Johannine'. What is more, the author has a definite predeliction for another word to describe the miracles of Jesus, which has a much sounder claim to the description of being

---

[17] R.E. Brown (1966) 224, 526.

distinctively 'Johannine', the word σημεῖον.[18] The author uses this word in narrative 8 times in the Gospel (in 2.11, 23, 4.54, 6.2, 14, 12.18, 37, 20.30), and elsewhere it is attributed to characters other than Jesus 7 times (in 2.18 to 'the Jews', in 3.2 to Nicodemus, in 6.30 and 7.31 to the crowd, in 9.16 to some of the Pharisees, in 10.41 to the 'many' who came to Jesus across the Jordan, and in 11.47 to the chief priests and Pharisees). Only twice is the word attributed to Jesus (in 4.48 and 6.26), and even here the use of the word in 4.48 is not the typically Johannine use but the Synoptic use, where the word is used in a derogatory way of the kind of spectacular demonstration of power which Jesus regularly refused to give.[19] The author's own use (which is reflected in 6.26) is to use the word positively to refer to miracles which signify something of Jesus' true identity (cf. 20.21).

The only other word used to refer to miracles in the Fourth Gospel is the word τέρας. This word is only used by Jesus in 4.48, and carries a derogatory meaning as it does in its two occurrences in the Synoptic Gospels (in Mt. 24.24 and Mk. 13.22).

The picture which has emerged from this brief review of the terminology of the Fourth Gospel in this area shows that the author himself prefers to describe Jesus' significant actions by means of the word σημεῖον, while he makes Jesus by contrast prefer the words ἔργον and ἐργάζομαι. It has been argued by some, as mentioned above in sections 1.5 and 4.1, that the author found the word σημεῖον in a 'signs source' and so included it in his Gospel but used the words ἔργον and ἐργάζομαι elsewhere as being expressive of a better theology,[20] but, quite apart from all the general objections made against source theories, of whatever kind, in chapter 1, we may reply that if such a creative and skilful an author as the author of the Fourth Gospel is commonly acknowledged to be was dissatisfied with the word σημεῖον, why did he allow it to stand in his own work, and indeed take such a prominent role in it? Surely the conclusion to the main part of the Gospel at 20.30-31 would have been phrased differently if the author really thought that the word σημεῖον was an inadequate one to use for describing Jesus' ministry, and that the words ἔργον and ἐργάζομαι were far better for the purpose. Again, if the author thought that these words were so important theologically for an understanding of Jesus' ministry, why are their occurrences limited almost entirely to Jesus' own speech? Why do they not occur in the Gospel's various summaries of Jesus' ministry, e.g. in the prologue, or at 2.23-25, or 10.40-42, or 12.37-43?

---

[18] It is recognised that ἔργα refers to more than simply miracles in the Fourth Gospel, but this is one of its primary meanings.
[19] Cf. C.K. Barrett (1978²) 76.
[20] See n. 5 above.

We are left, then, with the question: why are the words ἔργον and ἐργάζομαι so often attributed to Jesus in the Gospel and so little used outside his speeches by the author himself, who prefers to use another word in his narration of the story of Jesus' ministry? It appears that at least one plausible answer to this question is that these words actually reflect Jesus' own manner of speaking. The distribution of these words in the Fourth Gospel is a phenomenon not dissimilar from the case of the phrase 'son of man' which likewise is found almost exclusively in the sayings of Jesus in the Gospels. Most scholars take this to be a sign that the phrase was characteristic of Jesus' manner of speech. The same may be said about the words ἔργον and ἐργάζομαι. One criticism which may immediately be made of this view is that these words are not used by Jesus in the Synoptic Gospels to describe his activities. To this problem we must now turn.

4.5 Coherence with the Synoptic Evidence

Three types of coherence are relevant here: linguistic coherence, idiomatic coherence, and theological coherence.

We will look at each type in turn.

4.5.1 Linguistic Coherence

It was stated above that the words ἔργον and ἐργάζομαι are not used by Jesus in the Synoptic Gospels to refer to his own activities, and that this is a problem for accepting their 'authenticity' when they are attributed to Jesus in the Fourth Gospel. It is of course possible that this usage derives from a tradition which is not represented in the Synoptic material, as is the case with much that is found in the Fourth Gospel, but, quite apart from this consideration, the problem virtually disappears in the light of three linguistic facts about the Synoptic Jesus:

a. Firstly, though the words ἔργον and ἐργάζομαι are not used by the Synoptic Jesus to refer to his own activities, they are used by him to refer to the activities of others. Ἔργον is used by Jesus of others in Mt. 5.16, 11.19, 23.3, 5, 26.10 (par. Mk. 14.6),[21] Mk. 13.34 and Lk. 11.48, and ἐργάζομαι

---

[21] It is remarkable that the Fourth Gospel's parallel to the story of the anointing at Bethany in 12.1-8 does *not* have the phrase ἔργον ... ἠργάσατο, which is found both in Mark and in Matthew (at Mt. 26.10 and Mk. 14.6). This strongly suggests *either* that ἔργον and ἐργάζομαι are not particularly favourite Johannine words, *or* that the author of the Fourth Gospel was not dependent on Mark or Matthew in their present form. Both, of course, may be true.

is used by Jesus of others in Mt. 7.23, 21.28, 25.16, and 26.10 (par. Mk. 14.6). In addition, ἐργασία is used in Lk. 12.58 and ἐργάτης is used in Mt. 9.37, 38 (par. Lk. 10.2 twice), 10.10 (par. Lk. 10.7), 20.1, 2, 8, and Lk. 13.27. It is also relevant to note that ἔργον is only used in Mt. 11.2 and Lk. 24.19 outside the sayings of Jesus, ἐργάζομαι is only used in Lk. 13.14 outside the sayings of Jesus, and ἐργασία and ἐργάτης are not used at all outside the sayings of Jesus (as in the Fourth Gospel).

It is not essential to the argument to assert that all these verses reflect the *ipsissima verba* of Jesus. All that is being affirmed here is that the author of the Fourth Gospel is not alone in ascribing words from this word group to Jesus.[22]

b. Secondly, though the words ἔργον and ἐργάζομαι are not used by the Synoptic Jesus to refer to his own activities, the nearly synonymous verb ποιῶ *is*, and it is extremely likely that the same Aramaic words lie behind both ἐργάζομαι and ποιῶ (a verb which also, not surprisingly, occurs frequently in the Fourth Gospel as well).[23] Jesus is reported as using ποιῶ of his own activities in Mt. 4.19 (par. Mk. 1.17), 9.28, 12.12 (par. Mk. 3.4), 20.32 (pars. Mk. 10.51, Lk. 18.41), 21.24 (par. Mk. 11.29), 21.27 (pars. Mk. 11.33, Lk. 20.8), 26.18 and Mk. 10.36. It is also significant to note that in six of these verses the word is used in connection with the miracles of Jesus (in Mt. 9.28, 12.12 par., and 20.32 pars.), that twice elsewhere the verb is used of the miracle-working activities of others (in Mk. 9.39 of an unnamed disciple who was casting out demons in Jesus' name, and in some manuscripts of Mk. 13.22 of false Christs and prophets at the end of the age), and that eight times the verb is used of the activity of God (in Mt.

---

[22] ἔργον and ἐργάζομαι are therefore among the 433 words which are found *both* in the Synoptic Gospels *and* in the Fourth Gospel out of a total vocabulary of 530 words used in the Johannine sayings (cf. p. 57 above) i.e. a proportion of c. 81.7%. If we count these words in all their occurrences in the Fourth Gospel the figure rises to c. 97.3% (or 6287 out of 6461). If we discount all minor words (e.g. particles, conjunctions, prepositions, the definite article, the verb εἰμί, pronouns, possessive adjectives, and interrogative adverbs) the picture is not greatly different: c. 79.5% (or 369 out of a vocabulary of 464 major words) and c. 94.1% (or 2497 out of 2654 occurrences) respectively. Even if not every word is used in exactly the same way in the Synoptic Gospels as in the Fourth Gospel, this convergence is still impressive and scarcely noticed by Johannine scholars.

[23] As noted above in section 4.3 and nn. 15 and 16, the likely Aramaic words standing behind ἐργάζομαι are עבד or עשה. The latter is the standard Hebrew equivalent for ποιῶ also (it stands behind ποιῶ 2344 times out of 2624 when ποιῶ is used for a Hebrew word in the LXX, or a proportion of c. 89.3%) and was probably common in Jesus' time. The Targum of Onkelos mostly uses עבד for עשה (E. Brederek (1906) 90), reflecting later Aramaic usage, and this verb may also stand behind ποιῶ in the Gospel texts.

18.35, 19.4, par. Mk. 10.6, Mk. 5.19, par. Lk. 8.39, Lk. 11.40, 18.7, 8). True, there is no cognate noun derived from the verb ποιῶ to correspond with the noun ἔργον, but, as we saw, most of the possible Aramaic words for ἔργον are derived from the two verbs עבד and עשה, so this point loses its force. The result is that, if we are going to think of Jesus' Aramaic rather than the Greek of the Gospels, we have corroborative evidence from the Synoptic Gospels to suggest that Jesus indeed thought and spoke of his miracles and other activities as his 'works'/ 'deeds'/ 'actions', just as the author of the Fourth Gospel portrays him as doing.

c. Thirdly, we need to consider the alternative words for miracles in the Synoptic Gospels. The word τέρας is used twice in parallel verses in the Synoptic Gospels (in Mt. 24.24 and Mk. 13.22) in a negative sense of what false Christs and false prophets will do at the end of the age. Σημεῖον is used in the same sense in the same verses. Otherwise σημεῖον is used mostly either of the kind of demonstrations of power which Jesus refused to give (as in Mt. 12.39 twice and 16.4 three times, pars. Mk. 8.12 twice and Lk. 11.29 three times), or of signs which would happen at the end of the age (as in Mt. 24.30, Lk. 21.11, 25).

The only exceptions are Mt. 16.3 (the 'signs of the times') and Mk. 16.17 (of the signs accompanying believers), both of which verses are surrounded by textual uncertainty, and Mt. 12.39 (the third occurrence of the word, par. Lk. 11.30) which speaks of Jesus' death and resurrection as 'the sign of Jonah'. In no instance, therefore, with the possible exception of Mt. 16.3, does Jesus speak of his present activities as 'signs' in the Synoptic Gospels. This corresponds to Johannine usage, as we have seen (with the sole exception of Jn. 6.26).

There remains the word δύναμις, which is often said to be the Synoptic word for the miracles of Jesus. This assessment has some justification, though it needs to be stressed that, as far as the speech of Jesus is concerned, there is only one passage where he refers to his present works as δυνάμεις (Mt. 11.21, 23, par. Lk. 10.13). Elsewhere, the word has other meanings. In Mt. 7.22 he speaks of the miracles done by false prophets. In Mt. 22.29 (par. Mk. 12.24) he refers to the 'power of God' in connection with the resurrection from the dead. In Mt. 24.29, 30 (pars. Mk. 13.25f., Lk. 21.26f.) he refers to the powers at work at the end of the age. In Mt. 25.15 he speaks of the ability of men in the parable of the talents. In Mt. 26.64 (pars. Mk. 14.62, Lk. 22.69) 'power' is a periphrasis for God himself. In Mk. 9.1 he speaks of the power of the coming of the kingdom of God. In Mk. 9.39 he speaks of a miracle performed by another in his name. In Lk. 8.46 he speaks of the power which had gone out of him, in Lk. 10.19 of the power of 'the enemy', and in Lk. 24.49 of the power of the Holy Spirit.

Only in one passage, therefore, does Jesus speak of his miracles as δυνάμεις - hardly enough to establish his regular usage. Moreover, the evangelists themselves use the word δύναμις in their narratives (at Mt. 11.20, 13.58, par. Mk. 6.5, Mk. 5.30, Lk. 4.14, 5.17, 6.19, 9.1, 19.37), and do so on three occasions for the miracles of Jesus (in Mt. 11.20, 13.58 , par. Mk. 6.5, Lk. 19.37), so even in Mt. 11.21, 23, par. Lk. 10.13 the word δυνάμεις may be redactional rather than traditional. It may of course be that Jesus used the equivalent of both words,[24] but the credentials of ἔργον which occurs at least 21 times in the sayings of Jesus in the Fourth Gospel and nowhere in this sense in its narrative sections seem to be superior to those of δύναμις which occurs in one pericope only in the Synoptic Gospels and is used at least once by each of the Synoptic evangelists to refer to the miracles of Jesus in their narrative sections.

So far as the linguistic evidence is concerned, therefore, there is nothing in the Synoptic Gospels to discourage us from believing that Jesus did refer to his miracles and other activities as his 'works'/ 'deeds'/ 'acts' as the author of the Fourth Gospel portrays him as doing. The strange fact is that Jesus in the Synoptic Gospels so rarely uses a collective noun to refer to his activities, but that he did so in reality can hardly be doubted.

4.5.2 Idiomatic Coherence

One of the characteristics of Jesus' ministry as presented in the Synoptic Gospels is that he tends to reveal himself in a *veiled* way. This characteristic is brought out particularly clearly in C.E.B. Cranfield's commentary on Mark's Gospel, where he writes:

'It is a necessary part of the gracious self-abasement of the Incarnation that the Son of God should submit to conditions under which his claim to authority cannot but appear altogether problematic and paradoxical ... this veiledness is not simply designed to prevent men from recognising the truth. God's self-revelation is truly revelation; it is precisely veiled revelation'.[25]

One example he gives of this phenomenon is the use of the title 'son of man':

'This title, since it can denote both "The Man" with a capital letter and also "man" with a small letter, serves at the same time to indicate and to conceal with a discreet veil the

---

[24] There is a close Aramaic equivalent for δύναμις , meaning 'mighty deed', namely גבורה. See G. Dalman (1927²) 50, M. Jastrow (1903) 1.205, W. Grundmann in *TDNT* 2.301.

[25] C.E.B. Cranfield (1959) 157.

secret of His person. The hearer could take it to be merely a common periphrasis for the first person singular pronoun ... or he could recognise it as the majestic title'.[26].

The argument here is that the words ἔργον and ἐργάζομαι attributed to Jesus in the Fourth Gospel fit perfectly into this pattern. The words are, as we have seen, common and ordinary. They can refer both to good deeds and bad, both to the deeds of God and to the deeds of men, both to 'miraculous' deeds and 'non-miraculous'. On the surface, they need not carry any christological meaning, yet underneath they are capable of bearing a very rich and full christological meaning, as an examination of their use in the texts in which they occur will reveal. Their very ambiguity and 'veiledness' cohere well with Jesus' personal idiom in the Synoptic Gospels.

In addition, they may also be said to fulfil the criterion of anti-redactionalism. It is commonly accepted in the scholarly world that, whatever else the author of the Fourth Gospel is doing, he is 'heightening' the christology of the primitive Jesus-tradition. He tends to emphasise Jesus' divine status in a manner which exceeds anything found in the Synoptic Gospels, and makes Jesus' claims concerning himself more explicit than they do. In the light of this general tendency in the author's handling of his material, it is remarkable that he should choose a word for Jesus' miracles and other activities which is *the least* explicitly christological of all the words he might have chosen. The words τέρας, σημεῖον, or δύναμις would surely have suited his purpose much better if he had wanted to underline the supernatural character of Jesus' life and activities than the comparatively mundane words ἔργον and ἐργάζομαι. Here then is another indication that we may be at this point hearing Jesus' original style of speech.

4.5.3 Theological Coherence

If the Synoptic Gospels present us with no barriers to the acceptance of these words (or their Aramaic equivalents) as being used by Jesus with reference to his activities and ministry as a whole on the grounds of language and idiom, then neither do they on the grounds of theology. This point will not be developed here, since it belongs to the detailed discussion of the texts themselves, but part of what will be demonstrated in the ensuing chapters will be the fact that, to a very large extent, the way the words ἔργον and ἐργάζομαι are used in the sayings of Jesus in the Fourth Gospel reflects motifs which also belong to material which may reliably be attributed to the historical Jesus on the basis of the evidence of the Synoptic

---

[26] Ibid. 275f.

Gospels. Thus not only the words themselves, but also the way they are used, cohere with the Synoptic evidence and ring true to historical reality.

4.6 Conclusion

It has been argued in this chapter that the words ἔργον and ἐργάζομαι in the Fourth Gospel reflect Jesus' original style of speech. We have seen that these words were in common use in the Greek language, conveying some very basic concepts, figure prominently in Jewish literature in religious contexts, and correspond closely to some Aramaic words which Jesus almost certainly would have used in the course of his everyday life, quite apart from the evidence of the Gospels themselves. We have also seen that the author of the Fourth Gospel almost always puts these words onto the lips of Jesus, and never certainly uses them in his narrative sections (the only possible exception being 3.16-21). His own preferred word for the miracles of Jesus is clearly σημεῖον. Moreover, we have seen that though the Synoptic Gospels do not represent Jesus as speaking of his ἔργα, their evidence nevertheless coheres well with the usage of the Fourth Gospel: Jesus *does* use these words for the 'works' of others; he *does* use the closely synonymous verb ποιῶ of himself, even of his working of miracles; the only alternative word the Synoptics provide to correspond to ἔργον is δύναμις, but this is used in only one pericope by Jesus to refer to his present work, and even there it may be redactional in view of the clear preference of the Synoptic writers themselves for the word δύναμις; moreover ἔργον suits the personal idiom of Jesus in the Synoptic Gospels as expressing a 'veiled revelation'; it stands against the Johannine trend of 'heightening' the earlier christology of the church and making it more explicit; and its use in the Fourth Gospel coheres well with Jesus' understanding of his activities in the Synoptic Gospels, as will be fully shown in the textual studies which follow, where an attempt will also be made to show that some of the sayings in which these words occur probably stand in a close relation to something Jesus said (i.e. exhibit a 'type b' authenticity).

It is customary in Johannine scholarship either to dismiss the sayings attributed to Jesus in the Fourth Gospel as Johannine creations, or else to say that, though the author has to some extent preserved the original message of Jesus, he has written it up in his own way. As we have seen in this chapter, there is more to be said than is usually recognised in favour of the view that in some places, and in particular in its 'work' terminology, the Fourth Gospel preserves wording which corresponds with the *ipsissima verba* of Jesus. We should therefore be open to the possibility that this terminology may not simply be another example of 'Johannine' style, but may also be an example of the style of Jesus himself, and that sayings which include it may very well be 'authentic' in a strict sense of the term.

In the following chapters we will study first 9.3f., where Jesus is portrayed as expressing a sense of obligation to 'do the works' of God; then 4.34 and 17.4, where the word ἔργον is used in the singular to refer to the entire ministry of Jesus and where Jesus is portrayed as expressing his desire to see that ministry accomplished and his belief, at the end, that it had been accomplished; then we will look at 5.17 and 5.19f. where Jesus is presented as aligning himself with God and expressing his belief that he is at one with God in his actions; and finally we will look at 5.36, 10.25, 32, 37f., 14.10f., and 15.24 together, in which Jesus is found expressing his belief that his 'works' bear witness to his identity.

Chapter 5

The Divine Imperative

5.1 Introduction

In this chapter we will begin our study of individual sayings by taking a look at Jn. 9 3b-4 where both the noun ἔργον and the verb ἐργάζομαι occur twice.

The plan of the chapter will be to examine the context of the saying first, then to consider its authenticity, then to give an exegesis of it, and finally to show how it was used in the patristic era.

5.2 The Context of John 9.3b-4

We will narrow our focus on Jn.9. 3b-4 gradually by looking successively at its place in the Fourth Gospel as a whole, its place within ch. 9.1-10.21, its place within the healing story recorded in Jn. 9.1-7, and its place within the immediate context provided by the discussion recorded in 9.2-5.

5.2.1 The Johannine Context

The story of the healing of the blind man in Jn. 9 is sandwiched in between a record of what took place during a celebration of the feast of Tabernacles recorded in Jn. 7 and 8 and a celebration of the feast of the Dedication recorded in Jn. 10.22-39. These feasts appear to have been the last of such feasts that Jesus attended before Passion week, and J.A.T. Robinson plausibly connects his going up to Jerusalem in Jn. 7.1ff. with passages in the Synoptic Gospels which speak of him determining to go up to Jerusalem in the expectation of meeting his death there.[1]

The exact connection between Jn. 9 and Jn. 8 is less easy to determine. It is clearly unlikely that the events recorded in 9.1ff. followed chronologically immediately after 8.59, since in 8.59 Jesus is the object of

---

[1] J.A.T. Robinson (1985) 142.

an attempted lynching by stoning on the part of 'the Jews'.[2] Hoskyns' suggestion that the healing took place on the same day, the last day of the festival (cf. 7.37), is therefore extremely unlikely.[3] Nevertheless, the author clearly leaves the impression that the healing took place sometime between the feast of Tabernacles, which was held in October each year, and the feast of the Dedication, which took place in December,[4] and the fact that Jesus directs the man to wash in the pool of Siloam in 9.7 lends support to the view that it took place shortly after the feast of Tabernacles, since during the feast water from the pool was ceremonially transported up the altar ramp in the temple during each of the feast's seven water ceremonies.[5] Thus while we may agree that the healing was 'a new occasion',[6] we may doubt that there was no temporal connection at all between ch. 8 and ch. 9.[7]

With regard to the location of the healing, again we are given no specific information apart from the reference to Siloam in 9.7, 11 which implies that Jesus' conversation with the man took place in or near Jerusalem. Since the man was a beggar, according to 9.8, he was probably sitting in the Temple area or near one of the city gates, where there would have been plenty of people passing by.[8]

As far as the end of the story is concerned, there seems to be general agreement that ch. 9 and ch. 10 belong together, at least as far as 10.21, which refers back to the healing of the blind man and immediately precedes the next note of time.[9] According to J.A.T. Robinson, 'the whole narrative down to 10.21 ... appears to belong to the same Tabernacles visit'.[10]

---

[2] J.N. Sanders and B.A. Mastin (1968) 237, G.R. Beasley-Murray (1987) 153. R.C.H. Lenski's point, (1943) 674, that 9.1 could not have happened on the same day as 8.59 because 'the Jews' would not have picked up stones on the sabbath (9.14) is only valid if one believes that the sabbath motif is not a secondary addition to the healing story.

[3] E.C. Hoskyns (1947[2]) 2.405.

[4] D.A. Carson (1991) 361.

[5] B. Grigsby (1985) 228, R.E. Brown (1966) 376.

[6] B. Lindars (1972) 341.

[7] A view expressed by R. Bultmann (ET 1971) 330, R.C.H. Lenski (1943) 674, and R. Schnackenburg (ET 1980) 240.

[8] Cf. Acts 3.2 and B.F. Westcott (1908) 2.30, R. Schnackenburg (ET 1980) 240, J.N. Sanders and B.A. Mastin (1968) 237, and E.C. Hoskyns (1947[2]) 2.405. C.K. Barrett (1978[2]) 356 rules out the Temple because of 8.59, but this argument loses force if there is a gap in time between 8.59 and 9.1.

[9] Cf. J.H. Bernard (1928) 2.323, C.H. Dodd (1953) 354-357, and J. Becker (1979) 311.

[10] J.A.T. Robinson (1985) 217.

5.2.2 John 9.1-10.21

The original unity of 9.1-10.21 has been questioned by a number of scholars in recent years, most notably by those who hold to some kind of signs-source theory. Yet there has been little agreement as to how much the author may have derived from his source and how much he may have added himself. For R. Bultmann, the source contained 9.1-3, 6-21, 24-28, 31-38 (though editors of the Gospel have 'left their mark' on vv. 16f. and 35-38).[11] For J. Becker the oldest tradition only had 9.1, 6 and 7, to which the signs-source itself added vv. 2-3a before it reached the author.[12] For W. Nicol the source probably contained 9.1-3a, 6 and 7, the rest of the chapter being a Johannine composition, while J.L. Martyn thinks the source contained 9.1, 2, 6 and 7 and that the original ending to the story may have referred to the blind man's neighbours.[13] For R.T. Fortna 9.1, 2, 6 and 7, probably v. 3a and possibly v. 8 belonged to the source.[14] U.C. von Wahlde, on the other hand, believes that it contained 9.1, 6-17, 24-34.[15]

The differences of opinion held by the various source- theorists over this passage illustrate the difficulty of pinning down the content of any putative Johannine source, and constitute one of the objections to an acceptance of any of their theories, as explained in section 1.5 above. However, these scholars have raised historical doubts about the passage as a whole, and their belief that it contains a certain amount of Johannine elaboration is shared even by some who do not adhere to their particular source theories,[16] a fact which will have to be taken into account in our analysis of Jn. 9.3b-4.

At the level of history, then, there are doubts over the extent to which Jn. 9 contains an accurate report of what took place in Jerusalem some time after the feast of Tabernacles in the year before Jesus died, and the extent to which it contains a Johannine elaboration of the tradition he hands on. At the level of literature and theology, on the other hand, we are presented with a story of 'consummate artistry',[17] in which Jesus, on a sabbath day (9.14), heals a man blind from birth (9.1-7), whose spiritual eyes become gradually more and more open to see who Jesus is, while their opponents, variously

---

[11] R. Bultmann (ET 1971) 329.
[12] J. Becker (1979) 315-316.
[13] W. Nicol (1972) 35-6, J.L. Martyn (1979²) 26 n. 14.
[14] R.T. Fortna (1970) 70-73.
[15] U.C. von Wahlde (1989) 191.
[16] E.g. B. Lindars (1972) 339-341 and J. Painter (1991) 52f., 262-266, both of whom believe, for example, that the sabbath motif is secondary and that the excommunication from the synagogue referred to in 9.22 reflects the circumstances of the author's own time rather than those of Jesus' ministry.
[17] R.E. Brown (1966) 376.

called 'the Pharisees' and 'the Jews', angered at Jesus' transgression of the sabbath commandment, become progressively more hardened - 'blind' - in their unbelief (9.8-41). Jesus, who is the light of the world (9.5), also brings judgment, 'that those who do not see may see, and that those who do see may become blind' (9.39). This story then leads on into the Good Shepherd discourse, in which Jesus contrasts himself with the false leaders of God's flock.

5.2.3 John 9.1-7

There is a strong scholarly consensus that at the very least 9.1, 6 and 7 contain a traditional healing story.[18] Traditional elements can be seen at the following points:

a. The form of the story. The description of the illness, followed by Jesus' act of healing and a confirmation of the cure form a pattern familiar to us from the Synoptic Gospels and strengthen the impression that we are dealing here with traditional material.[19]

b. The word παράγων in v. 1 reminds us of Mk. 1.16, 2.14, Mt. 9.27, and 20.30 where the same word is used in what are regarded as traditional contexts.[20]

c. The fact that Jesus heals a man who is blind coheres well with a strong Synoptic tradition that Jesus healed blind men (cf. Mk. 8.22-26, 10.46-52 pars., Mt. 9.27-31, 12.22-23, 15.30-31, 21.14, Lk. 7.21-22). Of course, it should not be overlooked that healings were expected in the messianic age (cf. Isa. 29.18, 35.5, 42.7), and that there are pagan parallels to the healing of the blind,[21] but neither of these facts warrant the supposition that the healing stories were all created by the early church.

d. The use of saliva in v. 6 coheres well with Mk. 8.22-26, where Jesus spits on the eyes of a blind man. Likewise in Mk. 7.33 Jesus uses saliva in healing a deaf mute. It is perhaps significant that both Matthew and Luke

---

[18] Though even here exceptions are made. e.g. καί in v. 1 may be editorial - so J.H. Bernard (1928) 2.323. The phrase ἐκ γενετῆς in v. 1 may be an example of a Johannine 'heightening of the miraculous' - so C.K. Barrett (1978[2]) 356, E. Haenchen (1980) 377, 384, J. Painter (1991) 266. The phrase is noticeably less semitic than the expression ἐκ κοιλίας μητρός used in Mt. 19.12, Acts 3.2, 14.8, as R. Bultmann (ET 1971) 330 n. 6 notes, a fact which led B. Lindars (1972) 341 to believe that it is not from the author's source. ταῦτα εἰπών in v. 6 may be a Johannine resumptive clause - so W. Nicol (1972) 35, and ὃ ἑρμηνεύεται ἀπεσταλμένος in v. 7 is unanimously regarded as a Johannine explanation of the meaning of the word Σιλωάμ.
[19] J.L. Martyn (1979[2]) 24f., cf. C.H. Dodd (1963) 182.
[20] Cf. R.E. Brown (1966) 371, J. Becker (1979) 316, and B. Lindars (1972) 341.
[21] As that quoted by C.K. Barrett in (1978[2]) 353.

omit these references to the use of saliva, perhaps because they wanted to safeguard Jesus from the charge of engaging in magical practices.[22] A number of scholars regard this reference to saliva in Jn. 9.6, therefore, as a sign of the presence of a primitive tradition.[23]

e. The making of clay from saliva and dust is not paralleled in any of the Synoptic stories, but it is not necessarily invented either. Indeed it is the kind of vivid detail which leads a scholar like B.F. Westcott to the conclusion that the whole narrative bears the marks of 'the experience of an immediate witness'.[24]

f. The command to the man to go and wash himself coheres well with Jesus' normal method of healing in the Synoptic Gospels, i.e. by requiring some element of faith on the part of the one to be healed. As Dodd notes, this is not a specifically Johannine trait.[25] It is particularly reminiscent of Lk. 17.11-19 where the lepers are told to go and show themselves to the priests and are cleansed as they obey Jesus' words. The parallel with Elisha's command to Naaman in 2 Kings 5.10 does not detract from this point. Indeed, D.G. Bostock has argued that Jesus saw himself as a new Elisha.[26]

g. The reference to the pool of Siloam is true to life. As has already been noted, there was (and still is) a pool called Siloam in Jerusalem, which was moreover used in the ceremonies of the feast of Tabernacles. The fact that the author gives us an explanation of the meaning of the word does not necessarily mean that he introduced it here for the sake of the explanation (which clearly has a christological significance). It is much more likely that he is making christological use of an element in the tradition.[27]

h. The fact that Jesus takes the initiative here in healing the blind man is sometimes taken as a sign of the story's unhistorical character,[28] but, as R.T.

---

[22] Cf. C.K. Barrett (1978[2]) 358: 'the use of spittle was in general accompanied by magical practices which made it suspect in Judaism'.

[23] E.g. J. Painter (1991) 265, J.H. Bernard (1928) 2.327, R. Kysar (1986) 149, and R. Schnackenburg (ET 1980) 242. Since saliva was commonly regarded as having curative powers at the time, Jesus may have used it by way of accommodating himself to the man's own beliefs.

[24] B.F. Westcott (1908) 2.30, *contra* B. Lindars (1972) 343, who thinks that the author inserted it to bring out a creation motif on the basis of Gen. 2.6f., and A.E. Harvey (1982) 38, who thinks that the author inserted it because it portrays Jesus breaking the sabbath law, which Harvey believes he did not do in actual fact.

[25] C.H. Dodd (1963) 184.

[26] D.G. Bostock (1980-1) 39-41.

[27] So C.H. Dodd (1963) 184, W. Nicol (1972) 112, and J.A.T. Robinson (1985) 162.

[28] E.g. by W. Wilkens (1969) 42, R. Bultmann (ET 1971) 330, and J. Painter (1991) 264. Painter thinks that the story may have originally contained a request for healing which was removed when the evangelist made it the basis of a 'rejection story'.

Fortna[29] and G.R. Beasley-Murray[30] have pointed out, even in the Synoptic tradition Jesus takes the initiative in healing people (as, e.g., in Mk. 3.1-6, Lk. 7.11-17, 13.10-17, 14.1-6).

In view of these considerations, therefore, there are good grounds for believing that at least most of 9.1, 6 and 7 go back to an early tradition about a healing miracle of Jesus. As C.K. Barrett puts it: 'There is no need to suppose it invented as a whole; it was probably drawn from the still-flowing stream of tradition'.[31] Moreover, in view of its unique features, it is unlikely to have evolved from any of its closest parallels in the Synoptic Gospels. It is, in the words of R.E. Brown, 'a primitive story of healing preserved only in the Johannine tradition'.[32]

5.2.4 John 9.2-5

We come on, then, to the immediate context of 9.3b-4, which takes the form of a conversation between Jesus and his disciples.[33]

There is no need to doubt that a conversation of some sort did take place between Jesus and his disciples at this point in the story and in fact most scholars accept that at least 9.2-3a belongs to the tradition which pre-dated the final form of ch. 9.[34] As C.H. Dodd has shown, there are a number of Synoptic healing stories which include interventions by a third party or conversations of one kind or another,[35] and we are not necessarily to dismiss them as secondary additions simply because they do not fit in to the basic form of a healing story. As E.P. Sanders reminds us, stories could as easily contract as expand in size, or become more or less detailed in the period of the oral transmission of the Gospel tradition,[36] so a conversation in a healing story could theoretically be just as much an original element which has not dropped out as a later element which has been added in.

If we look first of all, then, at vv. 2-3a, we find the disciples' question and Jesus' answer entirely credible in this context. The disciples'

---

[29] R.T. Fortna (1970) 51.
[30] G.R. Beasley-Murray (1987) 71.
[31] C.K. Barrett (1978²) 354.
[32] R.E. Brown (1966) 379. Cf. C.H. Dodd (1963) 188, R. Bultmann (ET 1971) 330, and B. Lindars (1972) 339.
[33] Who these disciples were we do not know. They could have been the twelve, or some of the twelve, or some of the unknown disciples referred to in 7.3.
[34] The few exceptions include B. Lindars (1972) 341, U.C. von Wahlde (1989) 191, and J. Painter (1991) 264. J. Becker (1979) 317 believes that the 'signs source' itself inserted vv. 2-3a before it reached the author.
[35] C.H. Dodd (1963) 182, 189.
[36] E.P. Sanders (1985) 15.

assumption that, in the case of one born deformed in some way, either he or his parents must have sinned before his birth is one which is found in the rabbinic literature, and, in the case of parental sin, in the Old Testament itself.[37] Even the form of address in v. 2 suits the '*Sitz im Leben Jesu*'[38], while Jesus' initial reply in v. 3a coheres well with his approach to the problem of suffering shown in Lk. 13.1-5. Jesus does not deny that there may be a general connection between sin and suffering through the fall of mankind, nor that in some cases there may be a direct connection between the two (cf. Jn. 5.14, Mk. 2.5 pars.), but only that there is a necessary direct connection in every case. The author of the Fourth Gospel himself shows no interest in the problem of theodicy elsewhere,[39] and the question of the man's possible sin plays no part in the ensuing drama,[40] so we may with some confidence attribute vv. 2-3a to the original story.

Regarding v. 5, however, it has to be acknowledged that there are strong reasons for believing that these words concerning Jesus as φῶς ... τοῦ κόσμου have been added in here by the author:

a. Firstly, the author is clearly fond of using the image of light. In the prologue to the Gospel it is used no less than six times with reference to Jesus (1.4, 5, 7, 8 twice, 9). It is used five times in what is probably, though not certainly, a narrative passage in ch. 3 (3.19 twice, 20 twice, 21), and it is used in Jesus' speech in the following places: 5.35 (with reference to John the Baptist), 8.12 twice, 9.5, 11.9, 10, 12.35 twice, 36 twice, 46 (mostly with reference to Jesus himself). The image of light is also used in 1 Jn. 1.5, 7 twice, and 2.8 (with reference to the light of God).

b. Secondly, there is some doubt as to whether the historical Jesus would have spoken in such a direct way of himself as 'the light of the world', especially in view of the Synoptic evidence, which suggests that Jesus normally spoke in a more allusive or indirect way of himself. In the opinion of most modern scholars, the 'I am ...' sayings of Jesus in the Fourth Gospel are more likely to be the author's own way of describing Jesus' claims or significance than a direct reflection of Jesus' own style of speaking.

c. Thirdly, C.H. Dodd has drawn our attention to the fact that v. 5 does not cohere well with v. 4. Verse 4 speaks of Jesus as one man among many

---

[37] For parental sin, see Ex. 20.5, 34.7, Num. 14.18, Dt. 5.9, Ps. 79.8, 109.14, Isa. 65.6f. For rabbinic references to both kinds of causes, see S.-B. 2.527-529. It is unlikely that a belief in the pre-existence or transmigration of souls lies behind the disciples' question - so R. Bultmann (ET 1971) 331, R. Schnackenburg (ET 1980) 241, E. Haenchen (1980) 377, G.R. Beasley-Murray (1987) 155.

[38] Cf. J.H. Bernard (1928) 1.54-56.

[39] C.H. Dodd (1963) 187, W. Nicol (1972) 35.

[40] R.T. Fortna (1970) 71.

living *under* the sun, whereas v. 5 speaks of him *as* the sun.[41] While it is not impossible for Jesus to have changed his imagery in such an abrupt way (assuming for the moment that v. 4 was spoken by him in this context), it seems more likely that v. 5 reflects the author's own redactional activity.

d. Fourthly, the words of Jesus in v. 5 are clearly relevant to the theme of the spiritual enlightenment of the healed man which emerges at the end of ch. 9. Once again, this cannot of itself rule out the possibility that Jesus spoke them in this context, but, as E.C. Hoskyns has remarked, it is difficult to avoid the impression that the words have been inserted here to ensure the correct interpretation of the miracle.[42]

In view of the above considerations, it is not surprising that the vast majority of scholars regard v. 5 as a Johannine addition to the miracle story.[43] If this position is correct, then the initial ὅταν clause, which most commentators take as limiting the application of the saying to the earthly life of Jesus,[44] will probably have been inserted as a means of linking v. 5 to v. 4.

It is now time to consider vv. 3b-4 themselves in their present context. Are these verses also added by the author or did they belong to the original story? This question must of course be distinguished from the question of their 'authenticity', since, even if they have been added in here, it is still possible to believe that v. 4 at least was drawn from an authentic tradition of Jesus' sayings.[45] Nevertheless, it is still important to ask this question, because if the answer is that they *did* belong to the original story, and are in some sense authentic, then clearly they will take on fresh significance as a saying of Jesus in the light of their context. We will therefore review the arguments for and against the origination of vv. 3b-4 in this context.

First the arguments against:

a. The most frequently cited argument is the argument from style. Vv. 3b-4, it is said, are full of Johannine stylistic characteristics, most notably the words ἀλλ' ἵνα, φανερωθῇ, ἔργα, ἐργάζεσθαι, τοῦ πέμψαντός με and ἡμέρα ... νύξ. The last two characteristics will be dealt with in the next section where it will be argued that τοῦ πέμψαντός με may not be original

---

[41] C.H. Dodd (1963) 186.
[42] E.C. Hoskyns (1947²) 2.407.
[43] The only exceptions from modern commentaries consulted are those of L. Morris (1971) and D.A. Carson (1991).
[44] So J. Calvin (ET 1959) 240, J.H. Bernard (1928) 2.327, R.C.H. Lenski (1943) 679, R.H. Lightfoot (1956) 202, L. Morris (1971) 480, and D.A. Carson (1991) 362. B.F. Westcott (1908) 2.33, R. Kysar (1986) 149, and F. Grob (1986) 42, on the other hand, think it has no temporal limits.
[45] A possibility apparently recognised by R.E. Brown (1966) 379, and R.T. Fortna (1970) 72, who say that v. 4 may be 'traditional' even if not original to this context.

to v. 4, and that ἡμέρα ... νύξ are not typically Johannine as used here. Ἔργα and ἐργάζεσθαι were dealt with in chapter 4, where it was argued that, though they occur quite frequently in the speeches of Jesus in the Fourth Gospel, they should in fact be regarded as dominical. That leaves us with ἀλλ' ἵνα and φανερωθῇ. Ἀλλ' ἵνα is a common Johannine ellipsis, to be found at 1.8, 31, 11.52, 13.18, 14.31, 15.25 and 1 Jn. 2.19 as well as in 9.3, but it is also found in the speech of Jesus in Mark's Gospel at Mk. 4.22 and 14.49. Φανερῶ is also a fairly common Johannine word, being used at 1.31 (by John the Baptist), 2.11 (by the evangelist), 3.21 (probably by the evangelist), 7.4 (by Jesus' brothers), 9.3, 17.6 (by Jesus), 21.1 twice, 14 (by the author of ch. 21), and at 1 Jn. 1.2 twice, 2.19, 28, 3.2 twice, 3.5, 3.8, 4.9. Nevertheless, it needs to be remembered that this word also occurs in the saying of Jesus in Mk. 4.22, and that the whole concept of revelation which it expresses does not seem to have been at all alien to the mind of Jesus on the basis of the evidence of the Synoptic Gospels. In particular it should be noted that the word ἀποκαλύπτω, which is counted as synonymous with φανερῶ by G. Abbott-Smith,[46] is used twice by Jesus in Mt. 11.25-27 par., a saying widely regarded as authentic in some sense, once with the Father as subject and once with himself as subject. It is also found in sayings attributed to him at Mt. 10.26, 16.17, Lk. 12.2, 17.30, all probably referring to God's revealing activity. The stylistic argument should therefore not be given undue weight in assessing either the authenticity of vv. 3b-4 or their originality in this context. Some of the expressions are admittedly common in the Fourth Gospel, but they may also have their roots in the teaching of Jesus.

b. Secondly, it is thought inappropriate by some that v. 4 should have stood originally where it stands now on the grounds that it gives the impression of a Jesus who was under such pressure to work miracles while there was time that he had to do so even on the sabbath day - an impression which does not fit in with the rest of the Fourth Gospel.[47] Yet this argument loses weight when it is realised that in the Fourth Gospel the ἔργα of Jesus do not merely refer to the miracles of Jesus, but include the whole range of his activities (cf. e.g. 14.10). In the light of this observation, v. 4 is in fact plausible in this context as a general expression of a sense of urgency by Jesus in the face of the imminent termination of his ministry. This does not of course prove that it did originally belong to this context, but at least it shows that it could have done so.

Now the positive arguments for the origination of vv. 3b-4 in this context:

---

[46] G. Abbott-Smith (1936³) 50.
[47] This argument is advanced by J. Bligh (1966) 133 and J. Riedl (1973) 295.

a. Firstly, if the disciples actually did ask the question found in v. 2, and if v. 3a represents at least the beginning of Jesus' reply, then we are surely to suppose that a fuller reply was actually given. R. Bultmann clearly agrees with this point when he says that 'the original continuation of Jesus' reply has been suppressed'.[48] It does not require too great a stretch of the imagination to believe that in fact vv. 3b-4 contain at least the gist of the continuation of Jesus' reply.

b. Secondly, though v. 3b contains elements of Johannine style, as seen above, the thought it expresses is quite credible and fitting for the occasion, and something that Jesus might have actually said in some form. Note especially the underlying assumption of divine sovereignty - the very Jewish idea that God has a way of turning around even apparently evil things and using them for his glory; the way that Jesus focusses attention in the first place and overtly upon God rather than himself (contrast the more explicitly christological saying in 11.4); and the basic idea that God is going to do his work through Jesus, which, as we shall see later in this chapter, is quite compatible with Jesus' self-understanding as expressed in his Synoptic sayings.[49] If, then, v. 3b expresses the substance of the continuation of Jesus' reply, and if indeed Jesus did occasionally talk about his 'works'/ 'actions'/ 'deeds', there is no reason why v. 4, which, as we shall see, also coheres well with the Synoptic Jesus and may well be authentic in a strict sense, should not also belong to that continuation.

On the basis of considerations such as these, and some of those to be considered in the next section, C.H. Dodd came to the conclusion that vv. 3b-4 formed part of the original pericope, though he also believed these verses to have been reshaped in a Johannine way.[50] Nevertheless, one cannot ignore the weight of scholarly opinion on the other side, which, mainly for stylistic reasons, regards these verses as either Johannine creations or as placed here by the author from some other source.[51] So while Dodd's view is certainly plausible, and will be tentatively adopted here, it is recognised that this is an issue where one is especially conscious of the impossibility of historical certainty.

---

[48] R. Bultmann (ET 1971) 331 n. 2.
[49] Cf. especially Mt. 12.28 par. Lk. 11.20, C.H. Dodd (1963) 188, and R.E. Brown (1966) 1.372.
[50] C.H. Dodd (1963) 188.
[51] Cf.R. Bultmann (ET 1971) 331, R. Pesch and R. Kratz (1976) 76, W. Wilkens (1969) 42, R.T. Fortna (1970) 71f., W. Nicol (1972) 35, J. Becker (1979) 316, J.L. Martyn (1979²) 26 n. 14, R. Schnackenburg (ET 1980) 243, J. Painter (1991) 264.

5.3 The Authenticity of John 9.3b-4

5.3.1 Introduction

It was suggested above that the clause τοῦ πέμψαντός με may not be original to v. 4. This matter must now be discussed together with the question of the authenticity of this clause in general. Then it will be necessary to discuss the true text of what remains of the verse in view of the confusion of the textual tradition. Thirdly, the general meaning of the verse will have to be ascertained as a basis of a discussion of its authenticity, which will lead, fourthly, to an application of the various criteria of authenticity. Finally, the authenticity of the ἔργα motif in v. 3b-4 as a whole will be considered.

5.3.2 The Authenticity of τοῦ πέμψαντός με

Even the most casual reader of the Fourth Gospel is unlikely to miss its emphasis on Jesus as one 'sent' by God. The above participial clause occurs with God as subject and Jesus as object in Jesus' speech in the following places: 4.34, 5.23, 24, 30, 37, 6.38, 39, 44, 7.16, 28, 33, 8.16, 18, 26, 29, 9.4, 12.44, 45, 49, 13.20, 14.24, 15.21, 16.5. Jesus is also clearly thinking of himself when he uses the clause in 7.18, though the saying is cast in a general form. Otherwise the clause is used in a general form with mainly the disciples in mind in 13.16.

In addition to these occurrences where the verb πέμπω is used, there are also many instances where Jesus' speech has the verb ἀποστέλλω of the Father's activity in having sent him. This verb is used in the aorist indicative in the third person with this meaning in Jesus' speech in 5.38, 6.29, 57, 7.29, 8.42, and 10.36 (it also occurs in 3.17, but this is probably a narrative section). The verb also occurs with this meaning in the aorist indicative in the second person in 11.42, 17.3, 8, 18, 21, 23, 25 and in the perfect indicative in the third person in 5.36 and 20.21.

Scholars have long debated whether the verbs πέμπω and ἀποστέλλω have different meanings as used in the Fourth Gospel. B.F. Westcott, for example, believed that ἀποστέλλω 'conveys the accessory notions of a special commission, and so far of a delegated authority in the one sent. The simple verb πέμπω marks nothing more than the immediate relation of the sender to the sent'.[52] Similarly, K.H. Rengstorf, noting that the two verbs

---

[52] B.F. Westcott (1908) 2.358.

are used in different verbal forms consistently in the Fourth Gospel, comes to the conclusion that ἀποστέλλω is used when Jesus' concern is 'to ground His authority in that of God as the One who is responsible for His words and works and who guarantees their right and truth'. Πέμπω, on the other hand, affirms 'the participation of God in His work in the "actio" of His sending'.[53] Yet E.A. Abbott reverses the distinction when he says: 'we are perhaps justified in thinking that ἀποστέλλω means "sending away into the world at large", but πέμπω "sending on a special errand" '.[54] Most modern scholars, however, believe that the two verbs are used without any significant variation in meaning in the Gospel.[55] Such a conclusion is justified on the basis of the way the words are used,[56] as well as on the general observation that the author has a tendency to use virtually synonymous words merely as stylistic variants without intending to convey subtle distinctions of meaning.[57]

There are therefore at least 38 occasions in the Fourth Gospel on which Jesus is portrayed as referring to God as the one who 'sent' him. At the same time we need to note that the same idea crops up in Jesus' speech in the Synoptic Gospels, though less frequently. In the parable of the wicked vineyard tenants, Jesus speaks of the vineyard owner 'sending' his son, and surely he is thinking of himself at this point (Mk. 12.6 pars. Mk. and Mt. use ἀποστέλλω while Lk. uses πέμπω). In Mt. 15.24 Jesus says to the Syrophoenician woman: οὐκ ἀπεστάλην εἰ μὴ εἰς τὰ πρόβατα τὰ ἀπολωλότα οἴκου Ἰσραήλ. In Mt. 23.37 par. Jesus probably includes himself when he speaks of Jerusalem as λιθοβολοῦσα τοὺς ἀπεσταλμένους πρὸς αὐτήν. In Lk. 4.21 Jesus sees the words of the prophet Isaiah quoted in v. 18: ἀπέσταλκέν με κηρύξαι αἰχμαλώτοις ἄφεσιν, fulfilled in himself. (The words ἐπὶ τοῦτο ἀπεστάλην in Lk. 4.43 seem to be redactional in the light of Mk. 1.38.) Perhaps the greatest similarity with Johannine usage occurs, however, in Mt. 10.40 par. Lk. 10.16, and Mk. 9.37 par. where the very clause τὸν ἀποστείλαντά με occurs. It is disputed whether the clause belonged originally to one traditional saying only or to both,[58] but there are good grounds for believing that in at least one of these sayings it goes back to the historical Jesus. Note

---

[53] *TDNT* 1.405.

[54] E.A. Abbott (1905) 1723g, quoted in L. Morris (1971) 230 n. 78.

[55] So, e.g., J.H. Bernard (1928) 118-9, L. Morris (1971) 230 n. 78, C.K. Barrett (1978²) 569, J.A.T. Robinson (1985) 368.

[56] See especially 5.36-8, and compare 17.18 with 20.21.

[57] Cf. C.C. Tarrelli (1946).

[58] T.W. Manson (1949) 78 thinks that it probably belonged only to one. I.H. Marshall (1978) 397 thinks that it may do, but V. Taylor (1966²) 405 and R. Riesner (1988) 461f. are among those who think it belonged to both.

especially its attestation in both Mark and Q, as well as in the Fourth Gospel (cf. especially Jn. 13.20); the fact that both δέχεται, used in Mt. 10.40 and Mk. 9.37 par., and ἀκούει, used in Lk. 10.16, are naturally explicable as variant translations of the the Aramaic word קבל;[59] the climactic parallelism of Mt. 10.40, and the combination of climactic and antithetical parallelism in Lk. 10.16;[60] the four-beat rhythm of the Lukan saying;[61] the very fact that the clause is a circumlocution for God - a common phenomenon in Jesus' speech as in the Judaism of his time;[62] and the Jewishness of the expression when compared with similar sayings from the rabbis.[63]

We have, then, the curious situation of a clause which seems to be as 'authentic' as anything can be in the Synoptic sayings of Jesus and which is yet dismissed as 'inauthentic' from the Fourth Gospel because it is regarded as a mark of the author's distinctive style. The truth of the matter seems to be that the author has taken a clause which is indeed something Jesus said and has used it fairly indiscriminately in his Gospel in his reporting of the sayings of Jesus. As J.D.G. Dunn puts it: 'The fourth evangelist has greatly extended the motif, but this is one of the instances where we can detect the core of authentic tradition round which he builds'.[64] Whether, therefore, the clause originally appeared in the saying preserved in Jn. 9.4 or has been conflated with it by the author (after the manner of his treatment of Old Testament quotations) is a moot point over which certainty is impossible. Some scholars think it was inserted here and they may be right.[65] But, whatever the case on this question, there can be little doubt that the historical Jesus *did* describe himself as one sent by God.

5.3.3 The Textual Crux

One of the problems associated with Jn. 9.4 is the textual variation connected with the pronouns ἡμᾶς and με. The editors of the latest Bible Society text of the New Testament confess to 'a very high degree of doubt'

---

[59] T.W. Manson (1949) 78, I.H. Marshall (1978) 426.
[60] Both types of parallelism being noted characteristics of Jesus' manner of speech. Cf. C.F. Burney (1925) ch. 2.
[61] Another characteristic of Jesus' style. Cf. C.F. Burney (1925) 124.
[62] J. Jeremias (ET 1971) 10.
[63] S.-B. 2.167.
[64] J.D.G. Dunn (1975) 383 n. 86.
[65] E.g. R. Bultmann (ET 1971) 332 n. 1, J. Bligh (1966) 133, B. Lindars (1972) 342, K.E. Dewey (1980) 94.

concerning their reading of ἡμᾶς δεῖ ... τοῦ πέμψαντός με for this verse,[66] so we must look at this problem with care.

First, the textual evidence. Beginning with the initial phrase, the reading ἡμᾶς δεῖ is given by p66, p75, ℵ*, B, L, W, 0124, a syr[pal] ms, some cop[bo] mss, eth[ro], geo[1], Origen, Jerome, Nonnus, and Cyril, while δεῖ ἡμᾶς is given by D, it[d], and cop[sa]. On the other hand, ἐμὲ δεῖ is read by ℵ[a], A, C, K, X, Δ, Θ, Π, Ψ, f[1], f[13], a large number of other minuscules, several latin, syriac, and coptic versions, goth, arm, eth[pp], geo[2], the Diatesseron and Chrysostom. Turning now to the second phrase, πέμψαντός με is read by ℵ[a], A, B, C, D, K, X, Δ, Θ, Π, Ψ, 0124, f[1], f[13], a large number of other minuscules, several latin, syriac, and coptic versions, goth, arm, eth[pp], and geo. πέμψαντος ἡμᾶς on the other hand is read by p66, p75, ℵ*, L, W, cop[bo], eth[ro] and Cyril.

How is this evidence to be evaluated? It will be noticed first of all that some very good manuscripts support both readings in both cases. The Bible Society's 'very high degree of doubt' is therefore understandable. Secondly, it will be noticed that the vast majority of manuscripts *either* read ἡμᾶς δεῖ ... τοῦ πέμψαντος ἡμᾶς *or* ἐμὲ δεῖ ... τοῦ πέμψαντός με. The only manuscripts to stand against this trend are B and D. Could it be that their reading preserves the original and that all the others represent attempts to smooth out the awkwardness of combining ἡμᾶς with με in one sentence - a recognised scribal tendency? This is the solution adopted by most modern scholars,[67] and with good reason:

a. To take the second clause first, the reading τοῦ πέμψαντος ἡμᾶς, though supported by some very good manuscripts must be regarded as virtually impossible as an original reading because it runs counter to the author's otherwise consistent habit of writing τοῦ πέμψαντός με.[68] Sanders and Mastin's attempt to defend the reading τοῦ πέμψαντος ἡμᾶς here is therefore scarcely sustainable.[69]

b. If με is accepted for the second clause, then ἡμᾶς is the most likely for the first, as being the more difficult reading, without being an impossible one.

---

[66] UBS Greek New Testament3 xiii, 363 n. 1, 364 n. 2.
[67] E.g. R.C.H. Lenski (1943) 677, E.C. Hoskyns (1947[2]) 2.406, R.E. Brown (1966) 372, L. Morris (1971) 479, B. Lindars (1972) 342, C.K. Barrett (1978[2]) 357, J.L. Martyn (1979[2]) 28 n. 20, R. Schnackenburg (ET 1980) 2.241, R. Kysar (1986) 149, G.R. Beasley-Murray (1987) 155, D.A. Carson (1991) 362. B.M. Metzger (1971) 227 tells us that the UBS committee supported this reading because of its 'somewhat superior external support' and because it is slightly more probable that copyists would have altered ἡμᾶς to με than vice versa.
[68] J.H. Bernard (1928) 2.325f.
[69] J.N. Sanders and B.A. Mastin (1968) 238 n. 1.

c. The only scholars of note to support the reading ἐμὲ δεῖ ... τοῦ πέμψαντός με in recent years have been J.H. Bernard and R. Bultmann, but their arguments are not convincing: Bernard argues that Jesus did not associate his disciples with himself in the doing of 'the works of God' (taken by Bernard here to mean miracles), so the reading ἡμᾶς in the first clause is inappropriate.[70] It will be argued later that perhaps Jesus was not associating his disciples with himself at this juncture, but even if he was, it would not be an imposssible idea especially if the word 'works' mentioned here is understood in the broadest sense to cover any kind of action which God may require, as it may be in the Fourth Gospel. Passages such as Jn. 4.35-8, Mt. 10, and Lk. 10 suggest that Jesus *did* involve his disciples in some form of mission work during the time of his ministry, and other passages such as Jn. 3.11, 11.1-16, Mk. 4.30, 9.40, and Mt. 17.27 show that Jesus probably did on occasion link himself with his disciples in conversation. Bernard's second point that it is not in the manner of the evangelist to report a 'mere maxim of experience'[71] again begs the question (to be addressed later) whether this is what Jesus is doing here. Suffice it to say for now that other commentators who believe that this is what Jesus is doing have not felt it to be a difficulty as far as the textual question is concerned.

Bultmann argues that an original ἐμέ was changed to ἡμᾶς in the first clause 'since it was thought offensive that the night should put an end to Jesus' activity'.[72] Again, this point will also be considered later, but it is sufficient for now to note that the 'offence' remains even if ἡμᾶς is read, though perhaps it is softened a little. The point is therefore not strong enough to outweigh all other considerations.

One general point about both Bernard and Bultmann needs to be made, and that is that both were working without the evidence of p66 and p75, which are both earlier than all the uncials they quote. Perhaps if this evidence had been available to them they would not have been such strong advocates for the reading of ἐμέ in the initial clause.

We conclude therefore that the most probable original reading of the verse is the one adopted by the UBS 3rd edition text: ἡμᾶς δεῖ ἐργάζεσθαι τὰ ἔργα τοῦ πέμψαντός με ἕως ἡμέρα ἐστίν · ἔρχεται νὺξ ὅτε οὐδεὶς δύναται ἐργάζεσθαι.

---

[70] J.H. Bernard (1928) 2.326.
[71] Ibid.
[72] R. Bultmann (ET 1971) 331 n. 7.

5.3.4 General Maxim or Personal Statement?

Having decided that the text should read thus, it now remains to be discussed how the initial ἡμᾶς should be understood. Was Jesus making a general statement about himself and his disciples, that they should serve God as long as life lasts (if one may paraphrase the saying in this way), or was he making a statement specifically concerning himself?

At first sight the former alternative seems to be obviously correct, and this is how it is taken by the majority of modern commentators. Jesus was associating the disciples with himself in his work, they say,[73] some making the further point that the author is primarily thinking - anachronistically - of his own contemporary situation from a post-resurrection perspective.[74] None, however, take into account the suggestion made by J.T. Marshall in 1929 that this ἡμᾶς may in fact reflect in Greek a peculiarity of Galilean Aramaic whereby the first person plural is often used for the first person singular, even when a first person singular suffix immediately follows.[75] He gives the following example from the Palestinian Talmud where one Kahana says:

אמר מה סליקית מזכי ואנא איחטי
מה סליקית למיקטלה בני ארע דישראל
ניזיל וניחות לי מן הן דסליקית[76]

(He said: 'Did I come up here innocent and now I am led into sin? Did I come up to slay the sons of the land of Israel? I will go away, I will go down to the place whence I came up.) It is notable that in this sentence the first persons singular and plural are used apparently quite indiscriminately. Given the fact that the Greek of the Fourth Gospel is commonly recognised as bearing a heavy Aramaic stamp,[77] and that R.A. Martin can rank Jn. 9.1-12 as a 'clear translation from Aramaic', even apart from the observation just made,[78] there seems to be a strong possibility that the ἡμᾶς of this saying in fact refers to Jesus himself and him alone. This impression is only confirmed by the first person clause which follows: τοῦ πέμψαντός με, and by the fact that, however much Jesus associated the disciples with himself elsewhere (as already noted above), the disciples play no part in the

---

[73] E.g. R.C.H. Lenski (1943) 677, E.C. Hoskyns (1947[2]) 2.406, R.H. Lightfoot (1956) 202, R.E. Brown (1966) 372, J.N. Sanders and B.A. Mastin (1968) 238, W. Thüsing (1970) 63, L. Morris (1971) 479, J. Becker (1979) 318, R. Schnackenburg (ET 1980) 241, G.R. Beasley-Murray (1987) 155, D.A. Carson (1991) 362.
[74] So C.H. Dodd (1963) 188, W. Nicol (1972) 119, J.L. Martyn (1979[2]) 29f.
[75] J.T. Marshall (1929) 14.
[76] Ibid. 37, quoting from *Berakoth* 2.5c.
[77] Cf. The works of C.F. Burney (1922) and R.A. Martin (1989).
[78] R.A. Martin (1989) 10.

healing of the blind man.[79] Even if the saying was originally detached from its present context, the way the author uses it here strongly suggests that he understood it to have a personal reference to Jesus himself. While, therefore, Bernard and Bultmann may be wrong concerning the text, they may well be right concerning the meaning of the text.[80]

5.3.5 The Authenticity of John 9.4: The Criteria Applied

We are now in a position to apply the various criteria for authenticity to 9.4, considered in the first place as an independent saying, bearing in mind that on the basis of the above observations the original saying was probably intended to be a personal saying by Jesus about himself and that it may not have included a description of God as 'the one who sent me' (it could merely have referred to 'God', as in v. 3b). The criterion of multiple attestation fails to support authenticity here, since there is no parallel to the saying in the Synoptic Gospels. We will therefore apply the other four, in the following order: Language, Culture and Personal Idiom; Coherence; Dissimilarity; and Anti- Redactional Features.

(1) Language, Culture and Personal Idiom
Here a number of observations are appropriate:
  a. Firstly, the saying may easily be translated back into Aramaic, thus:

צריך לן למעבד עבידתא דמאן דשלחני מבעוד יום
אתי ליליא דלא יכיל למעבד נש

There is nothing from the point of view of language, therefore, which would prohibit it from being a saying of Jesus, if he was speaking in Aramaic at this point.
  b. Secondly, ἐργάζεσθαι ... ἔργα is a Semitic expression, as Bultmann notes.[81] It is true that he also notes that it also occurs in Greek literature, but the point being made here is simply that the expression would be entirely 'at home' in Jesus' speech.
  c. Thirdly, the use of ἡμέρα and νύξ here is also 'at home' in Jesus' speech. All the Gospels testify uniformly to the fact that Jesus was fond of using pictorial language in his teaching. Moreover, as noted above on p. 104f., the reference to day and night in this verse does not carry the

---

[79] As J.N. Sanders and B.A. Mastin (1968) 238 observe.
[80] At least at the level of the saying in its present form. R. Bultmann believes that in fact in the author's 'source' there were no personal pronouns at all in this saying - (ET 1971) 332 n. 1.
[81] R. Bultmann (ET 1971) 157 n. 6. See also chapter 4 for further arguments in favour of the view that these words formed part of the 'vocabulary' of Jesus.

characteristically Johannine spiritualising overtones as the word 'light' does, for example, in v. 5 and other verses such as 8.12, 12.35f., 46. It was partly for this reason that C.H. Dodd regarded vv. 4-5 as containing material 'for which the evangelist is not primarily responsible'.[82]

d. Fourthly, the image of daytime as the time for work is an Old Testament one, as seen from Ps. 104.23 ('Man goes forth to his work and to his labour until the evening'), and is reflected in a number of proverbial sayings found in the rabbinic writings, as, for example, the saying of R. Tarphon (c. 100 AD): 'The day is short and there is much work to be done; the workers are lazy and the reward is great and the Master of the house is urgent', or that of R. Simeon ben Eleazar (c. 190 AD): 'Work so long as you can and it is possible for you and it is still within your power'.[83] Jesus' saying here in Jn. 9.4 therefore to a certain extent matches his own cultural and religious background.

e. Fifthly, the saying as a whole takes the form of an aphorism which is commonly recognised as an aspect of Jesus' personal idiom as a teacher. J. Drummond includes it on his list of 'some of the most striking' in the Gospel,[84] a judgment which is endorsed by W.F. Howard, who describes the list as 'logia peculiar to the Fourth Gospel, which entirely suit the character and habit of Jesus as they are known to us from the Synoptics.'[85] This comment leads us on to the next criterion.

(2) Coherence

The saying coheres well with what we know of Jesus from the Synoptic Gospels at a number of points. Apart from the points already made above which are also relevant here, we may note the following:

a. The sense of 'necessity' conveyed by the word δεῖ is also a feature of Jesus' speech in the Synoptic Gospels (cf. Mk. 8.31 pars., Mt. 26.54, Lk. 2.49, 4.43, 13.33, 17.25, 22.37, 24.7, 26, 44). Jesus seems to have seen himself as a man of destiny, someone for whom God had a special plan which he felt constrained to fulfil.

b. Linked with this is the sense of the ultimate importance of obedience to the will of God, which is conveyed by the opening clause. This too is characteristic of the Jesus of the Synoptic Gospels (cf. Mt. 4.4 par., Mk. 3.35 pars., 14.36 pars.).

c. The sense of urgency conveyed by the imagery of day and night, with its implication of the shortness of the time available before death, is also

---

[82] C.H. Dodd (1963) 186.
[83] S.-B. 2.529.
[84] J. Drummond (1903) 19.
[85] W.F. Howard (1955[4]) 214f. Cf. L.M. Bridges (1987) 13, who includes 9.4 among the Johannine aphorisms in which the reader 'hears the penetrating voice of Jesus'.

thoroughly in tune with what we know of Jesus from the Synoptic Gospels (cf. Mk. 2.20 pars., 8.31 pars., 9.31 pars., 10.33-34 pars., 10.45 par., 14.21 pars., 14.27 par.). Jesus seems to have been aware of the likelihood of a violent death at an early point in his ministry, and therefore recognised that there was much to do in a short time.

d. If the saying includes a reference to miracles (which it does if taken in its present context) then the following words of J.A.T. Robinson are appropriate:

'The miracles [in John] are entirely and solely the works of the Father (5.36, 9.3f., 10.25, 32, 37f., 14.10, 17.4), and this is in close agreement with the Synoptic picture where all things are possible not to Jesus but to God (Mk. 10.27) and power is available to everyone who has faith (Mk. 9.23) ... He is a man of power because he is a man of prayer ... The Johannine picture is no different. All his power comes from prayerful dependence on the Father (11.22, 17.7f.). He can act because he is heard (11.41f.), and he is "always" heard because it is ever his meat and drink to do the Father's will and to be pleasing to him (4.34, 8.29)'.[86]

The saying thus coheres well with sayings in the Synoptic Gospels which we may reasonably regard as standing close to his original words.[87]

(3) Dissimilarity
In view of the rabbinic proverbs quoted above in the section on language, culture and personal idiom, it cannot be argued that the saying is greatly dissimilar from what any Jew might have said at the time of Jesus. Nevertheless, it needs to be pointed out that whereas the rabbinic proverbs are general in application, the saying of Jesus in Jn. 9.4, as we have seen, should probably be regarded as intensely personal, with connotations of the fulfilment of a particular destiny, the desire to obey God at all costs, and a sense of urgency in view of the threat of death, and as such suits the circumstances of his own unique ministry in a peculiarly appropriate way. These connotations do not characterise the parallels quoted by Strack-Billerbeck at this point.

A stronger case can be made, however, for the saying's dissimilarity from the tone of the early church. It is extremely unlikely that the early church would have created a saying which gave the impression that Jesus' work would come to an end at his death, still less one which gave the impression that at his death *no one* would be able to work. Yet that is precisely the impression this verse gives us.

---

[86] J.A.T. Robinson (1985) 349.
[87] There is a general agreement concerning the 'authenticity' of these gospel motifs. A more detailed defence of the authenticity, in a strict sense, of Mk. 3.35 will be given in chapter 6 in connection with Jn. 4.34, where the 'will' of God is explicitly referred to.

Many commentators have had difficulty with this verse on account of this disjunction between what the verse says and what we know of the early church. J. Calvin and B.F. Westcott are among those who struggle to make a distinction between the works which Jesus did before his death and those he did after his resurrection.[88] H. Odeberg makes a totally unconvincing attempt to spiritualise the concepts of day and night, making the 'night' refer only to the spiritual darkness which envelops unbelievers.[89] R. Bultmann correctly recognises the 'offensive' nature of the saying, but then proceeds needlessly to remove the offence by hypothesising, on the basis of an 'impression', that the author's 'source' only contained a harmless maxim at this point.[90] He fails to give a satisfactory explanation as to why the evangelist might have wanted to turn a harmless maxim into an 'offensive' statement and then inserted it into one of Jesus' speeches in his Gospel.

In short, the saying's dissimilarity from the way the early church generally regarded Jesus must be reckoned as a powerful argument against the view that it was created by the early church.

(4) Anti-Redactional Features
The argument from dissimilarity can be continued by looking specifically at the Johannine context itself. It is true that in the Fourth Gospel Jesus speaks elsewhere about his departure from the world (cf. e.g. 7.33f., 8.21, 12.35f., 13.33, 14.19, 16.16) but nowhere is his 'prognosis' of the future as bleak as it appears to be in this verse.

Once again, commentators have noticed the tension between this saying and the general trend of the Fourth Gospel. As Odeberg frankly acknowledges, 'It would be quite against the whole Johannine system of thought to say that the end of Jesus' earthly activity would mark the beginning of a "night", a period of darkness, when all spiritual activity would be excluded'.[91] Similarly J.L. Martyn sees 'a sharp contradiction' between 9.4b-5 on the one hand and 9.4a and 14.12 on the other,[92] a contradiction he is unable to resolve. In the former, Jesus says 'no one can work' when he goes. In the latter, Jesus prophecies that the disciples will do *greater* works *because* he goes. J. Bligh likewise sees this tension, and uses it, Bultmann-like, to reconstruct a possible original form for the saying which makes no reference to Jesus at all, but changes the ἡμᾶς into a ὑμᾶς.[93] Once again we are forced to ask: why would the author want to

---

[88] J. Calvin (ET 1959) 239f., B.F. Westcott (1908) 2.32.
[89] H. Odeberg (1929) 312.
[90] R. Bultmann (ET 1971) 332 n. 1.
[91] H. Odeberg (1929) 311.
[92] J.L. Martyn (1979²) 28.
[93] J. Bligh (1966) 133.

change an inoffensive saying into one which went against the general tenor of his Gospel ?

Other points along the same lines may be made. As we have already seen, the author is fond of using the light/ darkness distinction in a wholly spiritual way, yet in 9.4 this connotation is absent. He is fond of speaking of the cross as the hour of Christ's glory (cf. 12.23, 28, 13.31, 32, 17.5), yet here it is spoken of in terms of dereliction.[94] Perhaps most importantly of all, the author is usually thought of as viewing Jesus, even more than the Synoptists do, from a post-Easter perspective, of superimposing a picture of the post-Easter, heavenly Christ on that of the pre-Easter, earthly Jesus. Here, by contrast, we have a Jesus who, for the moment, seems to see no further than the cross.

Once again we have good grounds for believing that 9.4 stands in a close relation to something Jesus said, whether or not it was originally said in this particular context. Historical certainty is inevitably elusive in such matters, but on the basis of all the preceding arguments as good a case can be made out for the authenticity of this saying (in the strict, type b, sense of the word) as can be made for many sayings in the Synoptic Gospels which are regarded as 'authentic' by a majority of modern scholars.

5.3.6 The Authenticity of the ἔργα Motif in John 9.3b-4

No attempt will be made here to argue for a type b authenticity for v. 3b, though, as was noted on p. 107 above, it contains a number of motifs which cohere well with what we know of Jesus from the Synoptic Gospels. Rather, attention will be drawn to one particular motif which is implicit in vv. 3b-4 in their present context, and which will be found elsewhere in our studies of the 'works' sayings of Jesus, namely the motif that the works of Jesus are the works of God. As Jesus heals the blind man, so *God's* works are made manifest. What Jesus does is thus what God does through him. That this motif is true to the historical Jesus will now be shown from a close study of a well-known Synoptic saying: Mt. 12.28 par. Lk. 11.20.

This Q saying is found in the so-called 'Beelzebul controversy', recorded in all three Gospels, in which Jesus' opponents accuse him of casting out demons by Beelzebul, the prince of demons (Mt. 12.22-30 pars. Mk. 3.22-27, Lk. 11.14-23). The absence of Mt. 12.27f. par. Lk. 11.19f. from Mark's version of the controversy may mean that these verses have been

---

[94] Cf. F. Grob (1986) 41, who draws attention to the fact that 'not working' in the Fourth Gospel implies the absence of God, or the being in a wrong relationship with God (cf. 3.2, 5.19, 30, 9.16, 33, 10.21).

added in from another context, though they fit well where they are. Again there is uncertainty over whether Mt. 12.27 par. Lk. 11.19 originally belonged together with Mt. 12.28 par. Lk. 11.20,[95] but these issues are not of vital importance to the matter we are principally concerned with here, namely the authenticity and meaning of the saying in Mt. 12.28 par. Lk. 11.20 itself.

The authenticity of this saying in a strict sense is affirmed by the overwhelming majority of modern scholars. Indeed so sure are they of its genuineness that the impression is often given that if we cannot ascribe this saying to Jesus, then we might as well despair of being able to ascribe anything to him.[96] The only noteworthy exception to this general consensus at present is E.P. Sanders,[97] but he fails to give an adequate answer to the strong arguments which favour the saying's authenticity, and, as J.D.G. Dunn has argued in a recent article,[98] applies, as a requirement for authenticity, standards of precision in our ability to reconstruct Jesus' original Aramaic words which he fails to apply to other sayings which he is prepared to accept as authentic in his attempt to get back to the historical Jesus (e.g. Mk. 14.58).

The arguments advanced for the authenticity of the saying may be easily rehearsed. To begin with the saying satisfies the most stringent criterion of all for authenticity, namely that of double dissimilarity. On the one hand, there is no record of any Jew linking together the performance of exorcisms with the arrival of the kingdom of God,[99] and on the other it is well known that exorcism barely figures in the rest of the New Testament and does not seem to have had a prominent place in the life of the early church (the same

---

[95] Those who favour an original linkage include J. Jeremias (ET 1971) 15, I.H. Marshall (1978) 475, and W.D. Davies and D.C. Allison (1991) 2.339. Those who favour an independent origin for the two sayings include A.H. McNeile (1928) 176, W.G. Kümmel (ET 1957) 105, R. Bultmann (ET 1968²) 162 and B. Witherington (1990) 201.94.

[96] Thus: R. Bultmann (ET 1968²) 162 says 'Mt. 12.28/ Lk. 11.20 ... can, in my view, claim the highest degree of authenticity which we can make for any saying of Jesus ...'; J.D.G. Dunn (1975) 44 says 'If we cannot be sure that the Q saying preserved in Mt. 12.28/ Lk. 11.20 is a genuine saying of Jesus, we might as well give up all hope of rediscovering the historical Jesus, the man or his message'; in (1988) 38 n. 22 he speaks of 'a strong consensus in German scholarship in favour of the authenticity of Mt. 12.28/ Lk. 11.20 as a word of the historical Jesus'; E.P. Sanders (1985) 136 says 'there is probably no other verse in the Gospels about which there is so much unanimity'; W.D. Davies and D.C. Allison (1991) 2.339 say 'the authenticity of [Mt] 12.28 would seem to be one of the assured results of modern criticism'.

[97] E.P. Sanders (1985) 133-141.

[98] J.D.G. Dunn (1988) 47f.

[99] J. Jeremias (ET 1971) 32-34.

is true, though to a lesser extent, of teaching concerning the 'kingdom of God').[100] Secondly, despite the unusualness of the saying as a whole, the terms of the saying fit well into the Jewish religious culture of which Jesus was a part: exorcism *did* take place within that culture (as Mt. 12.27 par. Lk. 11.19 itself testifies); the phrases 'Spirit of God' (Mt.) and 'Finger of God' (Lk.) would both have been familiar to Jesus' hearers; and the same can be said of the phrase 'Kingdom of God'. Likewise, the use of the phrase 'Kingdom of God' and the idea of the presence of the kingdom inherent in the saying[101] are commonly regarded as characteristics of the teaching of the historical Jesus in particular, and the saying as a whole may be translated back into Aramaic,[102] so the saying satisfies the criterion of language, culture and personal idiom. Finally, the saying coheres well with the widespread belief, found not only in the Gospels but also in Jewish sources and accepted among modern scholars, that 'exorcism' in some form *did* form part of Jesus' ministry, and also with other sayings reliably attributed to Jesus in the Gospels in which claims are made concerning the fulfilment of the eschatological hopes of Israel in and through his ministry.[103] It is with good reason therefore that we may confidently attribute this saying to Jesus.[104]

---

[100] For the argument from double dissimilarity see especially J.D.G. Dunn (1988) 38-42. Philip and Paul are found casting out demons in Acts 8.7, 16.16-18, but there is no reference to exorcism at all in the letters of the New Testament or in the Fourth Gospel.

[101] That ἔφθασεν should be taken to mean that Jesus believed that the kingdom of God had in some sense arrived is still the common view. Cf., e.g., W.G. Kümmel (ET 1957) 106f., E. Ellis (1966) 165, J. Jeremias (ET 1971) 102, D. Hill (1972) 216, G. Bornkamm (ET 1973) 90, J.D.G. Dunn (1975) 44, (1988) 47 n. 45, I.H. Marshall (1978) 476, J.A. Fitzmyer (1985) 2.922, C.F. Evans (1990) 492, B. Witherington (1990) 202, W.D. Davies and D.C. Allison (1991) 2.340.

[102] Though certainty regarding the original words of Jesus is not possible at this point, the following is offered as a rendering of Luke's version of the saying back into Aramaic:

אלו באצבעא דאלהא מפיק אנא שדין מטא עליכון מלכותא דאלהא

[103] Such as Mt. 9.37f. par. Lk. 10.2, Mt. 11.5f. par. Lk. 7.22f., Mt. 11.11 par. Lk. 7.28, Mt. 11.12 par. Lk. 16.16, Mt. 12.41f. par. Lk. 11.31f., Mt. 13.16f. par. Lk. 10.23f., Lk. 17.20f. See J.D.G. Dunn (1988) 43-45. For the accepted fact that Jesus was an 'exorciser' see ibid. 31-33, B. Witherington (1990) 201.

[104] It is worth noting, in passing, that this confidence is not undermined by the existence of this saying in only one strand of the gospel tradition, namely Q, nor by its failure to satisfy the criterion of anti-redactional features (unless Luke's δακτύλῳ or Matthew's 'kingdom of *God*' is thought to fall into this category). This observation illustrates the fact that these two criteria should not be used negatively, a fact which has obvious relevance for Jesus' Johannine sayings.

As far as the original form of the saying is concerned, we need to note the major difference between the versions of the saying in Matthew and Luke, namely Matthew's πνεύματι as against Luke's δακτύλῳ. J.D.G. Dunn has put up a good case for Matthew's word as being more original on the grounds that Matthew's 'Kingdom of God' is unusual for Matthew, betraying a close following of his source here; that Matthew would have exploited the Moses typology inherent in δακτύλῳ if it had been in his source (cf. Ex. 8.19); that Luke may have changed πνεύματι into δακτύλῳ for the sake of an *Exodus* typology; and that he may not have wanted to portray Jesus as 'Lord' of the Spirit (as opposed to 'Man' of the Spirit) until after Pentecost.[105] The majority view is clearly in favour of Luke's version as the more original at this point on the grounds that Matthew is likely to have changed an original δακτύλῳ into πνεύματι in view of the comparative infrequency of the word δάκτυλος used as an anthropomorphism in the Biblical writings by contrast with the theologically more sophisticated and more common word πνεῦμα; that he may well have assimilated his source to the expressions in Mt. 12.18, 31f., with their references to the Spirit; and that it is difficult to see why Luke, who undoubtedly had a special interest in the role of the Spirit in the life of Jesus and that of the early church, would have wanted to change πνεύματι if he had found it in his source. In addition it has been argued that Matthew's unusual 'Kingdom of *God*' (rather than the more usual 'heaven') may have come about through the influence of the parallel expressions 'Spirit of *God*' in the same verse and '*his* kingdom' in v. 26, rather than through any close following of his source.[106] Fortunately not a great deal hangs on the outcome of this debate for our purposes, since both words

---

[105] J.D.G. Dunn (1975) 45f. Additionally, C.S. Rodd (1961) 157f. argued that as far as we know Matthew never added a reference to the Spirit to a source (though he does include verses unique to himself which do refer to the Spirit), and that despite Luke's liking for the word 'Spirit', he does not always preserve it when he finds it in his source (cf. Lk. 20.42 par. Mk. 12.36). This latter point is true but: a. this is the only such occurrence; b. it is about the inspiration of scripture not about the inspiration of Christ; and c. it is a case of *omitting* a reference to the Spirit, not of replacing it with something else. It is interesting to note that though Rodd believes Q probably had 'Spirit' rather than 'finger', he still believes that 'finger' may have been in L and may be 'nearer to the originality of the mind of Jesus' himself.

[106] A.H. McNeile (1928) 176, W.D. Davies and D.C. Allison (1991) 2.339. The view that Luke is closer to Q is held by A.H. McNeile (1928) 176, T.W. Manson (1949) 86, W.G. Kümmel (ET 1957) 106 n. 3, E. Ellis (1966) 165, J. Jeremias (ET 1971) 79, D. Hill (1972) 216, E. Schweizer (ET 1976) 287, I.H. Marshall (1978) 475f., J.A. Fitzmyer (1985) 2.918, F.W. Beare (1981) 279, B. Witherington (1990) 201, W.D. Davies and D.C. Allison (1991) 2.340.

effectually mean the same in this context, in that both are different ways of describing Jesus' belief that he was expelling demons by God's power.[107]

Having established, as far as possible, the authenticity and original form of this saying, we may now investigate its meaning. To begin with we note that the subject of the verb is Jesus. It is Jesus who casts out the demons, and the authority with which he does so is everywhere apparent in the exorcism stories of the Gospels. As has often been observed, Jesus does not invoke God or pray to God or use quasi-magical rituals in his exorcisms, but simply commands the demons to go.[108] Yet at the same time Jesus here claims that the power with which he exorcises demons is the power of God - the God of creation (Ps. 8.3), of revelation (Ex. 31.18, Deut. 9.10), and of judgment and redemption (Ex. 8.19). The action therefore is both the action of Jesus and the action of God. Or, as J.D.G. Dunn has put it: 'In his [Jesus'] action God acted'.[109] In other words, what Jesus did was what God did through him. At the point of Jesus' exorcisms, at least, their action coincided, the 'works' of Jesus were the 'works' of God. Thus despite the fact that exorcisms do not feature in the Fourth Gospel at all, we can see clearly that the same basic idea lies behind Jn. 9.3b-4 as lies behind Mt. 12.28 par. Lk. 11.20. Whatever the case concerning the wording of Jn. 9.3b-4, this ἔργα motif may be called authentically dominical.

5.4 The Exegesis of John 9.3b-4

5.4.1 Introduction

Quite a number of exegetical points have been made in the course of the discussion so far, so to some extent in this section we will be drawing these threads together, although a few new points will also be made.

One of the basic principles of exegesis is that the meaning of a text depends on its context, and that is why a considerable amount of space was devoted to a discussion of the context of Jn. 9.3b-4 in the earlier part of this chapter. However, it has also been recognised that v. 4 may have existed as a saying of Jesus independently of the context given it in ch. 9, though it was argued that it is more probable that this was not the case. Likewise it

---

[107] Cf. D. Hill (1972) 216, I.H. Marshall (1978) 475, W.D. Davies and D.C. Allison (1991) 2.340.

[108] E.g. B. Witherington (1990) 202.

[109] J.D.G. Dunn (1975) 47. Cf. C.F. Evans (1990) 492: '"Finger" ... stresses that the action of Jesus is nothing less than the personal redeeming action of God ...'. Cf. also J. Jeremias (ET 1971) 102, 254.

was seen that the phrase τοῦ πέμψαντός με may not have been original to the saying, and that v. 5 may not have been original to the context. On a broader front, it was seen that, at a historical level, doubts persist over the extent to which ch. 9 as a whole represents what took place during the ministry of Jesus on the one hand and the extent to which it represents the author's own creative writing up of what took place during his ministry on the other. All of this, of course, complicates the task of exegesis. Perhaps it would be best, therefore, to split up our comments into three sections, concerned with: 9.4 as an independent saying; 9.3b-4 in its presumed historical context; and 9.3b-4 in its total Johannine context.

5.4.2 John 9.4 as an Independent Saying

If Jn. 9.4 was originally an independent saying then its original context is lost, which makes it difficult for us to know its precise connotations. Nevertheless certain things may still be said about Jesus if the verse is taken in this way.

a. We learn in the first place that he felt a 'divine imperative', a strong sense of obligation to do what he believed God had given him to do. As L. Morris puts it: '"Must" reminds us that this is not simply what is advisable or expedient. There is the thought of a compelling necessity'.[110] In the light of the Synoptic sayings reviewed above on p. 115f. we may even say that this saying speaks of Jesus' sense of destiny, of his sense of need to fulfil the particular plan which God had for his life on earth.

b. In the second place, taking the phrase τοῦ πέμψαντός με to be authentic in a strict sense (whether or not it belonged to the original saying), we may say that Jesus had a consciousness of prophetic vocation.[111] The clause denotes one who has been commissioned by God, who represents God, who acts as God's agent, and who carries the authority of God,[112] and was usually associated with the prophet's calling (cf. Isa. 61.1, Jer. 1.5-7, Jn. 1.6, 33, 3.28).

c. In the third place, the saying shows us that Jesus was conscious of the brevity of the time available for him to fulfil his calling. His life was but a 'day'. 'Night' was coming. He was probably aware that his enemies were seriously plotting his death, and this gave him a sense of urgency in 'doing

---

[110] L. Morris (1971) 479.
[111] J.D.G. Dunn (1975) 83.
[112] Cf. *TDNT* 1.415, S.-B. 2.167, E. Haenchen (1962-1963) 208-216, A.E. Harvey (1982) 162, B. Witherington (1990) 136.

the works of God' while there was still opportunity to do so.[113] As was noted earlier on p. 118f., the saying sees no further than the cross, but this need not rule out the possibility that on other occasions Jesus spoke of his subsequent vindication and of the work that his disciples would do after his departure.

5.4.3 John 9.3b-4 in its Presumed Historical Context

If we take the whole saying to have been originally uttered on this occasion, as it was argued above we may, then it takes on new meanings. The 'works' then do not simply mean deeds or actions in general, but at least include the working of miracles, of which the healing of the blind man is an example, and the fact that these words immediately precede the action of Jesus in healing the blind man indicates that in saying them Jesus is in fact claiming to be actually 'doing the works of God', and not simply expressing a general sense of obligation to do so. In view of this, some further points may be made:

a. Firstly, Jesus may be making an implicit claim to messiahship. A number of commentators point out that in the Old Testament, the giving of sight to the blind is expected to be a mark of the messianic age (cf. Isa. 29.18, 35.5, 42.7).[114] Moreover, when Jesus himself is asked by the messengers of John the Baptist in Mt. 11.2 par. whether he is 'he who is to come', the very first thing he says by way of giving an affirmative reply is that the blind are receiving their sight (Mt. 11.5 par.). It needs to be remembered that there are no recorded instances of the healing of the blind in the Old Testament itself, so Jesus probably regarded himself as acting in an unprecedented way, as inaugurating a new era, and as being a 'messianic' figure.[115]

---

[113] The precise sense of the phrase 'doing the works of God' is difficult to pin down. It could mean 'doing the works which God commands', 'doing the works which God does in imitation of him' or 'doing the works which God does by being the means by which he does them'. If 9.4 was originally an independent saying, the first sense is the most natural in view of the word δεῖ, but in its context the third sense (which embraces and transcends the second) is also implied. See appendix B for a full discussion of this isssue.

[114] Cf. E.C. Hoskyns (1947²) 2.402, R.H. Lightfoot (1956) 199, R.E. Brown (1966) 378, L. Morris (1971) 475, J. Painter (1991) 265. F. Grob (1986) 45 sees further allusions to Isa. 42-43 in this passage, as, for example, in the 'blind' servant of the Lord (Isa. 42.19), who is 'created' for God's glory (Isa. 43.1, 7) and called to be God's witness (Isa. 43.10, 12).

[115] These important words of Jesus in Mt. 11.4f. par. Lk. 7.22 will be discussed more fully in chapter 9.

b. Secondly, Jesus is implicitly claiming that his 'works' are the works of God. He is conscious of being in such unity with God that he regards what he does to be at the same time what God does in and through him, and therefore something which 'manifests' what God does. As we saw in section 5.3.6 above, this understanding is comparable with Jesus' belief expressed in Mt. 12.28 par. Lk. 11.20 that what he did in his exorcisms he did by God's power.

c. Thirdly, in view of the reference to the sabbath in v. 14, if this may be taken to be part of the original story,[116] and the actions described in 9.6,[117] we find Jesus claiming, in effect, as he does in ch. 5, to have authority to dispense with the scribal interpretations of the sabbath which had built up over the years, to interpret scripture in his own way, and to act in accordance with an immediate perception of God's will. Such a claim indicates a very high view of his own status and not surprisingly is portrayed as alienating the guardians of the scribal traditions.[118]

5.4.4 John 9.3b-4 in its Total Johannine Context

Taking this saying in its broadest Johannine context, the following additional observations may be made:

a. The theme of light is clearly an important one for the author of the Fourth Gospel, as has already been said on p. 104 above, and it was argued there that he may well have introduced v. 5 into this context in order to bring out what he saw to be the spiritual significance of the story of the healing of the blind man. Jesus gives sight to the man, but he also enlightens his mind, as vv. 35-41 make clear. The giving of 'light', then, is one of the 'works' of God that Jesus does,[119] and those who follow him will have 'the light of life' (8.12, cf. 12.35-36, 46).

---

[116] We are not necessarily to take this detail as secondary and unhistorical. True, it appears as a kind of afterthought in the narrative, but consideration needs to be given to the possibility that it was part of the author's art to introduce pieces of information into a story only when they became functional and/or raised the tension of the narrative. Cf. Other such cases, as 2.6, 6.59, 13.30, 18.28, 19.14, 20.14.

[117] Both the making of the clay and the anointing of the eyes are probably intended to be seen as a breach of the sabbath commandments. Cf. R.H. Lightfoot (1956) 202, R. Bultmann (ET 1971) 332, J. Becker (1979) 317, R. Schnackenburg (ET 1980) 242. The Synoptic sabbath healing stories reveal that the Pharisees also objected to the sabbath healings of Jesus *per se*. Cf. Mk. 3.1-6 pars., Lk. 13.10-17, 14.1-6.

[118] This motif comes to clear expression in Jn. 5.16-18 and will be more fully dealt with in chapter 7.

[119] Cf. J. Riedl (1973) 298-306.

b. Allied to this, it must be considered possible that judgment was also seen by the author to be one of the 'works' of God performed through Jesus in this context in view of vv. 39-41. Jesus judges as well as gives life (cf. 5.22-30, 8.16). Not that this was the main reason for his coming into the world (cf. 3.17, 12.47), but rather that it was the inevitable by-product of his coming in the case of those who refused to receive the light he brought (cf. 3.18-21, 12.48).[120]

c. As was noted in n. 24, there may be a hint of the theme of a new creation in v. 6 in the mention of the clay which Jesus put on the blind man's eyes (cf. Gen. 2.6-7). This too may have been in the author's mind when he refers to the 'works' of Jesus. The language of vv. 4-5, with their references to 'works', 'light', 'day', 'night', and 'world', is certainly reminiscent of Gen. 1.1-2.3, where God performs the works of creation, and, in the case of 'light' and 'world', reminds us of Jn. 1.1-18 where Christ, the Word of God, is described as the agent of creation. Christ, who brought the old world into being, is here also seen at work in bringing about a new creation.[121]

d. A deeper christology can also be seen behind the phrase 'him who sent me' in v. 4. Though it is quite true to say that the phrase itself need mean no more than that Jesus had been called and commissioned by God to fulfil a prophetic role, within the context of the whole Gospel it is not difficult to see here a reference to his pre-existence with God from the beginning (cf. 1.1-3, 3.13, 6.38-39, 62, 8.58, 17.5). As J.D.G. Dunn puts it, the evangelist 'took the step of speaking of Christ as the Son sent *from heaven*, as a personal being sent from his pre-existent glory into the world' (italics his).[122]

e. Finally, we need to remind ourselves of the purpose of the evangelist in recording the miracle stories as he expresses it in 20.31, namely that his readers 'may believe that Jesus is the Christ, the Son of God, and that believing ... may have life in his name'.

5.5 The Exegesis of John 9.3b-4 in the Patristic Era

Jn. 9.3b-4 was not often discussed in the patristic era, if our extant literature is anything to go by.

A few times it is given a practical application, as when Jerome quotes 9.3. to comfort Castrutius, who was blind, to assure him that his blindness is not

---

[120] Cf. F. Grob (1986) 37f.
[121] Cf. F. Grob (1986) 43.
[122] J.D.G. Dunn (1989²) 245, *contra* J.A.T. Robinson (1985) ch. 8.

due to his sin,[123] or when Abbot Theodore, in his 'conference' with John Cassian, quotes 9.3 to say that some sufferings are brought upon us simply for the manifestation of the glory of God and his works. Augustine, on the other hand, characteristically makes the point that the fact that the blindness of the man was not due to the sin of the man or his parents does not mean that they were not sinners.[124]

Sometimes there is discussion over the length of the 'day' mentioned in 9.4. Ambrose distinguishes between the two natures of Christ at this point and says that as man Jesus was the light of the world for a season, but as God he exists at all times.[125] Augustine and Chrysostom see the day lasting as long as the world endures.[126]

Of more interest for our purposes, however, is the christological use to which Jn. 9.3b-4 is put. Tertullian cites 9.4, along with many other texts, in his work against Praxeas ch. 22, to show that the Son is distinct from the Father as against Praxeas' form of modalistic monarchianism. Irenaeus, on the other hand, uses 9.3 to show that Jesus shares with the Father in the work of creation. 'That which the artificer, the Word, had omitted to form in the womb', he says, 'He then supplied in public, that the works of God might be manifested in him in order that we might not be seeking out another hand by which man was fashioned, nor another Father; knowing that this hand of God which formed us at the beginning, and which does form us in the womb, has in the last times sought us out who were lost ...'.[127] Irenaeus' chief target is gnosticism, which imagined the Father of Jesus to be other than the creator of the world, but the interesting point here is that he sees the 'works' mentioned here to be the works of *creation*, and that he sees Christ's act of healing the blind man to be an example of Christ's creative activity as a whole as 'the Word' through whom God 'formed us at the beginning'.

This type of christological understanding of Jn. 9.3b-4 is developed further by later writers. Thus Hilary integrates Jn. 9.3f. into his exposition of

---

[123] Jerome, *Letter 68, to Castrutius*, sec. 1. Unless otherwise specified all patristic references in Chapters 5 to 9 will be taken from the *Ante-Nicene Fathers*, edd. A. Roberts and J. Donaldson, reprinted 1986-1990, and from *A Select Library of Nicene and Post-Nicene Fathers of the Christian Church*, first series reprinted 1975-1989, ed. P. Schaff, second series reprinted 1986-1991, edd. P. Schaff and H. Wace, all pub. by T. & T. Clark, Edinburgh, and Eerdmans, Grand Rapids. The referencing of the patristic writings cited has followed that of these editions. It is not claimed that these sections on the patristic exegesis of the relevant texts are exhaustive, but it *is* claimed that they give a fair portrayal of the major ways in which they were understood.

[124] Augustine, *Sermon 86*, sec. 1.
[125] Ambrose, *Of the Christian Faith*, 3.7.48.
[126] Augustine, *Tractate 44 on John's Gospel*, sec. 6.
[127] Irenaeus, *Against the Heresies*, 15.2.

Jn. 5 in his work 'On the Trinity' and explains: 'You see that in this case the work wrought by the Son is the Father's work; and the Son's work is God's work ... they are at one in their method of working'. So though they have a 'distinct existence' they have 'one nature'.[128] Augustine argues against the Arian use of Jn. 9.4 to prove the inferiority of the Son, because the Son is shown to obey the Father, by arguing that scripture teaches that in fact both Father and Son do the works of each other, so that they must share in the same 'power', 'will', and 'nature'.[129] Chrysostom perhaps goes the furthest of all, however, when he affirms that in Jn. 9.3 Christ, in speaking of the manifesting of the works of God was actually speaking about *himself* as the 'Architect of creation ... the Creator at the beginning' who does 'the same things' as the Father, sharing the 'same power with the Father'.[130]

This type of heightened christological understanding of the 'works' sayings of Jesus will be found in later chapters also in our study of the other sayings. Here we simply note that whereas Jn. 9.3b-4 may originally have had reference to the obedience of Jesus or the working of a miracle by the power of God, and only tangentially in the Johannine context to Jesus' creative power, it came to be seen as an example of a universal and eternal phenomenon, i.e. the total and continuous co-operation of Jesus as the Son with God the Father in absolutely everything he does, with his co-operation in the work of creation as the foremost thought.

5.6 Conclusion

The main conclusions from this chapter may now be briefly summarised:

a. The words attributed to Jesus in Jn. 9.3b-4 cohere extremely well with what we know of him from the Synoptic Gospels. As such they may be said to share at least in the looser, type c authenticity described in chapter 2 above. In addition we have seen reason to believe that v. 4 in particular stands in a close relation to the original words of Jesus (though τοῦ πέμψαντός με may be a secondary, yet independently authentic, addition), and therefore probably shares in a stricter, type b authenticity.

b. We learn therefore that Jesus felt himself to be a man of destiny. He was aware of a divine imperative, as one sent by God, to 'do the works of God' and of the shortness of time available to him for doing them. If v. 4 originally belonged to this context, there may also be here an implicit messianic claim and a claim to have the authority to overrule the scribal

---

[128] Hilary, *On the Trinity*, 7.21.
[129] Augustine, *Sermon 85*, secs. 4f.
[130] Chrysostom, *Homily 56 on John's Gospel*, sec. 2.

sabbath regulations. In addition we are reminded, from vv. 3b-4 as a whole, that Jesus believed that he had been sent by God and that what he was doing was actually what God was doing through him.

c. At the level of the Johannine redaction, we have seen reason to believe that the author regarded the 'works' of God performed through Jesus as including the works of light-giving and judging, in the case of the blind man and the Pharisees respectively, and participating in the creative activity of God. In addition the idea of Jesus being 'sent' has clear connotations of pre-existence in the Fourth Gospel.

d. Finally we have seen that in the patristic era the text is used christologically both the affirm the distinctness of the Father and the Son and to affirm their unity of nature. For Hilary and Augustine the works of the Father and the Son are absolutely and eternally one and the same, while for Irenaeus and Chrysostom Jn.9. 3b-4 is a reminder of the fact that Christ is the one through whom all things were made in the beginning.

Chapter 6

Accomplishing God's Work

6.1 Introduction

In this chapter we will consider Jn. 4.34 and 17.4. Only in these verses in the Fourth Gospel, and indeed in the New Testament as a whole, do we find Jesus describing his ministry as a 'work', using the word ἔργον in the singular. Elsewhere, Jesus is found to use this word in the singular at 6.29, 7.21, and 10.32, but in 6.29 he uses it of something his hearers are to do, namely believe in him, and in the other verses he is probably referring to his miracles.

As in the previous chapter, we shall consider the context of these sayings, then their authenticity, and their meaning, taking them one at a time, and then finally, taken together, their use in the patristic era.

6.2 The Context of John 4.34

6.2.1 John 4.1-42

Jn. 4.34 is found in what may be called a 'pericope' consisting of 4.31-34 embedded in the story of Jesus' encounter with the woman at the well in Sychar of Samaria. According to the story, Jesus is on a return journey from Judea to Galilee (4.3), following his visit to Jerusalem for the passover festival (2.13). Tired from his journey, he sits down beside the well in Sychar (4.6), and, while his disciples are away buying food (4.8), he engages in conversation with a Samaritan woman who had come to the well to draw water (4.7-26). The woman's perception of who Jesus is grows from the idea that he is an ordinary Jew (4.9), to the belief that he is a prophet (4.19), to speculation that he may be the Christ (4.29), and in the end, implicitly, to the conviction that he is 'the Saviour of the world' (4.42).

It is after the disciples have returned from their shopping expedition and while the woman is away talking to her fellow townspeople that Jesus has the conversation with his disciples which is recorded in 4.31-38 and which contains the saying to be studied here.

Doubts have been expressed concerning the historicity of the story as a whole. B. Lindars, for example, regards 4.1-26 as 'patently a Johannine construction', and, in view of Synoptic passages such as Mt. 10.5f., 15.24, and Lk. 9.51-56, doubts whether there ever was a mission to the Samaritans during the public ministry of Jesus.[1] He thinks the story may have been influenced by the later mission to Samaria in the post-Pentecost period recorded in Acts 8.4-25. Similarly, C.K. Barrett thinks it impossible to isolate a 'pre-Johannine nucleus' of the story.[2] Others, however, have been more positive. R. Schnackenburg, for example, admits the skilful construction of the passage, but thinks that this is no reason for doubting its historicity.[3] R.E. Brown, like Schnackenburg, is impressed by the evidence of local knowledge shown by the evangelist and concludes that there could well be a substratum of traditional material with a historical basis underlying the story. 'It is not at all impossible', he says, 'that even in the conversation we have echoes of a historical tradition of an incident in Jesus' ministry'.[4] Others go further still and in view of the vivid detail to be found in the passage affirm the presence of eyewitness material.[5] One problem with this view is, of course, that no one appears to have been in a position to witness the conversation between Jesus and the woman, since 4.8 gives the impression that the disciples had all gone off to the town. This is not an insuperable problem, however, because the woman herself clearly told others of her conversation with Jesus after the event (4.28f., 42), and it is highly likely that Jesus himself would also have later done so to his disciples, in view of its dramatic sequel. As for the passages which Lindars cites, Mt. 10.5f. and 15.24 refer to an official mission 'policy' which does not necessarily conflict with the kind of casual encounter described in Jn. 4, which takes place while Jesus and his disciples are en route between Jerusalem and Galilee, and Lk. 9.51-56 refers to a different kind of incident altogether.

Without going into all the details of this debate, we may safely say that a good case can be made for the basic historicity of the narrative, however much it may have been shaped by the author for the purposes of its

---

[1] B. Lindars (1972) 175.
[2] C.K. Barrett (1978²) 229.
[3] R. Schnackenburg (ET 1968) 1.420.
[4] R.E. Brown (1966) 1.176.
[5] Cf. B.F. Westcott (1908) 1.142, J.H. Bernard (1928) 1.152, and L. Morris (1969) 146-151, who also cites J.A. Findlay and C.J. Wright in support.

presentation in the Gospel, and it is this view which will be assumed in what follows.[6]

At this point, however, a further question arises. Granted that there is a basic historicity to the story, are we able to separate the original 'core' from secondary accretions? The source theorists would answer this question affirmatively, though not all agree on the exact extent of the original 'core'. For R. Bultmann, the original story contained vv. 5-7, 9, 16-19, perhaps some of 20-26, 28-30, and 40.[7] For R.T. Fortna, it contained vv. 4-7, 9, 16-19, 25-26, 28-30, 40 and 42,[8] for W. Nicol, vv. 5-9, 16-19, 28-30, and 40,[9] for U.C. von Wahlde, vv. 1-9, 16-19, 25-30, and 39,[10] for J. Becker, vv. 5-9ab, 16-19, 27-30, and parts of 40-42,[11] for E. Haenchen, vv. 4-7, 9-18, 28-30, and 39-42,[12] and for S. Temple, vv. 1, 3, 5, part of 6, 7, part of 9, 10-21, part of 23, 24-26, part of 27, and 28-35.[13] It will be noticed from this quick run through the various theories that all except for S. Temple regard 4.31-34, the 'pericope' in which our saying is to be found, as a secondary addition to the story. It is necessary to examine the arguments used for this conclusion, since not only do they challenge the link between 4.31-34 and the rest of the story, but in part they also challenge the historicity of 4.31-34 itself.[14]

Fortna produces no argument for this conclusion other than the fact that it appears to him to be 'quite obvious',[15] but this is no argument at all. Likewise, U.C. von Wahlde's comment that 4.31-38 interrupts 'the basic sequence of the narrative'[16] scarcely carries any weight unless one believes that the author is incapable of telling a true story which contains more than one scene. A more substantial argument, advanced by R. Bultmann and U.C. von Wahlde, is that the passage contains a misunderstanding (in v. 33),[17] which is commonly regarded as a mark of the author's style. Granted that the author seems to be fond of including misunderstandings in his

---

[6] In the words of I.H. Marshall (1974) 68 n. 3, 'Commentators are in general agreed that the narrative rests upon tradition, and that the tradition has a historical basis'.

[7] R. Bultmann (ET 1971) 175.

[8] R.T. Fortna (1970) 239.

[9] W. Nicol (1972) 40.

[10] U.C. von Wahlde (1989) 190.

[11] J. Becker (1979) 1.166f.

[12] E. Haenchen (1980) 255.

[13] S. Temple (1975) 111-113.

[14] For criticisms of source theories in general see chapter 1, section 5. Once again the point may be made that the very diversity of these theories is an argument against accepting any one of them.

[15] R.T. Fortna (1970) 189.

[16] U.C. von Wahlde (1989) 84.

[17] R. Bultmann (ET 1971) 194 n. 1, U.C. von Wahlde (1989) 87f.

narratives, the *a priori* exclusion from the realm of historicity of all misunderstandings in the Fourth Gospel is, however, surely unwarranted. There are good grounds for believing that as a matter of history Jesus was misunderstood by many of the people he came into contact with, as even R.A. Culpepper acknowledges,[18] and the Synoptic Gospels provide some very good examples of this phenomenon, including examples of the disciples failing to understand Jesus' teaching (Mk. 4.1-20, 7.14-23 par.) and even positively misunderstanding his teaching (Mk. 8.14-21 par.).[19] This last example is particularly relevant to Jn. 4.31-34, since here the misunderstanding turns on the meaning of a single word, the word 'leaven' (Mk. 8.15), which the disciples mistakenly think referred to ordinary bread while Jesus had a spiritual meaning in mind (said by Matthew to be the teaching of the Pharisees and Sadducees, Mt.16.12). In the light of this passage, if it can be taken to be basically historical, it is not at all impossible that the conversation recorded in Jn. 4.31-34 might have actually taken place. Moreover, as A. Plummer noted long ago, reports such as this one, which tell against the disciples, putting them in an unfavourable light, actually support a belief in the reports' trustworthiness.[20]

Two other arguments remain. One concerns the content of 4.31-34. R. Bultmann says that these verses are 'completely Johannine' in their thought,[21] while U.C. von Wahlde says that they exhibit a different theology from that of the original story.[22] This objection will be dealt with in the next sections, where it will be argued that Jesus' words in 4.31-34 are thoroughly consistent with what we know of him from the Synoptic Gospels and that what differences there are from what U.C. von Wahlde considers to be the original story stem simply from the fact that Jesus is holding a different conversation from the one he holds in 4.7-26. The other argument is the argument from style, which is perhaps most rigorously developed by W. Nicol.[23] Yet if we look closely at his statistics we find that he cannot prove his case, at least as far as 4.31-34 is concerned. If we take E. Ruckstuhl's list of 50 Johannine stylistic characteristics first,[24] we find that in the verses

---

[18] R.A. Culpepper (1983) 154 quoting C.K. Barrett (1955) 166 and J. Painter (1975) 82 in support. Cf. also D.A. Carson (1982) who cautions against excising misunderstandings in the Fourth Gospel on form critical grounds.

[19] Cf. J.H. Bernard (1928) 1.cxii, E.E. Lemcio (1978). E. Richard (1985) uses these phenomenological parallels as an argument against the existence of a 'signs source' altogether.

[20] A. Plummer (1882) 124.

[21] R. Bultmann (ET 1971) 194 n. 1.

[22] U.C. von Wahlde (1989) 84.

[23] W. Nicol (1972) 16-27.

[24] To be found in E. Ruckstuhl (1987²) 292-303.

Nicol believes belonged to the 'signs source' (given above), which contain 198 words, there are 9 occurrences of these characteristics, i.e. one for every 22 words on average, whereas in 4.31-34, which contains 52 words, there are only 2 occurrences, i.e. one for every 26 words on average. On this reckoning therefore 4.31-34 is actually *less* 'Johannine' in style than Nicol's proposed source material in the story. It is only when we add Nicol's own Johannine stylistic characteristics[25] that the picture changes to 11 occurrences for the 'signs source' material, or one for every 18 words on average, and 5 occurrences for 4.31-34, or one for every 10.4 words on average. The three extra Johannine stylistic characteristics he finds in 4.31-34, in addition to Ruckstuhl's, are the misunderstanding in v.32f., and the use of the phrase τοῦ πέμψαντός με and the word ἔργον in v. 34.[26] It has already been argued that misunderstandings should not be used as a means of separating out source material from secondary accretions; it will be conceded later that the phrase τοῦ πέμψαντός με may be a secondary addition in the saying of Jesus in v. 34, but this should not be used to rule out the whole 'pericope' as secondary; we are left then only with ἔργον, and it was argued in chapter 4 that this word is commonly found in Jesus' speech in the Fourth Gospel, and therefore in the 'discourse material', precisely because it was in fact a mark of Jesus' speech rather than being simply a feature Johannine style.

Without going into the case of the other proposed secondary additions in 4.1-42 we may nevertheless conclude that the arguments for assigning 4.31-34 to a separate source are unconvincing. It is quite possible that some such incident as that recorded in 4.31-34 did occur while the woman was absent from the scene. This issue does not, of course, of itself determine the authenticity of 4.34, since it could still be authentic even if spoken on another occasion, but it does set the saying in what is its most probable historical context.

6.2.2 John 4.31-34

The disciples have returned from their shopping expedition in Sychar (v. 27). They are now with Jesus and are in a position to witness what follows. C.H. Dodd is impressed by the 'Synoptic pattern' of what follows, with its address by the disciples to Jesus, its short interchange of one sentence only on each side, and its concluding 'pregnant saying' on the part of Jesus.[27] It

---

[25] Given in W. Nicol (1972) 23f.
[26] Ibid. 19.
[27] C.H. Dodd (1963) 325.

is for reasons such as these that A.M. Hunter came to the conclusion that 4.31-34 'must rest back on real tradition'.[28]

The disciples offer Jesus some food to eat (v. 31). As J. Bligh remarks, the conversation about food arises quite naturally out of the situation presupposed by the story so far.[29] The form of address used by the disciples in v. 31, 'Rabbi', is also a natural one for the disciples to use, being probably one which goes back to the religious environment of the historical Jesus.[30]

Jesus' reply (v. 32) takes the conversation on to a different level. As so often in his ministry, he uses the ordinary things of life to illustrate spiritual truth. His reply is not a quasi-docetic renunciation of the need to eat (otherwise the disciples would hardly have offered him food in the first place), but an allusive declaration of another type of sustenance by which he lives. The disciples now express their incomprehension in the form of a misunderstanding which has already been considered above (v. 33). This now gives Jesus the opportunity to explain himself in the form of the pronouncement in v. 34. To this saying we now turn.

6.3 The Authenticity of John 4.34

6.3.1 Introduction

Opinions have varied concerning the authenticity of this saying. In 1920 V.H. Stanton wrote of this and a few other sayings in the Fourth Gospel: 'No one will be disposed to doubt that these are genuine sayings'.[31] He seemed unaware that in fact many were and would continue to be so

---

[28] A.M. Hunter (1968) 45. Whether the disciples in this 'pericope' also represent Jews being catechised in the Johannine community, as suggested by J. Becker (1979) 136 and H. Leroy cited in D.A. Carson (1982) 75f. lies in the realm of speculation.

[29] J. Bligh (1962) 329.

[30] Cf. J.H. Bernard (1928) 1.54-56, L. Morris (1971) 157 n. 88. E. Lohse in *TDNT* 6.962 and S.-B. 1.916 both refer to the saying of Joshua b. Perahiah (c. 110 BC) preserved in Aboth 1.6, in which he says 'Get a teacher ...', using the word רב . According to Lohse, *TDNT* 6.963, by the end of the 1st century AD the word רבי was in common use in rabbinic literature and occurs on many Jewish inscriptions, especially burial inscriptions, in Palestine, Syria, Cyprus and Italy. There are no strong reasons, therefore, for doubting that the Gospel's use of this word as a form of address to Jesus stems from the time of his ministry, especially in view of the fact that the words do not occur elsewhere in early christian writings and must have quickly dropped out of use in christian circles in preference for other christological titles.

[31] V.H. Stanton (1920) 3.273.

disposed. Some time later, for example, R. Bultmann could write of 4.31-34: 'Of course no historical interest attaches to the scene'.[32] In this section an attempt will be made to tackle this question afresh, using the criteria for authenticity set out in chapter 2. Before this is done, however, two matters may be dealt with at the outset:

a. Firstly, there is the textual crux between the reading of ποιῶ and ποιήσω. ποιῶ is supported by ℵ, A, Γ, Δ, f¹³, and the Majority text, and, in modern times by Tischendorf and the 25th edition of the Nestle-Aland text among others. ποιήσω, on the other hand, is supported by p66, p75, B, C, D, K, L, N, Wˢ, Θ, Ψ, 083, 1, 33, 565, 1010 etc. and Clement, and in modern times by Westcott and Hort and the 26th edition of the Nestle-Aland text among others. J.H. Bernard and R. Bultmann supported the reading ποιῶ on the grounds that the alternative reading seemed to have come about through assimilation to τελειώσω,[33] but they both came to their conclusion without the benefit of the knowledge of the readings of p66 and p75. R. Schnackenburg comes to the same conclusion even with this knowledge on the grounds that it represents the *lectio difficilior* and brings out better the present nature of the action.[34] The latest edition of the Nestle-Aland text, however, comes down on the other side, perhaps because they feel that the weight of the earlier manuscripts is heavier than the argument from possible assimilation. It seems to be one of those cases where certainty is impossible in the present state of knowledge, but fortunately in this case little hangs on the outcome. The difference between an aorist and a present subjunctive in this context is minimal, and in any case cannot be reproduced in Aramaic.

b. Secondly, the same comments may be made about the phrase τοῦ πέμψατός με in this verse as were made in chapter 5 on Jn. 9.4. There it was observed that on the basis of the evidence of the Synoptic Gospels the phrase appears to be one which Jesus used as a description for God, yet at the same time its use appears to have been greatly extended by the author of the Fourth Gospel, who seems to insert it liberally in his representation of Jesus' speech. While therefore we need not doubt that Jesus spoke of God in this way, we cannot be sure that he used the phrase in the places in which it occurs in the Gospel, including 4.34. It is possible that another word for God was used instead.

---

[32] R. Bultmann (ET 1971) 195.
[33] J.H. Bernard (1928) 1.154, R. Bultmann (ET 1971) 194 n. 3.
[34] R. Schnackenburg (ET 1968) 1.447 n. 81.

6.3.2 The Criteria Applied

As far as the remainder of the verse is concerned, the criterion of multiple attestation clearly fails to support authenticity here, since no parallel for the saying exists in the Synoptic Gospels, so we are left with: Language, Culture and Personal Idiom; Coherence; Dissimilarity; and Anti-Redactional Features.

(1) Language, Culture and Personal Idiom
There are several observations to be made under this heading:

a. Firstly, as far as language is concerned the saying may be straightforwardly translated back into Aramaic, thus:

³⁵מיכלי הוא דאעבוד לרצונא דמאן דשלחני ודאשלים לעבידתיה

So there is nothing in the Greek before us which would prevent it from being by direct translation something that Jesus could naturally have said in his mother tongue.

b. Secondly, as far as culture is concerned, we find that the saying also fits naturally into Jesus' religious setting (though, as we will note later, there is also something distinctive about the saying). The use of the concept of food in a metaphorical sense is found in the Old Testament (e.g. Ps. 63.5, Prov. 9.5, Isa. 55.1f.), the intertestamental literature (e.g. Ecclus. 24.21), Rabbinic literature (e.g. *Qoh.R.* 2.24),[36] and Philo (*L.A.* 1.97, *Sacr.Ab.et C.* 86, *Opif.M.* 158, *Vit.Mos.* 2.69). The idea of doing the will of God is also common in the Old Testament (e.g. Ps. 40.8, 103.21, 143.10, Isa. 44.28, 48.14), in intertestamental literature including the Qumran literature (e.g. 1 Esd. 8.16, 9.9, 2 Macc. 1.3, 4 Macc. 18.16, 1 QS 9.13, 23),[37] and in Rabbinic literature (cf. S.-B. 1.467), and the idea of completing a work, which must in any case have been a common expression in everyday speech (not least for carpenters), is another common expression in the Old Testament (e.g. Gen. 2.2, Ex. 5.13, 40.33, 1 Kings 7.22, 40, 1 Chron. 28.20, 2 Chron. 4.11, 5.1, 29.34, Neh. 6.16) and in intertestamental literature (e.g. Ecclus. 7.25, 38.8, 27, 50.19, 1 Macc. 4.51, Judith 8.34). Moreover, the connection between eating and obeying God is made in Deut. 8.3 where God says that he gave the Israelites manna 'that he might make you know that man does not live by bread alone, but that man lives by everything that

---

[35] Several alternative Aramaic words could have been used, e.g. פרנסה or מזון could have been used instead of מאכל, עשה instead of עבד, צבי instead of רצון, כלה (Pi.) instead of שלם (Aph.), and מלאכה instead of עבידה.

[36] For further references to the rabbinic literature and also to the Mandean literature see H. Odeberg (ET 1968) 240-247.

[37] For discussion of the Jewish background to this phrase, see further S. Pancaro (1975) 369-371.

proceeds out of the mouth of the Lord' (cf. Deut. 30.15f., 32.46f.), as well as in some of the references given above. In the light of this evidence, the saying is perfectly credible on the lips of a first century Jew.

c. Thirdly, as far as personal idiom is concerned, we may begin by making the common point that the kind of pictorial language which we find in the saying is characteristic of the historical Jesus. We have already noted the close phenomenological parallel in Mk. 8.15, but this is just one example of a general trend whereby Jesus takes the ordinary things of life and uses them as vehicles of spiritual teaching.

d. Fourthly, attention may be drawn to the rhythm of the saying,[38] and the parallelistic structure to be found in it. This may best be illustrated if it is set out in the following way:

מיכלי הוא
דאעבוד לרצונא דמאן דשלחני
ודאשלים לעבידתיה

Whether we regard the final two clauses as an example of synonymous parallelism or of synthetic parallelism (and it will be argued later that the latter is more likely), they fit one of the characteristics of Jesus' teaching, since he used both.[39] Moreover the rhythm of the final two clauses fits the 'Kina' metre often used by Jesus for important sayings - whether the τοῦ πέμψατός με phrase is original (in which case the rhythm would be 4 + 2) or a simpler expression for God originally stood in its place (in which case the rhythm would be 3 + 2), since both occur, though the latter is more usual.[40]

e. Fifthly, we note that the saying takes the form of an aphorism, commonly recognised as a mark of Jesus teaching. As with the saying in 9.4 and 5.17, J. Drummond counts this saying as among the 'most striking' in the Gospel,[41] a judgment endorsed by W.F. Howard who regards them as entirely suiting 'the character and habit of Jesus as they are known to us from the Synoptics'.[42]

This leads us to the next set of evidence, the evidence from coherence with the Jesus of the Synoptic Gospels, which again shows that the saying is perfectly credible as one of the sayings of the historical Jesus.

---

[38] Cf. R. Schnackenburg (ET 1968) 1.446.

[39] C.F. Burney (1925) 63-71, 89-90.

[40] Ibid. 34-43, J. Jeremias (ET 1971) 25-27.

[41] J. Drummond (1903) 18.

[42] W.F. Howard (1955[4]) 214f. Similarly, S.S. Smalley (1978) 185 n. 163 regards Jn. 4.34 as an example of a 'pithy, memorable saying'.

(2) Coherence

There are a number of points at which the Synoptic evidence supports the authenticity of the saying in Jn. 4.34, at least in a loose sense:

a. Jesus' desire to put obedience to the will of God above the satisfaction of physical hunger finds an echo in Mt. 4.3f. par., where Jesus resists the temptation of the devil to turn stones to bread in the desert by quoting Deut. 8.3. The only problem here is the historical basis of the temptation stories, but if they at least preserve a tradition of Jesus' mental attitude in this sphere of life, then they lend support to the authenticity of Jesus' words in Jn. 4.34, where the same mental attitude is revealed.[43]

b. As regards the idea of the 'will of God', it is perhaps significant that of all the times the word 'will' occurs in the Synoptic Gospels (Mk. 3.35 par., Mt. 6.10 par., 7.21, 18.14, 21.31, 26.42 par., Lk. 12.47, 23.25) it occurs only once outside of Jesus' speech (in Lk. 23.25), and that in every other occurrence Jesus uses the word to refer explicitly or implicitly to the will of God. It is highly likely then that Jesus did speak of the will of God and showed an ardent desire to see it being done both in his life and in the lives of others.

c. A yet closer parallel may be found in Mk. 3.35 pars. in particular, because here Jesus not only commends others for doing the will of God but also implicitly claims to do so himself, and, moreover, 'sublimates' the idea of family relationships in terms of doing the will of God, just as in Jn. 4.34 he 'sublimates' the idea of food in the same way.[44] It will be worth pausing for a while to argue in detail for the authenticity, in a strict sense, of this saying, so as to strengthen our argument at this point.

Mk. 3.35 stands at the end of a pericope (Mk. 3.31-35, cf. Mt. 12.46-50 par. Lk. 8.19-21) in which Jesus' mother and brothers are depicted as coming and calling for Jesus while he sits in the middle of a crowd (apparently in a room). Jesus appears to ignore them and uses the occasion instead to teach his listeners about his spiritual kin.

It is highly likely that some kind of historical tradition lies behind this saying, since it is improbable that the early church would have wanted to create a story which could be interpreted as implying that Jesus had been

---

[43] Scholars differ over their assessment of the relationship between Jn. 4.34 and Mt. 4.3f. par. C.K. Barrett (1978²) 240 thinks the former to be possibly dependent on the Q narrative. B. Lindars (1972) 194 denies it. C.H. Dodd (1963) 326f. and S. Pancaro (1975) 387f. think that both are derived from a common tradition which has been modified in Jn. 4.34 in a Johannine way. D.A. Carson (1991) 228 thinks that Jesus echoes Deut. 8.3 in Jn. 4.34 and (independently) in Mt. 4.3f. par. In view of the formal differences between Jn. 4.34 and Mt. 4.3f. par. any view of their mutual or common dependence is bound to be precarious, but there is no doubt about their identity of outlook.

[44] As C.H. Dodd (1963) 326 saw.

disrespectful towards his own closest relatives, especially when we remember that in the post-Easter period they were among the believers (Acts 1.14), and James in particular was a prominent member of the Jerusalem church (Acts 12.17, 15.13-21, 21.18, Gal. 1.19, 2.9, 12).[45] The 'offensiveness' of Mark's narrative at this point is well illustrated by the omission of Mk. 3.21 (to which Mk. 3.31-35 was probably originally connected[46]) by both Matthew and Luke, and Luke's cutting out of those words in Mark which make a sharp distinction between Jesus' natural and spiritual kin.[47] The narrative is much more likely to belong to the time of the ministry of Jesus, when, according to Jn. 7.5, his brothers were not yet believers.[48]

The question whether v. 35 was an original part of the story or might have circulated as an independent saying is a little more difficult to determine. On the one hand, there is a certain amount of disjunction between v. 31-34 and v. 35 (cf. the introduction of the word ἀδελφή, the lack of personal pronouns after ἀδελφή and μήτηρ, and the introduction of a conditional element in v. 35 as against vv. 31-34), and the saying is quoted independently of its Synoptic context in 2 Clem. 9.11; but these are weak arguments, and are outweighed by the fact that it is difficult to imagine v. 35 circulating *without* some such context as it is given in the Synoptic Gospels for sense to be made of it at all.[49]

Could v. 35, then, have been added on to the original story, either by Mark or by one of the earlier tradents of the tradition? While this view is held by a number of scholars[50] and cannot be finally excluded, there are a number of good reasons for regarding it as an original saying of Jesus in

---

[45] J.D. Crossan (1973) tried to argue that Mark was actually engaging in a polemic against the doctrinal and jurisdictional authority of the Jerusalem church, but his theory has not been well received by other critics. Cf. J. Lambrecht (1974), H. Anderson (1976) 161, and J. Gnilka (1978) 153.

[46] So J.D. Crossan (1973) 84f., J. Lambrecht (1974) 249, E. Best (1976).

[47] So much so that J.A. Fitzmyer (1981) 1.723 can even argue that Luke presents Jesus' mother and brothers as *model* disciples.

[48] According to V. Taylor (1966²) 245 'the whole [pericope] leaves a strong impression of originality', and 'may have originated in the recollections of eyewitnesses'. B. Meyer (1979) 155 draws attention to the fact that the question-followed-by-statement pattern evident in Mk. 3.33f. seems to have been typical of Jesus' speech (cf. Mk. 8.12, 10.18 par., 11.17, Mt. 7.3-5 par., 12.27f. par., Lk. 12.51, 22.27). R. Bultmann's (ET 1968²) 29, 60 scepticism over the historicity of the basic story is unjustified. Cf. C.E.B. Cranfield (1959) 143.

[49] So, rightly, W.D. Davies and D.C. Allison (1991) 2.364, though even if they are wrong v. 35 could still be an authentic saying of Jesus.

[50] M. Dibelius (ET 1971) 57, 63, E. Schweizer (ET 1971) 84, J.D. Crossan (1973) 97, H. Anderson (1976) 125, J. Gnilka (1978) 147.

roughly its present form,[51] as we shall now see as we apply the criteria of authenticity.

(1) Multiple Attestation
The saying occurs in all three Synoptic Gospels, as we have seen. Matthew and Luke probably used Mark, of course, if we accept the most widely held solution to the 'Synoptic problem', but even so, their inclusion of this saying in their Gospels is a tacit witness to their own belief that Mark had passed on a genuine saying of Jesus. In addition, the saying is found in the Ebionite Gospel frag. 5, 2 Clem. 9 11, and the Gospel of Thomas 99. While the form of the Ebionite quotation suggests dependence on Matthew's Gospel, in the opinion of W.D. Davies and D.C. Allison the other two witnesses are not necessarily dependent on any of the Synoptic Gospels, in which case the argument from multiple attestation would be even stronger. It is difficult, however, to be certain on this issue.[52]

(2) Language, Culture and Personal Idiom
As far as language is concerned, Mk. 3.35 presents no problems since it can be easily translated back into Aramaic, thus:

מאן דעביד רצונא דאלהא הוא אחי ואחתי ואמי

If we accept the reading which omits the word γάρ after ὅς, we may also say that the asyndeton at the beginning of v. 35 suggests an Aramaic background for vv. 34f., as M. Black recognised.[53]

As far as culture is concerned, commentators have noted a number of features which this saying has in common with the Jewish religious milieu of which Jesus was a part. Thus, for example, 'doing the will of God', as we have already seen, is a concept with which a first century Jew would have been very familiar;[54] the words 'brother', 'sister' and 'mother' are used in a

---

[51] M.D. Hooker (1991) 119 has suggested that the word 'sister' may reflect the inclusion of women in the early christian community. Even if this word is a secondary addition, the case for the authenticity of the rest of the saying is not thereby damaged. In fact, the presence of the word 'sister' may equally be seen as an anti-redactional feature in view of Mark's failure elsewhere to give any prominence to the fact that Jesus' followers included women. Cf. P. Carrington (1960) 97: 'The words of Jesus show that the circle to which he referred included women as well as men, a point which Mark, generally speaking, passes over rather lightly.
[52] W.D. Davies and D.C. Allison (1991) 2.365. They also mention Jn. 15.14 and Clem. of Alex. *Ecl.proph.* 20, but Jn. 15.14 may have no connection with Mk. 3.35 and Clem. of Alex. is a relatively late witness.
[53] M. Black (1967[3]) 58.
[54] See n. 37 above. As M.D. Hooker (1991) 118 puts it, 'the idea that man's true life consists in doing the will of God is a thoroughly Jewish one'.

non-literal sense in the Old Testament;[55] and the idea of putting one's allegiance to God or one's community above one's allegiance to one's natural family also has its parallels.[56] The conjunction of these ideas in this particular form appears to be new,[57] but the 'building blocks' which went into the saying were already lying around in the world of first-century Judaism.[58]

As far as personal idiom is concerned, we note the saying's aphoristic and memorable qualities - qualities characteristic of so much of Jesus' teaching preserved in the Gospels. It was these qualities which no doubt contributed to the fact that the saying occurs an unusually large number of times in the extra-canonical literature of the early church.

(3) Coherence
The saying coheres well with the record of Jesus life and ministry which we find elsewhere in the Gospels. As we have seen, we find Jesus stressing the importance of doing the will of God. We find him warning those who would be his disciples that discipleship means putting him above the demands of the family in Mt. 8.21f. par. and 10.34-37 par. We find him assuring those who follow this path that a new 'spiritual' family awaits them in Mk. 10.29f. pars. And we find him calling his disciples 'brethren' in Mt. 25.40 and Jn. 20.17. Obviously the authenticity (in a strict sense) of some of these sayings would not be easy to maintain, but even if some of them closely represent Jesus' original teaching we have further evidence that Mk. 3.35 also goes back to him.

(4) Dissimilarity
As far as dissimilarity from the Jewish background is concerned, we have already noted that, although the verse contains some familiar 'building blocks', it is not itself paralleled, as far as we know, in any Jewish source. It required a creative mind to bring these elements together in such memorable way - the kind of creative mind which we may well believe Jesus possessed.

As far as dissimilarity from the early christian community is concerned, we have already noted the unlikelihood of such a saying naturally arising from that context, in view of the apparent aspersions it casts upon Jesus' natural family. Moreover, though the saying is *quoted* outside the Gospels in several places, we do not find its distinctive motifs in common use

---

[55] See F. Brown, S.R. Driver, and C.A. Briggs (1974^9) 26-28, 52 for references.

[56] See W.D. Davies and D.C. Allison (1991) 2.364 who cite Deut. 33.9, 1 QS 1-9, and Jos. *Bell*. 2.120-158. See also M. Hengel (1981) 13.

[57] It is significant that no entry is given under this verse in S.-B.

[58] J. Gnilka (1978) 152f. still calls this saying 'Diese jüdisch empfundene Maxime', even though he inclines to doubt its authenticity.

elsewhere in the New Testament. True, the New Testament often talks about the 'will of God', especially in the Epistles, and it uses 'brother' and 'sister' in a spiritual sense, but it does not normally talk about being a *spiritual* brother/ sister/ mother of *Jesus*, and never is such a relationship defined in terms of doing the will of God.[59] In addition, we may note that the saying contains nothing which could count as anachronistic christologically or from any other point of view. The saying therefore stands out both against its Jewish and its christian milieux. The criterion of double dissimilarity is fulfilled to a remarkable extent.

(5) Anti-Redactional Features
We have already noted the fact that the appearance of 'sister' in this verse is unusual for Mark, in that he fails elsewhere to stress that Jesus' followers included women.[60] In addition, we may note that nowhere else in Mark, or indeed in the Synoptic Gospels as a whole, do we find the phrase 'the will of God'. We find 'the will of my (or your) Father' at Mt. 7.21, 12.50, and 18.14 and 'your will' at Mt. 6.10 par. and 26.42 par., but nowhere else do we find 'the will of God' in the Synoptic Gospels, and the word θέλημα itself is a *hapax legomenon* in Mark's Gospel in Mk. 3.35. This is strange, especially when one thinks of the other phrases Mark might have used if he had been composing this saying himself, such as 'he who does my will' (cf. 8.38), or 'he who follows me' (cf. 8.34 etc. - the verb ἀκολουθῶ is used 18 times by Mark), or 'he who hears me/ my word/ God's word' (cf. 4.20 - the verb ἀκούω is used 45 times by Mark). In the light of such data, E. Best is surely right to conclude that 'it is most improbable that Mark himself created the saying of v. 35'.[61] The saying stands out as unusual in its Markan context just as it does in the context of the early church.

The evidence we have been reviewing has been mostly pointing in one direction, that is, in the direction of accepting Mk. 3.35 as a saying of Jesus, at least roughly in its present form. On this basis we have evidence that Jesus himself spoke explicitly in terms of doing the will of God and of the central importance of this commitment in the life of discipleship. Moreover, there is in this saying an implicitly high christology. If those who do God's will are the 'brothers'/ 'sisters'/ 'mothers' of Jesus, then what must Jesus himself be doing? The answer can only be that Jesus must have thought of

---

[59] Rom. 8.29 and Heb. 2.11 are the closest the New Testament gets to this saying of Jesus outside his other sayings, but in both cases the christians are called 'brethren' of Jesus because they have themselves become 'sons' of God by grace, not because they are doing the will of God.

[60] See n. 51 above.

[61] E. Best (1976) 315.

himself as doing the will of God in a consistent and exemplary way. 'Doing the will of God' must have been for Jesus both something he aimed at and something he felt he was actually achieving. The thought expressed in this saying is not at all distant from the words attributed to Jesus in Jn. 4.34.

d. The phrase 'accomplishing the work of God' is also in tune with what we know of Jesus from the Synoptic Gospels. As was noted in chapter 5, the Synoptic Gospels consistently present us with the picture of a man who felt a sense of destiny (cf. the use of δεῖ in Mk. 8.31 pars., Mt. 26.54, Lk. 2.49, 4.43, 13.33, 17.25, 22.37, 24.7, 26, 44), and who believed that he had been sent to fulfil a special mission (cf. Mk. 9.37 par., 12.6 pars., Mt. 10.40 par., 15.24, 23.37 par., Lk. 4.18, 21). Jesus was moreover conscious of the possibility of dying a violent death at the hands of his enemies, as some of the above texts show, and therefore of the limitations of time in carrying out what he believed he had to do. Two sayings found in Luke's Gospel are especially relevant to the use of the verb τελειῶ in Jn. 4.34, both with good claims to authenticity in a strict sense: Lk. 12.50, where Jesus says he is 'constrained' until his 'baptism' (i.e. his death) is 'accomplished' (τελεσθῇ); and Lk. 13.32, where he says that after he has cast out demons and performed cures 'today and tomorrow ... the third day I finish my course (τελειοῦμαι)'. We may take the first of these to show how the case for its authenticity may be made out.

It is possible that Lk. 12.50 was originally an independent saying. It is not particularly closely connected in thought with its Lukan context and could have been inserted here by Luke or Luke's source because of a perceived connection between 'fire' and 'baptism' (cf. Lk. 3.16, 12.49).[62] Again, it is quite likely that this saying has no connection with a similar one in Mk. 10.38, which is set in a conversation between Jesus and James and John and which has nothing corresponding to the second half of the saying in Luke. Most scholars justifiably therefore regard Q or L as the source for Luke's saying.[63] We have, then, a saying whose authenticity must be judged purely on its own merits. An application of the criteria of authenticity reveals that there are good reasons for believing it to be dominical, as we shall now see.

---

[62] C.F. Evans (1990) 539; cf. H. Conzelman (ET 1960) 109. On the other hand there may be a connection in thought between the 'fire' (the eschatological judgment?) which Jesus says he has come to cast upon the earth in v. 49 and the baptism (his death) which he says he must undergo in v. 50 in that he saw himself as sharing in the effects of the universal judgment. Cf. I.H. Marshall (1978) 547, and C.F. Burney (1925) 90, who sees here an example of synthetic parallelism.

[63] So V. Taylor (1939) 165 and J.A. Fitzmyer (1985) 2.994, who prefer L, and T.W. Manson (1949) 120 and H. Schürmann (1968) 213, who prefer Q. I.H. Marshall (1978) 545 is undecided, but thinks Luke used Q or L rather than Mark, *contra* H. Köster in *TDNT* 7.884.

(1) Multiple Attestation

As we have just seen, the saying is probably to be regarded as unparalleled in the Gospels, but in the light of Mk. 10.38 we may speak of a multiple attestation of *motif*, since in both Mark and Q or L we find Jesus speaking of his death as a kind of baptism.

(2) Language, Culture and Personal Idiom

The saying may be recaptured in Aramaic thus:

אית לי טנילות אטביל בה ומה צריר הוא לי עד דהוא שלם

The only Greek idiom which is not naturally translatable into Aramaic is the use of ἔχω with the infinitive, which is recognised as a Lucanism,[64] but the thought behind it can be adequately expressed.

As far as the cultural background is concerned, we may note that the Old Testament occasionally speaks about being 'flooded' with troubles (cf. Ps. 42.7, 69.2, 15), and that once the LXX uses the verb βαπτίζω to translate בעת (Pi., meaning 'overwhelm',[65] in Isa. 21.4). We should remember also that Jesus was working against the background of the ministry of John the Baptist, who had made the idea of a once-for-all baptism in water familiar to large numbers of Jesus' contemporaries, so even though the connection between baptism and death may have been new in the sayings of Jesus, the ingredients of such a connection were already in place in the religious environment of Jesus.[66] There is certainly no necessary connection between the 'anxiety' of Jesus expressed in this saying and the 'gnostic myth' as reconstructed by R. Bultmann.[67]

As far as personal idiom is concerned, the saying is typical of Jesus' method of taking something which is ordinary and familiar to his hearers and infusing it with new significance.[68] It is striking in its imagery and easily memorable, and as such may well go back to him.

---

[64] Cf. J. Jeremias (1980) 223 and J.A. Fitzmyer (1985) 2.996.

[65] F. Brown, S.R. Driver and C.A. Briggs (1974[9]) 130a.

[66] I.H. Marshall (1978) 547 notes the metaphorical use of βαπτίζω in the sense of being overwhelmed by catastrophe in Hellenistic sources (cf. A. Oepke in *TDNT* 1.530), but C.F. Evans (1990) 540 doubts whether such a usage would have been popular in Jesus' day and concludes that 'a connection between baptism and calamity could have been forged by Jesus himself'. A. Oepke, *TDNT* 1.538, also regards this as possible. Even if the phrase could be shown to have a purely Hellenistic origin, this alone would not be fatal to an argument for the authenticity of the saying in view of the permeation of Palestine by Hellenism in the centuries before Christ.

[67] R. Bultmann (ET 1968[2]) 154.

[68] J. Jeremias (ET 1971) 283 counts it as one of the passion 'meshalim'.

(3) Coherence

As already mentioned above, the saying may be seen as an example of a general trait of the Gospel presentation of Jesus as one who was conscious of fulfilling a divine plan and destined in particular to suffer and die at the hands of his enemies. Again it has to be said that not all sayings which convey this impression can be shown to be strictly authentic as they stand, but it would be quite unreasonable to assert that all sayings which refer to a coming crisis must necessarily be *vaticinia ex eventu*. As W.G. Kümmel and others have argued, it is extremely unlikely that Mk. 10.38f., for example, is a *vaticinium ex eventu* since, to the best of our knowledge, John the apostle was not a martyr at the time of the writing of Mark's Gospel, and possibly never was. Similarly the very vagueness and imprecision of some of these prophecies, including Lk. 12.50 itself, speak in favour of their authenticity.

(4) Dissimilarity

We have already noted the fact that, as far as Judaism is concerned, there is no exact parallel to this type of speech prior to the time of Jesus.[69] Though the 'building blocks' were there, a creative mind was need to put them together in the way they are in Lk. 12.50 and Mk. 10.38.

Likewise it needs to be said that the thought of Jesus' death as a baptism does not occur elsewhere in the New Testament. The closest parallel we find is Paul's description of christian baptism as a dying-with-Christ in Rom. 6.3f. and Col. 2.12, but this is a baptism in water symbolising a *spiritual* death, not a baptism of *suffering* resulting in *physical* death. It is not at all self-evident that Lk. 12.50 and Mk. 10.38, probably relying on independent sources, as we have seen, could have both been independently created out of these Pauline utterances.

There are further considerations which make it unlikely that this saying was created by the early christian community. The vagueness of the saying has already been mentioned. The lack of any reference to the resurrection or any kind of vindication beyond death is another factor to be taken into consideration. And, whatever the precise nuance of the word συνέχομαι,[70] the saying as a whole depicts a Jesus who is clearly limited in his options, filled with a sense of foreboding concerning the future, and longing for the coming ordeal to be undergone and finished with as soon as possible, in other words a picture of a very human Jesus which would not be the sort of picture to spring immediately to the minds of the early christians as they

---

[69] It is significant that S.-B. have no entry for this verse.

[70] Whether 'constrained', 'hemmed in', 'pressed' or 'governed'. Cf. H. Köster in *TDNT* 7.884. G.B. Caird (1963) 167 describes the tone of Lk. 12.49-53 as 'an agonizing mixture of impatience and reluctance'.

worshipped the risen and glorified Lord in the post-Pentecost period. It is much more likely to be a genuine reminiscence of something the earthly Jesus said as he approached Good Friday.

(5) Anti-Redactional Features
There is little that can be cited under this heading. The vocabulary of the saying cannot be said to be un-Lucan, and the thought also coheres well with the rest of Luke's presentation of Jesus. It is only the unusual use of 'baptism' in this verse which is unique to the Gospel. This factor, however, has considerable weight, as we have seen.

In conclusion, the balance of the evidence tips decisively in favour of this saying of Jesus being authentic in a strict sense.[71] What this means is that the historical Jesus believed that he had a mission to accomplish, a 'work' to do, which would ultimately take the form of a violent death, and that he had a strong desire to see it completed. The thought bears a remarkable resemblance to the words attributed to Jesus in Jn. 4.34.

There are many indications from the Synoptic Gospels, therefore, which suggest that the saying in Jn. 4.34 is the kind of thing Jesus might well have said. As A.M. Hunter put it: it has 'undoubtedly a Synoptic ring about it'.[72] The evidence adduced so far is surely sufficient to establish the authenticity of the saying in the broadest (type c) sense, but the cumulative case for a more direct correspondence with what Jesus originally said can be strengthened through an application of the final two criteria.

(3) Dissimilarity
It can hardly be claimed that the saying could not have been created by the early church - a powerful criterion when applicable positively, but not an absolute requirement for authenticity, as we saw in chapter 2. There are grounds, however, for affirming a certain amount of dissimilarity from the Jewish background. It was stated on pp. 137f. above that the concept of 'food' is used in a metaphorical sense in Jewish literature and that the saying as a whole fits naturally into Jesus' religious setting, but there is still something distinctive about the sense which is given to the concept of food here. In the parallels cited above, the 'food' is given a variety of senses. In Philo it stands for knowledge (*Sacr.Ab et C.* 86), or the discourses and doctrines of wisdom (*Opif.M.* 158), or 'viewing' God (*Vit.Mos.* 2.69), or the

---

[71] G.B. Caird (1963) 167 writes of Lk. 12.49-53 that here we have a 'rare glimpse into the inner mind of Jesus', and J.A. Fitzmyer (1985) 2.994 writes of Lk. 12.49-51: 'it is difficult to deny that this is a real prediction by Jesus'.
[72] A.M Hunter (1968) 91f.

practice of the virtues (*L.A.* 1.97). In 3 En. 8.1 (quoted by H. Odeberg as typical of early Jewish mysticism[73]) it stands for a variety of qualities: wisdom, understanding, life, grace, loving-kindness, love, the divine presence, meekness, mercy, peace, fear of heaven or fear of sin. Wisdom is the referent for food in Prov. 9.5 and Ecclus. 24.21, and the blessings of God in a more undefined sense in Ps. 63.5 and Isa. 55.1f. The closest analogy for the use of the concept of food in Jn. 4.34 is that hinted at in Deut. 8.3 and expressed more explicitly in the rabbinic literature (e.g. *Gen.R.* 54.1, 70.5, *Qoh.R.* 2.24, *Cant.R.* 1.4, and *TB Sabb.* 120a) where the food stands for the Law. Nowhere, however, is the concept of food linked with the discharge of a particular commission as it is in Jn. 4.34, where Jesus describes his 'food' not as being the fulfilling of the works of the Law or simply obedience to the will of God in general, but as accomplishing a special task which God had given him to do. For this sense there is no known parallel. To this extent, therefore, we may say that the saying is dissimilar from its Jewish environment.[74]

In addition R. Heiligenthal has drawn our attention to the unusualness of the phrase τελειῶ ... ἔργον as used in this context.[75] While there are instances of the two words τελειῶ and ἔργον occurring together in Jewish literature, they never occur together with the meaning of fulfilling a work which some-one has been sent to do, and while the idea of the latter is found in both Jewish and pagan literature, it is never expressed in these terms.

(4) Anti-Redactional Features
It has already been noted above that the use made of the concept of food in this saying is unparalleled in Jewish literature, as far as we know. It now needs to be said that it is also unparalleled in the Fourth Gospel itself. As many commentators have remarked, elsewhere, when the author uses the concepts of food or drink in a figurative sense, he uses them to denote gifts which Jesus is offering to other people (as, for example, water as symbolic of new life in 4.10-14, 7.37-39, and bread as symbolic of himself in 6.35-58); but here he uses the concept of food to denote that by which he himself lives, and his own food is not conceived of in terms of an offer from God but in terms of obedience on the part of Jesus in the fulfilling of a particular commission.[76] It would therefore be wrong to think of the discourse in ch. 6 as a development of 4.34, as R.A. Culpepper does, since

---

[73] H. Odeberg (ET 1968) 244f.
[74] It is perhaps significant that S.-B. have no entry under Jn. 4.34.
[75] R. Heiligenthal (1983) 137f.
[76] C.H. Dodd (1963) 325, R. Bultmann (ET 1971) 195, R. Schnackenburg (ET 1968) 1.445, G.R. Beasley-Murray (1987) 63.

the two passages speak of food in quite distinct ways.⁷⁷ It is perhaps symptomatic of this difference that the word βρῶμα is used in 4.34, and only here, in the whole of Johannine literature (though the word βρῶσις is found at Jn. 4.34, 6.27, 55) while the word ἄρτος is used 24 times in the Fourth Gospel, and 21 times in ch. 6. The saying in 4.34, therefore, stands on its own in the Gospel, and does not cohere at all well with the figurative use of the concept of food developed by the author elsewhere.

Once again, it has to be said that historical certainty is not possible in the case of assessing the degree of authenticity to be attached to a saying attributed to Jesus in the Gospels, but the above arguments do suggest at least that we have here a saying which not only reflects in a general way the mental attitude of the historical Jesus, but also stands close to something he actually said.

6.4 The Exegesis of John 4.34

6.4.1 Introduction

For the phrase τοῦ πέμψαντός με reference is made to pp. 122f. and 126 above. For the rest it would seem best once again to split up the comments made between the saying in its own 'pericope', the saying in its presumed historical context, and the saying in its total Johannine context.

6.4.2 John 4.34 within the Context of John 4.31-34

a. An initial exegetical question concerns the relationship between the two phrases ποιήσω τὸ θέλημα τοῦ πέμψαντός με and τελειώσω αὐτοῦ τὸ ἔργον. Are they the same or different in meaning? It is likely that the second is the case. Even if we accept the point made by R. Bultmann and U.C. von Wahlde that τελειώσω here does not mean completing a work begun by someone else (i.e. God), but executing or completing something one has been commissioned to do,⁷⁸ we are not obliged to accept Bultmann's conclusion that ποιεῖν τὸ θέλημα and τελειοῦν τὸ ἔργον are

---

⁷⁷ R.A. Culpepper (1983) 156. J. Riedl (1973) 100, 102, compares 4.34 with 18.11, but overlooks the differences: 18.11 concerns drink rather than food, and the cup stands for suffering rather than obedience. Moreover, ποτήριον only occurs here in the Fourth Gospel. It does not seem to be a motif he is interested in developing.

⁷⁸ R. Bultmann (ET 1971) 194 n. 3, U.C. von Wahlde (1980) 313 n. 30.

synonymous with the phrase ἐργάζεσθαι τὰ ἔργα in 9.4. τελειῶ carries the connotation of completing/ finishing/ accomplishing/ fulfilling/ bringing to an end a work which is absent from the simple verb ποιῶ. As F. Grob puts it: 'τελειῶ est formé sur l'adjectif τέλειος qui signifie parfait, complet, achevé. Le verbe souligne donc cette idée et va plus loin que le faire; il suggère que l'action est menée à son terme, qu'elle est achevée jusque dans ses dernières conséquences, qu'elle est conduite jusqu'à la plénitude et à la complétude de ses modalités.'[79] This holds good even if the phrase τοῦ πέμψαντός με is not a secondary addition to the saying but an original part of it. Certainly, it links Jesus' obedience with his commission and makes the phrase 'doing the will of God' more specific, as R.E. Brown notes,[80] but the phrase still lacks the connotation of carrying a task through to its appointed end which is present in the second phrase.

Jesus is therefore saying that his food is to do the will of God (or the will of the one who sent him) and to carry out[81] to the end the work of God (i.e. the task which God has given him to do, cf. 17.4). The parallelism is 'synthetic' rather than 'synonymous'.[82]

The content of the 'work' can only be clarified in the light of the wider context of the saying.

b. Most commentators are agreed that the word ἵνα in this context must be epexegetic rather than final.[83] What then does Jesus mean by describing his 'food' in this way? As has already been said on p. 135 above, we are not to understand this saying in a quasi-docetic sense, as though Jesus were saying that he had no need for ordinary food.[84] There is no evidence to suggest from the Fourth Gospel that Jesus was never genuinely hungry, and much to suggest that the 'flesh' he assumed (1.14) was the same as our own.[85] Rather, there seem to be two ideas here:

---

[79] F. Grob (1986) 97, cf. J. Riedl (1973) 58-63, A. Vanhoye (1960) 409-415 and W. Thüsing (1970) 51. The same distinction in meaning applies to the Aramaic verbs עבד and שלם.

[80] R.E. Brown (1966) 1.173.

[81] τελειώσω should probably be taken to be an aorist subjunctive rather than a future indicative, in view of the parallelistic nature of the saying, but the latter is not impossible. Cf. R. Schnackenburg (ET 1968) 1.447 n. 81.

[82] As S. Pancaro (1975) 386 says, τελειῶ 'adds the notion of "consummation"'.

[83] J.H. Bernard (1928) 1.154, L. Morris (1971) 277 n. 79, S. Pancaro (1975) 385, C.K. Barrett (1978²) 240, *contra* A. Plummer (1882) 124.

[84] Cf. J. Calvin (ET 1959) 105, C.H. Dodd (1963) 326 n. 1, F. Grob (1986) 86, W. Loader (1989) 183.

[85] Even in ch. 4 we find Jesus tired and thirsty (4.6f.). E. Käsemann's charge that the author 'changes the Galilean teacher into the God who goes about on earth' (ET 1968) 27 is surely a distortion of the truth.

Firstly, there is the idea that for Jesus doing the will of God and accomplishing his work was more important than eating ordinary food. His work took first place in his life, it was his top priority.[86] His devotion to his work put his natural physical hunger into the background.[87] He found greater sustenance and satisfaction in doing God's will than in any food which his disciples could offer him.[88]

Secondly, and more profoundly, there is the idea that doing God's will and accomplishing his work was an essential part of Jesus' very being, as though he could not exist apart from it.[89] Just as ordinary food is a *sine qua non* of our existence, so doing God's will and accomplishing his work was a *sine qua non* of Jesus' existence. He lived from it and by it.[90] It was his 'raison d'être' and 'la source de son être',[91] that which sustained his life[92] and gave him spiritual strength.[93] We have here, therefore, an expression of an awareness of being compulsively committed to the will and purpose of God, not through any external pressure, but through a strong inner desire.

c. The saying thus points in the direction of Jesus' moral oneness with God, but it also reminds us of his humanity and his subordination to the will of God in his incarnate state.[94] Jesus in the Fourth Gospel is not simply 'the God who goes about on earth', but also the man who submits himself to God's will, seeks to fulfil God's purpose for his life and is obedient even to the point of death on the cross.

6.4.3 John 4.34 within the Context of John 4.1-42

If the conversation recorded in 4.31-34 belongs historically to the context of the visit to Sychar described in 4.1-42, as was argued above in section 6.2.1, then extra significance is given to the saying in 4.34.

a. Firstly, the 'will' and the 'work' of God are more closely defined by the context as including the bringing of others to a recognition of who Jesus is and of the new life he can offer them. The woman at the well had

---

[86] J. Calvin (ET 1959) 105.
[87] C.H. Dodd (1963) 326 n. 1.
[88] D.A. Carson (1991) 228.
[89] R.C.H. Lenski (1943) 332: 'We could separate ourselves from our work, leave it undone, do a contrary work, but Jesus never'.
[90] C.H. Dodd (1953) 315, J. Riedl (1973) 48, E. Haenchen (1980) 247, R. Schnackenburg (ET 1968) 1.448, G.R. Beasley-Murray (1987) 63.
[91] F. Grob (1986) 94.
[92] C.K. Barrett (1978²) 241.
[93] J. Bligh (1962) 340.
[94] Cf. L. Morris (1969) 114, J.A.T. Robinson (1985) 349.

certainly been impressed with his words (4.19-29), and perhaps also Jesus could see people coming out of the town towards him on account of the woman's report of their conversation (4.30). E. Haenchen objects to T. Zahn's psychologically realistic understanding of the course of events,[95] but many other interpreters have found it entirely plausible.[96] The excitement of making an impact on the woman and the prospect of gaining even more followers from the village caused Jesus to lose his appetite for ordinary food as he realised that this was the work he had been sent to do.

b. Secondly, the immediate sequel to these verses shows that Jesus thought of his work as being something in which his disciples could to some extent have a share.[97] Without going into the problem of who the sowers are in 4.36-38, it is clear that the disciples are thought of as being among the reapers. Jesus invites them, in effect, to share with him in the task of reaping a harvest of followers from among the people of Sychar.

Contrary to the impression given by R. Bultmann and U.C. von Wahlde,[98] there is nothing in the thought or theology of 4.31-34 which requires us to believe that it did not originally belong to the context which the author gives it in ch. 4.

6.4.4 John 4.34 in its Total Johannine Context

If we stand back from the presumed historical context of this saying and see it in the light of the Gospel as a whole, the following tentative comments may be made:

a. It is rather far-fetched to see in the reference to 'food' in 4.34 even a 'remote preparation for the eucharistic doctrine of ch. 6',[99] a doctrine whose presence in ch. 6 itself is disputed. But perhaps it is less far-fetched, in the light of the Jewish parallels cited above which speak of the Law as 'food', and in the light of the nomistic connotations of the phrase 'doing the will of God',[100] to see here an allusion to Jesus as one who abides by, and therefore is the source of, a new Law.[101] This gives justification for the way in which

---

[95] E. Haenchen (1980) 246f.
[96] E.g. J. Calvin (ET 1959) 104f., J.H. Bernard (1928) 1.154, R.H. Strachan (1941³) 159, R.C.H. Lenski (1943) 332, L. Morris (1971) 277 n. 80.
[97] Cf. J .Riedl (1973) 66f. It is, of course, possible that 4.35-38 belong to another historical context. If so, the comment made here belongs to the next section.
[98] R. Bultmann (ET 1971) 194 n. 1, U.C. von Wahlde (1989) 84.
[99] J. Bligh (1962) 341.
[100] Cf. S. Pancaro (1975) 370f.
[101] F. Grob (1986) ch. 3. Grob develops this argument at some length from Jn. 4, but not all his arguments are convincing. For example, he thinks that the woman's five

later Jesus is seen to overrule a strict interpretation of the sabbath, for example, in Jn. 5 and 9, and insofar as 'doing the will of God' meant doing things which were not just peculiar to his own unique calling but applicable to the behaviour of his disciples, then Jesus is also claiming to set an example which his disciples are invited to follow.

b. Secondly, the rest of the Gospel can help us to understand more clearly how the author conceives the 'work' which God had given Jesus to do.

In 6.38-40 the will of God for Jesus is defined in terms of the granting of 'eternal life' to those who believe in him, or are 'given' to him, both in the present and at 'the last day', and in 17.3 'eternal life' is defined in terms of 'knowing' God and Jesus whom he sent. So the 'work' of Jesus, which is mentioned again in 17.4 immediately after the verse just cited, is conceived of as being primarily the work of leading those who believe in him to a knowledge of God. In other words, it is primarily a work of revelation.[102]

Is it also a work of atonement through his death on the cross? We need to remember that Jesus cries τετέλεσται (19.30) from the cross, using the word τελῶ which is closely related to the word τελειῶ in 4.34. W. Loader discusses this whole question at some length and concludes that while the theme of atonement through the sacrificial death of Jesus on the cross is present in the Gospel (cf. 1.29, 6.51c, 10.11, 15, 11.50-52, 18.14, 15.13), it remains subordinate to the theme of revelation, which clearly interested the author much more.[103] In particular, the fact that in ch. 4 revelation is made to a Samaritan may be a sign of a concern to show that the revelation Jesus brought was not intended purely for the Jewish nation.[104]

c. Finally, it was noted above on p. 150 that the phrase αὐτοῦ τὸ ἔργον means 'his work' in the sense of 'the work which he (i.e. God) gave him (i.e. Jesus) to do' (cf. 17.4), but, as a number of commentators have noted, the phrase is actually ambiguous and could mean 'the work which he (i.e. God) himself is doing'.[105] While the first sense was probably the one Jesus intended here (if, as has been argued, the saying goes back to him), it is not impossible that the author also had the deeper sense in mind in view of other verses in the Gospel which portray Jesus as one who can do nothing of

---

husbands (v. 18) stand for the five books of the Pentateuch, and that the sixth 'husband' stands for Simon Magus (p. 82).

[102] See especially G. Delling (1960) 32, W. Wilkens (1969) 85f. and W. Loader (1989) 94-107.

[103] Ibid. 94-107. Cf. J. Riedl (1973) 94-117, who sees the death and resurrection of Jesus as the act whereby his life-work was brought to completion.

[104] Cf. J .Bligh (1962) 346, J. Riedl (1973) 64.

[105] Cf. J. Riedl (1973) 63, U.C. von Wahlde (1990) 41.

himself and whose works are in fact the works which God does through him (cf. 5.19ff., 9.3f., 10.32, 37, 14.10).[106]

6.5 The Context of John 17.4

6.5.1 John 13-17

Jn. 17.4 is found in the opening section of the prayer which concludes the so-called 'Farewell Discourses' of Jesus given in the context of the Last Supper.

The more precise literary and historical setting of the prayer in ch. 17 is disputed among scholars, largely because of the 'aporia' at the end of ch. 14 ἐγείρεσθε, ἄγωμεν ἐντεῦθεν (14.31), which gives the impression that the discourses originally ended at that point and were followed by the narrative contained in 18.1ff. R. Bultmann saw here evidence for the dislocation of the text, and, because the prayer would not be suitable in the middle of the discourses, he believed that originally it was placed between 13.30 and 13.31.[107] However, there is no textual support for this view, and it has found little support among other scholars. From a purely literary point of view, a position at the close of the discourses is to be preferred.[108] J.H. Bernard's proposed re-arrangement of 13.1-31a, chs. 15-16, 13.31b-38, chs. 14, 17 satisfies this requirement,[109] but again his theory has no textual support and is unlikely anyway in view of the questions of the disciples in 14.5, 8, and 22, which are unnatural if placed after chs. 15-16, and in view of the way the Paraclete is introduced in 14.16f., which reads like a first-time introduction.[110] It is possible, of course, as some scholars believe, that chs. 15-17 were a later insertion into the Gospel,[111] but at the same time a more historically realistic solution cannot be excluded. Ch. 14.31 may have been a preliminary announcement of Jesus' intention to leave, though they did not actually leave until 18.1;[112] or chs. 15-17 may have been said on the way to the Garden of Gethsemane (in which case ἐξῆλθεν in 18.1 means that he

---

[106] Cf. W. Loader (1989) 80. See further appendix B. As we saw in chapter 5, this motif can also be traced back to the historical Jesus.

[107] R. Bultmann (ET 1971) 461.

[108] R.E. Brown (1966) 2.745, R. Schnackenburg (ET 1982) 3.167.

[109] J.H. Bernard (1928) 2.456-8.

[110] C.K. Barrett (1978²) 454, D.A. Carson (1991) 477.

[111] R.E. Brown (1966) 2.745, B. Lindars (1972) 486, R. Schnackenburg (ET 1982) 3.201, G.R. Beasley-Murray (1987) 223f.

[112] A. Plummer (1882) 298, D.A. Carson (1991) 479.

went out from the city, rather than from the upper room);[113] less convincing is L. Morris' view that Jesus was really talking about going on to another topic of conversation,[114] or C.H. Dodd's view that he was talking about rising to meet the devil in a purely spiritual sense.[115]

Quite apart from these literary problems, there is the historical problem of the extent to which the 'Farewell Discourses' report what was actually said on the night Jesus was betrayed. There can be little doubt that Jesus did share a final meal with his disciples, and that he probably spoke at some length during it, but it can hardly be maintained that the words attributed to him on this occasion represent his actual words in any close sense, even if the Fourth Gospel depends at this point on the testimony of one who was present at the Last Supper (cf. 13.23, 21.20-24). On the other hand, there is no need to assume that the 'Farewell Discourses' are purely Johannine creations *ex nihilo*.[116] The themes to be found in them may still reflect the substance of what Jesus said on this occasion, even if it has been written up in a Johannine way and from a post-Easter perspective.

6.5.2 John 17

Jn. 17 has traditionally been called the 'High Priestly' prayer of Jesus in view of the fact that he prays for his present and future disciples in much the same way as the High Priest in Old Testament days was called to intercede for the people of Israel (17.6-26). However, the prayer may also be called Jesus' prayer of consecration, since in it Jesus also prays for himself (17.1-5) and dedicates himself to God for his coming death and glorification (17.19).

Regarding the general authenticity of the prayer, it is not a valid objection to say that its note of quiet triumph is incompatible with the historically more credible anguish felt by Jesus in the Synoptic account of the prayer in the Garden of Gethsemane (Mk. 14.32-42 pars.). It accords well with his

---

[113] D.A. Carson (1991) 479. B.F. Westcott (1908) 2.239 suggests the Temple courts as a possible place for chs. 15-17 to have been said.

[114] L. Morris (1971) 661.

[115] C.H. Dodd (1953) 406-409.

[116] R. Bultmann (ET 1971) 459: 'Chapters 15-17 ... are fully Johannine in both content and form'. Cf. the following comments on ch. 17 itself: 'The present prayer is a summary of Johannine theology relative to the work of Christ', C.K. Barrett (1955) 417; 'John 17 certainly does not contain the words of the earthly Jesus', E. Käsemann (ET 1968) 77; 'The prayer cannot be securely traced back to Jesus himself', B. Lindars (1972) 517; 'The prayer undoubtedly originated in the Johannine school', R. Schnackenburg (1982) 3.201.

human nature that he should approach the cross with a mixture of feelings, both of calm resolution (cf. Lk. 9.51) and of horror.[117] As far as its detailed content is concerned, R.E. Brown believes that the chapter was probably constructed, as were the other chapters of the 'Farewell Discourses', 'by elaborating upon traditional sayings of Jesus, some of which were original in the setting of the Last Supper'.[118] Moreover, up to a point, the argument from coherence may be deployed, for a number of commentators have drawn attention to the fact that much of it accords well with what we are told of Jesus' prayers in the Synoptic Gospels, and especially with the 'Lord's prayer'.[119] As J.H. Bernard notes, these similarities 'show that the spirit which breathes throughout ch. 17 is similar to that with which we have been made familiar when reading Jesus' words as recorded by the Synoptists and elsewhere in John'.[120] Nevertheless, what was said above about the authenticity of the 'Farewell Discourses' in general obviously applies here: most of the time the most we can hope for is a substantial rather than a verbal form of authenticity.

6.5.3 John 17.1-5

The structure of Jn. 17 has been much discussed, and many theories proposed, but most commentators regard 17.1-5 as the opening section of the prayer, in which Jesus prays for himself as he faces the final crisis of his life on earth.[121]

The basic request of Jesus is that he might be 'glorified' with the glory he had with the Father before the world was made (vv. 1, 5). In other words, it is a request that through his coming death and resurrection, undergone in obedience to the will of God, he might be found acceptable to God and

---

[117] D.A. Carson (1991) 552, B.F. Westcott (1908) 2.239.

[118] R.E. Brown (1966) 2.745.

[119] J.H. Bernard (1928) 2.558f. notes how Jesus is portrayed as praying in times of crisis in the Synoptic Gospels (Mk. 1.35, 6.46, Lk. 3.21, 5.16, 6.12, 9.18, 28, 11.1), addresses God as 'Father' (Lk. 22.42, 23.34, 46, Mt. 11.25, cf. Jn. 17.1, 5, 11, 21, 24, 25), prays for a disciple (Lk. 22.32), has a concern for the name of God (Mt. 6.9 par., cf. Jn. 17.6, 11, 12, 26), does not want his disciples to be led into temptation (Mt. 6.13 par., cf. Jn. 17.12), but wants them to be delivered from evil (Mt. 6.13, cf. Jn. 17.15) etc. Cf. R.E. Brown (1966) 2.747, B. Lindars (1972) 518: 'John's picture ... is consistent with the impression of Jesus' personality which can be gained from the more varied evidence contained in the Synoptic Gospels'. Also J.A.T. Robinson (1985) 308f. and n. 33.

[120] J.H. Bernard (1928) 2.559; cf. L. Morris (1969) 183.

[121] E.g. R. Bultmann (ET 1971) 490, C.H. Dodd (1953) 417, C.K. Barrett (1955) 416, R.E. Brown (1966) 2.751, L. Morris (1971) 717, R. Schnackenburg (ET 1982) 3.169, D.A. Carson (1991) 553.

made to share again in the kind of divine splendour or radiance or majesty which was his before the incarnation. There is no selfishness in the request, because it is in effect a request for grace to fulfil the divine plan and Jesus sees the glory of God as the final outcome (v. 1).

It is in this context that Jesus is portrayed as looking back on the past (vv. 2-4). God gave him authority to be the one through whom 'eternal life' would be given to those destined to receive it (v. 2), and he has faithfully discharged his commission on earth (v. 4). Thus, already, in a sense, God has 'glorified' Jesus and Jesus has 'glorified' God. Now Jesus requests that this reciprocal glorification should taken to a new stage of operation.

Verse 3 is commonly taken by commentators to be a parenthesis on the part of the writer:[122] as a definition of eternal life, it hardly suits the language of prayer, but reads more like a confessional statement rather like those we find in 1 Jn. 2.25 and 5.20; again it is most unnatural for Jesus to call himself 'Jesus Christ', especially with 'Christ' as a proper name rather than a title; and vv. 2 and 4 connect up quite well. As C.K. Barrett notes, the author has grammatically incorporated the sentence into the prayer, but it functions more like a footnote.[123]

A further point to note about this opening section is its non-semitic Greek and its heavy concentration of typically Johannine words and expressions. R.A. Martin ranks 17.1-5 among the least semitic passages of the Gospel, such that, considered on its own, it would count as clearly having been written originally in Greek rather than in Aramaic.[124] As for words and expressions frequently found in the Gospel, we may note especially: ὥρα, δοξάζω, ζωὴ αἰώνιος, ἀληθινός, γινώσκω, ὃν ἀπέστειλας, ἔργον, and κόσμος. As has been argued at length in the case of ἔργον, the frequency of the use of these expressions does not necessarily rule them out as being inauthentic wherever they are found in the Fourth Gospel, but it does warn us against accepting too readily their authenticity in the narrow sense in every context the author gives them.

6.6 The Authenticity of John 17.4

In the light of this background, what are to say about the authenticity of 17.4? The *prima facie* case against its authenticity in the narrow sense of

---

[122] E.g. J.H. Bernard (1928) 2.561, C.K. Barrett (1955) 419, B. Lindars (1972) 578, R. Schnackenburg (ET 1982) 3.172, G.R. Beasley-Murray (1987) 296, though L. Morris (1971) 719 n. 11 and D.A. Carson (1991) 556 have reservations.
[123] C.K. Barrett (1978²) 503.
[124] R.A. Martin (1989) 11.

corresponding closely to something Jesus actually said on the night he was betrayed is strong, and may be confirmed by the following features from the verse itself:

a. The occurrence of the word δοξάζω, which seems to have been a favourite with the author. It occurs in his narrative sections as well as his reports of Jesus' speech (cf. 7.39, 12.16, 21.19 and the use of δόξα at 1.14, 2.11, 12.41, 43). In the Synoptic Gospels the word δοξάζω occurs in Jesus' speech only at Mt. 5.16 and 6.2, and only at Mt. 5.16 of men 'glorifying' God, and even here the word lacks the connotation of 'glorifying' through obedience, which is present in the Fourth Gospel.

b. The use of a subordinating participle τελειώσας is a Greek rather than a semitic construction and runs counter to the paratactic style which is normal in Aramaic and normally reflected in the Greek of the Fourth Gospel.[125] The verse is not straightforwardly translatable into Aramaic, so here at least we may be reasonably confident that the author is not relying on an Aramaic source.

c. Most of the other criteria fail to support the verse's authenticity. There is no multiple attestation for the verse. It is not aphoristic in form, and shows no signs of poetry or parallelism. It cannot be shown to run against the author's redactional trends, nor is the thought of glorifying God and accomplishing his work unparalleled in Jewish and christian literature.

The authenticity of Jn. 17.4 in the narrow, type b, sense of the word is therefore questionable, but by the criterion of coherence its authenticity in the broader, type c, sense need not be doubted. It was argued in chapter 5 and in the earlier part of this chapter that Jesus believed that he was a man of destiny, with a particular task to perform, given to him by God. If, as most commentators agree, the word ἔργον in this verse includes not only the task of revealing God but also of dying a sacrificial death on the cross, with τελειώσας looking forward proleptically to the accomplishment of that work,[126] and if, as the Gospels unanimously testify, Jesus was aware of the imminence of his death not only during the months which preceded his final passover, but most especially at the time of the passover itself, then there is nothing at all incongruous about his stating at this point that his life's work is complete. If, moreover, we may take the Synoptic Gethsemane tradition concerning the content of Jesus' prayer in the garden (Mk. 14.36 pars.) as historically trustworthy, along with some of the other

---

[125] Cf. C.K. Barrett (1978²) 7. The textual variant (καὶ D) τὸ ἔργον ἐτελείωσα is supported by D, Θ, Ψ, 054, f¹³, and the Majority text, but is almost certainly secondary when compared with the 26th ed. Nestle-Aland text which is supported by p66, ℵ, A, B, C, L, N, (W), 0109, 1, 33, pc.

[126] J. Calvin (ET 1959) 138, L. Morris (1971) 721 n. 19, R. Schnackenburg (ET 1982) 3.173, G.R. Beasley-Murray (1987) 297, D.A. Carson (1991) 557.

similar material from the earlier parts of the Gospels reviewed above on p. 139, then we may also say that Jesus believed that in his life and death he was consistently obeying the will of God. Perhaps the author has sharpened this idea by interpreting it in terms of 'glorification', but, if so, he has legitimately made explicit what is implicit, since in Jewish and christian thought obedience honours God (cf. 1 Sam. 2.30, Dan. 5.23, 1 Esd. 9.9, 2 Cor. 9.13).[127] So even if 17.4 is not a direct report of what Jesus said on this occasion, it may plausibly be said to reflect accurately the state of his mind as he approached his death. At least at this point the author is not painting a false picture or deceiving us by putting these words into Jesus' mouth.[128]

One further aspect of 17.4 has not yet been dealt with in this context, namely its resemblance to 4.34. Both use the phrase ἔργον τελειῶ. Both, in different ways, call the work God's work (in 4.34 αὐτοῦ, in 17.4 ὃ δέδωκάς μοι). And both use the verb ποιῶ in connection with the verb τελειῶ. In the light of R.E. Brown's comment that ch. 17 was probably constructed 'by elaborating upon traditional sayings of Jesus'[129], it would not be unreasonable to suppose that the author has here taken the language of 4.34 and used it as one of the 'building blocks' for the prayer in ch. 17, or as a piece in the mosaic. Rather like other features of Jesus' speech (e.g. addressing God as 'Father', or as 'he who sent me', and prefacing his sayings with 'Truly, truly I say unto you') the author may have taken this saying of Jesus which arguably goes directly back to him and has used its phraseology in this new context.

6.7 The Exegesis of John 17.4

Since there are not sufficient grounds for believing that 17.4 goes back directly to Jesus, we cannot speak of it as an independent saying. It remains for us therefore to give an exegesis of the verse briefly in its Johannine context, drawing together some of the exegetical points which have already been made and adding new ones where necessary.

As stated above, the words 'glorify' and 'glory' are quite common in the Fourth Gospel and serve as a vehicle for his theology.[130] The glory of God,

---

[127] Cf. C.H. Dodd (1963) 69 n. 2: 'In the context of Johannine thought, there is no substantial difference between θέλημα τὸ σὸν γινέσθω and δόξασόν σου τὸ ὄνομα.

[128] Contrast P.M. Casey (1991) 20, who calls the Johannine development of the tradition he received 'deceptive'.

[129] R.E. Brown (1966) 2.745.

[130] See J. Riedl (1973) 69-186 for an extended exposition of this theme.

his divine splendour/ radiance/ majesty,[131] is something in which Jesus himself shared before the world was made (17.5, 24, cf. 22). During Jesus' ministry on earth God continued to 'glorify' him (8.54), his glory being revealed particularly through his miracles (2.12, 11.4; cf. 1.14). At the same time Jesus 'glorified' God through the working of miracles and his general faithfulness in carrying out God's purpose (17.4, cf. 7.18, 11.4, 40, 12.28). The same mutual glorifying took place at and beyond the death and resurrection of Jesus, in which Jesus was 'glorified' (7.39, 12.16, 23, 13.31, 17.1, 5) and God 'glorified' through him (12.28, 13.31, 17.1). The Spirit also 'glorifies' Jesus (16.14), and through Jesus the disciples also share in the glory of God (17.22) and themselves bring glory to God (14.31, 15.8) and to Jesus (17.10).

In 17.4 Jesus is clearly portrayed as thinking of his earthly ministry and as claiming that through it God's 'glory' has been set forth, or manifested. The phrase ἐπὶ τῆς γῆς stands in contrast with παρὰ σεαυτῷ in v. 5 and points to the period between his birth and his death during which his own divine glory was to some extent veiled.

How did Jesus 'glorify' God on earth? The answer given here is that he did so by accomplishing the work which God had given him to do. Note here especially:

a. The content of the 'work'. As has already been said in connection with 4.34, the 'work' referred to here is primarily the work of revelation, whereby Jesus through word and deed revealed God and himself as the way to God, but also includes the work accomplished on the cross, whereby Jesus gave himself for the life of the world.[132]

b. The giver of the 'work'. The phrase ὃ δέδωκάς μοι brings out even more strongly than αὐτοῦ in 4.34 the fact that God is the source of Jesus' work. This is very much in tune with the rest of the Gospel, in which Jesus is portrayed as wholly dependent on God, the recipient of everything he has (cf. especially 3.35, 5.22, 26, 27, 36, 6.39, 12.49, 13.3, 17.2, 11, 24). The initiative in Jesus' work lies wholly with God. J. Riedl once again sees here the idea that not only is Jesus' work mandated by God, but actually performed by God through him.[133] While this latter idea is certainly to be found in the Gospel, it may be doubted whether it is present in 17.4 itself.

c. The accomplishment of the 'work'. The point made on pp. 149f. above about the distinction between ποιῶ and τελειῶ in 4.34 obviously applies here also, τελειῶ carrying the added connotation of bringing to a successful conclusion the commission which had been laid on Jesus. The aorist

---

[131] Cf. *TDNT* 2.233-249 for the background of the words δόξα and δοξάζω in the New Testament.
[132] See p. 153 and nn. 102 and 103 above. Also W. Thüsing (1970) 50, 71-75.
[133] J. Riedl (1973) 86-90, A. Vanhoye (1960) 392-409.

participle is not necessarily an anachronistic looking back at Jesus' work from a post-Easter perspective, as some have said,[134] but may be a proleptic anticipation of the work of the cross, which by this time for Jesus was imminent.[135] Jesus, therefore, on the eve of his death, having already done the work which God wanted him to do to this point, commits himself to carrying through that work to the end and is confident of his ability to do so.

6.8 The Exegesis of John 4.34 and 17.4 in the Patristic Era

As one might expect, Jn. 4.34 is used in the patristic era as a basis for exhortation. Thus, for example, Tertullian and Athanasius use it as a means to exhort their readers to the practice of fasting,[136] Cyprian to moderation in eating,[137] and Ambrose, Augustine and Chrysostom more generally to doing the will of God.[138] Clement of Alexandra gives the verse a different twist by saying that whereas for Christ doing His Father's will was food, for us Christ himself is food.[139]

Christologically the verse is used by Tertullian to demonstrate the Son's distinctness from the Father as against Praxeas' modalistic monarchianism,[140] while Origen, on the other hand, sees the verse as evidence for the unity of wills between the Father and the Son.[141] Gregory of Nazianzus saw that the mention of Christ being 'sent' could be used as an argument against the deity of Christ, but argues that it applies only to his human nature.[142]

As far as Jn. 17.4 is concerned, the nature of the 'work' the Son was given to do is variously defined. Augustine and Hilary conceive of it in terms of revelation,[143] whereas Athanasius conceives of it in terms of salvation.[144]

---

[134] E.g. R.E. Brown (1966) 2.741f., J. Riedl (1973) 117, R. Kysar (1986) 256.
[135] See n. 126 above.
[136] Tertullian, *On Fasting*, sec. 15; Athanasius, Festal Letters, 1.5.
[137] Cyprian, *Testimonies against the Jews*, 3.60.
[138] Ambrose, *Duties of the Clergy*, 1.31.163; Augustine, *Of Holy Virginity*, sec. 28; Chrysostom, *Homily 20 on John's Gospel*, sec. 3.
[139] Clement of Alexandria, *Instructor*, 1.6.
[140] Tertullian, *Against Praxeas*, sec. 21.
[141] Origen, *Commentary on John*, ad loc.
[142] Gregory of Nazianzus, *Theological Orations*, 3.17.
[143] Augustine, *Tractate 105 on John's Gospel*, 3, 5; Hilary, *On the Trinity*, 3.15f.
[144] Athanasius, *Orations against the Arians*, 3.25.23.

Novatian sees in Jn. 17.3-4 evidence for the Son's distinctness from the Father,[145] but both Augustine and Chrysostom are anxious to show that this does not mean that the Son is not God. Augustine interprets the Father's 'giving' as applying to the human nature of Christ which was assumed into the unity of Christ's person,[146] and Chrysostom stresses that Christ is here speaking in a 'condescending' way. It is not as though 'He ... waited to hear and learn'. In fact he came of his own will.[147]

Otherwise we find a tradition of interpretation which links this verse with others in the Gospels in order to demonstrate that there is a mutual glorifying between Father, Son and Holy Spirit, which illustrates their equality. This tradition is found in the works of Gregory of Nyssa, Basil, Ambrose, and Augustine.[148]

In summary, then, we find both 4.34 and 17.4 being used to affirm the distinctness of the Son from the Father. Both are also said not to contradict a belief in Christ's deity and both are used in the service of 'high' christologies (Origen in the case of 4.34, and Gregory of Nyssa, Basil, Ambrose and Augustine in the case of 17.4), though in neither case are the verses on their own used to affirm the deity of Christ in its fullest sense.

6.9 Conclusion

The main conclusions from this chapter may now be briefly summarised:

a. Jn. 4.34 and 17.4 need to be evaluated differently as far as their authenticity is concerned. We saw that 4.34 not only contains motifs which are present in Synoptic sayings which may be reliably attributed to Jesus, but also itself has a strong claim to authenticity in a strict, type b sense (though, as in 9.4, the phrase τοῦ πέμψαντός με may be a secondary, independently authentic, feature, added in here by a process of conflation). Jn. 17.4, by contrast, seems to be an attempt by the author to sum up Jesus' mood on the night on which he was betrayed, yet in words which recall 4.34 and which do not give a misleading impression of Jesus' character or state of mind.

b. We learn therefore from 4.34 of Jesus' strong feeling of commitment to obey God and fulfil the purpose of his coming, a feeling which was capable of superseding his physical needs and constituted a *sine qua non* of his

---

[145] Novatian, *Treatise concerning the Trinity*, sec. 26.

[146] Augustine, *Tractate 105 on John's Gospel*, sec. 4.

[147] Chrysostom, *Homily 80 on John's Gospel*, sec. 2.

[148] Gregory of Nyssa, *On the Holy Spirit*; Basil, *On the Spirit*, 18.46; Ambrose, *On the Christian Faith*, 4.10.137; Augustine, *On the Trinity*, 2.4.6; *Tractate 43 on John's Gospel*, sec. 14.

existence. The saying also points in the direction of Jesus' moral oneness with God, and yet his humanity and subordination as man to God. If 4.31-34 is placed in its original context, we may also say that Jesus saw his work as including making disciples of others and as being something in which his disciples themselves could be involved. We are also reminded from 17.4 of Jesus' awareness at the Last Supper of the imminence of his death, and of his belief that in his life and death he had faithfully discharged the task he believed that he had been given to do.

c. Within the context of the Fourth Gospel as a whole, we find the 'work' which Jesus has been given to do being defined principally in terms of revelation, which leads to the giving of life in the case of those who receive it, though the thought of Jesus' atoning work on the cross is also probably present as a subsidiary theme. The 'work' is conceived of as being done in obedience to God, but, in the light of the rest of the Gospel, there may also be the thought of God himself doing the work through Jesus. There may also be the idea that by the example of his obedience, Jesus became the source of a new Law for his disciples.

d. Finally we have seen that in the patristic era, these texts are used to affirm both the distinctness of the Father and the Son, and their unity. For Origen, 4.34 is evidence for their unity of will, while for Gregory of Nyssa, Basil, Ambrose and Augustine, 17.4 is part of the evidence adduced for the mutual glorifying, and therefore the equality, of the members of the Trinity.

Chapter 7

Doing what God Does (A)

7.1 Introduction

In this chapter we will take a look at the saying of Jesus found in Jn. 5.17. In the Johannine context this saying is closely related to that found in 5.19f., but because there is so much to say about each we will leave the latter passage to a separate chapter.

As usual, we will firstly set this saying in its context, secondly examine its 'authenticity', thirdly give an exegesis of it, fourthly give an account of its use in the patristic era, and finally draw some conclusions.

7.2 The Context of John 5.17

7.2.1 The Johannine Context

The saying is found in a chapter of the Fourth Gospel which has no direct parallel in the Synoptic Gospels, and which stands as a self-contained unit within the Fourth Gospel itself.[1] The chapter may be divided up as follows:
    5.1-9a. The healing of the man at the pool of Bethesda.
    5.9b-18. The sabbath question, arising from the healing.
    5.19-30. Jesus' discourse on his role as Son of God.
    5.31-47. Jesus' discourse on the witness borne to him.
The first two sections will be introduced here. The discourses will be touched on in the next two chapters.

---

[1] Though it is to be observed that the theme of life-giving, which is developed in ch. 5, is also found in the story of the healing of the official's son which immediately precedes it, at 4.50, 51, and 53. A further matter has been the ongoing, but so far inconclusive, debate among scholars as to whether ch. 5 originally followed ch. 6 in the Fourth Gospel, but there is no need to go into that question here, nor the question whether 7.14-24 and/ or 8.13-20 originally belonged to ch. 5.

7.2.2 John 5.1-9a

The story is set in Jerusalem at the time of a feast (v. 1).[2] Jesus comes to a pool (v. 2)[3] and finds a man there who had been suffering from some disability for thirty-eight years (v. 5). (The nature of his disability is not spelt out, but lameness of some kind would be consistent with the evidence). Jesus knows that the man has been there a long time (whether supernaturally or through some human agency the text does not make clear), asks whether the man would like to be healed (v. 6). When the man complains that he has no-one to put him in the pool when it is stirred (perhaps by an intermittent spring, v. 7),[4] Jesus tells him to rise, take up his pallet and walk (v. 8). 'At once the man was healed, and he took up his pallet and walked' (v. 9).

The historicity of this story has been questioned in various ways by a number of commentators. R. Bultmann, for example, argues that the story is a 'secondary composition',[5] but his reasons for so regarding it are not compelling. For example, on form-critical grounds he regards the detail in which the story is told to be a sign of lateness, but, as E.P. Sanders has said,[6] detail is not necessarily a sign of lateness. Stories can develop from the more detailed to the less detailed as well as in the opposite direction. The only other main reason Bultmann appears to advance against the historicity of the story is the fact that Jesus here seizes the initiative in healing the man (v. 6), whereas in earlier layers of tradition Jesus responds to needs which are brought to him, but as R.T. Fortna[7] and G.R. Beasley-Murray[8] have

---

[2] Which feast we do not know. Most commentators are agreed that the article should not be read in front of ἑορτή, but are not agreed as to which feast it was. The main suggestions are Passover and Pentecost. Which one it was is of no great importance for the meaning of the story itself.

[3] The textual problems of vv. 2-4 will not be dealt with here. Scholars are divided as to whether προβατικῇ qualifies πύλη (understood), or whether it should qualify κολυμβήθρα. There is also division as to the name of the pool where the man was lying, and where the pool was situated, though most believe that it should be identified with that excavated near St. Anne's church to the north of the temple area. Most are also agreed that all that follows ξηρῶν in v. 3 and the whole of v. 4 are later scribal additions to the text.

[4] If v. 4 carries a reliable tradition, the belief was that the first person to reach the pool after it had been stirred would be healed. R.T. Fortna (1970) 51, however, suggests that the belief originally was that anyone who reached the pool while it was being stirred would be healed.

[5] R. Bultmann (ET 1971) 237 n. 4, 239 n. 2.
[6] E.P. Sanders (1985) 15.
[7] R.T. Fortna (1970) 51.
[8] G.R. Beasley-Murray (1987) 71.

pointed out, even in the Synoptic tradition, Jesus takes the initiative in healing people (as, e.g., in Mk. 3.1-6, Lk. 7.11-17, 13.10-17, 14.1-6).

Some other commentators, who do not share in Bultmann's radical scepticism, are yet inclined to see in this healing story the influence of the story of the healing of the lame man recorded in Mk. 2.1-12. Direct dependence on Mark's story or even ultimate dependence on the same event is unlikely in view of the substantial differences between the two,[9] but a certain amount of cross-fertilisation between them at an early stage cannot be ruled out either in view of the striking phrase ἔγειρε ἆρον τὸν κράβαττόν σου which is found in both.[10]

However this may be, the early origin of the story of the healing of the man at the pool of Bethesda need not be doubted. As C.K. Barrett notes, there is 'no need to suppose that its origin is other than traditional'.[11] R.E. Brown also concludes that it comes from primitive tradition rather than being the creation of the evangelist,[12] while J.H. Bernard sees here the possibility that behind the story as recorded by the Evangelist there stands eyewitness testimony.[13] At least its historicity should be judged no more adversely than that of the many similar healing stories in the Synoptic Gospels which it generally resembles.

7.2.3 John 5.9b-16

Verse 9b clearly begins a new section, introducing as it does the sabbath motif and a quick succession of scenes which form the sequel to the healing itself:

Firstly, we have a conversation between 'the Jews' (probably to be understood as religious authorities opposed to Jesus here, as often in the Fourth Gospel) and the healed man, in which they object to his carrying his pallet as being a contravention of the sabbath commandment, and he in turn

---

[9] R. Schnackenburg (ET 1980) 2.96 mentions A. Loisy as the sole exception to this consensus.

[10] Cf. B. Lindars (1972) 52, 209. Some commentators draw attention to a further similarity between the two stories at Jn. 5.14 and Mk. 2.5, 9 - the introduction of the motif of the forgiveness of sins - but here the wording and setting of the motif is quite different in the two stories, and even B. Lindars (1972) 216-217 is less sure of a connection between the two at this point. The motif is more likely to go back to Jesus' tendency to see a connection between sin and sickness on different occasions. See further on v. 14 below.

[11] C.K. Barrett (1978²) 249.

[12] R.E. Brown (1966) 1.209.

[13] J.H. Bernard (1928) 1.225.

seeks to pass responsibility for his action on to the one who had healed him, though his name is as yet unknown to him (vv. 10-13).

Secondly, we have an encounter between the man and Jesus in the temple in which Jesus tells the man to sin no more lest something worse befalls him (thus apparently implying that his former paralysis had been caused in some way by his sin, and that continuance in sin would lead either to death, or, more probably, to eternal judgment, v. 14).

Thirdly, we have a further meeting between the man and 'the Jews' in which the man informs them of the name of his healer, not necessarily as an act of 'betrayal', but perhaps simply to comply with their request in v. 12 (v. 15).

These scenes conclude with a generalising statement which tells us that 'the Jews' used to (or began to) persecute Jesus because he used to (or began to) do 'these things' (presumably healings; cf. 7.23) on a sabbath (v. 16).

The link between the healing story recounted in vv. 2-9a and the sequel recounted in vv. 9b-14 has been much discussed in recent scholarship, with most scholars concluding that vv. 9b-14 has been added on as an afterthought by the author. In their view the original story made no mention of the sabbath. This view is naturally held by those who assign vv. 2-9a, in whole or in part, to a 'signs source',[14] but also by others who do not adhere to a 'signs source' theory.[15] The main arguments used to support this position are that the sabbath motif is not found in the body of the story itself, but is tacked on at the end, unlike similar sabbath-controversy stories in the Synoptic Gospels (cf. Mk. 2.23-3.6 pars., Lk. 13.10-17, 14.1-6), and that the author seems to want to introduce it here merely in order to prepare for the christological controversy which begins at v. 17, a controversy which could not flow from the sign without the sabbath motif being present.

A case may still be made, however, for the original unity of 5.2-15. In this connection the following points should be noted:

a. We are not necessarily to assume that the sabbath motif is secondary merely because it is introduced late in a story. As was mentioned above in connection with the healing story in ch. 9,[16] it is possible that it was part of the author's narrative art to introduce pieces of information into a story only

---

[14] They include: J. Becker (1979) 1.230, R. Bultmann (ET 1971) 177f., R.T. Fortna (1970) 48-54, J.L. Martyn (1979²) 68, cf. 166, W. Nicol (1972) 15f., 31f., R. Schnackenburg (ET 1980) 2.117, S. Schulz (1972, *Evangelium*) 83, H.M. Teeple (1974), U.C. von Wahlde (1989) 94-97. For a critique of the signs source theories in general see section 1.5 above.

[15] E.g. B. Lindars (1972) 209f.

[16] Chapter 5 n. 116.

when they became functional and/ or raised the tension of the narrative as seems to be the case with 2.6, 6.59, 13.30, 18.28, 19.14 and 20.14.[17]

b. As R.E. Brown has argued, the story from v. 9b to v. 14 has an air of verismilitude.[18] The man is true-to-life. He is no mere stereotype. He comes over as a rather dull, superstitious character, believing that the waters can heal him and grumbling about the others who get there first, failing to ask Jesus' name or find him later, then naively informing the Jews of Jesus' identity. He comes across as a real character.[19] Possibly, as J.L. Martyn argues, there were people in the evangelist's own situation who resembled this man,[20] but the characterisation could equally well be traditional.

c. Despite the tendency to regard 5.9b-15 as secondary in modern scholarship, a number of scholars still wish to hold on to v. 14 as an original part of the story.[21] This saying does not seem to be required for the elaboration of the christological themes in the later part of the chapter. Moreover, its theology of suffering seems to clash with that expressed in Jn. 9.2f., while it ties in very well with that expressed in Mk. 2.5.[22] In short, it seems more likely that v. 14 at least belongs to the original story than that it is a creation of the evangelist.

d. In a similar way, it is observable that vv. 9b-15 do not cohere very well with v. 16. In vv. 9b-15, the point at issue is the man's carrying of his pallet on the sabbath, whereas in v. 16 the point at issue is the fact that Jesus healed on the sabbath (though possibly Jesus' instruction to the man to carry his pallet is bound up in the word ταῦτα as well). If vv. 9b-15 had been a Johannine creation, would he not have focussed on the important issue straight away without introducing a second element which plays no part in the sequel? Again the impression is given that vv. 9b-15 is in the Gospel

---

[17] A point made by L.Th. Witkamp (1985) 31, though Witkamp himself thinks that this possibility is outweighed by other considerations concerning the author's general handling of his traditions. He believes that even vv. 2-9a show evidence of substantial Johannine redaction.

[18] R.E. Brown (1966) 1.208f. His further point that the sabbath motif is necessary to give the healing story significance is not strong. The healing story by itself still demonstrates Jesus' power and compassion, and can be held to symbolise Jesus' gift of life and forgiveness (cf. vv. 14, 21).

[19] *Pace* B. Lindars (1972) 210.

[20] J.L. Martyn (1979[2]) 68ff.

[21] E.g. R.T. Fortna (1970) 53, S. Pancaro (1975) 10-12, E. Haenchen (1959) 46-50.

[22] In fact no ultimate clash of theologies need be found here. It is quite possible to believe that suffering may be caused in particular cases by personal sin, but not in every case.

because it was a part of the original story, rather than being introduced by the author at a later stage.[23]

e. For what it may be worth, the argument may be added that there are no stylistic grounds for assigning vv. 9b-18 to a later hand. In fact, R.A. Martin has shown[24] that 5.9b-18 and 5.19-29 have a higher proportion of semitisms than 5.1-9a. Martin argues that most of the Gospel has been translated from an original Aramaic document, the rest showing signs of having initially been written in Greek, and therefore having a different origin, by its lower proportion of semitisms. The whole of ch. 5 is reckoned to be in the former category. Whatever our view as to Martin's main thesis, at least his statistics reveal that there are no stylistic grounds for believing that 5.2-9a and 5.9b-18 or 5.19-29 come from different sources.

Taking all these considerations into account, we may conclude that 5.2-15 may well have originally formed one unit, and may well describe an actual incident which took place during the ministry of Jesus. The whole story fits in well with what we know about Jesus from the Synoptic Gospels. That Jesus healed, that he healed occasionally on the sabbath day, and that as a result he came into conflict with certain religious authorities, is part of the bedrock of the Jesus tradition (cf. Mk. 3.1-6 pars., Lk. 13.10-17, 14.1-6; for another sabbath controversy story where healing is not involved cf. Mk. 2.23-28 pars.)[25]. Moreover, as we have seen, Jesus' words in v. 14 fit in well with what we know of him from other sources. In short, the whole pericope of vv. 2-15 is essentially credible as belonging to a *Sitz im Leben Jesu*.

Verse 16 clearly gives the evangelist's own comment on the situation. The imperfect tenses of ἐδίωκον and ἐποίει indicate that the sabbath story related in vv. 2-15 was just one in a series of similar happenings which led Jesus' religious opponents to the conclusion that he was a law-breaker and worthy of harrassment. This detaches the saying in v. 17 somewhat from the story.[26] Jesus is said to 'reply' to them,[27] but there is nothing for him to reply to, as far as the text is concerned, apart from the harrassment itself.

---

[23] R. Bultmann (ET 1971) 237f. believed that it was introduced at a later stage, but before the tradition reached the evangelist, but, as R.T. Fortna (1970) 52 n. 2 comments, this is an 'unnecessary complication'.

[24] R.A. Martin (1989) 9.

[25] Cf. E.C. Hoskyns (1947²) 253, J. Jeremias (ET 1971) 278 n. 8, E. Lohse (1973) 67, S. Westerholm (1978) 100, and M. Borg (1984) 148.

[26] Cf. J. Bligh (1963) 123.

[27] Commentators draw attention to the aorist middle ἀπεκρίνατο used here, which occurs in the Fourth Gospel only here and at v. 19 (the normal form being the aorist deponent passive ἀπεκρίθη), and believes it carries the connotation of a public, formal defence to a charge. Cf. J.H. Bernard (1928) 235, R.E. Brown (1966) 213, R. Bultmann (ET 1971) 244 n. 4, L. Morris (1971) 308 n. 40. Cf. Mk. 14.61 for the negative use at Jesus' trial.

Thus a temporal gap is quite likely between v. 15 and v. 17, but on the other hand, in the evangelist's mind at least, v. 17 was probably said while the incident of vv. 2-15 was still fresh in the minds of Jesus' opponents, since it still is at 7.23, as the words attributed to Jesus in that verse imply.

Having set the scene, we are now in a position to consider the authenticity of the saying contained in v. 17.

7.3 The Authenticity of John 5.17

The criterion of multiple attestation cannot be used to support the saying's authenticity, since the saying is not paralleled elsewhere, so we are left with the following four criteria: Language, Culture and Personal Idiom, Coherence, Dissimilarity, and Anti-Redactional Features.

(1) Language, Culture, and Personal Idiom
Here a number of points may be made:
   a. The saying can be translated straightforwardly into Aramaic, thus:

אבא עד כען עביד אף אנא עביד

Once again it should be said that we cannot be sure that these were the exact words which Jesus may have used,[28] but at least this attempted retroversion shows that the saying in 5.17 *could* have been said by him without serious loss or distortion of meaning.

   b. The whole idea of God and man as 'working' are very common in Jewish religion and culture.[29] Even the idea of God as 'working still' is at home in first century Judaism in view of the discussions in the works of Philo and the rabbis which seek to reconcile God's present activity with the statement in Gen. 2.3 that God 'rested' on the seventh day.[30] Of course it cannot be shown that either Jesus or the author of the Fourth Gospel were influenced directly by such discussions, but we do know that they belonged to their religious milieu. If the phrase ἕως ἄρτι relates to the imminent completion of Jesus' eschatological work, as O. Cullmann and S.

---

[28] For אבא as 'My Father' see G. Dalman (1905²) 90, 203, M. Black (1946) 198, 217f., and J. Jeremias (ET 1967) 55-60, (ET 1971) 64. In the light of Mk. 14.36 it seems highly likely that this word was one of Jesus' *ipsissima verba*, though, as J. Barr (1988 *JTS*) 28-47 and (1988 *Theology*) 173-179 has argued, we cannot be sure that Jesus used this unsuffixed form of the word on every occasion.

[29] Cf. the article by G. Bertram in *TDNT* 2.635ff. and chapter 4 above. For the idea of 'doing the work/ works of God' see further S. Pancaro (1975) 380-384 and appendix B at the end of this book.

[30] Cf. S.-B. 2.461. Some of these references will be quoted in the exegetical section below.

Bacchiochi have argued,³¹ this also would fit naturally into the *Sitz im Leben Jesu*.

c. Turning now to matters of Jesus' personal idiom, we note first of all that the manner of referring to God as his 'Father' was part of Jesus' idiom. Though there has been some discussion concerning the exact significance which should be attached to this word, as we shall see more fully below in the exegetical section, there seems to be general agreement that the historical Jesus did actually speak of God in this way.

d. The emphatic 'I' was also part of Jesus' personal idiom. We may compare the authoritative phrase 'Amen, I say to you', which is so often prefixed to Jesus' sayings in the Gospels, and which, as J. Jeremias argued,³² was surely part of his personal style. Jesus clearly had a strong sense of personal authority, both in his words and in his deeds, as the evangelists' frequent reference to his ἐξουσία demonstrate, and was not averse to speaking about himself in his teaching. In view of these facts, the emphatic 'I' in the phrase 'and I am working' is not out of place.

e. The saying is in the form of a parallelism, which again has been shown to be a mark of Jesus' personal speech.³³ C.F. Burney distinguishes four types of parallelism used by Jesus: synonymous paralellism, in which the two halves of the sentence make the same point; antithetical parallelism, in which the two halves of the sentence make the same point, but by way of contrast; synthetic or constructive parallelism, in which the second part of the sentence adds a new point to the first; and climactic parallelism, which is partly synonymous and partly synthetic, in which the second line takes up the thought of the first and develops it further. Burney does not mention this particular verse as an example of any of these types, but it could clearly fit into the third or fourth types of parallelism he mentions.

f. In addition to its parallelistic structure, the saying can be put into a form which illustrates its rhythm and rhyme, thus:

אבא עד כען עביד
אף אנא עביד

As Burney showed, rhythm and rhyme were also characteristics of Jesus' personal speech.³⁴ The particular rhythm the saying illustrates (a three-stress line followed by a two-stress line) is the Kina metre, a metre which was used to express strong inner emotion.³⁵

---

[31] O. Cullmann (1966) 187-191, S. Bacchiochi (1981) 3-19. It will, however, be argued below on pp. 187f. that this connotation may not be present in the phrase.
[32] J. Jeremias (ET 1971) 35f.
[33] C.F. Burney (1925) ch. 2, M. Black (1946) part 3.
[34] C.F. Burney (1925) 22-43, 100-175.
[35] C.F. Burney (1925) 34, J. Jeremias (ET 1971) 27.

g. As a result of these last two characteristics, this saying would have been very memorable. Its brief, pithy, aphoristic qualities are the qualities of many sayings regarded as being 'authentic', in a strict sense, in the Synoptic Gospels.[36] Similarly, its enigmatic, ambiguous qualities and lack of immediate context also deepen the impression that this saying could well go back to the Jesus himself.

(2) Coherence
We have already noted that the context of the saying (controversy with religious authorities resulting from a sabbath healing) rings true to what we know about Jesus from the Synoptic Gospels. It now remains to show that the same is true of Jesus' defence of his actions in this verse.

We have just seen that Jesus refers to God as 'Father' in the Synoptic Gospels. As far as the phrase '... is working still' is concerned, we may take it for granted (quite apart from the evidence of contemporary Jewish debates on the question) that Jesus would have agreed that God's working was not confined to six days in the week. The God who 'makes his sun rise on the evil and on the good, and sends rain on the just and on the unjust' (Mt. 5.45), who 'feeds the birds of the air' and 'clothes the grass of the field' (Mt. 6.26, 30) would not have been thought to suspend his providential and cosmological roles on the sabbath day. Indeed Jesus must have come to the conclusion that God was working *through him* on the sabbath day, since he evidently felt the power of God at work as he saw people being healed through his word and touch on that day.

This leads us to the final part of the saying: '... and I am working'. In chapters 5 and 6 we saw that Jesus in the Synoptic Gospels appears as a figure who believed that he was acting consistently in obedience to the will of God and by his power, such that it was God who was working in and through him. These ideas correspond very closely to the thrust of Jn. 5.17, which portrays Jesus' actions as being in some sense 'parallel' to God's.

What remains to be shown to be coherent with the picture of Jesus given in the Synoptic Gospels is that Jesus regarded himself as 'working' on the sabbath day in the sense of breaching the sabbath commandment to rest. Once this has been done, the saying in its entirety will have been shown to cohere with the attitudes of the historical Jesus as revealed in the Synoptic Gospels.

---

[36] Jn. 5.17 is found among J. Drummond's list of aphoristic sayings in the Fourth Gospel which W.F. Howard describes as 'entirely suiting the character and habit of Jesus as they are known to us from the Synoptics'. J. Drummond (1903) 17ff., W.F. Howard (1955[4]) 214.

That the word 'work' in Jn. 5.17 carries the nuance of that which was prohibited on the sabbath day need not be doubted, not only because Jesus is here seeking to defend actions he took on the sabbath day, but also because the words ἔργον and ἐργάζομαι and their Hebrew equivalents are regularly used in the Old Testament passages where the sabbath commandment is laid down. Thus the Greek expressions ἔργον ποιεῖν and ἔργα ποιεῖν are found in the LXX at Gen. 2.2f., Ex. 20.9, 23.12, 31.14, 15, 35.2, and Deut. 5.13, 14; the verb ἐργάζομαι is found at Ex. 20.9, 34.21, and Deut. 5.13; the Hebrew verb עבד is found at Ex. 20.9, 34.21 and Deut. 5.13 in this connection; the verb עשׂה at Gen. 2.2f., Ex. 20.9-11, 23.12, 31.14-17, 35.2, and Deut. 5.13, 14; the noun מעשׂה at Ex. 23.12; and the noun מלאכה at Gen. 2.2f., Ex. 20.9, 10, 31.14, 15, 35.2, and Deut. 5.13, 14.

In the light of these facts, as well as the indications given in Jn. 5.16 and 18, it is clear that in Jn. 5.17 Jesus is presented as admitting that he is breaching the sabbath commandment, and indeed as brazenly claiming the right to do so. He does *not* defend his healing on the sabbath on the grounds that it does not really count as 'work' (which he might have done since he had only spoken a few words, v. 8, and speaking as such was not prohibited on the sabbath day[37]), but on the grounds that, though it *was* a kind of 'work', it was justified 'work' because it was done in pursuance of the Father's will and in accordance with the Father's own activities.

It is at this point that we find an interesting link up between Jn. 5.17 and the evidence from other quarters concerning Jesus' attitude towards his sabbath activities. Not that Jesus elsewhere *explicitly* justifies his sabbath activities by reference to the Father's will or activities (this combination of motifs remains distinctive to this verse, though the individual motifs themselves have been found to be authentically present elsewhere), but that Jesus elsewhere *does* recognise some of his activities on the sabbath (and in one case the activities of his disciples) to constitute 'work', but *justified* 'work'.

This motif is strikingly found in every single major Gospel source - something which can be said of few Gospel motifs - as the following references will illustrate:

a. Mark. In Mk. 2.25f. (pars. Mt. 12.3f., Lk. 6.3f.) Jesus justifies his the actions of his disciples in plucking the grain on the sabbath by reference to the action of David, who, in an emergency, broke the law by eating the bread of the presence. In Mk. 3.4 (pars. Mt. 12.12, Lk. 6.9) he justifies his healing the man with the withered hand by saying (at least in Mark and Luke) that it falls into the category of 'saving life' - which his Pharisaic

---

[37] As G. Vermes (1983[2]) 25 points out. Additionally, E.P. Sanders (1985) 266 points out that even the laying on of hands (Lk. 13.13) does not necessarily constitute 'work'.

opponents would have regarded as a valid reason for suspending the sabbath rule.[38]

b. Q. In Lk. 14.5, par. Mt. 12.11, we seem to have a Q saying which is placed in different contexts by Matthew and Luke,[39] but which justifies Jesus' healings by reference to his opponents' readiness to 'work' on the sabbath by bringing out from a well/ pit a son/ ox/ sheep which has fallen into it.

c. M. In Mt. 12.5 we find Jesus justifying the disciples' action on the sabbath (as described above in a.) by reference to the 'work' the priests are commanded to do on a sabbath day.

d. L. In Lk. 13.15 he justifies his healing of the crippled woman on the sabbath by reference to the 'work' of untying an ox or ass on a sabbath and leading it to water.

e. John. In Jn. 7.22f. Jesus justifies his healing of the man at the pool of Bethesda by reference to the 'work' of circumcision which must take place on the eighth day, even if it be a sabbath day. In other words the circumcision commandment takes precedence over the sabbath commandment.

It may be argued, of course, that these utterances of Jesus are not authentic, and in order to counter that argument we will need to look at three of these sayings in more detail, but at this point we simply draw attention to this common motif found in no less than five independent sources. Whatever may be said about the accuracy of the details, there must surely have been a strong memory at a very early stage in the transmission of the Gospel tradition that Jesus had not only been accused of 'working' on the sabbath, but also that he had defended himself, not by denying that he had been 'working', but by affirming that the 'work' he had done was justified work in the circumstances.

We will now take a more detailed look at the first three passages mentioned above, where the words attributed to Jesus have a very strong claim to authenticity.

Firstly: Mk. 2.25f. (pars. Mt. 12.3f., Lk. 6.3f.)

Some critics have objected to the historicity of the scene described in Mk. 2.23f. pars. altogether, because they think it unlikely that Pharisees would have been found in a field on a sabbath day apparently spying on the activities of Jesus and his disciples.[40] Moreover it is said that the fact that

---

[38] Cf. I. Abrahams (1917) 132, S. Westerholm (1978) 94.

[39] M. Borg (1984) 335 n. 19 and J.A. Fitzmyer (1985) 2.1039 clearly do not regard these verses as true parallels, but the similarities are sufficiently strong for most scholars to believe in a common source for this saying. See further n. 57 below.

[40] E.g. E. Schweizer (ET 1971) 70, A.J. Hultgren (1972) 41, E.P. Sanders (1985) 265.

the Pharisees are objecting to the activities of the *disciples* rather than those of Jesus himself is a sign that the controversy originated in the time of the early church rather than the time of the ministry of Jesus.[41] Against this it may be said that the specific situation described in Mk. 2.23f. pars. is unlikely to have been a storm-centre in early christian-Jew relations, and that if the early church had wanted to invent a sabbath controversy story they would have chosen an incident of greater clarity and importance.[42] Again, the fact that Jesus is asked concerning his disciples' activities is not necessarily a sign of an early church origin for the story, since, as a number of scholars have pointed out, it was customary for rabbis to be held accountable for the actions of their disciples.[43] The scene, therefore, is credible and likely to be historical, but what of the words of Jesus which follow? We now need to apply the criteria for authenticity.

(1) Multiple Attestation
The saying occurs in all three Synoptic Gospels. Matthew and Luke have probably used Mark's gospel, but their inclusion of this material is a witness to their own belief that it is substantially dominical.

(2) Language, Culture and Personal Idiom
Since our argument here depends on the general thrust of Jesus' words rather than specific expressions, there is no need to translate these words back into Aramaic.

The argument of Jesus fits well in his religious culture. David was regarded as a model of piety in Jewish tradition.[44] The incident referred to is found in 1 Sam. 21.1-6. The appeal to scripture and the use of a counter-question as a way of answering an initial question was both a characteristic of the rabbis of Jesus' day, as far as we can tell, and also a mark of Jesus' personal idiom (cf. e.g. Mk. 7.1-13 par. Mt. 15.1-8; Mk. 12.10f. pars. Mt. 21.42, Lk. 20.17; Mk. 12.18-27 pars. Mt. 22.23-33, Lk. 20.27-40; Mk. 12.35-37 pars. Mt. 22.41-46, Lk. 20.41-44).[45] The words attributed to Jesus here are credible within the context of Jesus' ministry.

---

[41] E.g. R. Bultmann (ET 1968[2]) 16, A.J. Hultgren (1972) 41, E. Lohse (1973) 65.

[42] The historicity of the scene is well defended by I.H. Marshall (1978) 229, R.A. Guelich (1989) 120, and W.D. Davies and D.C. Allison (1991) 2.305.

[43] J. Roloff (1970) 55, F. Neirynck (1975) 266f., I.H. Marshall (1978) 229, M. Borg (1984) 152, B. Witherington (1990) 67.

[44] Cf. M.D. Hooker (1991) 103.

[45] For the rabbinic use cf. R. Bultmann (ET 1968[2]) 41, D. Hill (1972) 210, H. Anderson (1976) 110, and M.D. Hooker (1991) 104.

(3) Coherence

As we have seen, the substance of Jesus' argument coheres well with the type of argument Jesus uses in the other sabbath controversy stories found in all the other five major gospel sources. In particular, the apparent desire to place human need above a strict interpretation of the sabbath commandment is found elsewhere and seems to have been the usual way in which Jesus defended his actions.[46] In addition we may note the use of David as an example in Mk. 12.35-37 pars. Mt. 22.41-46, Lk. 20.41-44.

(4) Dissimilarity

It is here that the strongest arguments for authenticity may be deployed.

Firstly, there is a certain distance from the rabbinic style of argument here in that Jesus does not use a legal text to establish a legal principle, which would have been the normal rabbinic procedure, but a narrative passage instead. This use of haggadah for halakhic purposes is unusual.[47]

Secondly, there is also a certain distance from what might have been expected from the early church. The story is not particularly relevant to the case in hand (David's action did not take place on a sabbath,[48] and Jesus and his disciples could hardly be described as being in a similar state of danger and desperation as David was in the story), and is roughly recounted (the original story does not say that David's men were with him when he went to the priest, nor that David went into the house of God, nor that the incident took place when Abiathar was high priest). Moreover there is no exploitation of a David typology, which is unusual if this argument came from a church which believed that Jesus was great David's greater son.[49]

The argument of Jesus here therefore fits neatly neither into a wholly rabbinic mould, nor an early church mould, and therefore stands out as something which probably goes back to Jesus himself.

---

[46] So the majority of scholars. In addition a few scholars see Jesus' action as a desire to place his own mission, or the demands of the kingdom of God, above a strict interpretation of the sabbath commandment. Cf. T.W. Manson (1949) 190, E. Ellis (1966) 109, R.A. Guelich (1989) 127. This is likely in the case of the healing stories when taken in conjunction with passages like Mt. 11.2-6 par., but this theme is not evident in the passage we are dealing with here.

[47] Cf. S. Westerholm (1978) 97, M. Borg (1984) 153, R.A. Guelich (1989) 121f., W.D. Davies and D.C. Allision (1991) 2.308.

[48] Admittedly, later rabbinic tradition regarded the action as having taken place on the sabbath (S.-B. 1.618f.), but it is questionable whether Jesus himself knew of this interpretation, or, if he did, accepted it himself. Cf. M. Borg (1984) 337 n. 40.

[49] Cf. J. Roloff (1970) 58, I.H. Marshall (1978) 229, R.A. Guelich (1989) 123, 128, B. Witherington (1990) 67, W.D. Davies and D.C. Allison (1991) 2.305.

(5) Anti-Redactional Features

This argument cannot be strongly used in this case, since Mark elsewhere is concerned to show that Jesus offended the Pharisees by his behaviour on the sabbath (Mk. 3.1-6), that he had to answer for the actions of his disciples (Mk. 2.18, 7.5), that he used scripture and the counter-question method in his debates and so on. The only point to be made is that Mark here, as elsewhere, fails to fill out or embroider his narrative or iron out its difficulties.[50] We are left with the impression that he is faithfully passing on a tradition which he has received.

In conclusion, therefore, we may say that there are very good grounds for accepting Mk. 2.25f. pars. as coming from Jesus himself.[51] If so, then here we have evidence that he believed that a God-given law could be suspended for the sake of a higher God-given principle, in this case human need and well-being. This means that in the case of the sabbath in particular, the sabbath law could be suspended - i.e. 'work' could be done - for the sake of a higher principle.

Secondly: Mk. 3.4 (par. Lk. 6.9, cf. Mt. 12.12b)

This saying is generally regarded as 'authentic' in the fullest sense by the scholars.[52] The grounds of such confidence may be demonstrated once again as we go through the criteria:

(1) Multiple Attestation

The saying appears in much the same form in Mark and Luke, and in an abbreviated form as a statement in Matthew. No doubt both Luke and Matthew got it from Mark and thought it worth including in their Gospels.

(2) Language, Culture, and Personal Idiom

The saying in its Markan form may be translated back into Aramaic thus:

אריך בשבתא למעבד טובא או למעבד בישה
נפשא לאחאה או לאובדה

---

[50] Cf. C.E.B. Cranfield (1959) 114, H. Anderson (1976) 108.

[51] An increasing number of scholars seem to be coming round to this position, in contrast with a previous scepticism. In addition to the favourable judgments of scholars already mentioned (e.g. W.D. Davies and D.C. Allison, R.A. Guelich, I.H. Marshall, F. Neirynck, J. Roloff, S. Westerholm, and B. Witherington), we may note the comment of R. Banks (1975) 116: 'what we have here is a novel use of the Old Testament, christological in character, so striking that it must stem from Jesus himself'.

[52] Cf. R. Bultmann (ET 1968[2]) 147, J. Roloff (1970) 63f., E. Lohse (1973) 67, R. Banks (1975) 125, H. Anderson (1976) 112, I.H. Marshall (1978) 233, S. Westerholm (1978) 100, W.D. Davies and D.C. Allison (1991) 2.316.

If this translation can be accepted, a number of interesting possibilities arise, as will be explained at the close of this section.

As far as Jesus' religious culture is concerned, we note that the second half of the saying echoes the well-known exception which the rabbis made to the sabbath commandment, namely that if a life was in danger then 'work' was permitted on the sabbath day.[53] This idea had been developed at the time of the Maccabean wars when the Syrians were taking advantage of the Jewish sabbath laws by attacking them on that day (1 Macc. 2.32ff.).

As far as Jesus' personal idiom is concerned, we note the synthetic parallelism of the saying, and the antitheses within each clause, and its brief, pithy, memorable character.

(3) Coherence
The saying coheres well with the attitude Jesus adopts to the sabbath elsewhere in the Gospels, as we have already seen. For him 'doing good'/ compassion/ human need took precedence over a strict application of the sabbath commandment.

(4) Dissimilarity
The saying stands in contrast with its Jewish background through the striking way in which Jesus assimilates 'saving life' (which for the Pharisees was an acceptable 'work' on the sabbath) with 'doing good' (of which the healing of the man with the withered hand is presented as an example, and which therefore for the Pharisees would not have traditionally been acceptable 'work' - though by putting the question in this way Jesus forces the Pharisees to re-examine their position). As R. Banks puts it, the authenticity of the saying is 'generally unquestioned as a result of its radical character'[54].

The saying also stands in contrast with its christian background in that it has no overt christological element and is hardly the kind of saying the early church would have created as a weapon in its battle with Judaism over sabbath observance (contrast Mk. 2.28, which could well be Mark's own summarising comment on Jesus' sabbath teaching).

(5) Anti-Redactional Features
I am not aware of any un-Markan characteristics to this saying. The fact that this does not significantly damage the overall case for the saying's authenticity reminds us of the need for caution before we think of using this criterion negatively.

---

[53] See n. 38 above.
[54] R. Banks (1975) 125.

The case for the saying's authenticity in a strict sense is therefore justifiably strong. We note once again the fact that Jesus justifies his action of healing the man with the withered hand not by saying that it is not work, but by saying that it is legitimate work. He disagrees with the Pharisees, not because he does not accept the law, nor because, accepting the law, he regards his actions as falling within it, but because he is inclined to broaden the range of actions which may legitimately cause the law, as traditionally understood, to be suspended.

Three further points may be made on the basis of the Aramaic translation given above.

a. The translation uses the word עבד, which is one of the verbs used for 'work' in the sabbath commandment in the Old Testament. This confirms the point which is being made in this section.

b. Jesus may have seen his healings as an extension of the principle of 'saving life' through meditation on Deut. 32.39 where the word 'healing' stands in parallel to 'making alive' (Hebrew אחיה).

c. Further, Jesus may have seen his healings as a fulfilment of the law at a deeper level than that of the sabbath commandment considered in isolation, in that the purpose of the law was to 'give life' (cf. Lev. 18.5, Ezek. 18.4, 9, 20, 27f., 20.11 etc. Ezek. 18.27 actually uses the words את־נפשו יחיה of the man who does what is right).[55] It could well have been Jesus' view that the Pharisees, by insisting on their traditional understanding of the sabbath commandment, were blocking the fulfilment of the very purposes for which the law as a whole was given in the first place.

Thirdly: Lk. 14.5 par. Mt. 12.11

This saying occurs in different contexts in these two Gospels. In Luke it occurs in the story of the healing of the man with dropsy, and in Matthew it occurs in the story of the man with the withered hand. Since Mark does not have anything like this saying in the latter story, it is likely that Matthew has introduced it redactionally in his version of the story and has brought it in from the source which stands behind Lk. 14.5.[56] However this may be, we can be reasonably confident that the same saying of Jesus lies behind both Lk. 14.5 and Mt. 12.11, not just because of their general similarity but more specifically because the same Aramaic words can stand behind both βοῦς and πρόβατον (בעירא) and behind both φρέαρ and βόθυνος (בירא).[57]

---

[55] The RSV translates 'he shall save his life'. N.B. also the connection between the healing of the man at the pool of Bethesda and the theme of ζωοποίησις in Jn. 5.

[56] Therefore probably Q. The story in Lk. 14.1-6 could come from L, since it is not paralleled in the other Gospels, but the saying in v. 5 could have had a separate origin.

[57] So M. Black (1967³) 168f. The belief that a common source lies behind the two verses is held by J.M. Creed (1950) 188, I.H. Marshall (1978) 578, and W.D. Davies and

The inclusion of υἱός in Luke is likely to be textually original as being the *lectio difficilior*, but whether it was traditionally original is another question. M. Black and others have argued that it could have grown out of בעירא, since the word for son in Aramaic (ברא) is similar, but on the other hand the inclusion of the reference to a 'son' makes sense against the Jewish background of Jesus and the verbal similarity can be seen as an example of the poetic style of Jesus' speech.[58]

What now of the arguments for the saying's authenticity?

(1) Multiple Attestation
As has just been argued, Luke and Matthew are probably dependent on a common source, therefore probably Q. This at least takes us back to an early stage in the transmission of the Jesus tradition.

(2) Language, Culture and Personal Idiom
Because of the slight variations in detail between the two versions of the saying it would be difficult to be sure of the correctness of any Aramaic translation, but there is nothing in the core of the saying to prevent it from being said naturally in Aramaic, as the following attempted reconstruction will show:

מאן מנכון דאית ליה ברא או בעירא
נפיל בבירא בשבתא לא מקימה

As already indicated, the saying naturally falls into its first-century Jewish setting. The rabbis and the Qumran sectarians *did* discuss the issue of what to do if an animal or a person falls into a pit on a sabbath day, with differing conclusions, so the saying appeals to a practice which would have been common in Jesus' day.

The question method of challenging his opponents suits Jesus' personal style, so far as it can be gathered from the Gospels,[59] and the play on words in the Aramaic, as explained above, fits in well with his habit of using poetic elements in his teaching.

(3) Coherence
The saying coheres well with the attitude of Jesus to the sabbath as displayed in the other sabbath stories, in his opposition to the over-strict Pharisaic interpretation of the sabbath commandment and his defence of his own actions as falling into the category of permissible work.

D.C. Allison (1991) 2.319 among others, as against M. Borg (1984) 335 n. 19 and J.A. Fitzmyer (1985) 2.1039.

[58] See especially I.H. Marshall (1978) 580.
[59] Cf. W.D. Davies and D.C. Allison (1991) 2.317.

(4) Dissimilarity

Here it is worth noting that E. Lohse bases his belief in the saying's authenticity partly on the fact that the opening formula in Matthew's version, τίς ... ἐξ ὑμῶν, has no parallel in the rabbinic literature.[60]

As far as dissimilarity from the christian background is concerned, we have once again the fact that the saying contains no overt christology, nor would have been the kind of material the early church would have created later as ammunition in some sabbath controversy.

(5) Anti-Redactional Features

No such features are discernible. In fact, scholars tend to emphasise the Lucan characteristics of the whole pericope.[61] This factor, however, need not be decisive in our assessment of the authenticity of the saying, as we have already seen.

On balance, therefore, we can be fairly sure of assigning this saying in some form to the historical Jesus. The exact force of the saying is disputed, and depends partly on whether the Matthean or Lucan version is thought more original. It could be an *a fortiori* argument, saying 'if one may rescue an animal on the sabbath, how much more a person'[62] or 'if a person can rescue another on the sabbath, how much more can God'[63], or it could be an *a pari* argument, saying 'if a son can be rescued on the sabbath, so can a man with a physical ailment'[64]. But, whatever the exact force of the argument, Jesus compares his own activities with the activity of rescuing a son/ox/sheep on the sabbath, i.e. with what would have been regarded by his interlocutors as 'work', and argues that if that kind of 'work' may be permitted on a sabbath, then so can his 'work' of healing.

Enough has been said to demonstrate that the Synoptic Gospels reliably present Jesus as defending his sabbath activities and those of his disciples on the grounds that they fall into the category of permissible work.[65] Thus

---

[60] E. Lohse (1973) 70. Presumably this distinctiveness also belongs to Luke's τίνος ὑμῶν.

[61] Cf. J.A. Fitzmyer (1985) 2.1038, C.F. Evans (1990) 568.

[62] This is the thrust of Matthew's version. W.D. Davies and D.C. Allison (1991) 2.320 suggest that Matthew may have omitted υἱός from his version of the saying to turn it into an *a fortiori* argument.

[63] So I.H. Marshall (1978) 580 on the Lucan version.

[64] So J.A. Fitzmyer (1985) 2.1042 on the Lucan version.

[65] Thus E.P.Sanders' (1985) 266 statement that Jesus performed no work on the sabbath may be true from the point of view of a fairly slack interpretation of the law, but this does not affect the point being made here about Jesus' manner of self-defence.

when Jesus is presented as saying in Jn. 5.17 κἀγὼ ἐργάζομαι he is saying something which perfectly matches the attitude to the sabbath which he actually took so far as it can be deduced from the Synoptic evidence.[66]

Once this has been taken into account, we may now conclude that every motif included in the saying in Jn. 5.17 coheres with the historical Jesus as known to us from the Synoptic Gospels. It may of course be objected that while indeed the motifs are found elsewhere in the recorded teaching of Jesus, this particular *combination of motifs* is not. This is true, but not decisive, since otherwise one would have to make multiple attestation a *sine qua non* of strict authenticity in every case, an unreasonable condition (as was said in chapter 2). And in any case, the gap between the Synoptic sayings of Jesus and Jn. 5.17 in this respect is not actually as wide as this objection may suggest. By confronting the Pharisees in the manner recorded in the Synoptic Gospels, Jesus was in fact claiming a special insight into the mind, will and purpose of God and an ability to interpret the scriptures correctly. In other words, the Synoptic sayings presuppose a claim to a peculiarly close relationship with God, which is precisely the presupposition made explicit in Jn. 5.17.

(3) Dissimilarity
The saying in Jn. 5.17 is dissimilar both from Judaism and from early christianity for similar reasons:

Firstly, there is the christology of the saying. The manner in which Jesus aligns himself with God in this saying is not paralleled in Jewish literature, and is not the kind of claim an ordinary Jew of Jesus' day would make. Yet at the same time the very hiddenness and allusiveness of the saying's christology, and the absence of any christological title, makes it also unlikely to have been an invention of the early church. From different angles, therefore, the saying is dissimilar from both its Jewish and christian milieux on this account.

Secondly, there is the saying's relationship with Gen. 2.2f., which affirms that God *rested* when he had finished his work of creation. The radical contrast between the two illustrates the saying's dissimilarity from its Jewish background. True, there were debates in first century Jewish circles about how God could 'work' (in terms of creating, judging, saving etc.) while he 'rested', as we shall shortly see more fully, but in every case there is a conscious wrestling with the text of scripture which is totally absent from the Johannine context. Similarly, it is unlikely that early christians would have invented such a divergence from this creation ordinance unless

---

[66] For the consistency between the Fourth Gospel and the Synoptics over the sabbath question see also S. Pancaro (1975) 505 and M. Borg (1984) 161.

there was some dominical authority for doing so, and nowhere else in early christian literature does the critique of the sabbath ordinance implicit in this saying take this particular verbal form.[67]

(4) Anti-Redactional Features
The saying cannot be said to stand against the author's redactional tendencies, so far as they can be perceived, except in respect of the hiddenness and allusiveness of its christology, which *is* unusual for the Fourth Gospel. The absence of other such features, however, cannot be regarded as decisive against the saying's authenticity in a strict sense.

Sometimes scholars object to the saying's authenticity on the grounds that it contains 'Johannine coinage', such as πατήρ and ἐργάζομαι.[68] As against this argument, it was argued at length in chapter 4 above that the word ἐργάζομαι was also common 'coinage' and was probably (at least in its Aramaic form) part of Jesus' ordinary speech as well. The other word dubbed 'Johannine coinage' in this verse may serve as an illustration in this respect. The fact that the word πατήρ occurs 118 times in the Fourth Gospel with reference to God does not mean that Jesus himself did not use it in this way. The same may be said for the word ἐργάζομαι, which occurs but 8 times in the Gospel, and ἔργον which occurs 27 times. It is entirely plausible to suggest that the author's usage took its origin from some such original saying as that recorded in Jn. 5.17 rather than from his own imagination.[69]

We conclude this section, therefore, by saying that the words of the saying in Jn. 5.17 are the kind of words Jesus used, the thoughts the saying expresses are thoughts which were characteristic of him, and the way they are expressed is reminiscent of his style as known to us from the Synoptic Gospels. The saying is credible within the context of Jesus' milieu, and yet stands out against that milieu. There are therefore very good grounds for taking it to be an authentic saying of Jesus in a strict, type b, sense of the

---

[67] It was this aspect of dissimilarity, i.e. the dissonance between Jn. 5.17 and Gen. 2.2f. which particularly persuaded J.E. Davey (1958) 35, A.J.B. Higgins (1960) 71 and A.M. Hunter (1968) 94 of the saying's authenticity, while W.F. Howard (1955[4]) 223 agreed that 'this way of thinking about the sabbath came to the Evangelist from without rather than from within, by memory or tradition rather than by imagination'.

[68] E.g. L.Th. Witkamp (1985) 44 n. 108. Cf. J. Painter (1991) 185 and n. 38.

[69] Cf. K.E. Dewey (1980) 84 who suggests that some of the proverbs in the Fourth Gospel may have had an existence prior to their incorporation into the Gospel and may have been 'responsible for generating particular Gospel themes'. He cites 5.19-20a as an example. The same may be said for 5.17.

word.⁷⁰ At the very least its credentials as such an authentic saying are as good as, if not better than, those of many Synoptic sayings whose authenticity is generally accepted by a majority of New Testament scholars.

7.4 The Exegesis of John 5.17

7.4.1 Introduction

It has been argued above not only that the saying in Jn. 5.17 goes back directly to Jesus, but also that it belongs to the context it is given in the Fourth Gospel. Even if it is a stray saying from a different context, its content, with its reference to Jesus' 'working', would seem to demand some such context as it is given, i.e. the context of a sabbath healing which aroused the wrath of Jesus' enemies. So we will first consider the meaning of the saying at the level of Jesus' ministry in its presumed historical context, and then consider its meaning at the Johannine level in the light of its total Johannine context.

7.4.2 John 5.17 in its Presumed Historical Context

(1) 'My Father...'
While we cannot be sure that the Aramaic word אבא lies behind the expression ὁ πατήρ μου here, it is appropriate to mention the way it has been understood in recent scholarship as evidence for Jesus' filial consciousness, a consciousness which must have been in the background of Jesus' mind whenever he spoke of God as his Father.

It was J. Jeremias who popularised the notion that Jesus, in addressing God as אבא, was using a word which, to our knowledge, no one else had used in addressing God before, and which was customarily used by children in addressing their natural fathers. By using this word for God, therefore, Jesus was, according to Jeremias, expressing an unprecedented sense of closeness or intimacy with God: ''Abbā ... expresses the heart of Jesus'

---

⁷⁰ Other recent supporters of the 'authenticity' of this saying include F. Gryglewicz (1980) 10 and S. Bacchiochi (1981) 3, who cites F.L. Godet's description of it as 'a flash of light breaking forth from the inmost depths of the consciousness of Jesus'. The above presentation of the evidence should serve to strengthen this point of view as against the majority view which is to see the saying as a purely Johannine construction.

relationship to God. He spoke to God as a child to its father: confidently and securely, and yet at the same time reverently and obediently'.[71]

Jeremias' views have come under attack from scholars such as G. Vermes, J.D.G. Dunn, and J. Barr,[72] but have more recently been substantially vindicated by B. Witherington.[73] It remains the case that there is no known instance from the time prior to Jesus in which the precise Aramaic word אבא is used as a form of address to God, and it remains the case that this word was customarily, though not exclusively, used by children in addressing their parents. It also remains highly likely that it was a word which Jesus used in address to God, though he may also have used other forms of the noun. It does therefore suggest a consciousness on the part of Jesus of a peculiarly deep and intimate relationship with God. But does it also indicate a *unique* relationship with God?

Here the evidence is ambiguous. On the one hand, in the light of Rom. 8.15 and Gal. 4.6, we may safely assume that the word was *also* used by members of the early church in address to God. On the other hand, the Gospels seem to give the impression that the kind of sonship relationship which Jesus enjoyed with God was somehow different from that which the disciples enjoyed. As G. Bornkamm says: 'Although we find numerous passages where Jesus says "My Father (in heaven)" and "thy Father" or "your Father", there is nowhere a passage where he himself joins with his disciples in an "Our Father". We have no reason to doubt that this usage was truly characteristic for Jesus himself ...'.[74] Again Gal. 4.6 tells us that the use of אבא by the early christians was made possible through the Spirit of God's son, Jesus, and if the same word lies behind the word πάτερ in the Lucan form of the Lord's Prayer (Lk. 11.2), then it was a word which Jesus *gave* to his disciples for them to use *as* his disciples. This suggests that the sense of sonship that the disciples enjoyed was purely dependent on the prior sonship of Jesus and mediated through him.[75]

In the light of this evidence, the only sense in which we can definitely speak about the uniqueness of Jesus' sonship on the basis of the אבא form of address lies, as R. Bauckham has argued, in its capacity to be shared in his unique mission as the agent of God's eschatological salvation.[76]

---

[71] J. Jeremias (ET 1971) 67. For a fuller expositions of Jeremias' theme see (ET 1967) 11-65.

[72] G. Vermes (1983²) 210-213, J.D.G.Dunn (1975) 21-26, (1989²) 22-33, J. Barr (1988 *JTS*) 28-47, (1988 *Theology*) 173-179.

[73] B. Witherington (1990) 216-221.

[74] G. Bornkamm (ET 1960) 128.

[75] Cf. J.D.G. Dunn (1975) 24-26, B. Witherington (1990) 220-221.

[76] R. Bauckham (1978) 245-260.

This fact has a bearing on the interpretation of Jn. 5.18, which will be dealt with more fully in the next chapter. Even if Jesus used the precise word אבא here, to call God אבא could not *per se* have been a sufficient ground for the charge that Jesus was making himself 'equal with God'. It must therefore have been the *manner* in which Jesus spoke of this relationship, as exemplified in the saying in Jn. 5.17 as a whole, which gave rise to this charge. The anger of 'the Jews' must have been aroused by what they saw to be the implications of the rest of Jesus' utterance.

(2) 'My Father is working still...'
It was mentioned above on p. 170 that the idea of God as 'working still' was at home in first century Judaism. There is evidence that a number of Jews at that time were thinking about the problem of how to reconcile the statement in Gen. 2.2f. that God rested on the seventh day, after he had created the world, with the belief that he was still active in the world. Philo, for example, a rough contemporary of Jesus, wrote in his book on the Cherubim: 'There is but one thing in the universe which rests, that is God. But Moses does not give the name rest to mere inactivity. The cause of all things is by its nature active; it never ceases to work all that is best and most beautiful. God's rest is rather a working with absolute ease, without toil and without suffering ...' (ch. 87). In his book on the Allegory of the Laws, the contrast with the creation story is even more stark: 'God never ceases creating, but as it is the property of fire to burn and of snow to be cold, so it is the property of God to create' (1.5-6).

The rabbis too were coming to the same conclusion. It is, of course, notoriously difficult to date the rabbinic literature which has come down to us, and to date the origin of the traditions which it contains; but one tradition, which appears to go back to the first century, relates how R. Gamaliel II and three other rabbis were in Rome on one occasion and met a sectarian who challenged them to explain how God can be consistent with his words while breaking the sabbath. 'Wretch', they replied, 'is not a man permitted to carry on the sabbath in his own courtyard?' He replied: 'Yes'. Whereupon they said to him: 'Both the higher and lower regions are the courtyard of God, as it says: "The whole earth is full of his glory" (Isa. 6.3), and even if a man carries a distance of his own height, does he transgress?' The other agreed. 'Then', they said, 'it is written, "Do not I fill heaven and earth?" (Jer. 23.24)' (*Ex.R.* 30.9).

It will be noticed that all the references so far concern God's cosmological roles. A later rabbinic tradition, however, refers to God's work of judgment which resembles far more closely the content of Jesus' discourse in Jn. 5.19-30. According to this tradition, R. Phineas (c. 360 AD) said in the name of R. Oschaya (c. 225 AD): 'He rested from the work of creating the world, but not from the work of the wicked and the work of the righteous, for he works with the former and with the latter. He shows the former their essential character, and the latter their essential character. And how do we know that the punishment of the wicked is called work? Because it is said: "The Lord hath opened his armoury, and hath brought forth the weapons of his indignation, for it is a work that the Lord God hath to do" (Jer. 50.25). And how do we know that the bestowing of reward upon the righteous is called work? Because it is said: "Oh how abundant is thy goodness, which thou hast laid up for them that fear thee, which thou hast wrought for them that take refuge in thee, in the sight of the sons of men" (Ps. 31.20)' (*Gen.R.* 11.10).

Even if these parallels cannot be shown to have had any influence upon Jesus or the author of the Fourth Gospel, the thought expressed in the phrase 'My Father is working still' is unlikely to have seemed radically new to any Jew who was listening. As G. Bertram shows in his *TDNT* article on the 'work' word group, the idea of God working in creation, providence, redemption, judgment etc. is common throughout the Old Testament and the intertestamental literature even when words for 'work' are absent, and there is no suggestion that God ceases to be active in these ways on the sabbath day.[77]

This background may help us to clear up the uncertainty which surrounds the exact meaning of the phrase here translated 'still': ἕως ἄρτι. Literally it means 'up till now', but the question has been whether it is simply another way of saying that God continues to work now as he has been doing in the past, or whether it implies that there is a definite *terminus* to his work which is just around the corner. The expression itself can have either sense, depending on the context.[78] O. Cullmann argued for the second view, mainly on the grounds of Jn. 9.4 where Jesus speaks of the coming 'night ... when no one can work'. This shows, Cullmann argued, that Jn. 5.17 refers to a work which will soon reach its fulfilment and culmination in the death of Christ. God's true rest will begin on the day of the resurrection of Christ, when the work of salvation will in a decisive sense be complete. Thus

---

[77] *TDNT* 2.639f.

[78] As C. Maurer (1957) 136f. shows, comparing Jn. 2.10 and 16.24 on the one hand with 1 Jn. 2.9, 1 Cor. 4.13, 8.7, 15.6, Mt. 11.12 on the other. Maurer believes that the Hebrew עוד stands behind the Greek ἕως ἄρτι and that this word also is ambiguous. The same may be said of our proposed Aramaic translation. It is the general context which has to decide the right meaning in each case.

Cullmann saw here a hidden teaching about the christian Sunday which finds its origin in the resurrection of Christ on the first day of the week.[79]

The main problem with this view is that it is not a natural reading of Jn. 5.17, which attaches the phrase ἕως ἄρτι not in the first place to the working of Jesus, but to the working of *God*, and whereas Jn. 9.4 does indeed speak of a sense in which the working of Jesus will cease with his death, it is extremely unlikely that Jesus or the evangelist would have thought in terms of God himself stopping his work. This point is confirmed by the Jewish parallels quoted above which affirm the never-ceasing activity of God.[80] What Jesus seems to be saying, therefore, is that his work of healing the lame man on the sabbath is in some way connected with the never-ceasing activity of God who also in a sense 'works' during the sabbath. This brings us then to the final clause of the saying:

(3) 'My Father is working still, and I am working'
A number of points may be made here, in the light of the saying as a whole in its present context, concerning the way in which Jesus viewed his own activity:

a. Jesus is, of course, by saying these words, admitting his role in the healing of the the lame man at the pool. There are good reasons for believing that he saw healing miracles such as these not only as manifestations of God's power through him, but, more specifically, as signs of the arrival of the messianic age, and therefore of his own role as some kind of messianic figure. This point will be developed further in chapter 9, when we will look at those sayings in which Jesus speaks of his 'works' as witnessing to his identity.[81]

b. Jesus regards his healing of the man as a form of 'working'. The interesting point about this word and its cognate noun is that they can be used equally well of what we would call ordinary or natural deeds as they can of extraordinary or supernatural ones, and it is so used in the Fourth Gospel. As L. Morris says, the word 'work' as used in the Gospel 'reminds us that these are all of a piece, that Jesus' whole life was consistently spent in doing the will of God and accomplishing his purpose. Not only in the miracles, but in all his life he was showing forth God's glory'.[82] His miracles, therefore, are regarded as an integral part of his life and ministry.

---

[79] O. Cullmann (1966) 187-191. Cullmann's views were, to a greater or lesser extent, followed by J. Roloff (1970) 82, J. Riedl (1973) 191-193, and S. Bacchiochi (1981) 11-13.

[80] So C. Maurer (1957) 138-140. This view has been followed by E. Lohse in *TDNT* 7.27 and H. Weiss (1991) 316f.

[81] See also section 5.4.3.a above.

[82] Cf. L. Morris (1971) 691.

c. By 'working' on the sabbath day, Jesus came into conflict with Pharisaic teaching, and by his defence of his actions showed his freedom to interpret the law in his own way.

In the story there are two points at which Jesus clashed with the upholders of the law. Firstly, there is the healing itself. According to the scribal traditions preserved in the rabbinic literature, healing was regarded as a work, which was therefore not to be performed on the sabbath day. The only exception allowed was when life was in danger, as we saw above on pp. 173f. Since the man at the pool was not in danger of losing his life, Jesus will have been regarded as having transgressed the law by healing him, and the text confirms this (cf. 5.16, 18, 7.23). Secondly, there is the fact that the man carried his pallet. Jesus becomes the object of the enquiry in 5.10ff. because he told the man to carry his pallet, which means that he agreed to his action. The scribal traditions developed the prohibition of the bearing of burdens found in Jer. 17.21 and Neh. 13.19 (which seem to have originally related to commercial activity) to cover the carrying of anything from one place to another. *Shab.* 10.5 allowed a couch to be carried if someone was lying on it, but the implication is that to carry a couch on its own on the sabbath day was a sin.

On both these points Jesus showed a disregard for scribal teaching, and this attitude is consistent with what we know of Jesus from the Synoptic Gospels, as we have seen. Over a wide range of issues Jesus disputed the validity of the interpretations of the law given by his Pharisaic opponents,[83] and the right use of the sabbath was one such issue. Jesus' defence of his actions on the sabbath, therefore, demonstrates his freedom from scribal authority, and his claim to be able to interpret scripture in his own way. It is of a piece with the kind of authoritative teaching about the law which we find in the antitheses in Mt. 5, prefaced with their well known formula 'You have heard ... but I say to you ...'. All this has implications for Jesus' self-understanding. As B. Witherington puts it, after reviewing the evidence for Jesus' attitude to the Law: 'Jesus did not see himself as a Galilean hasid or another prophet, even one like Elijah. He saw himself in a higher or more authoritative category than either of these types familiar to Jewish believers ...'.[84] Similarly, R. Banks sees christological significance in Jesus' attitude to the law. Of the sabbath controversy in Mk. 2.23-28 he writes: 'All these accounts possess a christological orientation through which the issue of the legality or illegality of the disciples' actions is set in a different context to that of the Law ... He takes a position above it [i.e. the sabbath] so that it is incorporated into an entirely new framework and viewed from a quite

---

[83] See especially R. Banks (1975).
[84] B. Witherington (1990) 65, cf. 80f.

different perspective ... Jesus' teaching raises the question of the identity of the one who stands behind it'.[85] And in dealing with the healing stories on the sabbath in particular, he comes to a similar conclusion. Jesus does not just 'castigate rabbinic interpretations', but demands 'that the sabbath be orientated towards, interpreted by, and obeyed in accordance with, his own person and work'.[86]

It is this kind of freedom that we can also see in Jesus' words here in Jn. 5.17: 'My Father is working still and I am working'. With great daring and boldness he claims the right to 'work' on the sabbath day, to be free from the scribal restrictions, to be able to interpret and apply scripture in his own way without reference human traditions, to determine for himself what might be permissible on the sabbath day. There is little surprise that his attitude aroused such animosity from his opponents, since he seems to them to be rebelling against God himself in a most serious way (cf. 5.16, 18 correspond remarkably closely to Mk. 3.6 at this point), but Jesus believed that in fact he was acting in accordance with the will of God.

d. What then can the saying in Jn. 5.17 tell us about Jesus' view of his relationship with God, assuming its authenticity in a strict sense? Logically, of course, the words 'My Father is working still and I am working' do not necessarily imply that the works of Jesus are in any way related to the works of God, but the parallelistic structure of the saying strongly suggests that Jesus is in fact claiming at the very least to be working in harmony with God, and to be doing the kind of things that God does. In the light of passages such as Mt. 11.28 par., which we studied in chapter 5, we may also say that Jesus believed that God was working *through* him, so that Jesus' working and the Father's working were in a more immediate sense one. It was because of this sense of unity with God that Jesus felt he had the authority to override the scribal regulations in the way he did.

If we now ask the question how far Jesus saw this co-operation extending, the most we can certainly say, as far as the context of Jn. 5.1-18 is concerned, is that he saw it extending to his works of healing, which he considered to be part of God's activity through him. No doubt he also saw it extending to his ministry as a whole, as we saw in chapter 6, but exactly to what extent he believed he was sharing in the work of God it is impossible to know.

---

[85] R. Banks (1975) 122f.
[86] Ibid. 131.

7.4.3 John 5.17 in its Total Johannine Context

Perhaps three further comments may be made under this heading.

a. Firstly, as our study of the Fourth Gospel so far has shown, the author himself certainly regarded the works of Jesus and the works of God to be one, in the sense that whatever Jesus did was what the Father did through him.[87] Thus the 'working' of Jesus was nothing other than the 'working' of the Father in him.

b. Secondly, from the Johannine perspective we can say more about the extent to which the co-operation between the Father and Jesus went, in that, in the context of Jn. 5, we learn that Jesus would do the 'greater works' of life-giving and judging (5.19-30),[88] and, in the context of the Gospel as a whole, the work of revealing (cf. 17.1-6 etc.) and (more distantly) creating (cf. 1.3). In short, because the evangelist believed Jesus to be 'God' (cf. 1.1, 20.28), there can be no limit to the extent to which he conceived the works of the Son as coinciding with the works of the Father.

c. Finally, we may draw attention to the possible significance the saying may have had for the author in the context of his own community. Though it is hazardous to read off details concerning the author's own church life from the surface of the Gospel, it is quite possible that he included this story and presented it in the way he did because of a need to defend his community's freedom with regard to sabbath observance as against the accusations of local Jews, and because of a need to explain the relationship between God and Jesus in the light of Jewish misunderstandings. More than this it is difficult to say.[89]

7.5 The Exegesis of John 5.17 in the Patristic Era

Some of the Fathers use Jn. 5.17 solely with reference to the activity of the Father without seeking to make any christological points. Thus Methodius sees in the phrase 'My Father is working still' a reference to the process of procreation,[90] while Jerome uses it to support the creationist view of the

---

[87] Cf. sections 5.4.3.b, 6.4.4.c and appendix B.

[88] C.H. Dodd (1967) 183-198 has shown that the motifs contained in Jn. 5.19-30 also cohere remarkably well with what we can know of the teaching of Jesus from the Synoptic Gospels, but it is likely that they have mostly been re-expressed in a Johannine way in this discourse. The next chapter will make a detailed study of Jn. 5.19f., which may be said to contain material of an even stricter form of authenticity.

[89] Further elaboration of this aspect of the interpretation of Jn. 5 may be found in J.L. Martyn (1968) 68ff., J. Painter (1991) 175-213, and H. Weiss (1991) 311-321.

[90] Methodius, *Concerning Chastity*, 2.1.

origin of the soul,[91] and the view that freedom of will is a gift of grace, as opposed to the Pelagian position.[92]

Others put Jn. 5.17 to practical use, implicitly regarding Christ as an example to follow. Thus, for example, Clement of Alexandria uses it to exhort the christian teacher to keep on dispensing wisdom,[93] and Chrysostom uses it to exhort his readers to 'lay aside all carelessness' and to be 'zealous for virtue'.[94] Likewise in the *Disputation with Manes*, attributed to Archelaus, Jn. 5.17 represents the 'new Law', whereby we should cease from 'worldly work' and 'be devoted unceasingly' to the kind of work God does in 'saving men'.[95]

Most of the time, however, Jn. 5.17 is used in the patristic writings to refer to the relationship between Christ and the Father. Tertullian uses it as evidence that the Son is distinct from the Father, as against Praxeas' modalistic monarchianism.[96]

A far greater number use it as evidence for the unity of the Father and the Son. Thus, for example, Novatian sees in it the idea that Christ is the 'image' of the Father and an 'imitator of the Father's works'.[97] Athanasius, who often quotes this verse, goes further still in seeing in this saying a reference to the eternal co-operation between the Father and the Son in all that they do, including the works of creation and providence.[98] In this sense he finds it to be useful ammunition against the Arian doctrine of the createdness of the Son: if the Son does what the Father does, then on the Arian view the Son must have created himself, which is absurd;[99] and the fact that the Father is *always* working shows that he did not need to create a Son to do the work of creation for him.[100] Rather the Son is uncreated and always works with the Father in absolutely everything the Father does.

Similar understandings continued to be expressed throughout the Nicene period. Gregory of Nyssa, for example, in the context of quoting Jn. 5.17, makes the point that the sameness of works entails sameness of nature and being ('if anything should perform the functions of fire, shining and warming in precisely the same way, it is itself certainly fire'[101]). Cyril of

---

[91] Jerome, *Letter 126, to Marcellinus and Anapsychia*, sec. 1; *Letter to Pammachius against John of Jerusalem*, sec. 22.
[92] Jerome, *Letter 133, to Ctesiphon*, sec. 6.
[93] Clement of Alexandria, *Stromata*, 1.1.
[94] Chrysostom, *Homily 36 on John's Gospel*, sec. 2.
[95] Archelaus, *Disputation with Manes*, sec. 31.
[96] Tertullian, *Against Praxeas*, sec. 21.
[97] Novatian, *Treatise concerning the Trinity*, ch.28.
[98] Athanasius, *On Luke 10.22*, sec. 1.
[99] Athanasius, *Orations against the Arians*, 2.16.21.
[100] Ibid. 2.17.29.
[101] Gregory of Nyssa, *Against Eunomius*, 2.15.

Jerusalem sees in Jn. 5.17 an assertion that Christ is the maker of all things,[102] while for Gregory of Nazianzus it means that Christ is the creator, governor and preserver of the world.[103] The equality of the Father and the Son is also affirmed on the basis of Jn. 5.17 by Hilary, Augustine, and Chrysostom,[104] but perhaps Chrysostom goes the furthest of them all when he says that when Jesus said these words he was speaking 'as God'.[105]

In short, we find Jn. 5.17 being used to affirm both the distinctness of the Father and the Son, and their unity - their unity of works, nature and being. The 'works' the Fathers have in mind when they comment on this verse are almost invariably the cosmological works of creation, providence and rule; but there is in fact for them no limit to the extent of the co-operation of the Father and the Son.

7.6 Conclusion

We may now sum up some of our findings:

a. First of all we have discovered that the saying attributed to Jesus in Jn. 5.17 satisfies the criteria for authenticity in the stricter, type b, sense of that term to a remarkable extent. At the very least we may say that its credentials for authenticity are at least as good as many Synoptic sayings commonly regarded as 'authentic'. Moreover, these words were probably spoken in the context of a sabbath healing miracle, perhaps even the one they are actually given in Jn. 5. As part of our argument we saw in particular that the major motifs contained in the saying are also present in sayings which may be reliably attributed to Jesus in the Synoptic Gospels.

b. Secondly, we were reminded by this saying of Jesus' filial consciousness - his sense of a deep and intimate relationship with God, which, as the 'Abba' usage suggests, was both distinctive and to a certain extent unique. We were also reminded of Jesus' messianic role, and his claim to have authority to interpret the sabbath ordinance independently of the scribal regulations of his time. And finally we learnt that he viewed his activity as being in some sense 'parallel' with God's ongoing activities, probably meaning at least that it was the kind of activity in which God

---

[102] Cyril of Jerusalem, *Catechetical Lectures*, 11.23.

[103] Gregory of Nazianzus, *Theological Orations*, 4.11.

[104] Hilary, *On the Trinity*, 9.44f.; Augustine, *The Harmony of the Gospels*, 4.10.14; *Sermon 75*, sec. 6; *Tractate 17 on John's Gospel*, sec. 16; Chrysostom, *Homily on the Paralytic Let Down Through the Roof*, sec. 6; *Homily 38 on John's Gospel*, sec. 2; *Homily 39 on John's Gospel*, sec. 1.

[105] Chrysostom, *Homily 40 on Matthew's Gospel*, sec. 1, *Homily 38 on John's Gospel*, sec. 2.

himself was engaged, and that it was done in harmony with his will, and possibly also by his indwelling power.

c. Thirdly, in the context of the Fourth Gospel as a whole, we found confirmation that the author himself regarded the works of the Son to be the works of the Father and performed through the Father's indwelling power, and we found him describing the content of these works specifically in terms of life-giving, judging, revealing and (more distantly) creating. We also speculated concerning the possible relevance of this saying for the author's own community both in the area of sabbath observance and in the area of christology.

d. Lastly, we discovered that in the patristic era Jn. 5.17 was used to present Christ as an example to follow, and as being distinct from the Father, but also as being the image and imitator of the Father, and, most commonly of all, as being at one with the Father in his works, and thereby in his nature and being. For the Nicene and post-Nicene Fathers the works of the Father and the Son coincide completely and eternally, and particular emphasis is laid on the identity of their cosmological roles of creation, rule and providence.

Chapter 8

Doing what God Does (B)

8.1 Introduction

In this chapter we will take a look at Jn. 5.19f., which, as the title above indicates, continues the theme of Jn. 5.17 which we have just studied.

In view of the fact that neither ἔργον nor ἐργάζομαι occur in 5.19-20a, to which most of this chapter will be devoted, a word of explanation is in order as to why it is included in this book at all. The reasons may be set out as follows:

a. Though neither of these words occur in 5.19-20a, we do find the word ἔργα in v. 20b, and the parallelism of the clause in which it stands with the preceding clause indicates that the word is in this context functionally equivalent with the phrase ἅ ... ποιεῖ, which dominates the thought of 5.19-20a.

b. The verb ποιῶ is in any case broadly synonymous with the rarer Greek word ἐργάζομαι, which we have already found in the speech of Jesus at 9.4 and 5.17 and which is part of the object of our interest in these textual studies.[1]

c. The verb ποιῶ is used with christological significance in the Fourth Gospel. Examples of this significance in the speech of Jesus himself in the Gospel, apart from 5.19f., may be seen at: 4.34, 5.27, 30, 36, 6.38, 8.28f., 10.25, 37f., 14.10, 12-14, 31, 15.24, 17.4. In this respect also it resembles the use of ἐργάζομαι.[2]

d. Finally, 5.19-20a is of relevance to the particular historical perspective of this book *both* in respect of the fact that the saying contained in these verses may well go back to the historical Jesus in roughly its present form,

---

[1] Cf. J. Riedl (1973) 206-208. In LXX usage the verb עבד is translated both by ἐργάζομαι (41 times) and by ποιῶ (at least 30 times), though the latter is used more commonly to translate the verb עשׂה. It seems likely that here we have another instance of Johannine linguistic variation and that if 5.17, 19f., and 9.4 all closely correspond to something Jesus said, the same Aramaic verb may stand behind them all.

[2] S. Pancaro (1975) 151 refers to the 'christological overtones' of the verb ποιῶ in the Fourth Gospel, and says that with Jesus as subject, it 'designates the salvific activity of the Word made flesh'.

and *also* in respect of the fact that it played an important part in the development of patristic christology. Both these points will be elaborated in the course of this chapter.

The format of the chapter will be as usual. First we will look at the context of the saying (though much of this has already been covered in the previous chapter), then at the authenticity of its various parts, then at its meaning, both from Jesus' and from the author's perspective, and finally at its use in the patristic era.

8.2 The Context of John 5.19-20

The previous chapter fully dealt with the context of Jn. 5.19f. as far as Jn. 5.1-17 is concerned. It therefore remains for us here to look v. 18. This is clearly relevant for 5.19f. since the latter is said to be spoken in answer to the situation described in 5.18.[3]

It was noted on p. 169 above that 5.16 gives the evangelist's comment on the situation resulting from the healing of the man at the pool of Bethesda on the sabbath. The same point may be made here concerning 5.18, except that 5.18 describes a heightening of the tension between Jesus and the Jews resulting from Jesus' words in 5.17, which are taken by the Jews to be a claim to be 'equal with God', and leading to their desire, not just to persecute Jesus, but to kill him.

This form of generalised description once again serves to detach 5.19f. chronologically from the immediate context of the story of the healing and its aftermath related in 5.1-15, and the discourse which follows in 5.19-47 could in fact be made up of sayings drawn from different periods of Jesus' ministry and include the author's own interpretative comments.

J.N. Sanders and B.A. Mastin note that the verb λύω in this context can mean anything from 'break', 'infringe', or 'give a lax interpretation to', to 'cancel' or 'abrogate'.[4] Some scholars prefer the stronger sense of abrogating the sabbath commandment altogether,[5] but we need to bear in mind that the imperfect tense of λύω could equally well indicate repeated actions, in which case the softer sense of continually infringing the sabbath commandment as currently interpreted by the scribal authorities would be preferable. The second part of the accusation, that 'he ... called God his own

---

[3] For the particular nuance of the word ἀπεκρίνατο, which is used at the beginning of v. 19, see ch. 7 n. 27.

[4] J.N. Sanders and B.A. Mastin (1968) 164.

[5] Cf. B.F. Westcott (1908) 1.187, L. Morris (1972) 310 n. 48, R. Schnackenburg (ET 1980) 101.

Father, making himself equal with God', also needs careful handling. The difficulty here is that to call God one's own Father in both Jewish and christian traditions does not in fact necessarily amount to a claim to be equal with God in itself, and the author presumably knew this. The problem cannot be satisfactorily solved by saying that the phrase ἴσον ἑαυτὸν ποιῶν τῷ θεῷ constitutes a *third* charge against Jesus in the sentence,[6] nor by saying that the first part of the accusation looks back to the preceding verses but the second part looks forward to the verses which follow.[7] A better way is to see a special emphasis on the word ἴδιον in this context,[8] and to understand the author to mean that Jesus called God his Father *in such a way* that his hearers understood him to be claiming thereby a uniquely special sonship in relation to God amounting to equality with him - a manner of speaking of which 5.17 is set forth as an example.

Having said this, two important questions remain:

a. Is this understanding of the implications of Jesus' words one which the author himself endorses? And:

b. Do the accusations contained in 5.18 reflect the conditions of the period of Jesus' ministry or the conditions of the period of the author when he wrote the Gospel?

a. A number of commentators believe that the phrase ἴσος ... τῷ θεῷ is not something the author would have wanted to use himself for Jesus.[9] This point of view is understandable in the light of the fact that the phrase ἴσον ἑαυτὸν ποιῶν τῷ θεῷ would have been understood by Jews of Jesus' day to have been a blasphemous assertion of independence from and rebellion against God.[10] Nevertheless, within the context of the Gospel as a whole,

---

[6] As J. Bligh (1963) 124f. maintains. This does violence to the Greek.

[7] As A.C. Sundberg (1970) 28 maintains. This does violence to the words ἀπεκρίνατο οὖν in v. 19.

[8] Not that the word ἴδιος of itself necessarily carries such emphasis in the Fourth Gospel. Sometimes it does (e.g. 4.44, 5.43, 7.18), sometimes it does not (e.g. 1.41, 19.27). The point being made here is that in this particular context it does. So B.F. Westcott (1908) 1.187, W.F. Howard (1955⁴), B. Lindars (1972) 219, C.K. Barrett (1978²) 256, R. Schnackenburg (ET 1980) 101, J.A.T. Robinson (1985) 181. R. Bultmann (ET 1971) 244 n. 7 does not regard ἴδιος as important here, but still regards Jesus as claiming a particular relationship with God.

[9] J.H. Bernard (1928) 1.238 says that such a phrase, if affirmed, 'would seem to divide the Godhead'. Cf. C.H. Dodd (1953) 327f., J. Bligh (1963) 125f., R.E. Brown (1966) 1.214.

[10] Cf. H. Odeberg (ET 1968) 203. In rabbinic literature a son who rejected paternal authority is described as one who 'makes himself equal with his father'. S.-B. 2.462-465 give instances whereby it was acceptable for special individuals to be made to stand for God (e.g. Moses in Ex. 4.16, 7.1, or the 'gods' of Ps. 82.6), but unacceptable for any to make themselves as God (e.g. Hiram, Nebuchadnezzar, Pharaoh, and Joash). Cf. Philo

and especially in the light of verses such as 1.1, 10.30, and 20.28, it would seem equally plausible to regard the phrase ἴσος ... τῷ θεῷ as being acceptable to the author as long as it was qualified with an affirmation of Jesus' dependence on and subordination to God at the same time, as is in fact done in the verses which follow and elsewhere in the Gospel (e.g. 5.30, 6.38, 8.28f., 12.49, 14.10, 31).[11] A similar comment may be made about the phrase ἑαυτὸν ποιῶν. C.K. Barrett says that the author would have accepted ἴσος ... τῷ θεῷ but not ἑαυτὸν ποιῶν since, for him, Jesus *was* God, and did not need to make himself equal with God.[12] However, though from the point of view of his enemies Jesus was making an arrogant and unjustified claim, the author himself may equally have seen the phrase ἑαυτὸν ποιῶν as descriptive of Jesus' act of asserting the truth about his relationship with God.[13]

b. Again, a number of commentators have said that the charges levelled against Jesus in 5.18 at least to some extent really reflect the situation of conflict between the Johannine church and its local synagogue at the end of the first century rather than the situation of the historical ministry of the Jesus.[14] J.L. Martyn, for example, sees the conflict evolving out of a healing performed by a member of the Johannine church on a Jew in his city as a result of which the Jews persecute the christians because 'they worship Jesus as a second god'.[15] It is not impossible that the author's choice of language here has been influenced by the debates of his own time,[16] but we

---

L.A. 1.49: Φίλαυτος δὲ καὶ ἄθεος ὁ νοῦς οἰόμενος ἴσος εἶναι θεῷ. In 2 Macc. 9.12 Antiochus (called βλάσφημος in 9.28) remorsefully declares that a just man should not θνητὸν ὄντα ἰσόθεα φρονεῖν. In 2 Thess. 2.4 the 'man of sin' is described as ἀποδεικνύντα ἑαυτὸν ὅτι ἐστὶν θεός.

[11] This position is generally adopted by B.F. Westcott (1908) 1.187, J.N. Sanders and B.A. Mastin (1968) 164, R. Bultmann (ET 1971) 245, L. Morris (1971) 310, B. Lindars (1972) 219, M.L. Appold (1976) 23, C.K. Barrett (1978[2]) 256, G.R. Beasley-Murray (1987) 75, D.A. Carson (1991) 249f., J. Painter (1991) 186. W. Loader (1989) 163 perhaps gives the best expression to this position when he says: 'We ... see the author rejecting the Jews' meaning of equality with God, but like many statements with double meaning, taking it up as true in his own distinctive sense of equality in subordination'.

[12] C.K. Barrett (1974) 149.

[13] J. Painter (1991) 187 n. 50 sees a different kind of ambiguity: Jesus was equal with God in relation to the world, the Jews, the crowd, and the disciples, but was subordinate to God in relation to the Father himself. Up to a point this represents a false dichotomy since, as J. Painter himself admits on pp. 190 and 212, 5.19ff. teach equality *through* subordination.

[14] E.g. J.L. Martyn (1968) 52-57, B. Lindars (1972) 219-221, J. Becker (1979) 1.233, R. Schnackenburg (ET 1980) 101, R. Kysar (1986) 79, W. Loader (1989) 163, P.M. Casey (1991) 177, J. Painter (1991) 186.

[15] J.L. Martyn (1968) 56.

[16] As was said above in connection with Jn. 5.17 on p. 191.

need to remember that the Gospel is *primarily* about Jesus rather than the author's church and that there is important evidence from the Synoptic Gospels to suggest that Jn. 5.18 does in fact give an accurate summing up of the attitude of the religious authorities to Jesus during the time of his ministry. To substantiate this point, it is appropriate for us to consider three pericopae in particular:

Firstly, Mk. 3.1-6, pars. Mt. 12.9-14, Lk. 6.6-11.

Few doubt that as a matter of history Jesus had conflict with certain members of the Pharisaic party concerning his observance of the sabbath. As was stated on p. 169 above, this fact forms part of the 'bedrock' of the Jesus tradition, and the above pericope is one example of this tradition. The interesting point to note about it is that in Mk. 3.6, par. Mt. 12.14, the Pharisees (with the Herodians also, according to Mark) are said to have discussed how they might destroy Jesus as a result of his disregard for the sabbath commandment as traditionally understood. A number of scholars take this information at face value, even though it is acknowledged that the incident may not have occurred as early in Jesus' ministry as its placing in Mark's Gospel might suggest.[17] If so, we have a remarkable parallel with Jn. 5.18, in which, as a result of Jesus' healing of someone on a sabbath day 'the Jews sought ... to kill him, because he ... broke the sabbath'.

Secondly, Mk. 2.1-12, pars. Mt. 9.1-8, Lk.5. 17-26.

This is another healing story, but here the interest focusses not on the day on which it was performed but on the assurance of forgiveness which Jesus gives to the paralytic in Mk. 2.5, pars. Mt. 9.2, Lk. 5.20 and the response of the 'scribes' in Mk. 2.7, pars. Mt. 9.3, Lk. 5.21. Most commentators agree that Jesus' words of themselves do not necessarily imply a claim to exercise a divine prerogative, since they could constitute simply a prophetic declaration of God's forgiveness (cf. 2 Sam. 12.13),[18] but clearly the scribes themselves understand Jesus to be making a claim to exercise a divine prerogative and therefore regard him as guilty of blasphemy, a crime punishable with death.[19] The sentiment expressed in the words: 'Why does this man speak thus? It is blasphemy! Who can forgive sins but God alone?'

---

[17] E.g. C.E.B. Cranfield (1959) 122, G. Bornkamm (ET 1960) 153, V. Taylor (1966[2]) 220f., J. Jeremias (ET 1971) 279. E.P. Sanders (1985) 292 is, however, a dissenting voice.

[18] E.g. C.E.B. Cranfield (1959) 99, W. Lane (1974) 95, I.H. Marshall (1978) 214, E.P. Sanders (1985) 273f.

[19] It is also widely acknowledged that at the time of Jesus the charge of blasphemy applied to any violation of God's honour and did not necessarily have to include mention of the divine name as was later required (*Sanh.* 7.5). So C.E.B. Cranfield (1959) 98, V. Taylor (1966[2]) 569, W. Lane (1974) 538, I.H. Marshall (1978) 214, A.E. Harvey (1982) 170, as against E. Schweizer (1971) 331.

in effect implies the statement 'he is making himself equal with God', as made by Jesus' opponents, which we find in Jn. 5.18.

Thirdly, Mk. 14.60-65, pars. Mt. 26.62-68, Lk. 22.67-71.

Most scholars accept that Jesus was regarded as guilty of blasphemy at his trial before the Jewish religious authorities before being handed over to Pilate. The question is: what were the grounds of this charge? The claim to be the Messiah of itself was probably not sufficient to convict someone of blasphemy in Jesus' day.[20] It is more likely therefore that Jesus was regarded as guilty of blasphemy because he claimed to be a particular sort of Messiah, as the Synoptic Gospels themselves suggest when they report Jesus' claim to be the coming Son of Man sitting at the right hand of God.[21] It is also possible that the title 'Son of the Blessed'/ 'Son of God' in Mk. 14.61 and Mt. 26.63 should not be taken as a mere synonym for 'Messiah' but as a claim to a uniquely special relationship with God, and that Luke, who seems to be following a different source at this point, has preserved a tradition which confirms that Jesus' claim to a special sonship played a part in his trial (Lk. 22.70). As I.H. Marshall puts it: 'The Sanhedrin suspected that Jesus made claims to be the Son of God in an unusual sense and now had them [sc. their suspicions] confirmed, and this constituted the basis (or part of the basis) for the charge of blasphemy made in Mark'.[22] The claim to a uniquely special relationship with God of some kind, therefore, most probably played a part in the process which led up to the charge of blasphemy at Jesus' trial and to his death. If so, Jn. 5.18, as understood above, receives further confirmation as an accurate summing up of the situation at the time of the ministry of Jesus. There was a sense in which 'the Jews sought ... to kill him, because he ... called God his own Father ...'.[23]

We conclude, therefore, that though the language of Jn. 5.18 may have been influenced by the debates of the author's own time, the verse does not give a misleading account of the kind of accusations which were levelled against Jesus during his public ministry or the nature of the official reaction to him. Similarly, as will now be argued, we are not given a misleading

---

[20] C.E.B. Cranfield (1959) 445, G. Bornkamm (ET 1960) 163, E.P. Sanders (1985) 297f.

[21] C.E.B. Cranfield (1959) 445, V. Taylor (1966^2) 569f.

[22] I.H. Marshall (1978) 851. Cf. B. Meyer (1979) 180: 'In all probability the "blasphemy" (Mk. 14.64a par.) lay in dishonouring "the Blessed One" by the claim ... to be his "Son"'.

[23] It is likely, in view of the fact that Jesus was teaching publicly for a considerable period of time, that the charges made against him at his trial were already in the minds of his enemies well before that event.

account of the way in which Jesus defended himself against these accusations.

8.3 The Authenticity of John 5.19-20

The saying can be broken up into three sections, which will be dealt with separately, though the bulk of the discussion will focus on the longer middle section.

8.3.1 'Truly, truly, I say to you ...'

Few doubt that this phrase, at least in its Synoptic form of 'Truly, I say to you', goes back to the historical Jesus. It is found in all strata - 13 times in Mark, 9 times in Q, 9 times in M, and 3 times in L - and so satisfies the criterion of multiple attestation; it coheres well with the sense of authority with which Jesus evidently spoke in his teaching; it includes the Hebrew word אמן, which was taken over into Aramaic, and whose presence in the Gospels exclusively in the speech of Jesus is a strong indication that it was originally used by him; and, above all, the use of this word at the *beginning* of a sentence as a way of underlining the truth of its contents is totally unparalleled in Jewish literature. The phrase as a whole therefore satisfies most of the criteria for authenticity and so almost certainly goes back directly to Jesus.[24] If this is true, then the word 'Amen' must surely count as one of his *ipsissima verba*.

At this point two further questions arise. Firstly, what about the double 'Amen' used 25 times in the Fourth Gospel? Does this usage go back to Jesus also? J. Jeremias thought the duplication arose from Jewish liturgical usage,[25] but it is not impossible that Jesus himself on occasion repeated the word for extra emphasis at the beginning of an important saying, or in order

---

[24] Cf. J. Jeremias (ET 1967) 112-115, (ET 1971) 35f., (1973) 122f., I.H. Marshall (1976) 45f. and notes, both of whom defend the authenticity of this phrase against the attack of V. Hasler in his *Amen. Redaktionsgeschichtliche Untersuchung zur Einführungsformel der Herrenworte 'Wahrlich, ich sage euch'*, 1969, Zürich-Stuttgart, Gotthelf, and K. Berger in his *Die Amen-Worte Jesu*, 1970, Berlin, Gruyter. The scepticism of J.C.G. Greig (1968) 10-13 and of H.-W. Kuhn in *EDNT* (ET 1990) 1.70 on this point is also unjustified.

[25] J. Jeremias (ET 1971) 35 n. 8. So also F. Gryglewicz (1980) 11.

to make himself heard among a noisy crowd, and that the Fourth Evangelist fixed on this usage while the Synoptic tradition fixed on the other.[26]

This leads on to the second question: in view of the general flexibility with which the evangelists handled the traditions about Jesus, can we be sure that the sayings which this formula introduces are in every case as authentic as the formula itself? The answer must be that this conclusion cannot automatically be taken for granted, especially when one sees the formula being used in the Fourth Gospel in front of some typically Johannine phraseology (e.g. 3.11, 6.32, 47, 53, 10.7). We have already seen in former chapters how the author likes to use phrases such as 'him who sent me' and the word 'Father' liberally in his reports of Jesus' speeches where they may not have originally belonged, and it is likely that the same phenomenon recurs in the case of the phrase 'Truly, truly, I say to you'.

We conclude therefore that this opening phrase was very probably used by Jesus, but that it may not have originally been joined to what follows it in 5.19f.

8.3.2 '... the Son can do nothing of his own accord ...'

8.3.2.1 The Possible Background to the Saying

Before any discussion of the authenticity of the above part of the saying can begin, using the various standard criteria, an attempt must be made to come to terms with different views concerning its possible background.

R. Bultmann was of the opinion that 5.19f. reflects the language of the gnostic redeemer myth, which 'speaks of the sending of a pre-existent divine being, which in its metaphysical mode of being is equal to God, and was sent by him to carry out his work of revelation, for which he is commissioned and equipped by the Father, and which he achieves in unity with him'.[27] This proposed background is not, however, convincing for two reasons: firstly, most of the above ideas are in fact absent from 5.19f. when these verses are taken on their own: they do not refer to Jesus' pre-existence, nor (directly, at least) to his 'metaphysical mode of being', nor to his being sent, nor about a work of revelation to the people to whom he is sent, but rather to what Jesus *does* in the *present* in reaction to what he 'sees' the Father doing; and secondly, most of the literature Bultmann cites -

---

[26] Cf. J.H. Bernard (1928) 1.66f., who draws attention to other similar duplications in the Synoptic Gospels in speech attributed to Jesus (Mk. 15.34, Mt. 7.21f., Lk. 10.41, 22.31, to which we may add Lk. 13.34). Such an idiom is not, of course, peculiar to Jesus (cf. e.g. 2 Sam. 18.33, 19.4, 2 Kings 2.12, Ps. 22.1, 124.1-2, Isa. 38.19, Lk. 8.24, Acts 9.4), but it does seem to be one he used.

[27] R. Bultmann (ET 1971) 251; cf. J. Becker (1979) 1.239-240.

such as Philo, the Odes of Solomon, the Hermetic literature, Plotinus, 3 Enoch, and the Mandean literature -either post-dates the Fourth Gospel or else is unlikely to have had any influence on him at all, as is now commonly recognised in Johannine scholarship. It is not without good reason, therefore, that the majority of contemporary commentators on the Gospel have put Bultmann's view on one side.

A more plausible background for 5.19f. was suggested by C.H. Dodd in 1962, when he argued that the author has here incorporated into the discourse what was originally a parable about a son apprenticed to his father.[28] Dodd argued that parables were to be found elsewhere in the Fourth Gospel (e.g. at 3.29a, 8.35, 10.1-5, and 12.35); that the definite articles in 5.19f. could be taken in a generic sense to refer to any son and father (cf. Mk. 3.27, 4.21, Mt. 12.43, 23.24); that the picture conveyed by Jn. 5.19f. fits that of an apprenticed son in the ancient world and shares a similar background to the picture given in Lk. 6.40; that it would have been a natural picture for Jesus himself to have used in view of the fact that he is reported in the Synoptic Gospels to have been a carpenter and the son of a carpenter (Mk. 6.3, Mt. 13.55); that the idea of the son 'watching' the father is not taken up in the ensuing discourse and seems to be simply a touch of realism in the overall picture; and that the form of 5.19-20a (with its two general categorical clauses forming an antithesis, followed by an explanatory clause) is analogous to that of some of the Synoptic parables (Lk. 8.16, par. Mt. 5.15, Lk. 12.47f. being cited as fully analogous, and Lk. 6.40 and 11.21f. as partially analogous). Dodd concluded by saying: 'we may have here an echo of his [Jesus'] own words, recalling memories of the years of his youth when he learnt his trade in the family workshop'.[29]

Dodd's theory has at least two weaknesses. Firstly, it is clear that for the author himself, Jn. 5.19f. is not intended as parabolic, but as a straightforward christological statement. In the rest of the discourse (see especially vv. 21, 22, 23, and 26) the phrases 'the Son' and 'the Father' clearly refer to Jesus and God, and it is natural to suppose that the author intended his readers to understand these phrases in the same way in vv. 19f.[30] Secondly, none of the pre-Johannine literary evidence Dodd cites

---

[28] C.H. Dodd (1962) 107-115. This article, written in French, was later published in English in Dodd's *More New Testament Studies* (1968) 30-40. P. Gaechter (1963) 65-68 apparently came to the same conclusion independently of Dodd.

[29] C.H. Dodd (1968) 40. The additional argument of P. Gaechter (1963) 67, F. Grob (1986) 143 and J. Bernard (1977) 24 that φιλεῖ is used in 5.20 because it fits family affection better than ἀγαπᾷ cannot be pressed into use here in view of the commonly recognised synonymity of these two verbs in the Fourth Gospel.

[30] It is for this reason that C.K. Barrett (1978²) 259 finds Dodd's view unsatisfactory. Cf. J. Painter (1991) 189 n. 55. G.R. Beasley-Murray (1987) 75f. draws attention to the

actually uses the language of 'seeing' and 'showing',[31] while this same language is used frequently in the Old Testament in the context of revelation for people 'seeing' God's work or being 'shown' what God wants them to understand, say or do.[32]

Neither of these weaknesses are, however, insuperable. In the first place, it may be admitted that the author intends his words to be taken in a straightforward christological way; but it remains possible that he has taken what was originally a parabolic utterance and, by incorporating it into this discourse, given it a valid christological interpretation. And in the second place, while the Old Testament uses the language of 'seeing' and 'showing' in the context of revelation to various people, nowhere is it said that people are required to do what God does as a result of seeing God doing it.[33] The apprenticeship analogy fits more closely despite the lack of supporting contemporary linguistic evidence, and it is not without good reason that a large number of scholars have given Dodd's theory a warm reception. It seems highly likely either that the saying originally existed in the form of a parable, as Dodd affirmed,[34] or that apprenticeship imagery is being used as a basis for a straightforward christological statement.[35] The difference between these two views is perhaps not as great as those who adhere to the latter view appear to imagine. It is quite possible that ambiguity characterised the saying from the very beginning of its existence, since not only can the Greek definite article be taken in a generic sense, but, as is now commonly recognised, the emphatic state of the Aramaic noun may have lost the force of the definite article by the time of the first century AD,

---

prevalence of the οὐ ... ἀφ' ἑαυτοῦ motif in the Fourth Gospel (e.g. in 7.28, 8.28, 12.49, and 14.10) as a reason for rejecting Dodd's theory, but this motif may still have dominical roots, rather like the 'Amen' formula just considered, which also, it was argued, has dominical roots but is used quite liberally by the author in his Gospel.

[31] The closest he gets is the use of the verb δηλῶ in a papyrus dated at 183 AD (1968) 33.

[32] Cf. e.g. Ex. 14.13, 19.4, 34.10, Num. 14.22, Deut. 3.21, 24, 4.3, 11.7, 29.2f. for 'seeing' God's works; Ex. 25.9, 40, 26.30, Num. 23.3, Deut. 4.5, Jer. 24.1, Ezek. 11.25, 40.4, Amos 7.1, 4, 7, Zech. 1.9 for being 'shown' something to understand, say or do. The two verbs are more closely linked in Hebrew than in English and Greek since they represent the Qal and the Hiphil of the same root (usually ראה).

[33] F. Grob (1986) 129, 147f. notes these connections with Old Testament terminology, but likewise does not regard them as a sufficient explanation for the form of the words being studied in this section. It is also perhaps worth noting that S.-B. have no entry for 5.19f.

[34] A view supported by, e.g., R.E. Brown (1966) 1.214, 218, J. Jeremias (ET 1971) 58, B. Lindars (1972) 221, J. Riedl (1973) 198ff., J. Bernard (1977) 21, F. Gryglewicz (1980) 12, J.A.T. Robinson (1985) 319, 348, F. Grob (1986) 113ff.

[35] The preferred solution of L. Morris (1971) 312 n. 56, R. Schnackenburg (ET 1980) 2.102, W. Loader (1989) 161f., and D.A. Carson (1991) 250.

making it difficult for an Aramaic speaker to make a distinction between definite and indefinite references.³⁶ Such ambiguity would moreover not be uncharacteristic of the ministry of the historical Jesus.³⁷

With these introductory remarks, we can now begin to apply the criteria of authenticity.

8.3.2.2 The Criteria Applied

The criterion of multiple attestation cannot be used to support authenticity here. B. Lindars has suggested that the same 'parable' lies at the basis of Jn. 5.19f. and Mt. 11.27, par. Lk. 10.22,³⁸ but the differences are substantial enough to warrant caution on this point. Despite the references to 'the Son' and 'the Father' and the 'delivering' of everything to the Son by the Father, it is questionable whether the Q saying can be traced back to a parable,³⁹ and it lacks the crucial references to 'doing', 'seeing' and 'showing' which are integral to the Johannine saying. We cannot consider it a 'parallel', therefore, but there are sufficient similarities to warrant the extended treatment this passage will be given under the heading of coherence.

So we are left with the following criteria: Language, Culture and Personal Idiom, Coherence, Dissimilarity, and Anti-Redactional Features:

(1) Language, Culture, and Personal Idiom
Here the following points should be noted:
a. This saying can be translated back into Aramaic, thus:

לא יכיל ברא למעבד מן גרמיה כלום
אלא מא דחזי הוא עביד אבא
ארי אילין דעביד ההוא
כן עביד אף ברא
ארי אבא רחים לברא
ומחוי ליה כל דעביד הוא

Once again it needs to be said that it is difficult to be sure of the precise words and forms Jesus would have used,⁴⁰ assuming for the moment that the saying goes back to him, but the only point being made here is that there is

---

³⁶ Cf. W.B. Stevenson (1962) 23. The same problem is encountered in the speaking of Swahili today.

³⁷ Another approach which similarly overcomes this dichotomy is that of R. Bauckham (1978) 256, who suggests that the 'deparabolisation' of Jesus' parables may have begun with Jesus himself, and that he himself may have initiated the allegorical interpretation of Jn. 5.19-20a.

³⁸ B. Lindars (1972) 221.

³⁹ B. Witherington (1990) 226 *contra* J. Jeremias (ET 1971) 57f., R. Riesner (1988) 220f.

⁴⁰ See ch. 2 n. 33.

nothing of essential importance in the Greek of Jn. 5.19f. which could not be naturally translated back into Jesus' mother tongue.

b. It is especially noteworthy that the first and second pairs of lines above form an antithetical parallelism, which is well known to have been a characteristic feature of the teaching of Jesus.[41] No special rhythm can be discerned, but the fivefold repetition of the the verb עבד is a striking reminder of Jesus' other parallelistic sayings.

c. As was argued above, these words either use apprenticeship imagery or constitute a parable of apprenticeship. Either way they fit very well with what we know from the Synoptic Gospels of Jesus' teaching methods. That Jesus spoke in parables and used pictorial language in his teaching is not seriously in doubt. It was part of his personal idiom.[42]

d. As far as more general cultural and religious factors are concerned, it has already been mentioned above in section 8.3.2.1 that the apprenticeship imagery suits what we know of ancient practices whereby a father was accustomed to pass on the skills of his trade to his son, and that the language of 'seeing' and 'showing' are part of the Old Testament way of speaking about revelation by God to his people, which suits the christological interpretation of the words, and so on. Here we may add that the general idea of imitating the works of one's fathers is a *topos* found in both pagan and Jewish literature,[43] and that the specific idea of 'not doing anything of oneself' is found in the Old Testament at Num. 16.28, where Moses is represented as saying:

בזאת תדעון כי־יהוה שלחני לעשות
את כל־המעשים האלה כי־לא מלבי

The LXX actually translates the final word by means of ἀπ' ἐμαυτοῦ. Whether or not there is an allusion to Num. 16.28 in Jn. 5.19 it is difficult to say, but at least we can say that this idea is paralleled in the Old Testament.

For all its distinctiveness, therefore, the saying as a whole fits naturally into a first century AD Jewish background.[44]

(2) Coherence
The saying contains a number of motifs which are paralleled in sayings which may reliably be attributed to Jesus in the Synoptic Gospels.

---

[41] See especially C.F. Burney (1925) 71-88, J. Jeremias (ET 1971) 14-20.

[42] The same point is valid even if, with K.E. Dewey (1980) 84, 93 and R.F. Collins (1986) 53f., we categorise 5.19-20a as a 'proverb'.

[43] Cf. R. Heiligenthal (1983) 72-92, especially 89-92, where Jn. 5.19-20a is cited as an example of this phenomenon.

[44] As D.A. Schlatter (1902) 357f. shows, the language of not being able/ being able to do something of oneself, and of God showing certain things to certain people is also paralleled in the rabbinic literature.

The motif of obedience to the will of the Father has already been fully dealt with in chapters 5 and 6, so there is no more which needs to be added on this topic here. Likewise, we saw in chapter 7 that the description of God by Jesus as Father coheres well with the evidence of the Synoptic Gospels. What is new here is the fact that Jesus - whether in parable or straightforwardly - calls himself 'son' of the Father, and expresses his sense of dependence on the Father for revelation concerning what the Father is doing. Both motifs are present in the saying of Jesus at Mt. 11.27, par. Lk. 10.22, which will now be given extended treatment.[45]

In what follows we will take Mt. 11.27, par. Lk. 10.22, to be a straightforward christological statement. The suggestion made by J. Jeremias[46] and others that a parable about fathers and sons in general lies behind this saying is less convincing in this case than in the case of Jn. 5.19-20a, since it is very doubtful as a general truth whether *only* sons really know their fathers.[47] Moreover the context clearly refers to Jesus' own relationship with God.[48] If authenticity, in a strict sense of the word, can be demonstrated for this saying as taken in this stronger sense, then the case that Jesus also spoke Jn. 5.19-20a and intended it to be understood at least in part as a straightforward christological statement is also thereby strengthened.

But does Mt. 11.27, par. Lk. 10.22 go back to the historical Jesus? The older form critics were inclined to regard it as a Hellenistic revelation saying.[49] More recently, F.W. Beare has declared it to be a 'fragment of an incipient gnosticism',[50] and others have shared his scepticism concerning

---

[45] It is quite likely that Jesus saw himself as the 'son' in the parable in Mk. 12.1-12 pars. Mt. 21.33-46, Lk. 20.9-19, which is taken to be dominical by, e.g., V. Taylor (1966²) 472f., J.D.G. Dunn (1975) 35f., R. Riesner (1988³) 301, and B. Witherington (1990) 213. Likewise, Mk. 13.32 par. Mt. 24.36, in which Jesus calls himself ὁ υἱός is taken to be dominical by, e.g., V. Taylor (1966²) 522f., I.H. Marshall (1990) 139-140, and B. Witherington (1990) 228-231. Mt. 11.27 par. Lk. 10.22, however, provides a yet closer parallel to the motifs of Jn. 5.19-20a, and deserves closer attention for this reason at this point. Even if the word πάντα in Mt. 11.27 par. Lk. 10.22 does not refer to absolutely everything in the light of the context of Mt. 11.25 par. Lk. 10.21, it must at least refer to the totality of the revelation the Father had given to the Son, which must include the revelation of what he was doing. For the fundamental importance of Mt. 11.27 par. Lk. 10.22 for the Johannine presentation of Jesus as a whole, see W. Grundmann (1965-6) 42-49 and R. Garrison (1979).

[46] J. Jeremias (ET 1971) 58.

[47] Cf. J.D.G. Dunn (1975) 31 and E. Schweizer (ET 1976) 271.

[48] Cf. M. Miyoshi (1974) 130, J.D.G. Dunn (1975) 32, E. Schweizer (ET 1976) 271, I.H. Marshall (1978) 437, C.F. Evans (1990) 462.

[49] Cf. R. Bultmann (ET 1968²) 159, M. Dibelius (ET 1971) 245, 279-283.

[50] F.W. Beare (1981) 266.

its authenticity.[51] However, this view is not shared by all, and an increasing number of scholars have come round either to a cautious acceptance of the possibility of its authenticity,[52] or else to a firm inclination to accept its authenticity.[53] The major problem is, of course, that the saying sounds too 'Johannine', and its christology too 'high' and too explicit, and for these reasons it is thought by some to have emerged from the early church than from the historical Jesus.[54] A review of the evidence will however show that these objections are not insuperable, and that a good case can be made for accepting the saying as coming from Jesus roughly in the form in which it has survived.[55] We turn, therefore, to an application of the criteria for authenticity. The saying may be considered in isolation since it is not clear whether or not it belonged originally with Mt. 11.25f., par. Lk.10.21.[56]

(1) Multiple Attestation
The appearance of what is clearly the same saying in Matthew and Luke shows that the saying was in the source known as Q, according to the most commonly accepted theory of Synoptic relationships. Moreover, the presence in the Fourth Gospel of so much material which shares the same motifs as Mt. 11.27 par., but which yet cannot be shown to be directly dependent on Matthew or Luke or even Q itself, suggests an early origination of those motifs in a period prior to the formation of Q.

It needs to be said emphatically at this point that the 'Johannine' nature of Mt. 11.27 par. does *not* necessarily mean that it is derived from the Johannine tradition. In fact, it is more likely that the Johannine tradition grew out of some such sayings as this one, since without such sayings, as J.

---

[51] E.g. G. Bornkamm (ET 1973²) 227 and G. Vermes (1983²) 201.

[52] E.g. F. Christ (1970) 93, J.D.G. Dunn (1975) 33f., A.E. Harvey (1982) 160.

[53] T.W. Manson (1949) 79, V. Taylor (1959) 60-64, A.M. Hunter (1961-2) 244, O. Cullmann (ET 1963²) 286, I.H. Marshall (1967) 91-95, J. Jeremias (ET 1971) 56-61, M. Miyoshi (1974) 125-131, R. Garrison (1979) 202-257, B. Meyer (1979) 152, J.A.T. Robinson (1985) 359, R. Riesner (1988³) 220f., B. Witherington (1990) 221-228.

[54] The argument that it is too 'Hellenistic' has now lost its weight as will be made clear later.

[55] Matthew and Luke differ in small ways from each other in their versions of the saying, but Matthew is generally thought to stand closer to the Q form of the saying. Cf. M. Miyoshi (1974) 127, J.A. Fitzmyer (1985) 2.867, B. Witherington (1990) 225, W.D. Davies and D.C. Allison (1991) 2.281.

[56] The subject matter of Mt. 11.25f. par. is similar and has the same strophic structure, but Mt. 11.27 par. goes further than Mt. 11.25f. par. in declaring Jesus to be the unique mediator of the knowledge of God and refers to the Father in the third person rather than in the second. It could have been added to Mt. 11.25f. par. through the catchwords πατήρ and ἀποκαλύπτω.

Jeremias has said, it would be 'a complete puzzle' how the Johannine tradition could have originated at all.⁵⁷

(2) Language, Culture, and Personal Idiom
The saying may be translated back into Aramaic thus:

כלא מסיר לי מן אבא
ולא ידיע ברא אלא אבא
ולא ידיע אבא אלא ברא
ומאן דצבי ליה ברא לגלאה⁵⁸

As far as its cultural milieu is concerned, it has now long been recognised that the saying does not necessarily owe anything to Hellenism, let alone Gnosticism, other than in the Greek vocabulary used.⁵⁹ The precise Jewish background is still a matter for debate among scholars and does not directly concern us here,⁶⁰ but that it actually has a Jewish background can scarcely now be doubted. Moreover the semitic nature of the saying is clear from the central clauses, which use the common semitic way for expressing a reciprocal relationship in the absence of a reciprocal pronoun.⁶¹

The saying fits Jesus' personal idiom in a number of ways, in its concise, aphoristic, style, its poetic features (its strophic character, use of a double chiasm, synthetic parallelism, rhythm and rhyme),⁶² its rhetorical hyperbole,⁶³ and its threefold reference to God as 'Father'. It is also noteworthy that the word ἀποκαλύπτω occurs only on the lips of Jesus in Matthew's Gospel (at Mt. 10.26, 11.25, 27, and 16.17) and only once

---

⁵⁷ J. Jeremias (ET 1971) 59.
⁵⁸ Following Matthew's version rather than Luke's. Cf. n. 55 above.
⁵⁹ Of course, even if some Hellenistic ideas could be shown to lie behind the saying, its authenticity would not thereby be disproved since, as has been increasingly recognised in recent years, Palestinian Judaism had been influenced by Hellenism ever since the conquests of Alexander the Great in 333 BC.
⁶⁰ The main possibilities are a background in Wisdom speculation (cf. F. Christ (1970) 81-93, M.J. Suggs (1970) 71-97, S. Schulz (1972, *Q*) 222-228, C.F. Evans (1990) 458, B. Witherington (1990) 225, W.D. Davies and D.C. Allison (1991) 2.272, 287), Israel (cf. A.M. Hunter (1961-2) 245, J.D.G. Dunn (1989²) 199, W.D. Davies and D.C. Allison (1991) 2.286f.) and Moses (cf. D.C. Allison (1988) 477-485, and W.D. Davies and D.C. Allison (1991) 2.283-285). These backgrounds are not mutually exclusive. W.D. Davies and D.C. Allison (1991) 287 combine them in their exegesis of the saying thus: 'In a manner strongly reminiscent of Moses, Jesus, who is the perfect wise man and prophet, knows and reveals God, his Father, thereby fulfilling the calling of Israel while at the same time bringing to pass the prophecies of eschatological knowledge'.
⁶¹ J. Jeremias (ET 1971) 57.
⁶² C.F. Burney (1925) 133, 172, J. Jeremias (ET 1971) 57, R. Riesner (1988³) 220f.
⁶³ In the light of the Old Testament background, to say that only Jesus 'knows' God is clearly an exaggeration in the sense that it can only mean that Jesus alone knows him fully or properly.

outside his speech in Luke's Gospel (at Lk. 2.35, otherwise at Lk. 10.21f., 12.2, and 17.30). Mt. 11.25 par. Lk.10.21 has a particularly strong claim to authenticity in a strict sense,[64] so we can be fairly sure that Jesus *did* talk in terms of 'revelation'.

(3) Coherence
The first clause may be said to cohere well with Mt. 11.25 par., which, as we have just seen, has a good claim to authenticity. If Jesus can thank God for having revealed certain things to 'babes', then he must believe that he himself knows them already, and how else but by revelation at some previous point in his career?[65] The word πάντα may not mean more than all those things which Jesus believed he had learnt from God at the time of making this utterance.

Jesus' undoubted use of the intimate word 'Abba' to address God supports the view that Jesus regarded himself to be in a specially close relationship with God and thereby saw himself as God's 'son' in a special sense. As A. Harnack put it long ago: 'The consciousness he possessed of being the Son of God is, therefore, nothing but the practical consequence of knowing God as the Father and as his Father'.[66] Quite apart, therefore, from the other Synoptic texts in which Jesus refers to himself as the 'son' (Mk. 12.6 pars. Mt. 21.37, Lk. 20.13, Mk. 13.32 par. Mt. 24.36, Mt. 28.19), and the evidence that at his baptism he became aware of a calling to be God's son (Mk. 1.11 pars. Mt. 3.17, Lk. 3.22, cf. Ps. 2.7), there can hardly be any doubt that he thought of himself as being God's 'son' in a special sense, and, if he thought so, is it not possible that he expressed this filial consciousness occasionally, at least within the circle of his closest disciples if not while addressing the crowds?

The statement that no one knows the Son except the Father also rings true of the Synoptic tradition generally, as least with regard to the pre-Pentecost period. Despite Jesus' affirmation that the disciples had been 'given the secret of the kingdom of God' (Mk. 4.11 pars. Mt. 13.11, Lk. 8.10) and despite Peter's confession of him as 'the Christ' (Mk. 8.29 pars. Mt. 16.16,

---

[64] Cf. A.M. Hunter (1961-2) 242-244, R. Bultmann (ET 1968[2]) 160, J. Jeremias (ET 1971) 190, D. Hill (1972) 204f., J.D.G. Dunn (1975) 30, I.H. Marshall (1978) 433f., B. Meyer (1979) 192, R. Riesner (1988[3]) 336, W.D. Davies and D.C. Allison (1991) 2.278.

[65] J. Jeremias (ET 1971) 61 suggests that this point may have been his baptism.

[66] Quoted by J.D.G. Dunn (1975) 14. Cf. I.H. Marshall (1978) 433: 'It is a small step from addressing God as Father in this way to knowing oneself to be the Son of this Father'; R. Garrison (1979) 7: 'Jesus' consciousness of being God's son is certainly implicit in his use of Abba in addressing God'; B. Witherington (1990) 225: 'The Abba material ... implicitly supports the view that Jesus thought of himself as God's special son'.

Lk. 9.20), it is clear that they did not understand the nature of his messiahship until well after his death (cf. Acts 1.6), and if the disciples did not understand Jesus neither did the crowds. In these circumstances, well might Jesus have said that no one 'knew' him - i.e. truly, fully or properly - but the Father.

Jesus' claim to be the only one to know the Father must also be taken in the sense of a true, full or proper knowledge of God, since a knowledge of God of a sort was possible under the old covenant and indeed is implied by its terms, as Jesus himself must have known. That Jesus should have claimed a unique insight into the character of God perfectly matches his filial consciousness and his authoritative and unprecedented teaching about the nature of God's kingdom. That he should regard himself as the unique channel of this revelation to others flows from this presupposition. Only one who possesses knowledge can share it with others. Moreover, as the one who believed himself to be the means by which the Old Testament prophecies were being fulfilled and in particular the means by which the new covenant was to be inaugurated (cf. Mk. 14.24 pars. Mt. 26.28, Lk. 22.20), we may take it for granted that Jesus believed that through his death the true knowledge of God would spread throughout Israel and ultimately throughout the world (for the new covenant promise cf. Jer. 31.34; for more general prophecies cf. Isa. 11.9, 54.13, Hos. 2.20, Hab. 2.14). Thus though the formulation of Mt. 11.27 par. remains unique to the Synoptic tradition, the ideas it expresses are perfectly credible as the ideas of the historical Jesus himself in the light of the information we can reliably glean about him from other Synoptic evidence.

(4) Dissimilarity
There is no doubt that the claim being made here is radically dissimilar from anything that a first century Jew might reasonably be expected to make. The boldness and exclusivity of the saying is unprecedented within Judaism.[67]

The real problem comes with the relation between this saying and the theology of the early church. It sounds so much at home in an early church setting that it has been thought by many to belong there, rather than in the setting of Jesus' own life. But such a judgment fails to stand up to closer inspection, since the saying affirms the unknowability of *the Son*, which is not the kind of idea the early church might be expected to have invented in the days following Pentecost, when the disciples believed that they had at last come to an understanding of who Jesus really was (cf. the sermons of Acts). Both the Johannine and the Pauline traditions affirm not only the knowability of Jesus but also the crucial importance of knowing him as an

---

[67] Cf. M. Miyoshi (1974) 131, E. Schweizer (ET 1976) 271.

essential element in the christian life (cf. Jn. 14.7, 17.3, 1 Jn. 2.3, 2 Cor. 5.16, Phil. 3.10, 2 Tim. 1.12). To say therefore that 'no one knows the Son' is not the kind of thing to have naturally occurred to the minds of those who were moving in those circles, nor in any other christian circles of which we have any knowledge. This disjunction from the situation of the early church indicates that the saying has an origin in the pre-Pentecost period.

(5) Anti-Redactional Features
There is nothing of which I am aware which stands in tension with the evangelists' redactional tendencies here, but this is not important since it has already been established that the saying belongs to Q. At the level of Q, it is worth noting that only here is Jesus called 'Son' absolutely and only here is there mention of the mutual knowledge of the Father and the Son. The saying is indeed an 'erratic boulder' on the terrain of the early tradition of the sayings of Jesus, whose presence at that level is hard to account for unless it has some rootage in the ministry of Jesus himself.

Mt. 11.27 par. is an important saying, whose authenticity and meaning have been much discussed in New Testament scholarship. There is a widespread belief now that at the very least it reflects authentic motifs from the teaching of Jesus (and is therefore 'authentic' in the type c sense defined in chapter 2 above), but the considerations presented above taken cumulatively favour the view that the saying stands in a yet closer relationship with the original words of the historical Jesus, and this in turn adds to the credibility of the view that Jn. 5.19-20a also may have been spoken by him roughly as it stands.

Not every motif present in Jn. 5.19-20a can be paralleled from sayings in the Synoptic Gospels which may be reliably attributed to Jesus, notably the apprenticeship motif itself, but we may say at this point that to a very large extent the essence of Jesus' words in Jn. 5.19-20a is thoroughly in tune with the Jesus we meet in the Synoptic Gospels, and to that extent they qualify for authenticity in the most general sense of the word on this basis, quite apart from the other evidence which points towards an authenticity of a narrower kind.

(3) Dissimilarity
What has been said so far sets 5.19-20a firmly within the context of first century AD Judaism and of the ministry of Jesus - the language and thought forms used are entirely at home within that context. Yet at the same time the overall message of these words presents something unparalleled in the Judaism of Jesus' day since here we find him claiming, in effect, to be doing habitually the things that he sees God doing and only those things. Judaism

spoke of seeing what God does, of doing what God says, and even of being the means by which God does his own work (as will be made clear in appendix B), but it did not speak of anyone presuming to see what God does and then doing the same things himself. As F. Grob puts it after his review of the Old Testament background to these words: 'Dans la perspective du peuple-fils et du Dieu de l'Alliance, c'est une chose impensable. Que le peuple fasse lui-même les oeuvres que Dieu lui donne à voir et qui sont ses oeuvres, que le peuple se mette au niveau de l'oeuvre que Dieu fait, et non seulement au niveau d'une obéissance à la loi de Dieu par les oeuvres humaines qu'il peut faire en réponse et en reconnaissance à l'oeuvre de Dieu, cela est d'une outrecuidance non imaginable en terrain juif ... cette prétention introduit dans l'image de Dieu-père et du peuple-fils une incohérence radicale'.[68] At this point there is indeed a 'radical incoherence', a marked dissimilarity, with the Jewish background.

On the other side, is it likely that this claim on the part of Jesus could have been made up by the early church? Certainly the implications of a functional equality with God would no doubt have been welcome to the author of the Gospel and other christian groups, but if the saying began its life by comparing Jesus with an apprentice, as has been argued above, whether through parable or metaphor, then we may legitimately wonder whether this is the kind of imagery the early church would have created in the post-Easter situation. The idea of someone having no idea of himself as to what he ought to be doing, having to learn how to act at every step from God and being totally dependent on God's initiative in every circumstance, in short the idea of total 'weakness' from a human point of view, is not exactly the image which would have sprung immediately to mind among those who were celebrating Jesus' exaltation as Lord and Saviour to a place of supreme authority and power at the right hand of God.

The image as a whole, therefore, from different angles, cuts across what we might have expected both from first century AD Judaism and from the early church. This fact adds to the conviction that we are dealing here with words which stand in a close relation to what Jesus himself originally said about himself.

(4) Anti-Redactional Features
At first sight these words appear to be a typical piece of Johannine theology, and there is some justification in this view. Jesus is typically described as 'the Son' in the Gospel (1.18, 3.16, 17, 18, 35, 36, 5.21, 22, 23, 26, 6.40, 8.36, 14.13, 17.1); he is typically said not to be able to say or do anything 'of himself' (7.16-18, 28, 8.28, 42, 12.49, 14.10); the verb ποιῶ itself is in

---

[68] F. Grob (1986) 135.

frequent use in christologically significant sayings of Jesus as was shown above in the introductory section; God is regularly called 'the Father' throughout the Gospel and is also said several times elsewhere to love 'the Son' (3.35, 10.17, 15.9, 17.23, 24, 26). In addition W. Nicol picks out the following typical marks of the author's Greek style in this short passage: the independent pronominal use of the singular word ἐκεῖνος, ἀφ' ἑαυτοῦ, οὐ ... ἐὰν μή, ἐὰν μή τι, οὐ ... οὐδέν, a *casus pendens* and φιλῶ.[69]

It would seem a hopeless task to talk about anti-redactional features in the face of this evidence, yet it is still possible to do so. Note especially the following, which individually are only straws in the wind, but cumulatively count for something:

a. The verb βλέπω is normally used for ordinary seeing in the Fourth Gospel (1.29, 9.7, 15, 19, 21, 25, 11.9, 13.22, 20.1, 5, 21.9, 20). In 11.9 it may carry the secondary meaning of seeing Jesus as the light of the world and in 9.39, 41 it clearly refers to a spiritual seeing, but only here is it used with 'the Son' as subject and only here is it used of anyone 'seeing' God at work.

b. There are other verbs for 'seeing' in the Gospel but of these only ὁρῶ is used for Jesus 'seeing' God (6.46) or 'seeing' in the sense of receiving some kind of revelation from God (3.11, 8.38, cf. 3.32) and in each case the verb is used in the perfect tense, presumably referring either to Jesus' pre-existent state or to some moment of revelation earlier on in his ministry. In other words only in 5.19f. is Jesus in the Fourth Gospel said to 'see' God at work *in the present tense*.

c. Though it is likely that ἀγαπῶ and φιλῶ are to be regarded as synonymous in the Fourth Gospel, it is still noteworthy that, out of the seven places in the Gospel where the Father is said to love the Son, only here is the word φιλῶ used.

d. The verb δεικνύω is used seven times in the Fourth Gospel. Elsewhere Jesus is the subject of the verb, the object being variously a sign (2.18), 'many works' (10.32), the Father (14.8, 9), his hands and his side (20.20). Only in 5.20 (twice) is the Father the subject. Only here in the Gospel does he 'show' anything to anyone.

e. The above points, of course, all revolve around the apprenticeship imagery of the saying, and it is this imagery itself which once again stands out from the surrounding Johannine material as being particularly distinctive. As W. Loader has argued, the dominant motif used for Jesus' life and ministry in the Fourth Gospel is what he calls 'the revealer envoy model', which pictures Jesus as being sent from the Father to make the Father known and bring light, life and truth to those who believe in him. Jn.

---

[69] W. Nicol (1972) 20.

5.19f. represents a break from this dominant motif since it pictures Jesus as having some kind of experience of the Father in the present as a guide for his own actions. The only point of contact with the dominant motif comes in the sequel in which Jesus is presented as the giver of life (5.21ff.).[70]

All this points to the relative strangeness of Jn. 5.19-20a in the context of the Fourth Gospel, and adds weight to the argument for the authenticity of this passage in the narrower sense of the word. Moreover the presence of the 'Johannine' features noted above need not necessarily detract from this argument, since, as we have seen in the case of the 'Amen' formula and others, it is still possible for that which conforms to the general trends of the Gospel to have dominical roots, and the multiplied appearances of these phenomena elsewhere may well stem from some such saying as the one before us now.

In conclusion, therefore, there are strong indications from all the four relevant criteria which have been applied that the apprenticeship parable or imagery which forms the core of Jn. 5.19f. goes back, roughly in the form in which we now have it, to Jesus himself.

8.3.3 '... and greater works than these will he show him ...'

There is a general agreement among commentators that there is a certain break in continuity between v. 20a and v. 20b.[71] On the assumption that vv. 19-20a contain a parable, it is clear that by the time we reach v. 20b the parable is over. At the very least the ambiguity posed by vv. 19-20a is at an end, since, though Jesus is still using the apprenticeship imagery of vv. 19-20a in v. 20b, he is now unambiguously speaking about himself and 'the Jews' who have been accusing him.

A second general observation is that v. 20b obviously paves the way for the discourse which now unfolds. Whatever the phrase 'greater works' may mean precisely, a question which will be left to the exegetical section of this chapter, at least we can be fairly confident that they include the works of life-giving and judging which are referred to in vv. 21-22. Verse 20b therefore functions as a kind of bridge between the apprenticeship imagery and the ensuing discourse, which ranges far more widely than the healing

---

[70] W. Loader (1989) 206.

[71] E.g. P. Gaechter (1963) 67, R.E. Brown (1966) 1.221, C.H. Dodd (1968) 31, B. Lindars (1972) 222, S. Temple (1975) 129. W. Grundmann (1965-6) 45 n. 1, R. Bultmann (ET 1971) 253 and J. Becker (1979) 1.236, 240 regard v. 20b as a secondary intrusion into the passage.

miracle and the sabbath breaking with which the chapter began, and may well have been editorially attached to the saying in vv. 19-20a.[72]

Thirdly, it is noticeable that most of the standard criteria of authenticity fail to confirm this part of the saying as standing close to something Jesus said, except insofar as it shares in the apprenticeship imagery of vv. 19-20a itself. The focus on Jesus' 'greater works' of life-giving and judging cannot be said to stand in any way against the Johannine redaction nor to be dissimilar from early church theology, and the phrase '... that you may marvel' does not fit in well with the evidence of the Synoptic Gospels where Jesus deeds and words often excite wonder (Mk. 5.20, Mk. 7.37 par. Mt. 15.31, Mk. 12.17 pars. Mt. 22.22, Lk. 20.26, Mk. 15.5 par. Mt. 27.14, Mt. 8.27 par. Lk. 8.25, Mt. 9.33 par. Lk. 11.14, Mt. 21.20, Lk. 4.22, 9.43, 11.38, 24.41) but where he himself is never represented as using the word.

The likelihood is therefore that v. 20b is a piece of Johannine stitching to unite the saying in vv. 19-20a with the development of the theme of Jesus' equality of function with the Father which follows in 5.21ff. Nevertheless, some of the language used is characteristic of Jesus, as has already been argued in the case of δεικνύω and ἔργον, and, as C.H. Dodd has shown, the substance of the discourse which follows has close parallels in the Synoptic Gospels.[73] Jesus *did* regard himself in some sense as a life-giver and a judge, and no doubt, as v. 20b suggests, he regarded these roles as being more important in the long run than that of being a healer, and as being roles whose effect his enemies would not in the last resort be able to evade.

8.4 The Exegesis of John 5.19-20

8.4.1 'Truly, truly I say to you ...'

As we saw in section 8.3.1 above this phrase probably goes back to Jesus, though there is less probability that it was originally attached to the words which follow. As such, it is evidence for the great sense of authority with which Jesus spoke. In the Old Testament the word אמן was used to acknowledge as true, valid and binding what had been said by another

---

[72] R.E. Brown (1966) 1.221 believes that 5.30 was the original explanation of the 'parable' in 5.19-20a and that 5.21-25 and 5.26-29 were two different forms of the discourse which was originally attached to these verses, which the final editor brought together to form the discourse as we now have it. It will be noticed that 5.21-25 stresses realised and 5.26-29 future eschatology.

[73] C.H. Dodd (1967).

person, and in later Jewish literature it was used also at the end of a person's own prayers to express a strong wish for the accomplishment of what had been prayed for.[74] Against this background, therefore, when Jesus used the same word for the first time (as far as we know) at the *beginning* of his sayings he was affirming his own total commitment to the truth of what he was about to say and a belief that what he was about to say needed no further justification or external support.[75]

There is possibly a danger of reading out of this phrase more than it can reasonably bear. For example, while Jeremias helpfully observes that the formula should be seen as an alternative to the authoritative prophetic formula 'Thus says the Lord',[76] it would be going beyond the evidence, even if consistent with it, to say that Jesus thereby 'identifies himself ... with the God to whom he appeals'[77] if we are to take this identification in an ontological sense, or to claim that the one word 'Amen' expresses 'the whole of Christology "in nuce"'.[78] Even a prophet[79] or a rabbi[80] could say 'I say to you' in an emphatic way, so the sole distinguishing mark about the phrase is the word 'Amen', which certainly expresses a unique sense of authority and confidence on the part of Jesus that what he is saying is true and indeed the word of God, but perhaps no more.

The author's use of the phrase in this context, along with the unusually solemn introduction to the discourse (ἀπεκρίνατο οὖν ... καὶ ἔλεγεν αὐτοῖς),[81] clearly highlights the importance for him of what follows.

8.4.2 '... the Son can do nothing of his own accord ...'

As has been customary in these textual studies, we will seek to divide our comments between the meaning of the saying regarded as an original saying of Jesus, and its meaning for the author, though obviously the two overlap.

8.4.2.1 John 5.19-20a as a Saying of Jesus
It has been maintained in this chapter that the above words stand in a close relationship with something Jesus said and that originally they took the form

---

[74] Cf. H. Schlier in *TDNT* 1.335-338.
[75] Cf. J. Jeremias (ET 1971) 35f., I.H. Marshall (1976) 45f.
[76] J. Jeremias (1967) 112, (ET 1971) 36.
[77] L. Morris (1971) 170.
[78] H. Schlier in *TDNT* 1.338.
[79] As John the Baptist in Mt. 3.9 par. Lk. 3.8.
[80] Cf. D.A. Schlatter (1902) 40.
[81] See ch. 7 n. 27.

of a parable about an apprenticed son or a straightforward statement about himself as the Son of God in which Jesus uses apprenticeship imagery.

As was noted on pp. 204f. above the difference between these two ways of understanding these words as words of Jesus is not as great as may at first appear because of the ambiguity of the definite article in Greek and of the emphatic state of the noun in Aramaic. Here it should be added that the second understanding (taking the words as a christological statement) is suggested by the first (taking the words as a parable) as the natural interpretation of the parable, so whether or not Jesus intended these words to be a parable in the first place, he clearly intended to say something about himself through them. Or, to put the matter in another way, whether explicitly or implicitly, Jesus intended by means of these words to make a christological statement.[82]

This point might be challenged by those who make a sharp distinction between parable and allegory, as has been customary in New Testament scholarship in the wake of the pioneering studies of A. Jülicher, C.H. Dodd and J. Jeremias,[83] and who would claim that the christological statement would amount to an unwarranted allegorising of the parable. But more recent studies have gone some way towards minimising the distinction that used to be made between parable and allegory, showing that it is not illegitimate to talk of certain elements or characters in a parable as 'standing for' other things or people outside the parable.[84]

To illustrate this point from Jn. 5.19-20a itself, one is perplexed to read in C.H. Dodd's article on 'the Portrait of Jesus in John and the Synoptics' that 5.30 on the one hand corresponds with the 'application' of the parable in vv. 19-20a, and 'may be ... in touch with earlier tradition', and that 5.20b-29 on the other is 'a typical piece of Johannine exposition, in which the terms of the parable are treated allegorically, the working father standing for God the Father, the apprenticed son for Christ, and the trade which is taught and learnt for the work of ζωοποίησις and κρίσις'.[85] When Jesus is reported as saying in v. 30 'I can do nothing on my own authority; as I hear, I judge', assuming for the moment that this is an early application of the parable, how can he *not* be represented as understanding the father in the parable to 'stand for' God the Father and the son to 'stand for' himself and his work to 'stand for' judging? The distinction Dodd tries to draw at this point is quite unconvincing. While it is true that to say that Jesus is 'the Son' in a unique sense goes one step beyond saying that he is related to God as the son in the

---

[82] As we saw above in n. 37, R. Bauckham suggests that Jesus himself made the allegorical interpretation explicit.

[83] A. Jülicher (1899), C.H. Dodd (1935), J. Jeremias (ET 1954).

[84] See especially C.L. Blomberg (1990) ch. 2 and the literature cited there.

[85] C.H. Dodd (1967) 186.

parable is related to his father, there can be no doubt that if Jesus spoke these words as a parable he believed that the son in the parable 'stood for' himself.

Having said this, it is important to hold on to the valid aspects of the earlier studies and to avoid the over-allegorisation which was sometimes characteristic of the interpretation of the parables in the pre-critical period. We are not necessarily to squeeze spiritual meaning out of every detail of the Gospel parables, since the details may simply be part of the background scenery to give the picture some life and colour. Thus, for example, on the assumption that 5.19-20a is a parable, the 'seeing' on the part of the son and the 'showing' on the part of the father need not necessarily refer to some special ongoing *visionary* experience had by Jesus throughout his ministry, but may be just part of the apprenticeship scenery without any special spiritual significance.

What, then, did Jesus mean to say by means of these words? The following points may here be affirmed with some confidence:

a. At the very least he meant to convey his sense of possessing a filial relationship with God. His relationship with God is like that of the son in the saying. That he further believed that he was *the* Son of God, in a unique sense, cannot be certainly deduced from 5.19-20a itself, if taken to be a parable, but is likely to be the case in the light of other evidence,[86] and was also therefore probably present to Jesus' mind when he spoke these words. The thought that, as the Son, he was an agent of his Father is also no doubt included,[87] but we must remember that even those who are not sons may be agents, so the sonship language in the case of Jesus primarily connotes a uniquely deep, personal, intimate and loving relationship with God.[88]

b. Secondly, he meant to convey his sense of total dependence on God for guidance concerning his activities. In answer to the Jewish critics, who were accusing him of setting himself up as a rival to God and in rebellion against God (5.18, cf. section 8.2 above), Jesus affirms that, on the contrary, he can only act at God's initiative, just as the apprenticed son in the picture given is wholly dependent on his father showing him what to do. As noted on p. 206 above, there may also be an allusion to Num. 16.28, where Moses, similarly facing hostile critics, also defends himself by saying 'it has not been of my own accord'. If so, Jesus may be comparing himself with Moses, which

---

[86] As we saw in section 8.3.2.2 (2) above, especially in relation to Mt. 11.27 par. Lk. 10.22.

[87] Cf. W.A. Meeks (1976), A.E. Harvey (1987), H.S. Friend (1990), J. Ashton (1991) 317-329.

[88] The literature on the title 'Son of God' is, of course, vast, and will not be gone into here. See especially O. Cullmann (ET 1959) ch. 10, M. Hengel (1976), C.F.D. Moule (1977) 22-31, J.D.G. Dunn (1989²) ch. 2, I.H. Marshall (1990) 134-149.

would be a suitable defence to make in front of those who prided themselves on being Moses' disciples (cf. 5.45, 9.28).[89]

c. Thirdly, Jesus is implying that he actually is on the receiving end of revelation from God. He not only needs guidance before he can do anything, but he also receives it. Just as the apprenticed son is shown what he must do, so God reveals to Jesus the work which he wants him to do. We saw earlier that similar language is used at this point for the reception of revelation by the Old Testament prophets and others,[90] and there may be an implicit prophetic claim here.

d. Fourthly, Jesus is implying that he is not only receiving revelation from God but also obeying the revelation he is receiving, though not in the simple sense of doing what he is told after the Old Testament model, but in the sense of doing what he understands God to be doing on the assumption that he must do the same. He is conscious of a call to copy or imitate the activities of God.[91] What precise activities he may have had in mind when he spoke these words it is difficult to say with certainty, especially if 5.19-20a preserves an independent saying detached from its original immediate context, but it could well be that the saying was spoken originally with reference to Jesus' healing activities on the sabbath (cf. 5.18) and that the author has extended its applicability to the activities of life-giving and judging, as 5.20bff. suggests.

e. Finally, if we stand back and look at the saying as a whole in the light of the charge in 5.18 which it is said to answer, we find Jesus not denying that he is in some sense on a par with God, with the authority to act as God acts, but affirming that such a position stems from a total submission to the will and initiative of God. Paradoxically, it is an equality *through* subordination that he claims, a sameness of function achieved not through self-assertion but through self-abasement.[92] To go beyond these basic points would be either to over-allegorise the parable or else to rule out the possibility that it is a parable at all, neither of which options seem to be warranted, but, on the assumption that these words go back to Jesus in roughly their present form, the above points may reasonably be said to have been in his mind when he spoke them.

---

[89] R.E. Brown (1966) 1.214, J. Bernard (1977) 21-23. Bernard further points out that the Midrash Rabba on Num. 16.28 says the same about Elijah and Micaiah, and that by comparing himself with the biblical heroes and giving glory to God as he does here Jesus fulfils the two criteria in Jewish minds for having performed a divine miracle.

[90] See p. 204 and n. 32 above.

[91] Cf. B. Lindars (1972) 221.

[92] Cf. C.K. Barrett (1974) 149f., W. Loader (1989) 161f., J. Painter (1991) 188-190, 212.

8.4.2.2 John 5.19-20a in its Total Johannine context

By placing this saying where it is in the Gospel, the author has given it a sharper definition and a certain importance as we shall now see:

a. Firstly, the author has removed whatever ambiguity attached to the original utterance, especially as concerns the word 'son'. By placing 5.19-20a in its present context, which clearly speaks about 'the Son' in an absolute sense (5.21ff.), he indicates that the words ὁ υἱός in 5.19-20a should be understood as a christological title, and the saying as a whole understood as a christological statement.

b. Secondly, as has just been observed, whereas the original reference may have simply been to Jesus' healing activities on the sabbath, the author takes the saying to be a basic principle which applies to Jesus' entire work of salvation and judgment. As the ensuing discourse makes clear, Jesus assumes the divine prerogatives of life-giving and judging (5.21ff.) because he does everything the Father does, and that alone. In the context of the Gospel as a whole, the same may be said concerning the works of revelation and creation, as we saw in connection with 5.17 on p. 191 above, and in view of the fact that the Father loved the Son before the foundation of the world (17.24, cf. 3.13, 6.38, 17.3) and that the Son continues to work for the glory of the Father even in his post-resurrection state (14.13f.), 5.19-20a may have served for the author as a kind of portrait of the eternal relations between the Father and the Son and one way of describing the Son's deity.[93]

c. Thirdly, the motifs of dependence for guidance, reception of revelation, and obedience, although already alluded to in the Gospel, from now on become recurring features of the author's presentation of Jesus (for dependence cf. 5.30, 7.17f., 28, 8.28, 42, 12.49, 14.10; for reception of revelation cf. 3.11, 32, 34, 7.16, 8.26, 38, 14.24; for obedience cf. 4.34, 6.38, 9.4, 10.18, 12.50, 14.31, 15.10). Not all of these further sayings can claim the same degree of authenticity as 5.19-20a, so there are good grounds for believing that the author has taken this traditional saying and used its various motifs as 'building blocks' in other discourses.[94]

8.4.3 '... and greater works than these will he show him ...'

Most commentators are agreed that a contrast is being made here with the works of healing which Jesus has been performing, of which the healing of the paralytic described in 5.1-9 is an example, but there is less agreement

---

[93] As J. Giblet (1956) 97, 118 and J. Riedl (1973) 201-205 observe, the author would not have wanted to drive a wedge between the unity of action shared by the Father and the Son and their unity of being. Cf. A. Vanhoye (1960) 404f.

[94] A view also held by K.E. Dewey (1980) 84.

over the question of the identity of the 'greater works'. In the light of vv. 21ff., it must surely refer in some sense to the work of 'life-giving' and probably also to that of 'judging' (which for the author is the inevitable concomitant of life-giving; cf. 3.18-21, 9.39-41, 12.47f.),[95] but does it refer to the eschatological future,[96] the more immediate future,[97] or to the present as well as the future (whether conceived of as the 'present' of Jesus' ministry or that of the Johannine church)?[98] The last view is probably correct, though in view of the retrospective phrase 'Do not marvel at this' in 5.28, which commentators mostly ignore when commenting on the phrase 'that you may marvel' in 5.20, the emphasis would seem to be upon the final resurrection and judgment. In this case, the 'marvelling' does not necessarily lead to faith here, any more than it does in Jn. 7.21 or in Acts 4.13, but is just a human reaction of astonishment at God's action.[99]

In this context, therefore, the ἔργα of Jesus include not only his miracles but also his entire ministry of life-giving and judgment, in short, the 'work' which he was sent into the world to do.

8.5 The Exegesis of John 5.19-20 in the Patristic Era

In the patristic literature, we find similar comments being made about Jn. 5.19-20 to those made about Jn. 5.17, with which the former passage is not unnaturally often associated.

The theme of Christ as an example to follow is seen once again in the works of Clement of Alexandria, who conflates Jn. 5.17 with Jn. 5.19 and uses them to illustrate the work of the christian teacher who dispenses wisdom.[100] In a slightly different context, Eusebius of Caesarea compares Paulinus, bishop of Tyre, with the Christ of Jn. 5.19 on the occasion of the dedication of a new church building at Tyre.[101] Later, Chrysostom cites Jn.

---

[95] G.R. Beasley-Murray (1987) 76 thinks that greater miracles are primarily in mind on the grounds that they are 'works' which the unbelieving Jews must be able to 'see', but Jesus' life-giving work may cause 'wonder' in the minds of unbelievers even prior to the final resurrection (cf. Acts 4.13).

[96] So B. Lindars (1972) 222.

[97] So J. Marsh (1968) 261 who takes it to refer to Lazarus' restoration to life and Jesus' own resurrection.

[98] So J.H. Bernard (1928) 1.240f., C.K. Barrett (1955) 216 (who also adds Lazarus' 'resurrection' to the list), L. Morris (1971) 314f., D.A. Carson (1991) 252.

[99] So J.N. Sanders and B.A. Mastin (1968) 165f., J. Riedl (1973) 228, as against B.F. Westcott (1908) 1.190, L. Morris (1971) 314 n. 65, D.A. Carson (1991) 252.

[100] Clement of Alexandria, *Stromata*, 1.1.

[101] Eusebius of Caesarea, *H.E.*, 10.4.25.

5.19 as an example of an expression of humility, in that Jesus acknowledges that he does nothing of himself, and says that he thereby teaches others to exhibit a like modesty.[102]

Jn. 5.19 is also used along with Jn. 5.17 by Tertullian to illustrate the distinction between the persons of the Father and the Son, as against Praxeas' form of modalistic monarchianism.[103]

In particular he is at pains to stress that, despite the anthropomorphic language used with reference to the Father in 5.19, the Father is in fact always invisible, whereas the Son was visible.[104] Origen also uses 5.19 to affirm that the Son is other than the Father.[105]

In the post-Nicene period, we find a number of Fathers attributing the 'powerlessness' of Christ in Jn. 5.19 to his *human*, as opposed to his divine, nature. Theodoret's dialogues, for example, contain references to the view of Gregory of Nyssa that the statement that the Son 'could do nothing of himself' must apply to the human nature, and not the Godhead, of the only-begotten Son of God, and the same view is reported to have been said by Apollinarius with reference to the statement that the Son 'does what he sees the Father doing'.[106] So also Gregory of Nazianzus says that the statement that the Son 'can do nothing of himself' applies to Christ's human nature and cannot be used as evidence against the doctrine of his deity.[107]

The vast majority of references to Jn. 5.19 in patristic literature, however, use it to affirm the unity of the Father and the Son. This tradition goes back at least as far as Origen, who uses Jn. 5.19 in his exposition of Wisd. 7.25f., and says that, as the Wisdom of God, the Son 'mirrors' the Father's activity: 'the Son in no respect differs from the Father in the power of his works, and the work of the Son is not a different thing from that of the Father, but one and the same movement, so to speak, is in all things ... there is no dissimilarity whatever between the Son and the Father ... in the Gospel the Son is said to do not similar things, but the same things in a similar manner'.[108] Novatian similarly uses Jn. 5.19 to argue for the deity of Christ, since for him a mere man cannot do the 'heavenly' works of God.[109] It is noteworthy that in both cases the cosmological roles of God are in view.

---

[102] Chrysostom, *Homily 49 on John's Gospel*, sec. 2.
[103] Tertullian, *Against Praxeas*, sec. 21.
[104] Ibid. sec. 15.
[105] Origen, *Commentary on John's Gospel*, 10.21.
[106] Nicene and Post-Nicene Fathers 2nd series, 3.180, 215 (no sub-divisions of Theodoret's text are given in this edition).
[107] Gregory of Nazianzus, *Theological Orations*, 3.17.
[108] Origen, *De Principiis*, 1.2.12.
[109] Novatian, *Treatise Concerning the Trinity*, sec. 14; cf. sec. 21.

It was this type of exegesis which dominated the Nicene and post-Nicene periods. Thus, for example, Athanasius quotes Jn. 5.19 to refer to the work of the Son in creation and to demonstrate his equality with the Father,[110] and once again uses the argument that if the Son were a creature, as the Arians said he was, then, according to Jn. 5.19, he must have created himself, which is absurd.[111] So also Gregory of Nazianzus sees in the identity of the works of the Father and the Son expressed in Jn. 5.19 the implication that they share the same being.[112] The same basic thought is found in the writings of many other Fathers too, including Basil,[113] Hilary,[114] John of Damascus,[115] Ambrose,[116] Augustine,[117] and Chrysostom,[118] all of whom see the works of the Father and the Son as coinciding in every possible way.

In the later patristic period, this affirmation of the deity of the Son on the basis of Jn. 5.19 is accompanied by an explicit *denial* that Jn. 5.19 speaks of the Son as literally copying or imitating the Father.[119] Clearly the view that Jn. 5.19 pictured Jesus as an 'apprentice' to the Father was already in vogue in Augustine's day among the Arians, but Augustine urges his readers to take the language of Jn. 5.19 in a purely metaphorical sense. It is not as though the Son actually sees what the Father does and then does the same himself. Rather the language of seeing and doing likewise is only another way of stating what it is for the Son to be the Son in his eternal generation from the Father and his eternal sharing in the Father's divine being.[120]

In summary, therefore, we may say that, as with Jn. 5.17, Jn. 5.19f. is used to present Christ as an example, and as being distinct from the Father, but most of all as being of one being with the Father through a common,

---

[110] Athanasius, *Contra Gentes*, 3.46.7; *De Synodis*, 3.49.

[111] Athanasius, *Ad Afros*, sec. 7; *Orations Against the Arians*, 2.16.21. Cf. his use of Jn. 5.17 as cited on p. 192 above.

[112] Gregory of Nazianzus, *Theological Orations*, 4.10.

[113] Basil, *On the Holy Spirit*, 8.19; *Letter 8, to the Caesareans*, sec. 9.

[114] Hilary, *De Synodis*, secs. 19, 75; *On the Trinity*, 7.17, 18, 21, 11.12; cf. 9.43-47, 72.

[115] John of Damascus, *Exposition of the Orthodox Faith*, ch. 8; cf. ch. 18.

[116] Ambrose, *Of the Holy Spirit*, 2.12.135f.; *Of the Christian Faith*, 1.2.13, 2.8.69; cf. 4.6.67.

[117] Augustine, *On the Trinity*, 2.1.3; *On the Creed*, sec. 5; *The Harmony of the Gospels*, 1.47; *Sermon 76*, secs. 5, 10; *Tractate 20 on John's Gospel*, sec. 8.

[118] Chrysostom, *Homily 38 on John's Gospel*, secs. 3f.; *Homily 64 on John's Gospel*, sec. 1.

[119] Cf. Hilary, *On the Trinity*, 7.17; Ambrose, *Of the Christian Faith*, 4.4.44f., 4.5.59f.; Augustine, *Sermon 76*, sec. 9; *Tractate 18 on John's Gospel*, sec. 5; *Tractate 21 on John's Gospel*, sec. 2; Chrysostom, *Homily 38 on John's Gospel*, sec. 4.

[120] Augustine, *Sermon 76*, secs. 13-15; *Tractate 18 on John's Gospel*, secs. 6f.; *Tractate 20 on John's Gospel*, sec. 8; *Tractate 21 on John's Gospel*, sec. 4; *Tractate 23 on John's Gospel*, sec. 11.

total and eternal sharing in all the Father's works, of which his cosmological works are primarily in mind. In addition, and as an accompaniment to this affirmation of the deity of Christ, we find an explicit denial that the 'apprenticeship' imagery of this saying should be taken literally, and the assertion that the 'powerlessness' which the saying attributes to Christ in independence from the Father should be attributed only to his human, and not to his divine, nature.

8.6 Conclusion

We are now in a position to draw together some conclusions:

a. Firstly, we have seen that whereas the opening 'Amen ...' formula in Jn. 5.19 probably represents Jesus' original style of speech, but may not have been originally attached to the saying which follows, and v. 20b probably represents a piece of Johannine 'stitching', the central saying in Jn. 5.19-20a probably goes back to Jesus in roughly its present form, either as a parable about an apprentice which he applies to himself, or as a straightforward statement about himself which uses apprenticeship imagery. We have also seen that most of the motifs contained in Jn. 5.19-20 as a whole cohere extremely well in content with material we may reliably attribute to Jesus in the Synoptic Gospels.

b. Secondly, we have learnt from these verses about Jesus' sense of absolute authority as he spoke, his filial consciousness, his sense of dependence on his Father for guidance concerning his activities, his belief that he was in fact receiving revelation from his Father, and his conviction that he was actually obeying his Father and doing the kind of things his Father was doing. In short, we may say that he believed that he was at one with his Father in action through subordination to his Father's will. In addition we may possibly see an implicit claim to be his Father's agent and to be a prophet, indeed a new Moses.

c. Thirdly, we have seen that the author has taken up this saying, removed its possible earlier ambiguities and woven it into a discourse which emphasises Jesus' role as life-giver and judge. In other words the range of 'works' in view has been made to broaden out from the original healing miracle to include the entire work which Christ was sent to earth to perform. However, within the context of the Gospel as a whole, with its affirmation of the deity of Christ, the author may well have seen this sameness of works shared by the Father and the Son to have been an absolute and eternal phenomenon which expresses that deity.

d. Finally, we have seen how that while Jn. 5.19 is used in the patristic era to present Christ as an example and as other than the Father, it is mainly used to emphasise his essential unity with the Father. For the later Fathers, the cosmological works of Christ are given greater prominence than his salvific works, all subordinationist elements are attributed to his human nature, and the apprenticeship imagery is seen to be a purely metaphorical way of expressing the Son's eternal generation from the Father.

Chapter 9

Indicators of Jesus' Identity

9.1 Introduction

In this final textual study, we will consider the remaining passages in which the ἔργα of Jesus are mentioned in his Johannine sayings, all of which are found to revolve in some way around the theme of indicating Jesus' identity. The sayings in question are found at 5.36, 10.25, 32, 37f., 14.10f., and 15.24. Since in no case will it be argued in this chapter that these sayings stand in any close relationship with the original words of Jesus (though it *will* be argued that to a large extent they can be shown to exhibit a more general, type c, authenticity), a different procedure will be followed from that which has been followed in the previous four chapters.

The procedure will be as follows: firstly, an exegesis of the sayings will be given, taking due account of their contexts; secondly, an attempt will be made to establish, as far as may be possible, the extent to which their content coheres, in a strict sense, with other material, Synoptic and Johannine, which may reasonably be said to go back to the historical Jesus roughly in the form in which it has survived; thirdly, the ways in which the author seems to have creatively handled the material at his disposal will be determined; and fourthly, as before, the ways in which these sayings were understood in the patristic era will be surveyed.

With these introductory comments we may now turn to the sayings themselves.

9.2 The Exegesis of the Sayings

9.2.1 John 5.36

9.2.1.1 The Context of John 5.36
As has already been seen in the previous two chapters, Jn. 5 begins with the story of the healing of the lame man at the pool of Bethesda in Jerusalem (vv. 1-9), short dialogues between the healed man and the 'Jews', the healed

man and Jesus, and Jesus and the 'Jews' (vv. 10-18), and a discourse by Jesus on his God-given roles of life-giver and judge (vv. 19-30). At v. 31 the discourse takes a new turn as Jesus begins to talk about those people and things which 'bear witness' to him and thereby support the claims he makes for himself. It is in this context that we find Jesus saying that the works he performs bear him witness that the Father had sent him.

The theme of witness is extremely common in the Johannine writings. The verb μαρτυρῶ is used 47 times and the noun μαρτυρία 30 times in them, and in the Fourth Gospel itself a wide variety of people and things are said to bear witness to Christ: God (5.32, 37, 8.18), Jesus himself (8.14, 18, cf. 3.11, 32), the Holy Spirit (15.26), the works of Jesus (5.36, 10.25), Scripture (5.39), John the Baptist (1.7f., 15, 19, 32, 34, 3.26, 5.33), the Samaritan woman (4.39), the disciples (15.27, cf. 19.35, 21.24) and the crowd (12.17). The legal connotations of the word are confirmed by the reference to the Old Testament law concerning witnesses in 8.17, though, as R.E. Brown notes, the author broadens the principle originally related to the condemning of a criminal to make it apply to the confirming of a person's testimony (in this case Jesus' self-testimony).[1] Thus Jesus is pictured as being under attack and as summoning various witnesses to his defence so that his claims might be upheld.[2]

Jesus concedes in effect in v. 31 that self-testimony on its own need not be accepted as true,[3] but immediately goes on to say that there is 'another' (v. 32) who bears witness concerning him. Though a few scholars have thought that this refers to John the Baptist,[4] the vast majority rightly agree

---

[1] R.E. Brown (1966) 1.223. The same broadening occurs in the Mishnaic tractate *Kethuboth* 2.9. For the legal air of the word μαρτυρῶ in this context, cf. S. Pancaro (1975) 193-208, A. Trites (1977) ch. 8, and J. Painter (1991) 195f. The author may also have been influenced by the religious application of this legal term in Isa. 43.9-13, 44.7-11; cf. *TDNT* 4.483f., J. Riedl (1973) 234f.

[2] A number of scholars draw attention to the appropriateness of this theme to the author's own perceived context of conflict between his community and local Jews, e.g. R.E. Brown (1966) 1.228 and J. Becker (1979) 1.249. Others connect it more generally with the christian mission to Jews in the post-Pentecost period, e.g. C.H. Dodd (1963) 297, J. Bligh (1963) 133, B. Lindars (1972) 220f., S. Pancaro (1975) 208, C.K. Barrett (1978[2]) 258, E. Haenchen (1980) 297, G.R. Beasley-Murray (1987) 80. While this relevance is in no way denied, nor the fact that the passage is in some sense a Johannine composition, it must not be forgotten that Jesus was in conflict with the Jews in his own life-time also, and that many of the individual themes of 5.31-47 correspond to elements in the Synoptic tradition concerning the ministry of Jesus, as will be seen in more detail later in the chapter in the case of the theme of the 'works' as witnesses to Jesus.

[3] Though in his case it is in fact true, as the (apparently contradictory) statement in 8.14 makes clear.

[4] J. Bernard (1979) 9, F. Grob (1986) 163.

that it refers to God.⁵ Verses 33-35, which do refer to the Baptist's testimony, seem to be a kind of digression, included as a concession to his followers, but Jesus himself refuses to accept the testimony of a mere man (v. 34), and depends rather on a 'greater testimony' than that which John gave to him.⁶ Hence the ἄλλος referred to in v. 32 must be God rather than John the Baptist, and we are probably also for the same contextual reasons to see the witness of the works of Jesus in v. 36 and the witness of the scriptures in vv. 39f. to be different forms of the Father's witness which is more directly mentioned in vv. 37f.⁷ Thus the works which the Father gives to Jesus to perform are one way in which the Father witnesses to the truth of Jesus' claims in the face of those who doubt or oppose them.

9.2.1.2 The Scope of the ἔργα in John 5.36

How are we to understand the word ἔργα in this context? Some scholars see in this word a reference to the miracles Jesus worked.⁸ Others see a reference to the works of life-giving and judging which are mentioned earlier in the discourse at vv. 20-22.⁹ Others again see a reference to the totality of Jesus' ministry, all his deeds and words, and recall the words in 5.19f. which speak of Jesus being wholly dependent on the Father for *everything* he does, and the reference to 'work' in the singular at 4.34 and 17.4, which seems to embrace the whole of Jesus' ministry.¹⁰ It is difficult to decide between these alternatives. Perhaps R. Heiligenthal is nearer the mark when he says that there is a deliberate ambiguity here (a not uncommon feature of the Fourth Gospel).¹¹ There seems to be a specific reference to the miracles here (since their evidential value is obviously more clear-cut and 7.3f., 21, 9.4 show that the word can be used with this meaning), but in the background there stands the more general meaning of

---

⁵ E.g. R.E. Brown (1966) 1.224, R. Bultmann (ET 1971) 264, B. Lindars (1972) 228, C.K. Barrett (1978²) 264, J. Becker (1979) 1.252, E. Haenchen (1980) 292, R. Schnackenburg (ET 1980) 2.121, U.C. von Wahlde (1981) 386.

⁶ This seems to be the meaning of the elliptical phrase μείζω τοῦ Ἰωάννου in v. 36. So, e.g., R.E. Brown (1966) 1.224, R. Bultmann (ET 1971) 265, L. Morris (1971) 328, B. Lindars (1972) 229, C.K. Barrett (1978²) 266, R. Schnackenburg (ET 1980) 2.123, D.A. Carson (1991) 261.

⁷ So C.H. Dodd (1963) 297, R.E. Brown (1966) 1.227, S. Pancaro (1975) 211, R. Schnackenburg (ET 1980) 2.120, U.C. von Wahlde (1981) 386.

⁸ So E.C. Hoskyns (1940) 1.303, J. Bligh (1963) 120, R.E. Brown (1966) 1.224, B. Lindars (1972) 229, J. Bernard (1979) 22.

⁹ So C.H. Dodd (1953) 329, H. Odeberg (ET 1968) 221f., and A. Trites (1977) 101.

¹⁰ So R. Bultmann (ET 1971) 265, W. Thüsing (1970) 61, J. Riedl (1973) 239, S. Pancaro (1975) 215, R. Schnackenburg (ET 1980) 2.123, F. Grob (1986) 168f., D.A. Carson (1991) 261f.

¹¹ R. Heiligenthal (1983) 139-141.

the entire ministry of Jesus, which is more concretely summed up in Jn. 5 in the notion of life-giving and its obverse of judgment for those who refuse to accept the offer of life.[12]

9.2.1.3 The Exegesis of John 5.36
a. The Commission of the Father

Jesus describes the 'works' as ἔργα ἃ δέδωκέν μοι ὁ πατὴρ ἵνα τελειώσω αὐτά. The works are 'given' by the Father. J. Riedl characteristically sees here a reference to the empowering of Jesus to do the works of the Father,[13] but though this idea is undoubtedly present elsewhere in the Gospel, as we shall see later in this chapter (especially when we consider 14.10), the present reference may mean no more than that the Father has commissioned Jesus to do certain works. It is in this sense that they have a divine origin here (cf. 17.4).

Whether the word ἵνα should be understood as completive, equivalent to an infinitive, or as final, expressing purpose, is another moot point. Certainly the former understanding is possible in the Johannine context,[14] but A. Vanhoye, followed by J. Riedl, has argued strongly in favour of the latter understanding in this case,[15] and, though not much hangs on this decision, the final sense should probably be accepted. The word τελειώσω carries the connotation of completion or fulfilment,[16] so the clause as a whole means that the Father has commissioned Jesus to do certain works with the purpose that he should bring them to completion. As 17.4 makes clear, these works must be the works Jesus has been given to do on earth.

b. The Obedience of Jesus

The verse continues with Jesus saying that these works are ἔργα ἃ ποιῶ. Jesus thereby claims to be fulfilling the purpose of the Father, to be on the way towards completing the work he has been given to do, to be obedient to the Father's will. The theme of Jesus' obedience to the Father is, of course,

---

[12] Cf. B.F. Westcott (1908) 1.199, W. Loader (1989) 80.

[13] J. Riedl (1973) 240f. Cf. S. Pancaro (1975) 215f.

[14] C.K. Barrett (1978²) 266.

[15] A. Vanhoye (1960) 377-419, J. Riedl (1973) 242f. Cf. B.F. Westcott (1908) 1.199, J. Bernard (1979) 22. The strongest arguments in favour of this understanding are: a. the presence of αὐτά after τελειώσω means that the relative pronoun ἃ must be the object of δέδωκεν and not of τελειώσω, which in turn means that δέδωκεν is not 'free to govern' τελειώσω; b. τελειῶ is given special weight in the Fourth Gospel, for which a completive ἵνα would not do justice, in contrast with the completive ἵνα ποιήσω clause in 17.4; and c. the presence of the clause which follows, which would be redundant if the preceding clause were merely completive.

[16] See pp. 149f. above.

a constantly recurring one in the Fourth Gospel and reaches its triumphant conclusion in the 'high-priestly' prayer (17.4) and on the cross (19.30).

c. The Witness of the Works

The works Jesus does μαρτυρεῖ περὶ ἐμοῦ ὅτι ὁ πατήρ με ἀπέσταλκεν. As a number of commentators have remarked, the works do not compel faith; they do not amount to demonstrable proof which leaves no choice to those who witness them.[17] On the other hand it is doubtful if we should simply say that they presuppose faith to be effective at all, as some of these commentators suggest, otherwise what would be the point of citing them as evidence? A better understanding is that which sees them as indicators of Jesus' identity which indeed do not compel faith but rather evoke faith among unbelievers or confirm the faith of those who to some extent already believe (cf. 14.8-11), and increase the guilt of those who continue in unbelief despite the evidence the works provide (cf. 10.25-39, 15.24).[18]

In this particular saying Jesus' identity is expressed by means of the phrase ὁ πατήρ με ἀπέσταλκεν. Jesus is the Father's 'sent one'. Since this description of Jesus has already been fully discussed in chapter 5 there is no need to go into it again here. Suffice it to say that it points in the first place to a prophetic role, though in the context of the Gospel as a whole the thought of pre-existence also lies in the background.

9.2.1.4 Conclusion

In conclusion we may say that the saying in Jn. 5.36 presents Jesus as claiming: that the Father had commissioned him to complete certain tasks; that these tasks comprised his entire ministry (though his miracles seem to be specially in mind in this verse); that he was actually in the process of obediently discharging that commission and performing those tasks; that the tasks he was performing served as indicators of his identity as one sent by the Father; and (taking the broader context into account) that this was one way in which the Father himself was confirming the truth of his claims in general in the face of those who doubted or rejected them.

---

[17] E.g. H. Odeberg (ET 1968) 221f., R. Bultmann (ET 1971) 260, J. Riedl (1973) 235, E. Albrecht (1977) 152, J. Becker (1979) 1.254, E. Haenchen (1980) 293. Cf. also C. Brown (1984) 324.

[18] J. Bernard (1979) 23f. reminds us of the Old Testament background whereby signs may serve to validate a spokesman of God (Ex. 4.1-9), and yet not be an absolute guarantee of his genuineness (Deut. 13.1-5). Thus they have evidential value without being 'proofs', as in the Fourth Gospel. R. Heiligenthal (1983) 141f. cites pagan Greek and Jewish-Hellenistic parallels for the general idea of miracles as signs of legitimation. More importantly, the idea is also present in the Synoptic Gospels, as we shall see later.

232   *Jesus and His 'Works'*

The question of the extent to which these ideas may be traced back to the historical Jesus and the extent to which the author has creatively adapted the tradition at his disposal will be addressed after the other relevant sayings on this theme have been dealt with.

9.2.2 John 10.25, 32, 37f.

9.2.2.1 The Context of John 10.25, 32, 37f.
These verses are found in a section of the Gospel (10.22-39) which purports to describe what took place at the feast of Dedication in Jerusalem, the last such feast before Jesus' death. This section stands at the end of a longer section (chs. 7-10) which purports to describe the conflict between Jesus and the religious authorities in Jerusalem from the time of the feast of Tabernacles onwards, and in a sense forms its climax: here we find Jesus publicly and explicitly claimimg to be one with God and the Son of God (v. 30, 36), and the 'Jews' publicly charging Jesus with blasphemy (v. 33) - both features being unique to this passage in the Fourth Gospel.

A number of scholars relate the story to the needs of the church in its conflict with the synagogue at the end of the first century.[19] While this relevance is not denied, certain features of the story point to its 'anchorage' within the ministry of Jesus himself: the feast of the Dedication itself, instituted to commemorate the rededication of the Temple in 164 BC by Judas Maccabaeus after its desecration by Antiochus Epiphanes, was a relatively unimportant feast, and, as R.E. Brown notes, it is hard to imagine why this setting would have been invented without some historical basis;[20] vv. 23ff. are peculiarly vivid, as if the report of an eyewitness;[21] the question of the 'Jews' in v. 24 rings true to strong Synoptic tradition that Jesus had a tendency of revealing his identity and role in a veiled way;[22] the shepherd discourse in vv. 27-29 would have been appropriate to the setting given it in the feast of Dedication;[23] and the scriptural argument in vv. 34-36

---

[19] E.g. J. Becker (1979) 1.338, E. Haenchen (1980) 394. Cf. J. Giblet (1965) 23.
[20] R.E. Brown (1966) 1.405.
[21] So B.F. Westcott (1908) 2.64, J.H. Bernard (1928) 2.343, J.A.T. Robinson (1985) 217.
[22] A point noted by E.C. Hoskyns (1940) 2.449, C.K. Barrett (1978[2]) 378 and J. Painter (1991) 303. C.E.B. Cranfield (1959) has drawn out this trait of the Synoptic Gospels particularly well in his commentary on Mark's Gospel.
[23] Cf. R. Schnackenburg (ET 1980) 2.305, and A. Guilding (1960) 129-132 who note the fact that readings with the shepherd theme in the Old Testament (Ezek. 34.1ff., 37.16ff.) were often read at the feast of Dedication. For this reason also, it is quite

also fits, both in terms of its style[24] and in terms of its content.[25] Some scholars have indeed seen a similarity between this scene and the Synoptic trial scenes,[26] but we are not necessarily to imagine that the author has inserted here material which originally belonged to the passion story. It is not at all unlikely that Jesus' Jewish trial was the culmination of a steadily worsening relationship between him and the Jewish authorities rather than something which happened 'out of the blue'.[27]

Yet, despite such signs of an historical 'anchorage', we cannot be sure of the historical integrity of the passage as it stands. While the shepherd discourse in vv. 27-29 and the scriptural argument in vv. 34-36 may have been uttered at the time of the feast of Dedication, there is no assurance that the 'works' sayings originated in the same context. The most we can say is that the author has woven them into the narrative as part of his programme to present Jesus as one who not only claimed a uniquely close relationship with God but also appealed to his 'works' in support of his claims.

9.2.2.2 The Scope of the ἔργα in John 10.25, 32, 37f.

In v. 37f. the appeal to the ἔργα is made at a point when the appeal to Jesus' verbal self-testimony is not enough on its own to convince Jesus' opponents, so miracles seem to be primarily in mind at this point,[28] and if here then probably in the other verses as well. This is confirmed in the case of vv. 32f. where the singular ἔργον/ἔργου must refer to some kind of dramatic action on the part of Jesus. Nevertheless, in view of the more

---

possible that 10.1-18 originally belonged to 10.27-29, as a number of scholars have argued, e.g. J.H. Bernard (1928) 2.341.

[24] Its typically rabbinic style is noted by J.H. Bernard (1928) 2.367f., R.E. Brown (1966) 1.409f., and J.A.T. Robinson (1985) 311 as being suitable for a dominical origin, though the evidence does not require such an origin, as R. Bultmann (ET 1971) 389, B. Lindars (1972) 373, C.K. Barrett (1978²) 385f. and R. Schnackenburg (ET 1980) 2.310 observe.

[25] A number of scholars note the suitability of the theme of consecration (ὃν ὁ πατὴρ ἡγίασεν) in v. 36 to that of the rededication of the temple, e.g. E.C. Hoskyns (1940) 2.447, A. Guilding (1960) 128, R.E. Brown (1966) 1.404, B. Lindars (1972) 375, G.R. Beasley-Murray (1987) 177, D.A. Carson (1991) 399. Num. 7.1, which speaks of Moses consecrating the tabernacle and its furnishings, used to be read out at the festival.

[26] Cf. C.H. Dodd (1953) 362, (1963) 91f., S. Pancaro (1975) 67-71, C.K. Barrett(1978²) 379, A.E. Harvey (1982) 63, J.A.T. Robinson (1985) 250, J. Painter (1991) 304.

[27] As R.E. Brown (1966) 1.405 and G.R. Beasley-Murray (1987) 174 note. It must not be forgotten that the Synoptic Gospels say nothing about Jesus' visits to Jerusalem during his ministry prior to the final week of his life, yet presuppose that such visits took place (Mt. 23.37 par., Mk. 11.3 pars., 14.13-15 pars.). Scenes such as those which the author describes are not impossible during these otherwise unrecorded visits.

[28] So E. Albrecht (1977) 146f.

general sense given to the word in ch. 5, a secondary reference to the whole of Jesus' ministry is not impossible in v. 25.

9.2.2.3 The Exegesis of John 10.25

In v. 24 the 'Jews' challenge Jesus to declare openly whether he is the Christ of Jewish expectation.[29] His initial reply in v. 25 that he had told them but that they had not believed is perplexing, because he had not in fact told them plainly that he was the Christ (though he had told the Samaritan woman in 4.26, and he had told the man cured of blindness in 9.35-37 that he was the 'Son of Man'). Probably the author regards Jesus as having given them an answer *indirectly*, through his teaching (e.g. at 2.16, 19, 5.39, 8.24, 56, 58, and in those places where he calls God his Father and speaks of himself as the Son) or his 'works' or both.[30] If the 'Jews' had had ears to hear they would have learnt that Jesus was indeed the Christ, but not exactly the kind of Christ they were expecting. In fact, however, they did not have ears to hear. They did not 'believe' - a statement which corroborates the general impression we have from all the Gospels that Jesus' ministry did not force faith on anyone but left those who witnessed it with room to make their own decision.

The main idea of the saying itself, repeated in almost identical words, is the same as that in 5.36 which has already been discussed, namely that Jesus' 'works' bear witness to his identity.[31] The only major differences are the addition of the phrase ἐν τῷ ὀνόματι τοῦ πατρός μου and the context itself. The additional phrase probably means no more than that Jesus acts on behalf of or on the authority of his Father and therefore in accordance with his revealed will and character.[32] We note also the characteristic phrase 'my Father', which has also been fully discussed in chapter 7 above. As far as the context is concerned, it indicates that, according to this verse, Jesus' miracles and ministry in general, including both his words and his deeds,

---

[29] Commentators differ over whether the phrase τὴν ψυχὴν ἡμῶν αἴρεις means 'keep us in suspense' (so B.F. Westcott (1908) 2.63, J.H. Bernard (1928) 2.343) or 'annoy us'/ 'provoke us' (so R.E. Brown (1966) 1.402f., B. Lindars (1972) 367, C.K. Barrett (1978[2]) 380, G.R. Beasley-Murray (1987) 173, D.A. Carson (1991) 392). Most agree that it does not mean 'take away our life' in a literal sense. All agree that the question is asked with hostile intent.

[30] So E.C. Hoskyns (1940) 2.450, J. Riedl (1973) 256, C.K. Barrett (1978[2]) 380.

[31] The only differences here are the additions of the emphatic ἐγώ and the resumptive ταῦτα in 10.25.

[32] Cf. B.F. Westcott (1908) 2.65, L. Morris (1971) 520, J. Riedl (1973) 256, J.A.T. Robinson (1985) 386 n. 129, J. Painter (1991) 305 n. 53, D.A. Carson (1991) 393. The additional idea of acting by the Father's power (suggested e.g. by J.H. Bernard (1928) 2.344, D.A. Carson (1991) 393) is not necessarily present here.

bear witness to the fact that he was indeed the Christ - though perhaps not of a traditional sort.

9.2.2.4 The Exegesis of John 10.32

Following the previous saying there stands the short section of the shepherd discourse which culminates in Jesus' declaration that he and the Father are 'one' (v. 30). The 'Jews' take this to be a blasphemous assertion of his own divinity (v. 33) and so take up stones to throw at him, stoning being the penalty for blasphemy according to Lev. 24.16.[33] It is in this context that we have the above saying.

Jesus defends himself from Jewish objections to his claim to be 'one' with the Father by once again appealing to his 'works' which he describes as many and good (καλά, meaning fine, beautiful, admirable, excellent etc.). The verb ἔδειξα suggests once again the idea that Jesus saw his 'works' as indications of his identity, as σημεῖα in the Johannine sense, and therefore as evidence of which his opponents needed to take account in their assessment of him.[34]

The following phrase ἐκ τοῦ πατρός tells us why they are good. They are good because they are from the Father.[35] They have their source in the Father. It is difficult to pin down the precise meaning of the preposition ἐκ here, but it is possible that the phrase means not only that Jesus does the works that the Father gives him to do, but also that he does them by the Father's power,[36] a thought certainly present in 14.10, as we shall see. Either way they point to the unity between the Father and the Son.[37]

The final question is clearly ironical. The word ποῖον points to the quality of Jesus' 'works'. Are they such as to warrant the stoning of the one

---

[33] We need not take this scenario as a sign of the author's ignorance of conditions in Palestine in the pre-70 AD period, as does C.K. Barrett (1978²) 383. If Stephen could be subjected to similar treatment on lesser grounds (Acts 7.58), then so could Jesus a few years earlier. Similarly, as C.K. Barrett (1978²) 384 himself recognises, the law of blasphemy could well have been broader in application in the first century than it was at the time when the Mishnah was written. See further ch. 8 n. 19.

[34] Cf. R. Heiligenthal (1983) 88.

[35] So S. Pancaro (1975) 75.

[36] So A. Vanhoye (1960) 394, G.R. Beasley-Murray (1987) 175.

[37] Most scholars today are agreed that the 'unity' Jesus claims with the Father in 10.30 need be no more than a moral unity, or a unity of action. Whether this kind of unity, in the context of the Fourth Gospel as a whole, is grounded in a deeper ontological unity is, of course, another question, but see ch. 8 n. 93 above.

who does them?[38] Clearly not, as far as Jesus himself is concerned.[39] They are 'good' and 'from God', and justify Jesus' claim to unity with him.

9.2.2.5 The Exegesis of John 10.37f.

Jesus' appeal to scripture in vv. 34-36 concludes with his assertion that he had said: υἱὸς τοῦ θεοῦ εἰμι. Since Jesus is not recorded as having made such a statement in those exact words, it is likely that the author meant us to understand that this assertion was implied in Jesus' claim to unity with the Father in v. 30,[40] or in those places where Jesus calls God 'my Father' and himself 'the Son' (e.g. 5.17-23). Having justified the use of this terminology in his appeal to scripture, he now continues to support it by reference to his 'works' once again, though now the way the argument is expressed is fuller and more developed than it was in 10.25 and 32.

We note first of all the implicit claim made by Jesus in these verses 'to do the works' of his Father.[41] This expression, more succinct than those which preceded it in 5.36, 10.25 and 32, though closely similar to that in 9.4, is open to three distinct meanings, all of which may be paralleled from other 'works' sayings of Jesus in the Fourth Gospel and all of which may be present here. It may mean:

a. to do the works which his Father has given him to do;[42]

b. to do the works which his Father is doing;[43] and/ or

c. to do the works which his Father is doing by being the means by which he does them.[44]

a. implies that Jesus is obedient to the Father. b. that Jesus is working in parallel with the Father, doing the kind of things the Father does, and c. that it is the Father himself who is at work in him, giving him the power to do what he is doing and accomplishing his purpose through him. That this last sense, which presupposes the truth of the first two also, is the sense to be accepted here will be argued for at length in appendix B.

---

[38] As many commentators note λιθάζετε is conative. E.g. L. Morris (1971) 525, B. Lindars (1972) 371, R. Schnackenburg (ET 1980) 2.511 n. 122.

[39] Cf. 6.14, 7.31, 51, 9.25, 10.21, 11.45, 12.11 for other positive reactions to Jesus' 'signs'.

[40] So W. Loader (1989) 164. For M.L. Appold (1976) 33f., 137 the oneness motif is the 'heartbeat' of the author's christology, and 'the constitutive and underlying theme' of the Gospel.

[41] For the expression 'my Father' see section 7.4.2 (1) above.

[42] Understood thus by R. Bultmann (ET 1971) 390 n. 1. Cf. 4.34, 5.36, 10.25, 32, 17.4.

[43] The imitative sense, supported by R. Heiligenthal (1983) 87-89, who also illustrates the idea from pagan and Jewish sources, pp.72-84. In the Fourth Gospel itself, cf. 5.17, 19f., 8.39-41.

[44] So A. Vanhoye (1960) 394, J. Riedl (1973) 264. Cf. 14.10f.

Secondly we note the fact that Jesus encourages his hearers to believe in him on the basis of the works he does. This is a further elaboration of the by now familiar motif of the works as a form of 'witness' to his identity, a witness which does not force faith but rather provide evidence on which faith may be based. The verb πιστεύω with the dative usually means 'accept as credible' in an intellectual sense in the Fourth Gospel (rather than 'trust' in a personal and moral sense, which is usually expressed by πιστεύω εἰς),[45] so Jesus is saying here that, even though his opponents do not accept his self-testimony as true, they should consider the testimony of his works and realise that they are 'the works of God',[46] so that they might arrive at a right judgment concerning his relationship with God.[47] The 'works' can thereby become a stepping stone towards a full and personal faith in Jesus himself.

Thirdly, we note the distinctive way in which Jesus describes his relationship with the Father in v. 38: ἐν ἐμοὶ ὁ πατὴρ κἀγὼ ἐν τῷ πατρί. What are we to make of these words? It would be easy at this stage to be over-influenced by the later patristic doctrines of co-inherence, and not a few scholars seem to go too far in that direction.[48] An important fact to hold on to here is that the same sort of language is used in the Johannine literature for *believers* in their relationship with God and Christ as is used here for the relationship between God and Christ (e.g. Jn. 15.4f., 17.21, 23, 26, 1 Jn. 3.24, 4.15f.). The degree to which Christ and God are related may exceed the degree to which believers are related to each, but there must be some analogy between the two types of relationship. A further important fact to hold on to is that it is commonly recognised that the author was thinking in Aramaic while writing in Greek (even if the Gospel was not originally written in Aramaic), and in Aramaic the equivalent for ἐν would be the extremely common preposition ב, which has a wide range of

---

[45] L. Morris (1971) 335-337, 528, J. Riedl (1973) 265-267, R. Schnackenburg (ET 1980) 2.312. The distinction should not be over-pressed, however. 5.24, 38, e.g., appear to be exceptions to the rule.

[46] S. Pancaro (1975) 75.

[47] The aorist and present subjunctives of the verb γινώσκω are probably used in v. 38 to denote coming to know and going on knowing that Jesus and the Father are 'in' each other. So E.C. Hoskyns (1940) 2.457, L. Morris (1971) 529, J. Riedl (1973) 268, R. Schnackenburg (ET 1980) 2.313.

[48] E.g. J. Painter (1991) 307f. thinks that the phrase implies 'ontological sonship'. M.L. Appold (1976) 283 thinks it excludes any kind of 'subordinal role' for Jesus. S. Pancaro (1975) 74 speaks of a total unity with God 'which implies some sort of identity', while C.H. Gordon (1981) 612f. interprets the phrase to mean that Jesus is 'the same' as the Father. To speak of identity or sameness, of course, is to go beyond Nicene orthodoxy into some form of modalism.

meaning.[49] Moreover, the lack of a reciprocal pronoun in the semitic languages[50] means that this phrase could be reduced to 'I and the Father are in/ with each other'. Those commentators are justified therefore who see in this expression simply another way of describing the uniquely deep and intimate relationship which Jesus claimed to have with God.[51]

9.2.2.6 Conclusion
In conclusion we may say that the sayings of Jesus in Jn. 10.25, 32 and 37f. present him as claiming that his 'many good works', which are also the Father's works, done in his name and (probably also here) by his power, show that, so far from being a blasphemer, he is intimately related to the Father and (in some sense) the Christ. As such they may be a ground for faith in Jesus and knowledge of the truth of his claims.

9.2.3 John 14.10f.

9.2.3.1 The Context of John 14.10f.
These verses are found in the so-called 'farewell discourses' spoken by Jesus at the last supper.[52] At the beginning of ch. 14 Jesus speaks about going to the Father and about being the way to the Father for the disciples. This prompts Philip's request in v. 8 that Jesus should show the Father to the disciples. We are not necessarily to regard this as purely a literary device to enable the evangelist to move the discussion on to a new stage, as some scholars maintain,[53] and if such a request was genuinely made we are probably to understand it in the light of Old Testament precedents and

---

[49] In biblical Hebrew ב can mean: in, on, through, among, within, into, as, at, by, against, down to, upon, with, by means of, for, at the cost of, on account of, although, in spite of, about, when, and though (F. Brown, S.R. Driver and C.A. Briggs (1974^9) 88-91). A similar range of meanings is found in late Hebrew and Aramaic (cf. J. Levy (1876) 1.186f.).

[50] Cf. J. Jeremias (ET 1971) 58.

[51] Cf. *TDNT* 2.543, W.F. Howard (1955^4) 220, B. Lindars (1972) 376, J. Riedl (1973)268, R. Schnackenburg (ET 1980) 2.313, W. Loader (1989) 166. E. Boismard (1974) 166 believes the phrase is a development of the idea that God was *with* Jesus (cf. Ex. 4.12, Jn. 3.2). C.H. Dodd (1953) ch. 6 sets out pagan, Philonic and Pauline 'parallels' to this language, and E. Malatesta (1978) 42-77 goes into the Old Testament antecedents, but both recognise the distinctiveness of the Johannine usage.

[52] For a brief introduction to the farewell discourses see section 6.5.1 above.

[53] As suggested by C.K. Barrett (1978^2) 459 and R. Schnackenburg (ET 1982) 3.68. Contrast J.A.T. Robinson (1985) 301.

therefore in terms of a request for some kind of theophany.⁵⁴ Jesus' reply, as given by the author, is in effect a claim to be the revelation of God, such that no further revelation need be given (v. 9), and an appeal to Philip (v. 10) and to all the disciples present (v. 11)⁵⁵ to believe him when he says that he has a particularly close relationship with the Father. It is in this context that we have the sayings which refer to Jesus' 'works'.

9.2.3.2 The Scope of the ἔργα in John 14.10f.

This exegetical problem is not so easily resolved here as it was in the case of the verses we have looked at so far. In view of the unusual content of 14.10, where Jesus' 'works' stand in parallel with his 'words', three positions seem to be possible:

a. The 'works' *are* the words Jesus speaks. This is the position of R. Bultmann, followed by W. Wilkens and E. Haenchen.⁵⁶ It is very difficult to sustain, however, in view of the fact that in v. 11 (cf. also 10.37f. and 15.22, 24) there seems to be a distinction between believing on the basis of Jesus' words and believing on the basis of his works, and in view of those places (e.g. 7.3, 21) where the word ἔργον seems to be used unambiguously to refer to miracles.

b. The 'works' are not the words Jesus speaks but the miracles he performs. This is the position of R. Schnackenburg and L. Cerfaux, and apparently also of G.R. Beasley-Murray and D.A. Carson, who make a sharp distinction in their commentaries at this point between Jesus' words and his works, and understand the word 'works' to refer to Jesus' miracles.⁵⁷ The problem with this view is that the natural meaning of v. 10b is that at the very least the Father's works done through Jesus *include* the words which Jesus speaks, and 8.28, where Jesus' speaking is taken at the very least as an example of his doing, gives the same impression.

c. The best position therefore seems to be a mediating one. We need to remember that elsewhere the ἔργα may stand for the ministry of Jesus as a whole - both his deeds and his words - and may also in certain contexts have

---

⁵⁴ So B.F. Westcott (1908) 2.171, J.H. Bernard (1928) 2.540, E.C. Hoskyns (1940) 2.535, R.E. Brown (1966) 2.632, L. Morris (1971) 643, J. Riedl (1973) 276. Cf. Ex. 24.9-11, 33.18, Isa. 6.1. On this understanding R. Bultmann's suggestions concerning the 'epoptia' of the mysteries, the experience of philosophical meditation and the gnostic eschatological vision of God, (ET 1971) 608 n. 4, are wide of the mark.

⁵⁵ Note that the singular πιστεύεις in v. 10 becomes the plural πιστεύετε in v. 11.

⁵⁶ R. Bultmann (ET 1971) 609, cf. 388, 390, W. Wilkens (1969) 86, E. Haenchen (1980) 475. Bultmann is not in fact wholly self-consistent. Thus in one sentence he can say *both* that Jesus' words are 'part' of his ἔργα *and* that they 'alone' are his ἔργα.

⁵⁷ L. Cerfaux (1958) 137, R. Schnackenburg (ET 1982) 3.69, G.R. Beasley-Murray (1987) 254, D.A. Carson (1991) 494f.

special reference to his miracles. In v. 10 the ministry as a whole seems to be primarily in view, since the 'works' embrace the 'words', whereas in v. 11 the emphasis seems to be particularly on the miracles themselves as a form of witness to Jesus which is distinct from his speech. In other words 14.10f. illustrates the ambiguity which we have already seen to be present elsewhere in the word ἔργα as used in the Fourth Gospel.

9.2.3.3 The Exegesis of John 14.10f.

A number of the motifs to be found here have already been discussed in this and previous chapters, so there will be no need to go over them again here. This includes Jesus' statement that he cannot say anything ἀπ' ἐμαυτοῦ (for which see chapter 8), the phrase ἐγὼ ἐν τῷ πατρὶ καὶ ὁ πατὴρ ἐν ἐμοί (for which see above on 10.38 - where the same phrase occurs with only minor variations), the use of πιστεύω with the dative case (for which see above on 10.37f.), and the appeal for belief on the basis of the works Jesus does when his words on their own are reckoned to be insufficient evidence for the truth of his claims (for which see above on 5.36, 10.25, 32, 37f.).

What then is new in this passage?

a. Firstly, as noted above, the appeal to faith on the basis of works is here made to the *disciples* rather than the 'Jews', illustrating the shallowness of the disciples' faith in the pre-resurrection period which is a feature of the author's presentation.

b. Secondly, as argued above, the ῥήματα of Jesus, i.e. the individual utterances which make up his message, are here said to be as much derived from the Father as are his 'works' in general, because they are included in his 'works'. What Jesus says[58] has its source in the Father as much as what he does (cf. 10.32).

c. Thirdly, and most importantly, only here is it said in the Fourth Gospel that the Father 'dwells' (μένων) in Jesus, and does his works through him. We can now look back and see the progressively increasing role attributed to the Father in Jesus' works in the verses we have been examining. In 5.36 it was said that the Father had 'given' Jesus works to accomplish; in 10.25 it was said that Jesus did his works 'in the name of' his Father; in 10.32 that his works were 'from' the Father; and in 10.37 that his works were his Father's works. Now the Father himself is said to do them through him. As C.H. Dodd puts it (in another connection) 'Father and Son are subjects of

---

[58] No distinction in meaning should be made between λέγω and λαλῶ here as L. Morris (1971) 156 n. 86, 644 n. 26 and J. Riedl (1973) 278 argue, *pace* B.F. Westcott (1908) 2.173. This seems to be another example of the author's love of stylistic variation.

the same activity',[59] and the power as well as the authority to do them come from the Father.

9.2.3.4 Conclusion

In summary we may say, therefore, that 14.10f. presents Jesus as appealing to his disciples to accept his claim to a uniquely close relationship with the Father - a relationship in which his 'works' (including his words) are done (or spoken) at the initiative and through the power of the Father who dwells within him - and urging them to accept this claim on the evidence of the 'works' he performs (especially the miracles), if they are not persuaded by Jesus' self-testimony on its own.

9.2.4 John 15.24

9.2.4.1 The Context of John 15.24

The above verse occurs in the part of the farewell discourses which deals with the subject of the hatred and persecution from the 'world' which the disciples will encounter as they go about their mission in obedience to Christ (15.18-16.4). A number of commentators remind us of the suitability of this theme for the perceived situation of the author's own community at the end of the first century,[60] but we must not forget that the same theme is also prominent in the Synoptic Gospels[61] and that it is not at all improbable that, as Jesus faced his own death at the hands of the Jewish and Roman authorities, he foresaw that those of his own disciples who remained faithful to him might well encounter similar opposition.

Within this section 15.22-25 forms a sub-section, dealing with the culpability of the 'world' for its hostility towards Jesus during his ministry, which lies at the root of its hostility towards the disciples. It is culpable because it has rejected the evidence provided by Jesus' words (v. 22) and deeds (v. 24) for the truth of his message. It has sinned against the light, and because Jesus is one with the Father its rejection of Jesus is at the same time a rejection of the Father (v. 23). Its behaviour, Jesus claims, is a fulfilment of Old Testament scripture (v. 25).

---

[59] C.H. Dodd (1953) 257.

[60] E.g. B. Lindars (1981) 66f., J. Becker (1981) 2.489, R. Schnackenburg (ET 1982) 3.114, 116, A.T. Hanson (1991) 265.

[61] Cf. Mk. 8.34f. pars. Mt. 16.24f., Lk. 9.23f., Mk. 13.9-13 pars. Mt. 10.17-22, Lk. 21.12-17, Mt. 5.11, 10.23-39, Lk. 6.22, 12.2-9, 51-53, 14.25-27, 17.33.

9.2.4.2 The Scope of the ἔργα in John 15.24

It is doubtful if the parallelism between the words of Jesus and his 'works' (in vv. 22 and 24) should be seen as synonymous,[62] especially in the light of the reference to 'seeing' in v. 24, which is not appropriate for words, and in the light of the implicit distinction between words and works which we have already seen operating in 10.38 and 14.11. The parallelism is rather climactic, and once again it is likely that the word ἔργα stands for the ministry of Jesus as a whole, but with special reference to his miracles. The reference to the miracles is confirmed by the fact that the 'works ' are here said to be ones ἃ οὐδεὶς ἄλλος ἐποίησεν a phrase which recalls 9.32, and possibly also 7.31, both of which verses clearly refer to miracles, but the broader meaning should not be excluded either in the light of the way the word is used elsewhere in the Gospel.[63]

9.2.4.3 The Exegesis of John 15.24

Jesus first of all affirms that if he had not done the unique works which he had done among his opponents 'they would not have sin'. The word εἴχοσαν[64] stresses the responsibility of his opponents for their sin,[65] and through its imperfect tense stresses the continuing reality of their guilt.[66] At first sight this might seem an extraordinary thing to say. Would they not still be guilty of sin even if they had not witnessed Jesus' ministry inasmuch as all people are sinners by nature? In a sense this also must be affirmed, but Jesus is here talking about a special kind of sin, the ultimate and unmistakable manifestation of our sinful natures which consists in refusing to believe in the one who is the perfect revelation of God.[67] Even the Old Testament and the rabbis acknowledged that 'witting' sins were of greater severity than 'unwitting' ones,[68] and Jesus here in effect applies that general principle to the reactions of his contemporaries to his ministry. The 'works', as well as the words, of Jesus had provided the evidence they needed for them to believe in him, so their failure to do so only served to increase their guilt before God. The motif of Jesus' 'works' as indicators of his identity,

---

[62] As R. Bultmann (ET 1971) 551 n. 1 claims.

[63] Cf. L. Morris (1971) 681, J. Riedl (1973) 376.

[64] This form, with its unusual ending, was perhaps favoured as avoiding the ambiguity in person which attaches to the more normal form εἶχον. Cf. H. St. J. Thackeray (1909) 213. The -σαν ending for both second aorists and imperfects is a frequent occurrence in the LXX. Cf. ibid. 212, BD 44 sec. 84.

[65] B.F. Westcott (1908) 2.211, L. Morris (1971) 681 n. 53.

[66] R.E. Brown (1966) 2.688.

[67] Cf. R.E. Brown (1966) 2.688, R. Bultmann (ET 1971) 551, J. Riedl (1973) 373-375, C.K. Barrett (1978²) 481 (on v. 22). Cf. also 16.8.

[68] Cf. Lev. 4, Num. 15.27-31, Ps. 19.12f., S.-B. 2.523, 536, 565.

which we have seen illustrated in the other verses we have examined in this chapter, is implicit in this statement also.

Secondly, Jesus declares that his opponents had 'seen and hated' both him and his Father. Commentators are agreed that the perfect tenses here indicate a permanent attitude,[69] but they are not agreed as to the object of ἑωράκασιν. Some think the understood object is the same as for the verb μεμισήκασιν which follows, namely Jesus and the Father,[70] while others think that the object is the 'works' which Jesus has referred to in the preceding clause.[71] In favour of the first view is the fact that it takes the word καί (used four times in this clause) in its normal and natural sense. Against the first view and in favour of the second is the thought that it is unlikely that the author would want to say that *unbelievers* had 'seen' the Father, especially in view of the fact that in this very context they are said not to 'know' the Father (15.21, 16.3). On this second view, the fourfold καί would have to be understood to mean 'although ... yet ... both ... and', or something similar, respectively in its four occurrences. Against the second view it may be said that the author does speak of unbelievers 'seeing' Jesus in 6.36, and in 14.9 represents Jesus as stating (admittedly to a disciple but at the same time quite categorically as a general truth) that those who have seen him have seen the Father. It would perhaps be more true to the Gospel to say that for the author unbelievers both see and do not see (cf. 9.41, 12.40 - they are not blind and yet they are blind). They see Jesus (and thereby the Father, though they do not recognise him as such) only from the outside, and fail to see through the outward appearance to the inner reality of his person and of his relationship with the Father.

Finally we note in this verse the way Jesus once again calls God 'my Father' and claims to be so fully representative of him that the attitude that others take to him (hatred in this case) is at the same time inevitably the attitude they take to the Father (cf. 5.23, 15.23, and the positive counterpart to these sayings in 13.20). This is another way of claiming that oneness with the Father which we have already seen expressed in other ways in the verses we have studied.

9.2.4.4 Conclusion
In conclusion, this verse presents Jesus as (implicitly) claiming that his unique 'works' (his miracles especially, but also his entire ministry)

---

[69] E.g. J.H. Bernard (1928) 2.495, L. Morris (1971) 682, J. Riedl (1973) 377, C.K. Barrett (1978²) 481.

[70] B.F. Westcott (1908) 2.211, J.H. Bernard (1928) 2.495, L. Morris (1971) 681f., G.R. Beasley-Murray (1987) 276.

[71] R.E. Brown (1966) 2.688, R. Bultmann (ET 1971) 551 n. 1, J. Riedl (1973) 376, C.K. Barrett (1978²) 481, R. Schnackenburg (ET 1982) 3.116.

constitute evidence for the truth of his message such that those who reject him despite that evidence are guilty of a far more serious sin than if he had not done them in the first place. Their rejection of Jesus is moreover not simply a rejection of him, but also of the Father with whom he is one.

9.2.5 Exegetical Conclusions

It would not be possible here to sum up the content of the verses we have studied so far in such a way as to include every nuance of every word and turn of phrase. However, it *is* possible to sum up the main motifs that we have found expressed in these verses, and this will now be done. They may be drawn up under three headings:

a. The claims of Jesus

We have found Jesus making various claims for himself in these verses, mostly connected with his relationship with God, whom he calls 'my Father' (10.25, 37, 15.24). He claims to be sent by the Father (5.36), to be (in some sense) the Christ (10.25), to be obedient to and dependent on the Father (5.36, 10.25, 32, 37f., 14.10), to be intimately related to the Father (10.38, 14.11), to be indwelt by the Father (14.10), and to be fully representative of the Father (15.24).

b. The 'works' of Jesus

We have seen that the 'works' of Jesus in these verses are his words and deeds in general and (usually) his miracles in particular. They are said to be given by the Father for Jesus to accomplish (5.36), to be done in the Father's name (10.25), to come from the Father (10.32), to be the Father's works (10.37), and to be done by the Father through Jesus (14.10). As explained above, these expressions overlap in meaning, and together mean that the works Jesus does are works which the Father himself does and which he commissions and empowers Jesus to do also. In addition, they are said to be many in number, good in quality, and unique in kind (10.32, 15.24).

c. The evidence of the 'works' of Jesus

The 'works', and the Father who does them through Jesus, witness to who Jesus is (5.36, 10.25, 32, 37f., 14.11, 15.24), in particular to his having been sent by the Father (5.36), to his being (in some sense) the Christ (10.25), and to his being one with the Father (10.38, 14.11). They do not force faith, but evoke it, and supplement the witness of Jesus' verbal claims (10.38, 14.11, 15.22, 24). To fail to believe in Jesus in the light of such evidence is to be guilty of serious sin (15.24). Jesus presents his works as evidence both to his disciples (ch. 14) and his enemies (chs. 5 and 10), though with differing expectations.

Our task is now to determine, as far as we can, to what extent these motifs may be traced back to the historical Jesus.

9.3 Coherence with the Historical Jesus

9.3.1 Introduction

A number of motifs which are found in the verses we have been studying in this chapter are also found in the sayings attributed to Jesus in 4.34, 5.17, 19f., and 9.3f., which were studied in previous chapters, and which, it was argued, probably stand in a close relationship with the original words of Jesus himself. These motifs include the following: the motif of God as the Father of Jesus in a special sense (5.17, 19f.; cf. 10.25, 37f., 14.11); the motif that Jesus had been sent by the Father to accomplish a certain task and therefore was called to be the Father's agent and representative (4.34, 9.4, cf.5.36, 10.25, 32); the motif that Jesus was actually being obedient to the Father's will (4.34, 5.19f.; cf. 5.36, 10.25, 32, 37f., 14.10); and the motif that the works which had been commissioned to do were works which the Father himself does (5.17, 19f.; cf. 10.37f.) and was doing through him, such that he was dependent on the Father for the doing of them (9.3f.; cf. 10.37f., 14.10).

In addition, most of these motifs were shown to be coherent, in a strict sense, with what may be reliably attributed to Jesus from the Synoptic Gospels. That Jesus felt an especially close relationship with God is attested by his use of the word ἀββά (Mk. 14.36), the Q saying in Mt. 11.27 par. Lk. 10.22 and other verses where he calls himself 'the Son' or sees himself as God's son in a special sense (Mk. 13.32 par. Mt. 24.36, Mk. 12.1-12 pars. Mt. 21.33-46, Lk. 20.9-19); that he felt called and commissioned to accomplish a particular task is attested by his speaking of being 'sent' (Mk. 9.37 par. Lk. 9.48, Mk. 12.6 pars. Mt. 21.37, Lk. 20.13, Mt. 10.40 par. Lk. 10.16, Mt. 15.24, 23.37 par. Lk. 13.34, Lk. 4.18, 21), and of it being necessary for him (Mk. 8.31 pars. Mt. 16.21, Lk. 9.22, Mt. 26.54, Lk. 2.49, 4.43, 13.33, 17.25, 22.37, 24.7, 26, 44) to do certain things until they were accomplished (Lk. 12.50, 13.32), in short his sense of destiny (cf. Mk. 2.20 pars. Mt. 9.15, Lk. 5.35, Mk. 9.31 pars. Mt. 17.22f., Lk. 9.44, Mk. 10.33f. pars. Mt. 20.18f., Lk. 18.31-33, Mk. 10.45 par. Mt. 20.28, Mk. 14.21 pars. Mt. 26.24, Lk. 22.22, Mk. 14.27 par. Mt. 26.31); that he believed himself to be obedient to the will of the Father is attested by a number of passages (cf. Mt. 4.1-11 par. Lk. 4.1-13, Mk. 3.31-35 pars. Mt. 12.46-50, Lk. 8.19-21, Mk. 14.36 pars. Mt. 26.39, Lk. 22.42); and that he believed that what he was doing was actually what God was doing through him, such that he was dependent on the Father for the doing of them, is also a motif attested in the Synoptic Gospels (cf. Mk. 9.23, 10.27 pars. Mt. 19.26, Lk. 18.27 for a sense of dependence; Mt. 12.28 par. Lk. 11.20 for a sense of co-operation; and further Lk. 4.18-21 and Mt. 5.3 par. Lk. 6.20, where Jesus assumes the role of the Spirit-anointed prophet of Isa. 61.1, for a sense of empowering).[72]

This leaves us with the following major motifs:

a. that the works Jesus does, which he holds to be many, good, and unique, witness to his having been sent by God, to his being (in some sense) the Christ, and to his being intimately related to God; and

b. that this witness is regarded as evoking faith in Jesus rather than forcing it, yet in such a way that those who refuse to believe in him despite this witness are regarded as especially guilty of sin.

We will now examine two Synoptic sayings of Jesus which provide evidence that the historical Jesus did in fact think in these terms.

9.3.2 Matthew 11.2-6 par. Luke 7.18-23

This Q pronouncement story is longer in Luke than it is in Matthew. We cannot be sure of its exact original wording in the Q source, of course, but most scholars are inclined to believe that Luke has added to his source rather than that Matthew has subtracted from it.[73] In addition, both have given the story slightly different introductions (Mt. 11.2a, Lk. 7.18). We can be fairly sure, however, that the substance of what they have in common was in Q and that is all we need concern ourselves with here. Both agree that John the Baptist sent some of his disciples to Jesus from prison (Mt. 11.2, Lk. 3.20, 7.18b-19a) to ask him whether he was ὁ ἐρχόμενος or whether they should wait for another (Mt. 11.3, Lk. 7.19b).[74] Jesus' reply (Mt. 11.5f., Lk. 7.22f.) is given in almost identical words.[75]

The historicity of the story as a whole is entirely plausible. All the Gospels agree that John the Baptist was indeed expecting someone greater

---

[72] See sections 5.3.2, 5.3.5 (2), 5.3.6, 6.3.2 (2), 7.3 (2) and 8.3.2.2 (2) above.

[73] The addition of Lk. 7.21 is suggested by T.W. Manson (1949) 66, W.G. Kümmel (ET 1957) 109, J. Jeremias (ET 1971) 105, I.H. Marshall (1978) 290, F. Bovon (1989) 370 and C.F. Evans (1990) 352. The addition of Lk. 7.20f. is suggested by J.A. Fitzmyer (1981) 1.663 and W.D. Davies and D.C. Allison (1991) 2.242.

[74] There is no necessary distinction in meaning between ἕτερος (Mt. 11.3) and ἄλλος (Lk. 7.19).

[75] The only differences are that Lk. 7.22 has ἃ εἴδετε καὶ ἠκούσατε instead of ἃ ἀκούετε καὶ βλέπετε which is found in Mt. 11.4, and that Matthew has a καί in front of χωλοί, νεκροί, and πτωχοί.

than himself to come after him (Mt. 3.11, Mk. 1.7, Lk. 3.16, Jn. 1.27), so when reports of Jesus' activities came to him in prison it would have been natural for him to want to know whether Jesus was in fact the one he had been waiting for.[76] The fact that John is here presented as a doubter rather than a confident witness for Jesus militates against the view that we have here an early church creation,[77] as does the vague phrase ὁ ἐρχόμενος. The early church would no doubt have found a more definite title for Jesus if it had been making up the story from scratch.[78] Moreover the words of Jesus given in reply, whose authenticity will shortly be argued for, require the sort of narrative context which they are given here,[79] and the absence of any response of faith on the part of John at the end still further supports the historicity of the story.[80]

The arguments against the historicity of the narrative are not weighty. G. Vermes questions whether anyone would have been able to visit John in prison,[81] R. Bultmann whether Jesus began his ministry before John's death.[82] J.D.G. Dunn reports the objection that the early church would have wanted to portray John as recognising Jesus as the Messiah *before* his death, and the opposing objection that John would hardly have thought of identifying the coming judge with Jesus.[83] Meanwhile, R. Leivestad thinks

---

[76] Commentators are divided as to whether they think that John had previously believed that Jesus was the one he had been waiting for and was now beginning to doubt it - whether through depression or through reports that Jesus was not fulfilling the judging role he expected him to fulfil (cf. T.W. Manson (1949) 67, E. Ellis (1966) 121), or that John was only now for the first time tentatively coming to believe that Jesus was the one he had been waiting for (cf. W. Manson (1930) 78, J.M. Creed (1950) 105f., A.R.C. Leaney (1958) 144, G.B. Caird (1963) 111, B.Meyer (1979) 295 n. 96, C.F. Evans (1990) 351). This issue is not important for the purposes of our argument.

[77] W. Manson (1930) 78, W.G. Kümmel (ET 1957) 110, E. Schweizer (ET 1976) 255, I.H. Marshall (1978) 288, B. Witherington (1990) 42, W.D. Davies and D.C. Allison (1991) 2.244.

[78] W.G. Kümmel (ET 1957) 110, I.H. Marshall (1978) 288, A.E. Harvey (1982) 83, R. Leivestad (ET 1987) 93, R. Riesner (1988³) 300, B. Witherington (1990) 42.

[79] J.D.G. Dunn (1975) 59f., W.D. Davies and D.C. Allison (1991) 2.245.

[80] W.G. Kümmel (ET 1957) 111, R. Leivestad (ET 1987) 93, B. Witherington (1990) 165. Strangely, R. Bultmann (ET 1968²) 23 sees this as a sign that the narrative context is a community product.

[81] G. Vermes (1983²) 32. Contrast I.H. Marshall (1978) 289: 'they would have been able to visit him in prison without difficulty'.

[82] R. Bultmann (ET 1968²) 23, an uncommon view. His other objection, that Jesus was not actually referring to his miracles but only to passages of scripture which paint a picture of final blessedness now beginning is an unnatural dichotomy.

[83] J.D.G. Dunn (1975) 56. The problem here is that the story *fails* to portray John as recognising Jesus to be the Messiah, and presents him as a doubter quite possibly precisely *because* Jesus was not the fiery judge he was expecting.

that the warning tone of Mt. 11.6 par. Lk. 7.23 would have been unduly harsh as a reply to an enquirer.[84] As can be seen, a number of these objections cancel out each other. They are hardly sufficient to overturn the positive reasons enumerated above for regarding this story as essentially historical.

Turning now to the saying itself in Mt. 11.4-6 par. Lk. 7.22f., which should be taken as a unit,[85] a number of considerations favour its authenticity. Firstly, the criterion of double dissimilarity is satisfied by the fact that Jesus' reply does not fit neatly into either the contemporary Jewish or early christian contexts. On the one hand, the implicit claim (to be explored shortly) that the age of the fulfilment of God's promises had arrived was, to say the least, extremely audacious and unusual in the Jewish context. Again, Jesus makes no claim to be the Messiah in any traditional sense. On the other hand, Jesus' self-description as the 'coming one' shows no sign of early church theologising either. There are no christological titles, no reference to the cross and resurrection, or to a final coming in judgment, but just references to Jesus' healing and preaching activities.[86]

Secondly, the criterion of language, culture and personal idiom is satisfied. Most of the saying is taken straight out of the Old Testament and the whole can be easily turned back into Aramaic, thus (following Matthew's version):

זילו אמרו ליוחנן מא דשמעין וחזין אתון
עוירייא חזין וחגרייא מהלכין
מצטרעין מתדכין וחרשייא שמעין
ומיתייא מתקמין ועניא מתבשרין
וטוב דלא מתכשל בי

---

[84] R. Leivestad (ET 1987) 93. Yet Jesus knew of John's doubts, according to the story, and presumably was aware that he might not be matching all John's expectations. In any case Mt. 11.6 par. Lk. 7.23 takes the form of a macarism, not a woe.

[85] As J.D.G. Dunn (1975) 59 has argued. If the story is genuine and Mt. 11.5f. par. Lk. 7.22b-23 is authentic, then Mt. 11.4 par. Lk. 7.22a is an inevitable link between the two. F.W. Beare (1981) 258 regards Mt. 11.6 par. Lk. 7.23 as originally independent, but without good reason. It belongs well together with Mt. 11.5 par. Lk. 7.22b, as Dunn has shown, and if the saying had been originally independent we might have expected it to crop up elsewhere in the Gospel tradition, but in fact it fails to do so. F. Bovon (1989) 370 doubts the authenticity of Mt. 11.6 par. Lk. 7.23 on the grounds that its christology is too explicit. No such qualms are felt, however, by W.G. Kümmel (ET 1957) 109-111, R. Bultmann (ET 1968[2]) 23, 126, 151, J.D.G. Dunn (1975) 57-60, I.H. Marshall (1978) 288, J.A. Fitzmyer (1981) 1.664, A.E. Harvey (1982) 83, 141, R. Riesner (1988[3]) 299-301, B. Witherington (1990) 165, or W.D. Davies and D.C. Allison (1991) 244, all of whom accept at least Mt. 11.5f. par. Lk. 7.22b-23 as an 'authentic' unit.

[86] Cf. R. Bultmann (ET 1968[2]) 151, J.D.G. Dunn (1975) 58, B. Witherington (1990) 165.

Moreover, the style is typical of that of Jesus, as shown by the presence of parallelism and rhythm,[87] and the indirect, enigmatic quality of Jesus' reply to John's question.[88]

Finally we note the coherence of this saying with others attributed to Jesus which speak in similar terms of the arrival of the time of salvation or of the fulfilment of God's promises (e.g. Mt. 5.3 par. Lk. 6.20, Mt. 13.16f. par. Lk. 10.23f., Lk. 4.18-21), and the possibly anti-redactional element of the absence of any reference to exorcisms, an aspect of Jesus' ministry which looms large elsewhere in the Synoptic Gospels.[89] Taken together these considerations strongly suggest the authenticity (in the strict sense of the term) of the words attributed to Jesus in this pericope.

Having established, therefore, as far as is possible, the historicity of the story and a strict form of authenticity for the words here attributed to Jesus, we may now go on to reflect on the significance of Jesus' response to John the Baptist's question.

We note first that Jesus' response is couched in the words of scripture, specifically from Isa. 26.19, 29.18f., 35.5f., 61.1, with a possible allusion to the story in 2 Kings 5 for the reference to the cleansing of lepers. Secondly, it is clear, not only from the immediate context of Mt. 11.4 par. Lk. 7.22a, but also from the context of the Gospels of Matthew and Luke as a whole, that Jesus is using these passages of scripture to describe what was happening in his own ministry. The clear implication is that Jesus regarded these passages as prophecies and regarded the prophecies as being fulfilled in his own ministry. When, in the third place, we note that some of these passages were understood in Jewish tradition to refer to the conditions which would be experienced in the messianic age,[90] then we may legitimately deduce that Jesus believed that that messianic age was being inaugurated through his activities.[91]

Whether this means that Jesus is here claiming to be the Messiah himself is a more difficult question to answer, but the evidence does point in that direction:

---

[87] J. Jeremias (ET 1971) 23, 103.
[88] W.G. Kümmel (ET 1957) 111, J. Jeremias (ET 1971) 30, J.D.G. Dunn (1975) 57, I.H. Marshall (1978) 288, R. Leivestad (ET 1987) 93, R. Riesner (1988³) 301, B. Witherington (1990) 42.
[89] Cf. B. Witherington (1990) 165.
[90] See S.-B. 1.593-596.
[91] Cf. W.G. Kümmel (ET 1957) 111.

a. Whatever John may have meant by ὁ ἐρχόμενος,[92] Jesus' reply is clearly a guarded affirmative and implies that John and his disciples should not look for any figure on the future horizon as inaugurator of the messianic age other than himself;

b. Though a Messiah does not figure in every Jewish apocalypse or vision of the future, and though the various Jewish expectations concerning the shape of the future differed considerably from one another, where a messianic figure does occur, he *is* thought of as inaugurating a new stage in God's plan for Israel and the world; and

c. One of the texts Jesus uses, Isa. 61.1, speaks of a prophet being 'anointed' (the MT uses the verb משׁח, from which 'Messiah' comes) to bring good news to the poor. Jesus clearly sees himself as that person in this passage as he does elsewhere in the gospel tradition (cf. Lk. 4.18-21, Mt. 5.3 par. Lk. 6.20). In other words Jesus did see himself as an 'anointed' one.

In the light of this evidence, it is perhaps best to conclude that, as far as this passage is concerned, Jesus believed himself to be the Messiah,[93] not, however, the political, warring, earthly Messiah of one strand of Jewish expectation, nor (for the moment at least) the transcendental 'Son of Man' Messiah who would come on the clouds of heaven, but rather the eschatological-prophet type of Messiah portrayed in Isa. 61.1. In other words, Jesus believed himself to be a Messiah only of a certain kind, and his general reticence in accepting the title of Messiah stemmed from his awareness that he was giving that role a unique definition.

By now the links with the Johannine motifs which we studied in the earlier part of this chapter should be clearer. Especially noteworthy are the following remarkable correspondences:

a. Jesus here appeals to his 'works' as evidence that he has been sent by God (a description appropriate for all prophets),[94] and that he is, in some sense, the Messiah, the Christ. The words attributed to Jesus in Jn. 5.36: τὰ ἔργα ἃ ποιῶ μαρτυρεῖ περὶ ἐμοῦ could hardly be improved upon as a summary of Mt. 11.4f. par. Lk. 7.22 taken in context.

b. The 'works' he has in mind are especially his miracles, but all his activities, his words as well as his deeds, are also in mind as the reference to his preaching makes clear. This corresponds exactly to the definition given

---

[92] Whether it be the Messiah himself (cf. D. Hill (1972) 197), or Elijah redivivus (cf. Mal. 3.1, 4.5, J.A. Fitzmyer (1981) 1.666), or the Prophet of Deut. 18.18 or Michael (cf. R. Leivestad (ET 1987) 92, who is open to all these options).

[93] Cf. J. Giblet (1955) 53f., F. Bovon (1989) 375, W.D. Davies and D.C. Allison (1991) 2.242. J.D.G. Dunn (1975) 58, 61 and I.H. Marshall (1978) 292 do not go beyond saying that Jesus conceives of himself in this passage as being the eschatological prophet of Isa. 61.1.

[94] Cf. Isa. 6.8, 61.1, Jer. 1.6, Ezek. 3.5, Jn. 1.6, 33, 3.28.

to ἔργα in the Johannine passages studied above. In the light of the description given here, those 'works' may also well be described as 'many' and 'good'.

c. Jesus clearly hopes that John will grow in faith (or have a lost faith restored) on the basis of the evidence of these 'works', but that he did not regard his 'works' as in any way forcing those who saw them or heard about them to believe in him is apparent in the final macarism.[95] The choice as to whether they 'stumble' over Jesus or not is theirs.

We may now turn our attention to the second Synoptic passage.

9.3.3 Matthew 11.20-24 par. Luke 10.12-15

The original context of this saying is unclear, since Matthew and Luke provide it with different contexts and neither is likely to be original. Matthew has inserted this material after his section on John the Baptist in Mt. 11.1-19, apparently as another illustration of the way in which Jesus, like John, was rejected. He may have been led to do so on account of the reference to Jesus' δυνάμεις in vv. 21 and 23, which ties in very well with the reference to his ἔργα in vv. 2 and 19.[96] Luke, by contrast, has inserted this material in his account of Jesus' mission charge to his disciples in Lk. 10.1-16. The theme of judgment on the unrepentant towns of Galilee hardly suits a mission charge to the disciples and does not fit the account of their success in Lk. 10.17-20 either.[97] In view of these considerations it is likely that the original setting of the saying has been lost.[98]

There are strong grounds, however, for believing that the saying itself goes back to the historical Jesus. In the first place, it is unlikely to have been created by the early church, both because it highlights Jesus' *failure* to bring people to repentance, despite his miracles,[99] and because there is no evidence of any christian mission in these parts of Galilee in the post-Pentecost period which might have given rise to it, let alone one which depended on the working of miracles for its success.[100] The supposition by some scholars that the saying reflects early christian polemic[101] is therefore

---

[95] Cf. W.G. Kümmel (ET 1957) 111, E. Schweizer (ET 1976) 256.
[96] Cf. D. Hill (1972) 203.
[97] Cf. A.R.C. Leaney (1958) 178, J.A. Fitzmyer (1985) 2.850, C.F. Evans (1990) 451.
[98] So B. Witherington (1990) 166.
[99] Cf. F.W. Beare (1981) 264, B. Witherington (1990) 166.
[100] Cf. J.D.G. Dunn (1975) 70f., B. Witherington (1990) 166, W.D. Davies and D.C. Allison (1991) 2.270.
[101] R. Bultmann (ET 1968²) 113, E.P. Sanders (1985) 110, 114, 117. F.W. Beare (1981) 264 regards this as 'possible' but only after acknowledging that the saying is

without foundation. At this point the saying satisfies the criterion of dissimilarity.

Secondly, the saying satisfies the criterion of language, culture and personal idiom. It contains the semitic word σάκκος,[102] and the whole may be turned back into Aramaic, thus:

וי ליך כורזין וי ליך בית־צידא
דאלו הוון בצור ובצידן גבוריא
דהוון בכון כבר הוון תיביין בסקא ובקטמא
ברם לצור ולצידן יהוי נייח ברינא מלכון
ואת כפר־נחום לא עד־שמיא יתרומם ייחות עד־שאול [103]

The saying reflects Old Testament terminology and style,[104] and its use of antithetical parallelism,[105] strophic parallelism,[106] assonance[107], and periphrases for the activity of God[108] all suit the personal style of Jesus.

Thirdly, the saying coheres well with other sayings of Jesus and records of his activity. Its apocalyptic vision of the coming final judgment, and its striking teaching that members of Israel will be judged more severely than non-Israelites both fit in well with other sayings which may be reliably attributed to Jesus.[109] Moreover, its picture of Jesus working miracles in the area surrounding the lake of Galilee fits in well with the Synoptic accounts of his ministry. As W.D. Davies and D.C. Allison have put it 'If Jesus did not perform healings in and around Capernaum, then about him we know nothing at all'.[110]

'probably a true reflection of the disappointment of Jesus in the results of his work in Galilee'.

[102] Cf. Hebrew שק, Aramaic סקא, F. Brown, S.R. Driver and C.A. Briggs (1974^9) 974a.

[103] Where Matthew and Luke vary, the simpler form has been followed. The penultimate sentence has been turned into a statement since Aramaic does not seem to have had an interrogative particle, except in the phrase הלא. In the spoken form, of course, a question could be indicated by tone of voice.

[104] For terminology cf. Isa. 14.13-15 and the words addresssed to Capernaum in Mt. 11.23a par. Lk. 10.15. For style cf. the 'woe'-indictment-verdict pattern in Isa. 5.11-17, 29.15-21, 33.1, Mic. 2.1-5, Hab. 2.9-11 and Mt. 11.21f. par. Lk. 10.13f.

[105] In Mt. 11.23a par. Lk. 10.15.

[106] In the case of Mt. 11.21f. and 23f. So T.W. Manson (1949) 77, B. Meyer (1979) 295 n. 100. Some scholars believe, however, that Mt. 11.23b-24 may be a Matthean addition. Cf. I.H. Marshall (1978) 426, B. Witherington (1990) 166.

[107] Between Bethsaida and Sidon. So B. Witherington (1990) 166.

[108] In the use of γίνομαι in Mt. 11.21 par. Lk. 10.13 twice and Mt. 11.23 twice, and in the use of the 'divine passive' ὑψωθήσῃ in Mt. 11.23 par. Lk. 10.15. Cf. J. Jeremias (ET 1971) 10f.

[109] Cf. J.D.G. Dunn (1975) 70, B. Witherington (1990) 166.

[110] W.D. Davies and D.C. Allison (1991) 2.270.

Finally we note that there is no reference to Jesus' preaching ministry here,[111] and that the town of Chorazin is not mentioned elsewhere in the Gospels, nor indeed in the Bible as a whole.[112] Both these factors make the saying stand out as unusual, as being to some extent in tension with the general run of gospel material. Thus while the saying is credible in its Jewish context and in the context of the Gospels and what we know of Jesus' ministry, it yet stands out against its background with all these special characteristics which make it unlikely to have been created by the early church. It is not surprising therefore that a large number of scholars accept the saying as 'authentic'.[113]

As far as the original Q form of the saying is concerned, as noted above (under n. 106) there is some doubt as to whether Mt. 11.23b-24 was added in here, though in view of Lk. 10.12 and Mt. 10.15 it is likely that Sodom was in fact in some way mentioned in Q in this connection. Be that as it may, there can be little doubt that Q had at least what Matthew and Luke have in common in Mt. 11.21-23a par. Lk. 10.13-15,[114] and that these words go back to Jesus in roughly their present form.[115]

Having established the authenticity (in a strict sense) of at least this core, as far as is possible, what are we to make of its meaning, especially in relation to the Johannine texts we have been studying?

First, we note that Jesus obviously expected the inhabitants of these towns to repent on the basis of the 'mighty works' (δυνάμεις) which he had performed in their midst. In other words he regarded his miracles as 'witnessing' to a spiritual reality (here unspecified) in such a way that action was required by way of response. This motif is already familiar to us from both the Johannine and the Synoptic texts which we have studied in this

---

[111] Noticed by J.D.G. Dunn (1975) 71.

[112] Noticed by T.W. Manson (1949) 77, J. Jeremias (ET 1971) 92, E. Schweizer (ET 1976) 266, J.A. Fitzmyer (1985) 2.852 and B. Witherington (1990) 166.

[113] Apart from the scholars already mentioned in connection with arguments in favour of the authenticity of this saying, one may note also the verdicts of F. Mussner (cited by J.D.G. Dunn (1975) 379 n. 15): 'If there is one pre-Easter logion, then it is the lament of Jesus over these three cities of his native Galilee'; and of R. Riesner (1988[3]) 476: 'die Echtheit dieser Worte nicht erschuttert werden kann'.

[114] That is omitting Matthew's λέγω ὑμῖν and ἡμέρᾳ in v. 22 and Luke's καθήμενοι in v. 13, though it is of course possible that one or all of these expressions may have been in Q. The difference between Matthew's ἐγένοντο in v. 21 and Luke's ἐγενήθησαν in v. 13 is insignificant.

[115] It is relevant at this point to recall the suggestion on pp. 93f. above, that δύναμις as a word for Jesus' miracles could in fact be redactional here and that it is more likely that Jesus actually referred to his miracles as ἔργα (or one of the possible Aramaic equivalents of this word).

chapter. The only difference is that here repentance rather than faith is looked for as the required response.

Secondly, we note that Jesus did not regard his 'mighty works' as being capable of forcing the required response. They were not such as to leave those who witnessed them with no alternative but to repent. The miracles functioned as evidence but not 'proof' of the divine origin of his mission. This too is a motif we have come across above in both sections 9.2 and 9.3.2.

Thirdly, and more importantly for our purposes, we note that Jesus here expresses a belief in different degrees of sin, and therefore of culpability, corresponding with the rejection of different degrees of revelation. All the places he mentions here, Chorazin, Bethsaida, Tyre, Sidon, Capernaum, and Sodom are said to be fit for judgment, but the towns which had rejected Jesus' ministry in particular, Chorazin, Bethsaida and Capernaum, are said to be *more* fit for judgment than the others (for whom the day of judgment will be 'more tolerable'). Why? Because they are guilty of greater sin. Why so? Surely because Jesus had brought a fuller and clearer manifestation of God than had been available to Tyre, Sidon and Sodom, all of them pagan towns outside the boundaries of the covenant people of God (and all of which would have repented, Jesus says, if that manifestation had been available to them). The clear implication of Jesus' words is that if he had not come and done the works he had done, they would not have been guilty of the same degree of sin as they are now.[116] Though the form and the referents are different, the thought is surely the same as that which lies behind Jn. 15.24 as understood above.[117]

9.3.4 Conclusion to the Argument from Coherence

There are other passages in the Synoptic Gospels which might have been used to support the case being made here. For example, Jesus' belief that his 'works' were bearing witness to his special role might have been supported further from passages such as Mk. 8.17-21 par. Mt. 16.8-12 and Mt. 12.28 par. Lk. 11.20,[118] and more generally from those passages in which he

---

[116] Cf. W. Manson (1930) 124f., E. Ellis (1966) 155, D. Hill (1972) 203.

[117] It is worth noting in passing also the implicit claim Jesus makes here to know what is going to happen on the day of judgment and the implicit assumption that the eternal fate of the inhabitants of the towns he mentions will depend on their reaction to his activities in them.

[118] The latter passage was dealt with extensively in chapter 5 above. It implies that Jesus regarded his exorcisms as evidence for the arrival of the kingdom of God. In view of the fact that in Jewish tradition the Messiah was associated with bringing about the

teaches that a person's 'works' will always reveal their true character, such as Mt. 5.16, 7.16-20 par. Lk. 6.43-45, Mt. 12.33-35, 15.10-20 par. Mk. 7.14-23, Mt. 23.1-12 pars. Mk. 12.37b-40, Lk. 20.45-47; and his belief that greater revelation involves greater responsibility on the part of those who receive it might have been supported further from Lk. 12.47f. However, little would be gained from going further into these passages here, partly because the 'authenticity' of some of them cannot be so easily defended as that of those which have already been examined in some detail, and partly because none of them adds anything substantially new to what has already been demonstrated.

We conclude, therefore, on the basis of our study of Mt. 11.2-6 par. Lk. 7.18-23 and Mt. 11.20-24 par. Lk. 10.12-15 that almost all the motifs mentioned above in section 9.3.1 as requiring corroboration by the principle of coherence from sayings which may firmly be attributed to the historical Jesus have in fact been so corroborated. The only major motif which has not been corroborated is that of the uniqueness of Jesus' works (ἔργα ... ἃ οὐδεὶς ἄλλος ἐποίησεν, Jn. 15.24) but clues to its possible corroboration may be found within the Fourth Gospel itself, as was noted on p. 242 above. The reference may be to the unparalleled *number* of miracles Jesus worked (cf. 7.31), or to the unparalleled healing of the man *born* blind (cf. 9.32).[119] Whether or not Jesus made such an explicit claim, therefore, the author may still have been putting into his mouth a description of his miracles which had some basis in historical fact.

We come to the conclusion, therefore, that even though these Johannine sayings in their present form cannot be shown to correspond closely to the original words of Jesus they nevertheless express motifs which for the most part can be traced back to him. In the strict sense of the word they 'cohere' for the most part with the historical Jesus as understood from material which can be more firmly attributed to him. Jesus *did* regard his various activities as commissioned and empowered by God, with whom he claimed a close filial relationship, and *did* regard them as faith-evoking evidence for the validity of his God-given messianic role, such that those who failed to respond positively to that evidence would be accounted especially guilty of sin. This is not to say that every nuance of the Johannine sayings can be corroborated from other evidence, but it is to say that, in this area at least,

---

kingdom of God, we need not doubt that some kind of messianic claim is being made here. Cf. W.G. Kümmel (ET 1957) 108 n. 11, B. Witherington (1990) 165.

[119] This miracle, as far as we are aware, was not attributed to anyone else in the ancient world. Cf. E.C. Hoskyns (1940) 2.413, R.E. Brown (1966) 1.375, D.A. Carson (1991) 374. It is also possible, of course, that Jn. 15.24 has some of the nature miracles in view.

the author's presentation of Jesus rings historically true and that he and the Synoptists are presenting us with recognisably the same person.

This fact is perhaps not sufficiently appreciated by Johannine scholars today, not only by those who regard the Johannine Christ as a figment of the author's imagination and his words as having no connection with historical reality, but also by some who take a more cautious line. R.E. Brown, for example, in his commentary on Jn. 15.18-16.4a duly notes the many 'parallels' which exist between Jn. 15.18-21, 26-16.2 and the Synoptic Gospels, but when he comes to comment on Jn. 15.22-25 he appears to regard these verses as a purely and peculiarly Johannine elaboration of the Synoptic persecution material, without seeming to recognise that these verses contain motifs which *also* have a very firm anchorage in the Synoptic Gospels, though the connection is not so apparent at first sight.[120] Examples of this type of omission in the commentaries could be multiplied.

9.4 The Johannine Redaction

What then can we say about the distinctively Johannine presentation of Jesus' words? Here we have to be more cautious, partly because we simply do not know for sure what sources of information were available to the author of the Fourth Gospel, as was shown in chapter 1, and partly because we cannot be sure that Jesus did not say something the author attributes to him simply on account of its 'Johannine' style, as was shown in chapter 3. Nevertheless, a tentative way forward was suggested on the basis of our study of the way in which the author handles Old Testament quotations in the Gospel, and we may suggest here that the kind of freedoms we saw him using in that area were probably at work in this area also, and indeed in the Gospel as a whole. In particular we may detect the author's use of the freedoms to summarise, conflate, paraphrase and interpret the material at his disposal. Let us look at some possible examples from the texts we have studied:

a. Summaries
We saw that the evangelist tended to telescope, simplify or abbreviate his Old Testament quotations, and it was suggested above on p. 251 that the words we find in Jn. 5.36 (τὰ ἔργα ἃ ποιῶ μαρτυρεῖ περὶ ἐμοῦ) could hardly be improved upon as a summary of what we find in Mt. 11.4f., par. Lk. 7.22, taken in context. This is not to say that the author had this Q passage before him as he wrote, but he might have had access to this

---

[120] R.E. Brown (1966) 2.694, 698.

tradition or something similar to it and wrote it up in summary form in 5.36. The same precedure may well have been at work in 5.31-40 as a whole, where Jesus is represented as listing the various people and things which bear witness to him, and in other passages too.

b. Conflations
We have noted that the Synoptic Gospels represent Jesus as claiming a close filial relationship with God, and also as claiming that his works point to the advent of the kingdom of God and (implicitly) his own special messianic role, but there is no Synoptic passage where Jesus' appeal to his 'works' is directly linked with his Sonship relationship with God. It is at least possible that the evangelist himself combined the Father-Son motif with the works-as-evidence motif in the texts we have been studying, and the same procedure may well have been at work in the case of other motifs also.

c. Paraphrases
We have noted the distinctively Johannine phrase ἐν ἐμοὶ ὁ πατὴρ κἀγὼ ἐν τῷ πατρί in Jn. 10.38, and a very similar formulation in 14.11, and said that this seems to be 'simply another way of describing the uniquely deep and intimate relationship which Jesus claimed to have with God' (p. 239 above with n. 51). The total absence of this formulation from the Synoptic Gospels and from Jewish literature generally gives rise to the suspicion that the author is here expressing the reality to which the Synoptic tradition bears witness in his own way, that he is paraphrasing Jesus' claims after his own idiom, and if here, then perhaps elsewhere too.

d. Interpretations
Even to follow procedures a. - c. above inevitably involves an element of interpretation, since the author has to decide how to simplify and paraphrase, and what to conflate, and these decisions necessarily reveal the author's particular understanding of his material.

Particularly noticeable in this respect is the author's consuming interest in christology, and his endeavour to focus his material concerning the works of Christ explicitly on the person of Christ himself and his relationship with God. Likewise his putting of 5.36 in the context of 5.19-47 has the effect both of broadening out the meaning of the 'works' to cover the activities of life-giving and judging, and also of showing that Jesus' actual acivities in this regard justify his claim to have the right to give life and judge. The author's practice of synthesising and recontextualising motifs has the effect of shedding fresh light on them all.[121]

Yet despite the use of these freedoms, not only is the content of the sayings studied in this chapter remarkably faithful to what we can know of the historical Jesus, as has been argued at length above, but the vocabulary used may not be far removed from him either. It is worth noting that out of the vocabulary of 47 different words used in these sayings, only two of them are not found on the lips of Jesus in the Synoptic Gospels, the reflexive pronoun ἐμαυτοῦ and the verb λιθάζω, which is used in an incident the Synoptic Gospels do not record. The Johannine Jesus is not so totally removed from the Jesus of the Synoptic Gospels as has sometimes been suggested. Despite the different ways in which the different evangelists relate his teaching, in this area at least it is one and the same person who stands behind them all.

9.5 The Exegesis of the Texts in the Patristic Era

Jn. 5.36 is rarely quoted in the patristic era. Tertullian uses it, alongside many others, to confirm the distinction in person between the Father and the Son.[122] Athanasius uses it to help his argument that Prov. 8.22 refers to Christ's incarnation, not his origin.[123] Hilary uses it, possibly uniquely among the Fathers, to support his doctrine of the divine Sonship of Christ, whereby the Father and the Son share 'one inseparable nature'.[124] Chrysostom, by contrast, thinks that at most Jn. 5.36 proves the obedience of the Son to the Father.[125] Otherwise, however, the verse is barely mentioned in the patristic literature.

The same comment may be made about Jn. 10.25 and 32. Tertullian quotes both, and Novatian the latter, to show that the Son is other than the Father in their expositions of the Trinity,[126] and Theodoret and Pseudo-Athanasius take up the latter into their expositions of 10.32-38 as a

---

[121] A similar phenomenon occurs in the Synoptic Gospels as well, of course, though there the re-arrangements take place much more at the level of pericopae, whereas in the Fourth Gospel they appear to take place rather at the level of much smaller units.

[122] Tertullian, *Against Praxeas*, ch. 21.

[123] Athanasius, *Orations against the Arians*, 2.21.66.

[124] Hilary, *On the Trinity*, 6.27, 9.20.

[125] Chrysostom, *Homily 40 on John's Gospel*, sec. 3.

[126] Tertullian, *Against Praxeas*, ch. 22; Novatian, *Treatise concerning the Trinity*, ch. 15.

whole,[127] but otherwise these verses are not given much independent attention in the patristic period.

The case is quite different, however, with Jn. 10.37f. and 14.10f., where enormous attention is paid to the assertion that the works Jesus does bear witness to the fact that the Father is 'in' the Son and the Son 'in' the Father.[128] Occasionally the point is made that this expression demands the confession, as against all forms of modalism, that the Son is other than the Father,[129] and John Cassian sees the statement that the Father dwells in Jesus and does his works as an example of humility, and believes that it is spoken from the point of view of Christ's human nature,[130] but on the vast majority of occasions this affirmation of the mutual indwelling of the Father and the Son is woven into an exposition of the Godhead as evidence of the unity which is believed to exist in some form between the Father and the Son.

This use of the formula began even in the pre-Nicene period. Thus Tertullian uses it to affirm the eternal inseparability of the Father and the Son as against Valentinus' emanationism,[131] and Origen uses it to justify the worship of Christ since the Father and Son are 'one in unity of thought, in harmony and in identity of will'.[132] Similarly, Dionysius of Rome uses the statement that the Son is 'in' the Father to affirm his eternity,[133] and Alexander of Alexandria, at the beginning of the Arian crisis, quotes the formula of mutual indwelling, along with other verses, to oppose the Arian view that the Son is mutable.[134] But it is with Athanasius and other Nicene and post-Nicene Fathers that the formula became one of the most commonly quoted texts to support the doctrine of the true and full deity of Christ. For them the 'co-inherence' of Father and Son implies unambiguously their essential unity and therefore the Godhead of the only-begotten Son of God

---

[127] Theodoret, *Dialogues*; Pseudo-Athanasius, *Orations against the Arians*, 4.16 (this work is now commonly recognised to have been written by someone other than Athanasius himself).

[128] These passages will be treated together here for the sake of convenience, since it is often difficult to tell whether a writer has 10.37f. or 14.10f. in mind when he uses this formula. True, in 10.38 the Father is mentioned before the Son, whereas in 14.10f. the Son is mentioned before the Father, but sometimes a writer will quote material from the other passage in the same context in such a way as to indicate that he has conflated the two in his own mind and is quoting from memory.

[129] E.g. Tertullian, *Against Praxeas*, chs. 22 and 24; Cyril of Jerusalem, *Catechetical Lectures*, 11.16.

[130] John Cassian, *Institutes*, 12.8, 17.

[131] Tertullian, *Against Praxeas*, ch. 8.

[132] Origen, *Against Celsus*, ch. 12.

[133] Dionysius of Rome, *Against the Sabellians*, sec. 2.

[134] Alexander of Alexandria, *Catholic Epistle*.

with all that that means in terms of his eternity, omnipotence, unchangeability and so on.[135]

Sometimes alternative explanations of this formula of 'co-inherence' are recognised. Thus Eusebius of Caesarea interprets the formula in the light of Jn. 17.21f., where the same language is used about the disciples' relationship with the Father and the Son, and concludes that the formula depicts a oneness which does not go beyond that which even ordinary christians may possess.[136] Athanasius, Hilary, and Augustine, by contrast, seem to be aware of this possible interpretation, but reject it. Athanasius maintains that if Jesus had meant that he is in the Father and the Father in him as others are, he would have said 'I too am in the Father and the Father is in me *too*'.[137] Hilary says that Jn. 14.10 does *not* mean that 'the Father works in the Son through his own omnipotent energy', but rather 'through the Son's possession, as his birthright, of the divine nature'.[138] Augustine similarly, in commenting on this formula, distinguishes between what may be ours through grace, and what belongs eternally to the Son by right: 'the prerogative of the Lord is equality with the Father: the privilege of the servant is fellowship with the Saviour'.[139]

Little needs to be said about Jn. 15.24. Augustine is at pains to point out that though the 'works' are said to be Christ's in this verse, they are still the works of the Father and the Spirit also.[140] Chrysostom uses the verse to illustrate the fact that we cannot claim exemption from punishment on account of our office.[141] And both discuss the meaning of the uniqueness Christ claims for his works in this verse: Augustine thinks it means those which are otherwise unparalleled (e.g. walking on water, changing water

---

[135] Cf. e.g. Athanasius, *De Incarnatione*, 18.2-6; *De Decretis*, 5.21; *Orations against the Arians*, 2.15.12, 3.23, 3.25.16, 3.26.32, 3.27.37; Theodoret, *Dialogues*; *Letter to Monks of the Euphratensian, the Osrhoene, Syria, Phoenicia, and Cilicia*; *Eccles. Hist.*, 2.6; Gregory of Nyssa, *Against Eunomius*, 1.39, 2.4, 2.9, 4.8, 6.3, 8.5, 9.4, 10.4; Hilary, *On the Trinity*, 3.1ff., 3.23, 7.12, 7.26, 7.38-41, 8.4, 8.52, 9.52, 9.69f., 11.12; Cyril of Jerusalem, *Catechetical Lectures*, 11.16; Basil, *Letters*, 38.8; John of Damascus, *Exposition of the Orthodox Faith*, chs. 8, 18; Ambrose, *Of the Christian Faith*, 1.3.22, 1.3.25, 5.11.133; Leo the Great, *Sermons*, 51.6; Augustine, *The Harmony of the Gospels*, 1.4.7; *Sermon 2*, sec. 14; *Tractate 71 on John's Gospel*, sec. 2; *On Ps. 86*, sec. 20; *On Ps. 110*, sec. 8; Chrysostom, *Homily 3 on John's Gospel*, sec. 4; *Homily 40 on John's Gospel*, sec. 3; *Homily 61 on John's Gospel*, sec. 2f.; *Homily 64 on John's Gospel*, sec. 1; *Homily 74 on John's Gospel*, sec. 2.

[136] Eusebius, *De Eccl. Theol.*, 3.19.4 (cited by T.E. Pollard (1970) 295f.).

[137] Athanasius, *Orations against the Arians*, 3.23.3; cf. 3.25.23.

[138] Hilary, *On the Trinity*, 7.41.

[139] Augustine, *Tractate 48 on John's Gospel*, sec. 10.

[140] Augustine, *Sermons 21*, sec. 25f.

[141] Chrysostom, *On the Priesthood*, 4.1.

into wine, feeding a multitude, and opening the eyes of a man born blind) and reminds us that even miracles others performed were really performed by Christ working through them,[142] while Chrysostom refers to Mt. 9.33, Jn. 9.32 and the story of Lazarus, and says that Jesus' mode of wonder-working was 'new, and all beyond thought'.[143] Otherwise, however, references to this verse are hard to find.[144]

In summary, therefore, we find these verses being used in a variety of ways. As far as their christological use is concerned, we have found Jn. 5.36, 10.25, 32, 37f., and 14.10f. all being used to affirm the distinction between the Father and the Son, and the 'co-inherence' formula of Jn. 10.37 and 14.10f. being used to affirm their unity. Clearly, there were some in the patristic era, such as Eusebius, who regarded this unity to be nothing other than that which believers also may experience with the Father and the Son, but, for the majority, it denoted a unity of being, and as such could be used to support arguments for the deity of Christ and his membership of the Holy Trinity.

9.6 Conclusion

We may now draw some of the threads of this chapter together:

a. We have seen that while none of the sayings dealt with in this chapter can be shown to stand in a close relationship with Jesus' original words, they yet contain many basic motifs which can be traced back to him. To a very large extent, therefore, they can be shown to share in what we have called a type 'c' authenticity.

b. We have been reminded therefore in this study of some of the elements of Jesus' self-awareness: his filial consciousness; his sense of call to be his Father's agent in carrying out the specific task which he believed he had been given to do; his belief that he was actually carrying out his Father's plan through his Father's power and in obedience to his Father's will; his belief that his deeds indicated his special messianic role, such that those who failed to respond to their faith-evoking witness were especially guilty of sin; and so on. However the author of the Fourth Gospel may have shaped his material, he may be said faithfully to have represented these elements of the mental make-up of the historical Jesus.

---

[142] Augustine, *Tractate 91 on John's Gospel*, secs. 1, 3f.
[143] Chrysostom, *Homily 77 on John's Gospel*, ad.loc.
[144] There are no references to this verse in the indices of the Ante-Nicene Fathers or of either series of the Nicene and Post-Nicene Fathers outside the works of Augustine and Chrysostom.

c. As far as the Johannine redaction is concerned, we have tentatively suggested that the author has used certain freedoms in compiling his representation of Jesus' message. He seems to have felt free by paraphrase and summary to 'write up' Jesus' words in his own way, to combine motifs in new ways, and to draw out their meaning in certain directions. Particularly striking in this connection is his concentration on christology, and his broadening out of the concept of Jesus' 'works' to cover his works of preaching, life-giving and judging, indeed his ministry as a whole.

d. Finally, as we have just seen, in the patristic era these verses were mostly used for christological purposes. While most of them were used to affirm the distinction between the Father and the Son, the 'co-inherence' motif of Jn. 10.37f. and 14.10f. in particular was used for the most part, and especially in the Nicene and post-Nicene periods, to affirm their essential unity.

Chapter 10

General Conclusions

We have now completed our review of those passages in the Fourth Gospel in which Jesus is represented as speaking about his 'works', 'work' or his 'working', and it is time to draw together our conclusions from the book as a whole. They may conveniently be summed up under five headings:

10.1 The Possibility of Finding 'Authentic' Sayings of Jesus in the Fourth Gospel

On the basis of our discussion of the relevant issues in chapters 1 and 3, we may confidently affirm that *there is nothing in contemporary Johannine scholarship which need prevent us from finding 'authentic' material among the sayings attributed to Jesus in the Fourth Gospel.*

On the question of authorship, we saw that there is still no consensus as to who put the Gospel together and that it is still possible to argue that the evangelist was either an eyewitness of the ministry of Jesus, or else a close associate of such an eyewitness. On the question of the relationship of the Fourth Gospel with the Synoptic Gospels, we saw that the majority view was that the Fourth Evangelist was writing independently of the Synoptic Gospels, but that whether this is so or not, it is quite possible, even likely, that he was drawing on an independent tradition of the ministry of Jesus which could be at least as historically trustworthy as that contained in the Synoptic Gospels. On the question of the possible use of other sources, we saw that the evangelist may have drawn on a signs-source, but that even if he did it is no longer possible for us to determine its extent within the Gospel, and in any case its presence in the Gospel, if proven, does not necessarily rule out the possibility that what lies outside it may also contain historically trustworthy information about Jesus. On the question of the possible stages of development through which the Gospel may have passed, we saw that there is no consensus on this matter, and a great deal of speculation, and that even if a certain amount of development in the formation of the Gospel is accepted, it still has to be acknowledged that later additions to the Gospel may yet contain information which has an early origin, as even some of the development theorists themselves concede.

Turning now to issues specifically connected with the sayings of Jesus in the Fourth Gospel, we saw that his sayings cannot be dubbed 'inauthentic' in a wholesale way on the grounds that they reflect a non-Palestinian milieu. The Dead Sea Scrolls have done much to cast doubt on that position, along with the recent trend in scholarship which has appreciated more than was formerly the case that Palestine had been heavily permeated by Hellenism for some centuries before the coming of Christ. Nor can the sayings of Jesus in the Fourth Gospel be dubbed 'inauthentic' in a wholesale way on the grounds of their difference in style from the Synoptic sayings of Jesus, since, quite apart from the occasional verbal parallels which exist between the two, there are a number of sayings of Jesus in the Fourth Gospel which have a Synoptic 'stamp', and at least one notable instance of a saying of Jesus in the Synoptic Gospels which has a Johannine 'stamp' (Mt. 11.27 par.). Moreover, we cannot simply assume that Jesus spoke in one way all the time, and it may be that the Johannine tradition has captured more of his informal, discursive style of speaking, whereas the Synoptic has preserved more of his aphoristic style.

It is admitted that all these conclusions have a negative character in that they simply show that it is unjustified to rule out the possibility that some of the sayings attributed to Jesus in the Fourth Gospel in some way actually go back to him. They do not prove that they *do* go back to him, only that they *may*. But it was necessary to go over these issues in order to clear the way for the more positive assessment of some of the sayings attributed to Jesus in the Fourth Gospel which was carried out in the later part of the book.

10.2 The Nature of 'Authenticity'

Our second general conclusion is derived from the argument presented in chapter 2, and it is that *'authenticity' should be seen as a complex rather than as a simple phenomenon.*

The majority of New Testament scholars today treat the concept of 'authenticity' in a simplistic manner, as though sayings attributed to Jesus in the Gospels can be neatly compartmentalised into the categories of 'authentic' and 'inauthentic'. It was argued in chapter 2 that reality demands a more nuanced appreciation of the nature of the Gospel material before us, and that 'authenticity' should rather be seen as a *spectrum* of possibilities, ranging from a transcription of the very words the historical Jesus used in his own language, through a reasonably close translation of those words into Greek (on the assumption that he originally regularly spoke in Aramaic), to looser representations of his original speech, which may include summaries, paraphrases and interpretative clarifications, either singly or in combination. Even the three 'types' of 'authenticity' which were distinguished in that chapter are not to be seen as hard and fast distinctions, because they merge into one another, and the latter two contain within themselves a range of options, each bearing different degrees of closeness to the original words of Jesus.

All this was asserted at a theoretical level, and as such it holds good for the analysis of any body of literature which contains words purported to have been spoken by figures from the distant past, but further evidence that this way of approaching the words attributed to Jesus in the Fourth Gospel is potentially fruitful was gathered from the way in which the Gospel records Old Testament quotations. Here it was discovered that the author quotes the Old Testament in different ways on different occasions, sometimes exactly, sometimes with a fair degree of freedom, using the same kind of freedoms as those mentioned above. Moreover, it was suggested that this approach could be further developed by: using the same criteria for 'authenticity' which are used in the case of the Synoptic sayings of Jesus in order to identify sayings of Jesus in the Fourth Gospel which are not paralleled in the Synoptic Gospels and yet which may be said to stand in a reasonably close relationship with his original words; and by using the criterion of coherence (understood in the sense of identity of content with sayings which manifest a stricter type of 'authenticity') to identify sayings which may at least be said to represent his original words more loosely.

Having, therefore, established the possibility of finding 'authentic' material among the sayings of Jesus in the Fourth Gospel through our discussion of the introductory questions, and having armed ourselves with an adequate understanding of the nature of 'authenticity', we then felt able to approach one particular strand which makes up the tapestry of Jesus' Johannine sayings, or one theme of the Johannine 'fugue', namely the group of sayings in which he speaks about his 'works', 'work' or 'working', in order to discover what could be said about them as far as their authenticity was concerned, as well as to see how they were used in the Fourth Gospel and understood in the patristic era.

10.3 The Authenticity of the Works-Sayings of Jesus in the Fourth Gospel

This question was extensively discussed in chapters 4 to 9. Our general conclusions may now be summed up under three subheadings:

a. We have discovered that *to a very remarkable degree the works-sayings of Jesus can be shown to be 'authentic' at least in a loose sense of that term.*

This has been done by comparing the content of these sayings with the content of some sayings attributed to Jesus in the Synoptic Gospels which can be shown to stand in a close relationship with the original words of Jesus and which are normally regarded as possessing such a status by a majority of New Testament scholars today. The motifs which these Synoptic sayings have in common with the Johannine sayings we have been studying include the following:

- Jesus' consciousness of God as being his Father in a special sense, and of himself as being God's son in a special sense;

- Jesus' custom of speaking with absolute authority through the unparalleled use of the word 'Amen' at the beginning of statements he made;

- Jesus' belief that he had been 'sent' by God to perform a particular task, and his sense of destiny, urgency and strong desire in the carrying out of that task in the limited time available to him;

- Jesus' belief that he was actually in the process of carrying out that task in obedience to the will of God and in dependence on the power of God, such that what he was doing was at the same time what God was doing through him;

- Jesus' belief that he had the authority to overrule the scribal regulations concerning the observance of the sabbath;

- Jesus' belief that what he was doing was witnessing to who he was, such that those who saw him in action were at least expected to recognise his messianic role or else be held especially guilty of sin for failing to do so.

All these motifs can be shown, and have been shown in this book, to be motifs which underly *both* sayings which can confidently be attributed to the historical Jesus from the Synoptic Gospels *and also* the works-sayings attributed to Jesus in the Fourth Gospel. To this extent at least, by the application of the criterion of coherence (in the sense of identity of content), the works-sayings of the Fourth Gospel must share at least in the loose, type 'c', sense of authenticity as defined in chapter 2.

b. In addition we have found that *some of the works-sayings of Jesus in the Fourth Gospel bear the marks of sayings which stand in a close relationship with the original words of the historical Jesus.*

This has been shown at some length in the case of Jn. 9.4, 4.34, 5.17 and 5.19-20a. In each case, an application of the 'criteria of authenticity', as traditionally used with reference to Jesus' Synoptic sayings, has shown that these sayings also may well go back to him in roughly their present form. One of the arguments traditionally used against this position, namely that the ἔργον/ἐργάζομαι vocabulary is Johannine 'coinage', was answered in chapter 4, where it was argued that these words (or their Aramaic equivalents) are in fact the *most likely* words the historical Jesus would have used in making collective references to his activities. Of course, historical certainty is elusive in this matter, as it is for all the sayings material in all the Gospels, but at least we can say with confidence that the grounds for accepting the 'authenticity' of these Johahnnine sayings (in a strict, type b, sense) are *at least as good* as the grounds for accepting the authenticity (in a similarly strict sense) of many Synoptic sayings of Jesus whose 'authenticity' is normally accepted by a large number of contemporary New Testament scholars.

From a cumulative point of view, therefore, it highly probable on the basis of our study of these verses that the christologically significant use of a word for 'work' goes back to the historical Jesus himself, and, if so, it is likely that *all* the works-sayings of Jesus in the Fourth Gospel reflect this usage, however dimly, and not simply those which seem to share in a higher form of authenticity. In other words, just as in the case of expressions such as 'Truly, truly, I say to you', or 'him who sent me', or 'Father', the christologically significant use of a word for 'work' is likely to be *both* a usage which has a firm basis in the spoken ministry of the historical Jesus *and also* one which the author of the Fourth Gospel felt inclined to use liberally in his looser representations of Jesus' message.

Moreover, if we can regard these four sayings as 'authentic' in a strict sense, we learn, in addition to being reminded of motifs in the Synoptic Gospels some of which have been set out above, that for Jesus obedience to the divine will was as important and as necessary as food is to the body (4.34); that he regarded himself as acting, so to speak, 'in tandem' with God (5.17); and that he regarded himself as a kind of apprentice to God in doing the things which he saw God doing (5.19-20a).

c. The upshot of all this is, of course, that *in this area at least the author of the Fourth Gospel has presented us with a faithful and accurate portrait of the Jesus of history.*

As we have demonstrated in the detailed arguments of chapters 5 to 9, there is very little indeed in the sayings we have been studying, as far as content is concerned, which cannot be shown at least to 'cohere' (in the strict sense given) with sayings which may reliably be attributed to Jesus from the Synoptic Gospels, and this material is *either* insignificant, *or* contained in the Johannine works-sayings which are probably 'authentic' in a stricter sense, *or* (as in the case of the claim to work 'unique' works) possibly 'authentic' in some sense even if it cannot be shown to be such from the normal application of the criteria of authenticity.

In other words, the statements sometimes made by scholars to the effect that the sayings of Jesus in the Fourth Gospel are 'completely unhistorical', 'misleading' and 'deceptive', or that the author has presented us with a 'legendary figure' have been shown, *in this area at least*, to be considerably wide of the mark, and insensitive to the true character of the material, and if this so in this area, then it could well be so in other areas also. Especially if one accepts, as was argued in ch. 1, that the author had access to, or himself carried, traditions about Jesus which are not represented in the Synoptic Gospels, it would not be at all unreasonable to suppose in the light of the fresh evidence and argumentation which has been presented in this book that there may well be more 'authentic' material of various kinds in the Johannine sayings of Jesus than many scholars have previously imagined.

10.4 The Johannine Presentation of the Works-Sayings of Jesus

Special care is required in this area, since we have no sure knowledge as to the exact nature and extent of any sources the author of the Fourth Gospels may have used. If we could know for sure, for example, that he used the Synoptic Gospels, and only they, as sources for his work, then a lot could be said with confidence about his redactional creativity, but since there is no assurance that they were even among his sources, we cannot draw such firm conclusions. Similarly, if the author used a signs-source, we do not know how extensive it was nor whether it was his only source, so redaction critical work on the basis of a signs-source theory is precarious indeed. Moreover, the facts that the author probably had access to independent traditions about Jesus, and that the criteria of authenticity discussed above in chapter 2 cannot legitimately be used absolutely to rule out from the realm of authenticity sayings which cannot be positively identified as 'authentic' in a strict sense by their use, should warn us against assuming too readily that certain material in the Fourth Gospel is redactional rather than traditional.

Nevertheless, despite these justifiable caveats, it seems probable, as was suggested in chapter 3 and in our discussion of the farewell discourses in chapter 6, that the author has moulded whatever traditions were available to him in his own way and has composed the speeches he attributes to Jesus in the Gospel by weaving together sayings and motifs which may originally have had a separate origin. Again, at the level of the individual sayings, it was suggested in chapter 3 through the analogy of his use of Old Testament quotations, and in chapter 9 through our study of the group of sayings which speak of Jesus' works as indicators of his identity, that the author probably felt free on occasion to give loose representations of the original teaching of Jesus, by summarising it, paraphrasing it, conflating originally separate motifs, and generally giving it an interpretative slant by concentrating on its christological significance and filling traditional words with fresh content through a process of recontextualisation.

We saw possible examples of these processes at work in the sayings dealt with in chapter 9, but even in the case of the other sayings, which we had reason to believe stand in a closer relationship with the original words of Jesus, we concluded that the concept of the 'works' of Jesus seems to have taken on a broader significance from the one it may originally have had through the context in which the author has placed the sayings in which the word occurs. Thus, to mention some specific examples, a saying which may originally have referred only to the miracles of Jesus may have had its range of reference broadened by its being placed in a context which refers to the work of Jesus as light- or life-giver, or judge, or revealer or even as creator (cf. 9.4, 5.17, 19f., 36). Or a statement which originally spoke about Jesus as a doer of God's works in the sense of doing what God had commanded may have had its meaning broadened out in the Johannine context so as to take on the additional meaning of doing God's works by being the means by which God does them (cf. 9.4, 4.34). Or a parabolic or metaphorical saying about a son and a father may have had its ambiguities cleared up through its being placed in a discourse which speaks unambiguously about Jesus as the Son of the Father (5.19-20a). Or the statement that Jesus was 'sent' from God, which may originally have merely had the connotations of a prophetic role, in the Johannine context may be said to have taken on the extra connotation of pre-existence. In general, we may say that the author's explicit belief in the deity of Christ (cf. 1.1, 18, 20.28) has caused the sayings of Jesus to appear in a new light both for the author himself and through him for his readers.

In other words it is being tentatively suggested here that, at least as far as the passages we have studied in this book are concerned, *the author's redactional tendencies are comparable with those discernible in his handling of Old Testament quotations, and lie in the direction, not so much of creating material 'de novo', nor of radically changing the original teaching of Jesus into something quite different, but rather of concentrating on its christologically significant elements, placing originally separate motifs alongside one another in a mutually interpretative way, clarifying previously obscure or ambiguous elements in the tradition, and generally re-expressing traditional sayings and motifs after his own manner, though occasionally also preserving sayings in roughly their original form.*

10.5 The Patristic Development of the Johannine Presentation of the Works-Sayings of Jesus

The processes at work in the Johannine redaction may be seen to have been developed further in the patristic era. As we have seen from our study of the references to the works-sayings of Jesus in the patristic literature, while they are used sometimes to make the point that the Son is distinct from the Father, or to portray Jesus as an example to follow, in most cases *these verses are used, especially in the post-Nicene period, to set forth the doctrine that the Son and the Father share in the same nature and being.*

For the later Fathers at least, the assertion that the works of Jesus are the works of God is not simply true with reference his earthly ministry, in his work of healing, preaching, revealing, light- and life-giving, judging and so on, but is also true *for all time* and with respect to *every activity* in which the Father is engaged without exception, including, indeed especially, his cosmological roles of creating, preserving, and ruling the universe. In other words the sameness of the works of the Son and the Father is seen as an eternal fact, without any limitation of time or scope. Likewise the statement that the Son is 'in' the Father and the Father 'in' the Son, found in 10.38 and 14.10f., is taken to be not merely an assertion of an intimately close relationship between the Son and the Father enjoyed on earth, but also an assertion of their eternal 'co-inherence'. Thus the works-sayings of Jesus in the Fourth Gospel are explicitly connected with the doctrine of the deity of Christ, and the unity in action between the Father and the Son which they affirm is taken to be a sign of a unity of being.

All this represents a development from the Johannine presentation. In the Fourth Gospel, as we have seen, the 'works' of Jesus refer in the first place to the works of his earthly ministry and are limited in time and scope to the specific earthly 'work' which he had been given to do. It is true that the Gospel *also* speaks about Jesus as the pre-existent Word of God through whom the world was made (1.3), and creation motifs have been seen to hover in the background of the author's presentation of the stories of healing in Jn. 5 and 9, as we have seen in our exegesis of those passages. It is also true that the Gospel speaks about what Jesus *would do* in the future after his departure from his disciples, in answering their prayers (14.13f.), sending the Spirit (15.26), and so on. But, while the author may well have seen the works-sayings of Jesus in light of Jesus' pre- and post-existence activities, none of these activities is *explicitly* called a 'work' in the Gospel. It was left to the Fathers to make an *explicit* connection between the works-sayings of Jesus and the (equally Johannine) doctrine of his deity, and to broaden once again the scope of the 'works' of Jesus so as to embrace eternity and to refer not only to works of revelation and salvation, but also to works of creation, preservation and rule, indeed the full range of divine activities.

Thus we may trace a trajectory of understanding of Jesus as a doer of the works of God, stemming originally from Jesus himself, who saw himself as working 'in tandem' with God, doing God's work(s) by God's power, through the author of the Fourth Gospel, who took this motif and coloured it in his own way, to the Fathers of the early church who saw it as one way of expressing their belief in his deity in the fullest sense. At each stage in this development, as we have seen, the original motif was freshly understood in the light of convictions about Jesus which had origins outside the motif itself. To what extent these convictions also have an anchorage in the ministry of the historical Jesus it has not been part of the purpose of this book to explore.

Appendix A

U.C. Von Wahlde's Source Theory

U.C. von Wahlde's recent book *The Earliest Version of John's Gospel* (1989) differs from other works on Johannine source criticism in that, among other primary criteria, it counts the special use of ἔργα to refer to the miracles of Christ and of ἔργον to refer to the whole ministry of Christ as a primary criterion in determining the second as opposed to the first edition of the Fourth Gospel.[1]

Von Wahlde's proposed source contains the miracle stories, a passion narrative and several other dialogues and narratives. His basic criterion for discerning different layers in the Gospel is the presence of aporias, but the decision as to which layer belongs to which edition rests with 22 further criteria, mostly of a linguistic, ideological and theological kind, of which 3 linguistic criteria are regarded as 'primary': the use of the terms 'Pharisees', 'chief priests', and 'rulers' as opposed to 'the Jews' as terms for the religious authorities; the use of the term 'sign' as opposed to 'work' for miracles; and the use of the term 'Jews' to refer to Judaeans rather than to the religious authorities.[2] Passages which bear these marks are assigned to the first edition of the Gospel, while those which bear the alternative marks are assigned to the second edition. The passages so identified are then used as a basis for working out the subsidiary criteria.[3] The character of the proposed source is thus built up: it was a product of a Jewish christian community in Judaea c. 70-80 AD before the exclusion of christians from the synagogue, a missionary document with a relatively 'low' christology which progressively stressed the magnitude of Jesus' miracles, the increasing numbers of people who came to belief in Jesus as a result, and the increasing hostility against him on the part of the Jewish religious authorities. The source is not influenced by a θεῖος ἀνήρ concept, but

---

[1] U.C. von Wahlde (1989) 36-41, 182-186. W. Nicol (1972) 23 also counts the use of ἔργον and ἐργάζομαι for 'the Messianic works of Christ' as a mark of Johannine style rather than that of his postulated source. S. Temple (1961) 225f., (1975) 44-50, on the other hand, regards this terminology as a mark of the original 'core' of the Gospel. Neither, however, give it quite the same prominence as a criterion for separating out different strata in the Gospel.

[2] U.C. von Wahlde (1989) 30-43.

[3] Ibid. 43.

rather develops a Moses typology for Jesus, and does not polemicise against John the Baptist, but regards him simply as a herald for Jesus.[4]

Clearly von Wahlde's theory shares in some of the weaknesses of the source theories mentioned so far. There is no external evidence for his proposed source; the newness of his theory has the effect of broadening the range of options on offer, thus weakening still further whatever consensus there may have been in the area of source-critical methodology; the aporias he claims to detect are often susceptible of alternative explanations; and his claim to detect source material on the basis of content criticism takes insufficient account of the possibility that variety of expression and theological faceting may have been part of the evangelist's own style. In addition, von Wahlde's theory assumes that parts of the signs material he postulates are not represented in the Gospel, which gives him the liberty to assign small snippets of Gospel material to the source without the need to find a context for his excisions in the source, or even for the excisions to make complete sense as they stand.[5] Furthermore, there are serious weaknesses in the very foundations of his theory, in the application of his three 'primary' criteria, as we shall now see, and if the foundations are faulty, what hope is there for the superstructure?

On p. 41, speaking of the terms 'Pharisees'/ 'chief priests'/ 'rulers'/ 'signs' on the one hand and 'Jews' (in the sense of religious authorities)/ 'works'(in the sense of miracles) on the other, von Wahlde says: 'The correlation of these terms with one another is both consistent and exclusive throughout the gospel'. It is worth testing the validity of this proposition since it is so fundamental to von Wahlde's whole theory:[6]

a. First, it should be observed that, in order to maintain his case, von Wahlde has to distinguish not only between different meanings of the word 'Jews',[7] but also between different senses of the word σημεῖον and different uses of the word ἀρχιερεύς. Thus at 2.18 'the Jews' (meaning the

---

[4] Ibid. 156-175.

[5] E.g. 2.23, 3.1-2, 7.25-27, 31-32, 12.20-22, 18.28-29, 33-35 are assigned to the source, detached from their Johannine context. Von Wahlde believes that their original context is lost.

[6] We may leave out of account here the third primary linguistic criterion, namely the use of 'Jews' to mean 'Judaeans' in the signs material, partly because this meaning for the term in the Fourth Gospel is disputed, and partly because its appearance in the Gospel with this meaning attached to it by von Wahlde (at 3.25, 11.19, 31, 33, 36, 45, 54, 12.9, 11) is not sufficiently scattered to make it a significant criterion. Apart from 3.25 (where the word appears in the singular anyway) all the other references are connected with the Lazarus episode.

[7] The distinctions he draws between different senses of the word 'work' are not actually necessary for determining the source, since for him *all* uses of this word fall outside the signs material.

religious authorities) ask for a 'sign'. Von Wahlde can only maintain his case by saying that in this non-signs-material passage 'sign' is being used in a negative sense, whereas in the signs material it is used in a good sense.[8] The same explanation has to be given at 4.48 and 6.30 where Jesus is being asked to perform a 'sign'. 4.48 occurs in a signs-material passage and so is excised;[9] 6.30 occurs in a non-signs-material passage and so can remain.[10] More doubtful is the relegation of 6.26 to non-signs-material,[11] since here Jesus seems to be using the word in a good sense. If the author of the 'second edition' could have written this verse, could he not also have written verses in the 'first edition' which refer to signs in a positive sense? Likewise the word ἀρχιερεύς when used in the singular to refer to the High Priest as it does at 11.49, 51, 18.10, 13, 15 twice, 16, 19, 22, 24, and 26 occurs *both* in signs-material *and* in non-signs-material, so it is only the plural use of the word which counts as a mark of signs material according to von Wahlde. For him the use of ἀρχιερεύς in the singular does not determine a source, but its use in the plural does. These observations are not of themselves necessarily sufficient to overturn von Wahlde's theory, but they do make it more precarious.

b. Secondly, it needs to be observed that the correlation of which von Wahlde speaks can be illustrated only from a handful of passages, and that there are many passages in which these terms appear in isolation from each other. As far as the correlation between 'Pharisees'/ 'chief priests'/ 'rulers' and 'signs' is concerned, nowhere do they appear all together in close proximity; 'Pharisees' and 'signs' occur together at 3.1f. (which also has 'ruler' in the singular), 9.13-16 and 12.18f.; 'Pharisees', 'priests' and 'signs' occur together at 7.31f. and 11.46f.; and 'Pharisees', 'rulers' and 'signs' occur together at 12.37-43. Otherwise they appear many times apart. 'Pharisees', 'priests' and 'rulers' occur individually apart from 'signs' at 1.24, 4.1, 7.45 twice, 47, 48 twice, 8.13, 9.40, 11.57 twice, 12.10, 18.3 twice, 35, 19.6, 15, 21; and the term 'signs' appears apart from 'Pharisees', 'priests' and 'rulers' at 2.11, 23, 4.48, 54, 6.2, 14, 26, 10.41, 20.30.

As far as the correlation between 'the Jews' (referring to the religious authorities) and 'works' (referring to miracles) is concerned, only 5.10-20, 7.1-21, and 10.24-38 can be cited. Otherwise, the phrase 'the Jews' (referring to the religious authorities) occurs apart from the term 'works' (referring to miracles) at 2.18, 20, 6.41, 52, 7.35, 8.22, 31, 48, 52, 57, 9.18, 22, 10.19, 11.8, 13.33, 18.12, 14, 31, 36, 38, 19.7, 12, 14, 31, 38, 20.19; and the term 'works' (or 'work' in the singular, which von Wahlde also counts

---

[8] Ibid. 37.
[9] Ibid. 93, where other reasons are also given for the excision.
[10] Ibid. 37. Jn. 6.22-71 as a whole is omitted from the signs source, ibid. 190.
[11] Ibid. 102.

as a mark of the second edition of the Gospel) occurs apart from the phrase 'the Jews' at 4.34, 9.3f., 14.10, 11, 12, 15.24, 17.4.

In view of this evidence, the question arises as to whether the correlations of which von Wahlde speaks are fortuitous rather than indications of the existence of separate authors.

c. Thirdly, not only are the supposed correlations weakly supported, but there are also passages in which words from opposite pairs are found together:

In 1.19 we are told that 'the Jews sent priests and Levites from Jerusalem' to interrogate John the Baptist. To maintain his theory, von Wahlde has to say that the phrase 'the Jews' here does not refer to the religious authorities but to the Judaeans.[12] This can hardly be right in view of the fact 'the Jews' here evidently have priests and Levites in some sense at their command. If this single point is accepted then von Wahlde's basic proposition collapses instantly.

In 7.35 'the Jews' are mentioned in close connection with the 'chief priests and Pharisees' in 7.32. Von Wahlde's answer is to include 7.31-32 in the proposed signs source and to exclude 7.33-39, yet the only reasons for doing so (apart from the mention of 'the Jews' itself) are a supposed aporia at the beginning of v. 33, Jesus' 'supreme indifference and superiority to the plans of men', and the Jews' misunderstanding of Jesus' words in v. 35.[13] The aporia is surely only in the mind of the beholder. Jesus' attitude is not dissimilar to that he shows in ch. 18, in material which von Wahlde acknowledges as part of the signs source (18.1-3, 7, 8, 10, 11, 19-24), and misunderstandings are also not foreign to the signs source he proposes (e.g. 11.11-14). Von Wahlde cannot justifiably assign 7.32 and 7.35 to separate authors.

In 18.31 'the Jews' are mentioned in close connection with the 'chief priests' in 18.35. Von Wahlde's answer is to excise 18.30-32 from 18.28-35. The only reasons for doing so (apart from the mention of 'the Jews' itself) are an aporia created by v. 33 (the Jews had not charged Jesus with being the King of the Jews in 18.30ff., so perhaps an original part of the charge has been lost), and the theme of the fulfilment of Jesus' words which occurs in 18.32.[14] 18.32 may indeed be some kind of secondary addition, but this argument affects 18.32 alone and not 18.31. The aporia mentioned also definitely exists, but whether it warrants the supposition of two different authors for 18.30-31 and 18.33-35 may be doubted.

---

[12] Ibid. 67 and n. 2.
[13] Ibid. 105f.
[14] Ibid. 141.

In 18.36 and 18.38 'the Jews' are mentioned in close connection with the 'chief priests' in 18.35 again. Von Wahlde's answer is to excise 18.36-38 from 18.33-19.6a. His reasons for doing so (apart from the mention of 'the Jews' itself) are that the phrases 'of this world' (v. 36) and 'testify to the truth' (v. 37) do not in his view belong to the signs material; that Pilate's repeated declarations of Jesus' innocence in 18.38, 19.4 and 6 must be a sign of editing; and that Pilate's movements described in 18.29, 33, 38, 19.4, 9 and 13 are too complicated not to have been a result of editing (he 'goes out' twice in 18.38 and 19.4, without our being told of his going back in the intervening period).[15] That Pilate would have repeated his declarations of Jesus' innocence in his conversations with the religious authorities is entirely plausible both from a historical and from a dramatic point of view; his re-entry is probably implied in 19.1; and it is doubtful whether the two phrases mentioned are of sufficient weight to demonstrate a change of author.

In 19.7, 12 and 14 'the Jews' are mentioned in close connection with the 'chief priests' in 19.6 and 15. Once again, von Wahlde's answer is to excise 19.6b-12 and 19.14b-15a. His only reason for the excision of the first passage (apart from the mention of 'the Jews') is the use of the phrase 'Son of God' in 19.7.[16] Yet von Wahlde has no objection to having 1.49 and 20.31 in the signs material, both of which verses call Jesus 'Son of God'. As for 19.14b-15a, there is no reason given at all (apart from the mention of 'the Jews').[17] Von Wahlde simply speculates that the author of the second edition may have inserted this material to 'reaffirm the intensity of the religious authorities' desire to have Jesus crucified'.[18]

So one might go on. Von Wahlde is on slightly stronger ground when he maintains that in the Fourth Gospel the term 'works' is not associated with the terms 'Pharisees'/ 'chief priests'/ 'rulers', and the term 'signs' is not associated with the phrase 'the Jews' (though, as we have seen, the counter-instance of 2.18 has to be explained away), but his theory depends on the supposition that the different word groups as a whole are derived from different editions of the Gospel and we have adduced sufficient evidence to show that this supposition can scarcely be maintained without a considerable amount of special pleading.

The whole theory is therefore unsafe. It depends on some over-subtle distinctions between different meanings and usages, and on a correlation between groups of words which is supported only by a handful of passages and for which we have found several important exceptions. The application

---

[15] Ibid. 142.
[16] Ibid. 144f.
[17] Ibid. 146f.
[18] Ibid. 147 n. 161.

of the theory leads von Wahlde to excise from his proposed signs source material which is inconvenient for the theory, for whose excision there is little or no justification on other grounds, and little or no support from the other source theorists. Such a procedure, which can also be seen at work in his book elsewhere, hardly inspires confidence in the theory itself. The 'signs'/ 'works' terminology cannot be used with any confidence to separate out a first from a second edition of the Gospel.[19] It is much more likely, as is maintained in chapter 4 above, that the distribution of the words 'signs' and 'works' is as it is because the author preferred to use the former word for his own comments and the comments of others on the miracles of Jesus, and the latter word for Jesus' own speech in the Gospel, and that this is so because it reflects the historical situation of Jesus' ministry.[20]

---

[19] This last point can be reinforced by the following consideration. Von Wahlde argues that in a number of places the author of the second edition has suppressed parts of the signs source material in favour of his own (cf. 140f. and n. 149). But if he did so, why did he leave unchanged the conclusion of the signs source material in 20.30f., with its reference to the 'signs' which Jesus did, when, according to von Wahlde, he personally preferred to speak of Jesus' miracles as 'works' rather than as 'signs'? If he felt free to change the less important, why did he not feel free to change the more important?

[20] H.H. Wendt (1902) 58-66 came to this conclusion long ago, though he went on to argue that the terminology was a sign of a special discourse source, composed by John the apostle, which the Fourth Evangelist (considered as other than the apostle) used in compiling his Gospel.

Appendix B

Jesus' Claim to 'Do the Works of God' in John 10.37f.

1 Introduction

This appendix will examine in greater detail the possible meanings of the implicit claim attributed to Jesus in Jn. 10.37f. to be 'doing the works of God'. Though this claim comes to its clearest expression in this form in these verses, it has also been seen in various ways to underlie a number of other verses where Jesus speaks about his works, work or working (e.g. 4.34, 5.17, 19f., 9.3f.) and may justifiably be said to lie at the centre of what may be called the 'works-christology' of the Fourth Gospel. Our purpose here is to try to see this claim against its Jewish, New Testament and specifically Johannine background so that we may be able properly to understand its meaning.

It is important to state at this stage what will count as primary evidence in this appendix. There is understandably a very large number of general references to 'the works of God' in Jewish and christian literature - both in the sense of what God does (creating, providing, ruling, delivering, judging etc.) and in the sense of those things which God *has made* - and an even larger number of general references to the 'works' which human beings do or have made,[1] but both groups of references are only of tangential importance for our purposes. What will be of primary importance will be those references or passages where *human beings* are specifically called upon to do, or are said to do, the works of *God*, since only these provide a direct analogy to the phrase we are considering in this appendix.

A framework for this study has already been suggested in chapter 9 above (on pp. 236f.). In the light of the framework given there we may say that the phrase to 'do the works of God' may mean one or more of the following:

---

[1] For a helpful summary of the relevant material see G. Bertram's article in *TDNT* 2.635-650 and S. Pancaro (1975) 380-384. In the Fourth Gospel itself there are references to human works in 3.19-21, the works of the world in 7.7, the works of Abraham in 8.39, and the works of the devil in 8.41. In every case the people mentioned are the agents of the works done (though 8.39 and 41 have secondary meanings, as we shall see). In no case in the Fourth Gospel are the 'works of God' unconnected with what Jesus does.

a. to do the works which God commands;
b. to do the works which God does in imitation of him; and/or
c. to do the works which God does by being the means by which he does them.

We may illustrate the differences between these possible interpretations of this phrase by referring to the words of President Bush to the American troops who were sent to Somalia to facilitate the relief work going on there to feed the starving in December 1992, when he said that they were 'doing God's work'. What did he mean in saying these words? Did he mean that what they were doing was in accordance with God's will? Or that they were doing the kind of things God does (i.e. provide food for the hungry etc.)? Or that God was actually using them and enabling them, and so working through them, to accomplish his purposes in Somalia at this time? Or a combination of two or all of these possibilities? A similar problem of interpretation faces us as we seek to understand this phrase in Jn. 10.37f., and we must be prepared for the same possibility that the phrase may carry more than one meaning at the same time. Such ambiguity, if it is found to exist, would, of course, not be an isolated phenomenon in the Fourth Gospel.

With these introductory remarks, we may now proceed to look at the evidence.

2 Doing the Works which God Commands

There are a number of instances in which the phrase 'doing the works of God', or something similar, is found in Jewish, New Testament, and Johannine literature with the meaning of 'doing the works which God commands'. We may consider the chief examples:

2.1 Jewish Literature

In Num. 8.11 we find Aaron offering the Levites to the Lord that they might do his work:
MT   והיו לעבד את־עבדת יהוה
LXX   καὶ ἔσονται ὥστε ἐργάζεσθαι τὰ ἔργα κυρίου

If we look at the context, we find that Num. 3-8 is filled with the Lord's instructions to his people, largely concerning the duties of the priests and Levites and the requirements for the tabernacle in the desert. The Levites are repeatedly said to be called to do work in the 'tent of meeting' (e.g. 4.3, 23, 31, 33, 35, 39, 43, 47), twice said to be called to do the work of the 'tent of meeting' (4.30, 7.5, i.e. what is prescribed by the Lord for the tent of meeting) and once said to be called to do the work of the 'sons of Israel' (8.19, i.e. prescribed by the Lord for the sons of Israel). In the light of this context, it is most unlikely that Num. 8.11 means that the Levites are called to do what God himself does, and highly likely that it means rather that they are called to do what God requires of them.

The same usage is found in the Apocrypha and Pseudepigrapha. In 1 Esd. 7.9 the priests and Levites are said to have stood ἐπὶ τῶν ἔργων τοῦ κυρίου θεοῦ Ἰσραήλ, and in 7.15 the Lord is said to have strengthened his people ἐπὶ τὰ ἔργα κυρίου θεοῦ Ἰσραήλ. In both cases a cultic form of service is in view, as in Num. 8.11. In 1 Bar. 2.9 the ἔργα of the Lord are specifically described as ἃ ἐνετείλατο ἡμῖν. In 4 Esd. 7.24 the unrighteous are said to have failed to 'perform his [i.e. God's] works'. 2 Bar. 57.2 speaks of 'the works of the commandments'. In T.Levi 19.1, Levi's children are invited to choose between ἢ τὸ φῶς ἢ τὸ σκότος ἢ τὸν νόμον κυρίου ἢ τὰ ἔργα τοῦ βελιάρ, where the word 'works' stands in parallelism with the word 'law' (though there is textual uncertainty as to whether the word ἔργα is original here). In all these cases the word 'works' stands for that which has been commanded, and 'the works of the Lord' that which has been commanded by the Lord. A similar usage has been found at Qumran,[2] and in the rabbinic literature, where the word 'works' is often used interchangeably with the word 'commands'.[3]

2.2 The New Testament

Perhaps the clearest example of this usage in the New Testament outside the Fourth Gospel itself is in Rev. 2.26 where the 'conqueror' is described as ὁ τηρῶν ἄχρι τέλους τὰ ἔργα μου. The 'works' of Jesus must here be what Jesus requires. Any other sense would not fit in with the word 'keep'. Some commentators would add 1 Cor. 15.58 here,[4] but this verse is perhaps best kept for section 4, as we shall see.

---

[2] At CD 1.1, 2.14f. Cf. R. Bergmeier (1967) 254f., S. Pancaro (1975) 384, U.C. von Wahlde (1980) 310.

[3] E. Lohmeyer (1929) 183, S. Pancaro (1975) 382, U.C. von Wahlde (1980) 310, S.-B. 3.160ff.

[4] E.g. J.H. Bernard (1928) 1.192, R. Bultmann (ET 1971) 222 n. 4.

2.3 The Fourth Gospel

Virtually all scholars are agreed that the phrase τὰ ἔργα τοῦ θεοῦ in Jn. 6.28 and the phrase τὸ ἔργον τοῦ θεοῦ in 6.29 refer to that which God requires.[5] Apparently the crowd misunderstand Jesus' use of the word ἐργάζεσθε in v. 27 and think he is demanding some kind of moral effort on their part in order to win the 'food which endures to eternal life'. The author may be representing them as thinking here specifically of the works of the law, as most scholars believe,[6] or in a more general sense of the will of God, as U.C. von Wahlde has argued.[7] Either way, the discussion is about what God wants the crowd to do in order to gain eternal life, and the answer Jesus gives is that only one thing is necessary,[8] namely faith in the one whom God has sent.

2.4 Conclusion

In conclusion, then, we may say that, in the light of Jewish, New Testament and Johannine usage, it is quite possible that when Jesus claims to be 'doing the works of God' in Jn. 10.37f. at least part of what he means is that he is doing what God is requiring of him, or what God is commanding him to do. This, at least, is the natural understanding of the similar expressions in 4.34

---

[5] So B.F. Westcott (1908) 1.225, J.H. Bernard (1928) 1.192, E.C. Hoskyns (1940) 1.330, R.E. Brown (1966) 1.262, R. Bergmeier (1967) 253-260, L. Morris (1971) 360, R. Bultmann (ET 1971) 222 n. 4, J. Riedl (1973) 317-339, S. Pancaro (1975) 390-393, C.K. Barrett (1978²) 287, U.C. von Wahlde (1980) 304-315, and G.R. Beasley-Murray (1987) 91. J. Riedl (1973) 337-339 argues that the phrase τὸ ἔργον τοῦ θεοῦ in 6.29 *also* means that which God does, but the parallelism between the two phrases in 6.28 and 6.29 is too strong to make this likely. Nevertheless, as R. Bergmeier (1967) 253-260 argues, the author's predestinarian teaching implies that the 'work' of faith *is* a gift from God, even if that thought is not necessarily included in 6.29. Similarly, B.F. Westcott (1908) 1.225, E.C. Hoskyns (1940) 1.330, C.K. Barrett (1978²) 287, D.A. Carson (1991) 285.

[6] So H. Odeberg (ET 1968) 256, L. Morris (1971) 360, S. Pancaro (1975) 391, E. Haenchen (1980) 320, G.R. Beasley-Murray (1987) 91.

[7] U.C. von Wahlde (1980) 304-315. The difference between these two views cannot have been great for a first century Jew. The view that ἔργα in 6.28 refers to miracles, held by R. Heiligenthal (1983) 139 and J. Painter (1991) 230, is most improbable. There is no suggestion elsewhere in the Gospel of the 'crowd' seeking the ability to work miracles.

[8] It is difficult not to see significance in the fact that ἔργον is singular in 6.29 in contrast with the plural ἔργα in 6.28. So B.F. Westcott (1908) 1.225, E.C. Hoskyns (1940) 1.330, R. Bultmann (ET 1971) 222, S. Pancaro (1975) 392, and R. Schnackenburg (ET 1980) 2.31, as against R. Bergmeier (1967) 259 and U.C. von Wahlde (1980) 314, who see it as a mere stylistic variation.

and 9.4, as was argued in chapters 6 and 5 respectively above. In 4.34 the phrase 'accomplishing the work' of God stands in parallel with 'doing the will of God' and carries a similar meaning,9 and in 9.4 'doing the work' of God is seen as an obligation to be fulfilled.10

3 Doing the Works which God Does in Imitation of Him

3.1 Jewish Literature

There are no clear instances of this usage in the Old Testament or in the intertestamental literature, though Jer. 48.10, which will be considered in the next section, may be said to imply it, and though the *idea* of imitating God (as of imitating other great men of the past), is present in this literature, even if not in the *wording* which interests us here.11

However, there are some relevant examples in the rabbinic literature, as can be seen from S.-B. 2.524. *A.Z.* 10b quotes Obad. 18: 'there shall be no survivor to the house of Esau', and continues by saying that this applies to 'he who does the work of Esau' (מעשה עשו). *Ex.R.* 3 (69d) comments on Ex. 4.3, where the Lord changes Moses' rod into a serpent, and says that this was done to transmit a message to the unbelieving Israelites mentioned in Ex. 4.1 that they had 'done the work of the serpent' (מעשה נחש). *S.Nu.* 5.15.8 (4a) speaks of the deed of an adulterous woman as being like the deed of a beast (מעשה בהמה), and *p.Bik.* 3.65d.22 speaks of the 'works of Abraham' (מעשיו של אברהם), which were reckoned by *Aboth* 5.19 to be 'a benevolent eye, a modest mind, and a humble spirit'. In all these cases the 'works' of the people mentioned mean what they did, or their general character, and for others to 'do the work' of Esau or the serpent or a beast or Abraham means to be like them in character, or to do the kind of things they did or do. There is no thought here of the work(s) being commanded by the persons or animals in question.

---

9 See pp. 149f. above. True, the parallelism is synthetic rather than synonymous, but at least there is a parallelism present. A deeper meaning in the total Johannine context is, however, not impossible, as was noted on pp. 153f.

10 See p. 123 above, though again a deeper meaning is evident if Jn. 9.4 is joined together with 9.3b rather than being regarded as an independent saying. See p. 125.

11 Cf. R. Heiligenthal (1983) 78-84.

3.2 The New Testament

There is an interesting example of the usage we are considering in this section in 2 Tim. 4.5, where the author (traditionally held to be Paul) exhorts Timothy with the words: ἔργον ποίησον εὐαγγελιστοῦ. Clearly there is no evangelist to whom Timothy is required to go for instructions. Rather the writer is exhorting Timothy to behave like an evangelist, or to do the work characteristic of an evangelist. He is to do the work an evangelist does, in imitation of him.

3.3 The Fourth Gospel

Within the Fourth Gospel itself, we have a clear example of this usage in 8.39, where Jesus is represented as saying to some Jews who were seeking to kill him (v. 37, 40): εἰ τέκνα τοῦ Ἀβραάμ ἐστε, τὰ ἔργα τοῦ Ἀβραὰμ ἐποιεῖτε.[12] It is not clear precisely what 'works of Abraham' are in mind here, whether they are his faith,[13] or his good behaviour and obedience to God,[14] or, more specifically, his willingness to receive messengers from God,[15] or his joy at 'seeing' Jesus' 'day' (8.56),[16] or a combination of these, but, whatever they are, Jesus is clearly rebuking these Jews for failing to live up to their Abrahamic descent by 'doing the works' which Abraham did. In other words, if they were truly descendants of Abraham in every sense, they would be behaving as Abraham did, they would follow his example, they would imitate him. There is no thought here of Abraham issuing instructions to them, or working through them in any way, but simply of them doing the kind of things he did.

This idea is also present in 8.41 where Jesus tells the same Jews: ὑμεῖς ποιεῖτε τὰ ἔργα τοῦ πατρὸς ὑμῶν. The 'father' in question turns out in v. 44 to be the devil. The fact that the devil is there described as a murderer

---

[12] This is the Nestle-Aland text, the 26th ed. Though ποιεῖτε is well attested, and supported (as an imperative) by J.H. Bernard (1928) 2.310 and C.H. Dodd (1963) 331, ἐποιεῖτε (expressing an unfulfilled condition) is to be preferred as the *lectio difficilior* following ἐστε (which is much better attested than the alternative reading ἦτε), and as fitting better the words νῦν δέ which follow at the beginning of v. 40. So E.C. Hoskyns (1940) 2.392, R.E. Brown (1966) 1.357, L. Morris (1971) 461, R. Bultmann (ET 1971) 442 n. 4, B. Lindars (1972) 327, G.R. Beasley-Murray (1987) 126.

[13] Cf. Gen. 15.1-6 and R. Bultmann (ET 1971) 442 n. 6, J. Riedl (1973) 401, S. Pancaro (1975) 396, J. Becker (1979) 1.304, R. Schnackenburg (ET 1980) 2.211.

[14] Cf. Gen. 22.15-18, 26.5 and C.H. Dodd (1957) 12f., D.A. Carson (1991) 352.

[15] Cf. Gen. 18.1-8 and J.H. Bernard (1928) 2.311, E.C. Hoskyns (1940) 2.392, R.E. Brown (1966) 1.357.

[16] Cf. J. Becker (1979) 1.304.

and a liar[17] confirms the impression that Jesus in v. 41 is saying that the Jews are doing the same things that the devil is doing, that they are imitating him, since they are seeking to kill Jesus (v. 37, 40) and refuse to believe one who is speaking the truth (v. 45f.). However, there may be more to the expression in 8.41 than this, since the Jews are also said in v. 44 to want to do the devil's wishes, and to be 'of' (ἐκ) the devil, which may imply that they are actually the devil's agents.[18] In other words the expression in v. 41 may be said to embrace all the three senses which we are distinguishing in this appendix.

3.4 Conclusion

We have seen, then, in all the three types of literature represented here, grounds for believing that when Jesus is said to 'do the works of God' in Jn. 10.37f., at least part of what is meant is that he is behaving like God, or imitating God, or doing the things which are characteristic of God. This is corroborated still further by 5.19f., where, as we saw in chapter 8, Jesus likens himself to an apprenticed son who watches carefully all that his father is doing and then does the same himself. Even though the actual phrase 'doing the works of God' is absent from those verses, the thought of doing what God does in imitation of him is certainly present.

4 Doing the Works which God Does by Being the Means by which He Does Them

This sense of the phrase 'doing the works of God' transcends and embraces the two senses already considered. Here the thought is not only that of doing what God commands, nor simply of doing the kind of things he does, but of actually being assisted and used by him in carrying out his own work in the world.

---

[17] The early chapters of Genesis are probably in mind here, with the story of the fall and death of Adam and Eve through the devil's deceit in ch. 3 and the murder of Abel in ch. 4.

[18] Cf. B.F. Westcott (1908) 2.21: they are the devil's 'voluntary organs'; E.C. Hoskyns (1940) 2.394: they are the devil's 'willing agents'; H. Odeberg (ET 1968) 303: Satan's will 'has been infused into them'; B. Lindars (1972) 328: they are 'under the control' of Satan; J. Riedl (1973) 405: the devil is the 'treibende Kraft' in the background, and they are his 'Werkzeuge'.

4.1 Jewish Literature

We deferred our consideration of Jer. 48.10 to this section, though a number of commentators see it as simply an example of the first usage given above.[19] It runs as follows:

MT ארור עשה מלאכת יהוה רמיה

LXX (31.10) ἐπικατάρατος ὁ ποιῶν τὰ ἔργα του κυρίου ἀμελῶς

The important point to note is the context. Jer. 48 is about the Lord's judgment on Moab, yet it is a judgment wrought through the hands of men and v. 10 pronounces a curse on the one who fails fully to align himself with the purposes of God in this regard. In other words 'doing the work of the Lord' in this context is not simply a matter of obedience to his command but of being his agent, a tool in his hand, so to speak, such that the Lord acts in and through human beings. This is confirmed by Jer. 50.25 when the same Hebrew word (מלאכה) is used to describe the Lord's own activity of judgment in the land of the Chaldeans.

The actual phrase 'doing the work(s) of God (or the Lord)' is not found elsewhere in Jewish literature with this meaning clearly attached, but, as E. Lohmeyer has shown,[20] the *idea* is prevalent throughout this body of literature, especially with regard to doing good works. Commenting on Ps. 89(90).17, Ps.Sol. 6.3 and 16.9, for example, he says: 'So ist jedes "Wirken", soll es gültig sein, gleichsam zweifachen Ursprunges: Gott wirkt es, und der Mensch muss es wirken oder wirkt es gleichfalls',[21] or, as S. Pancaro has put it: 'The good works of men ... are worked by God and by man at one and the same time'.[22]

4.2 The New Testament

There is a striking parallel to the Johannine language we have been considering in 1 Cor. 16.10, where Paul[23] writes of Timothy: τὸ γὰρ ἔργον κυρίου ἐργάζεται ὡς κἀγώ. Similarly in 1 Cor. 15.58 he exhorts the

---

[19] So J.H. Bernard (1928) 1.192, R. Bergmeier (1967) 254, R. Bultmann (ET 1971) 222 n. 4, U.C. von Wahlde (1980) 308.

[20] E. Lohmeyer (1929) 183f., 188-192.

[21] Ibid. 184.

[22] S. Pancaro (1975) 399. Isa. 26.12 (כי גם כל־מעשינו פעלת לנו) would provide further evidence for this view except that there is textual uncertainty over the words גם כל.

[23] In this section Paul will be named as the author of the Pauline letters without prejudice to the question of their true authorship.

Corinthians to be always περισσεύοντες ἐν τῷ ἔργῳ τοῦ κυρίου. These expressions may be said to share in the ambiguity of the Johannine ones, yet there are certain other verses in the Pauline corpus which may incline us to the view that Paul is here speaking of the work the Lord himself was doing *through* Timothy and the Corinthians. Paul is quite fond of using the compound verbs κατεργάζομαι and ἐνεργῶ, and his use of them well illustrates the concept we are considering in this section. Thus he speaks in Rom. 15.18 of what Christ has 'wrought through' him (κατειργάσατο Χριστὸς δι' ἐμοῦ) to win obedience from the Gentiles; in Col. 1.29 he speaks of 'striving with all the energy which he [God] mightily inspires' within him (κατὰ τὴν ἐνέργειαν αὐτοῦ τὴν ἐνεργουμένην ἐν ἐμοί); in Gal. 2.8 he speaks of God 'working through' (ἐνεργήσας) Peter in the mission to the Jews and 'working through' (ἐνήργησεν) himself in the mission to the Gentiles; in Phil. 2.12f. he tells the Philippians to 'work out' (κατεργάζεσθε) their own salvation, since God is 'at work' in them (ὁ ἐνεργῶν ἐν ὑμῖν) to will and to work (τὸ ἐνεργεῖν) for his good pleasure; in Gal. 3.5 and 1 Cor. 12.6, 11 he speaks of miracles and spiritual gifts respectively as taking place in the church in consequence of the 'working' (ἐνεργῶ is used in all three cases) of God, or the Holy Spirit; and finally, in the letter to the Ephesians, we find the verb ἐνεργῶ being used to describe God's work in the raising of Jesus from the dead (1.20), in the lives of believers (3.20), and in all that he decides to do (1.11). In short, Paul had a strong conception of dual agency in the lives of christians, including his own. He thought of christians as the arena and channel of God's own work, such that what they did was also what God did through them by his power. As Paul himself puts it in one of his more striking sayings: ἐκοπίασα, οὐκ ἐγὼ δὲ ἀλλὰ ἡ χάρις τοῦ θεοῦ ἡ σὺν ἐμοί (1 Cor. 15.10). In this sense also, he 'did the work of the Lord'. He was the means by which the Lord did his own work.

4.3 The Fourth Gospel

There are three passages within the Fourth Gospel which give the impression that for the author part of what is meant by the phrase 'doing the works of God' is doing what God does by being the means by which God does it.

The first is 3.21, where we find the curious and possibly unparalleled expression τὰ ἔργα ... ἐν θεῷ ... εἰργασμένα. It is not absolutely clear who is the subject of 3.21. The view of F. Grob, that it is Jesus,[24] is

---

[24] F. Grob (1986) 23-29.

ingenious but unlikely. The close parallelism with v. 20, and the fact that there the 'light' almost certainly stands for Jesus, makes it highly likely that the 'light' in v. 21 also stands for Jesus, in which case the one who comes to the light must be other than him. Otherwise, we may see here a reference to the christian believer who keeps on coming to the light,[25] or to one who is coming to the light for the first time,[26] or both.[27] Of these options the second seems to be the most natural in the context, since v. 19 speaks of the historical coming of Jesus into the world and of the reaction of the majority of people to him when they encountered him. Jn. 3.20f. generalises the different types of reaction, but a first-time encounter still seems to be in mind.

The more important question is what exactly is meant by the phrase τὰ ἔργα ... ἐν θεῷ ... εἰργασμένα. The problem is once again (as we found when discussing 10.38) the ambiguity of the preposition ἐν. It could imply that the 'works' have been done in fellowship with God,[28] or by the action of God.[29] But it clearly means more than simply that the 'works' are done in accordance with God's will, and appears to suggest that God is at work in the lives of people even before they come to Christ, so that they are ready to come to the light of Christ when they first hear of him.

The second passage is 14.12-14, where Jesus is represented as speaking of the 'greater works' which his disciples would do after his departure. One initial question concerns the reason why the works which the disciples will do are described as 'greater' than the works Jesus has done. The view that greater miracles are meant is usually rejected by commentators, who either favour the view that a greater number of conversions is meant (on account of the coming of the Spirit, and the greater geographical spread and temporal duration of the church),[30] or the view that a greater number of blessings is meant (on account of the coming of the Spirit who will apply the benefits of Christ's death and resurrection, give greater clarity of

---

[25] Cf. J. Riedl (1973) 395.

[26] Cf. B. Lindars (1972) 161.

[27] Cf. J.H. Bernard (1928) 1.123, R. Heiligenthal (1983) 228-230.

[28] Cf. B.F. Westcott (1908) 1.124, R. Bultmann (ET 1971) 157 n. 6.

[29] The view of M. Goguel (1947) 491, cited by R. Bultmann (ET 1971) 157 n. 6. Cf. J. Riedl (1973) 380: 'Die guten Werke der Menschen sind also nicht nur von den Menschen getragen, sondern auch in irgender Form von Gott (mit)gewirkt'; and F. Grob (1986) 29: 'Dieu est le sujet réel qui opère l'oeuvre'.

[30] Broadly the position of B.F. Westcott (1908) 2.174, J.H. Bernard (1928) 2.543, E.C. Hoskyns (1940) 2.538, L. Morris (1971) 646, B. Lindars (1972) 475, and C.K. Barrett (1978[2]) 460.

understanding concerning the meaning of the words of Jesus etc.).[31] It is not impossible, however, that 14.12 is a Johannine version of the saying of Jesus preserved in Mt. 21.21, which *does* (at least superficially) refer to the working of a greater miracle (casting a mountain into the sea) than one that Jesus has just worked (causing a fig tree to wither), and that the author has given it a fresh meaning by placing it in a fresh context (a procedure which we have seen at work in other places).[32]

However that may be, the important point to note is that in the author's conception the disciples will do the works of Jesus not simply by obeying him or imitating his example but by being the means by which Jesus himself will do them. This thought is present in 14.13f.,[33] where *Jesus* is said to do the things which they will ask of him in his name as they go about their mission. We may compare also 15.5, where it is said that the disciples will not be able to do anything apart from Jesus, and 10.16 where Jesus says that *he* will bring in other sheep from another fold - referring, surely, to the missionary task which the disciples would carry out. This thought is also implicit in 14.12 itself where Jesus gives the fact of his return to the Father as the reason why the disciples would do 'greater works'. His return to the Father, according to 16.7, is the prelude to the coming of the Spirit, who, as Jesus' *alter ego* and agent (14.16f., 26, 15.26f., 16.7-15) would give the disciples the necessary power for their ministry (20.21-23). We see then in this passage another example of the use of 'works' terminology to express the concept we have been examining in this section.

The third passage is 14.10f. itself, of which a full exegesis was given in chapter 9 and which therefore needs no further treatment here. This time it is Jesus himself who is involved, and in whom the Father lives and 'does his works'. Here is the clearest indication of all that when Jesus is said to do the works of God in 10.37f., what is meant is that he is one through whom God himself works and does what he chooses to do.

4.4 Conclusion

We have seen, then, that the idea of God actively using people as the means by which he does his own work and accomplishes his purposes is present in

---

[31] Broadly the position of R.E. Brown (1966) 2.633, R. Bultmann (ET 1971) 610, J. Riedl (1973) 287-289, G.R. Beasley-Murray (1987) 255, W. Loader (1989) 56, 60, 127, 209, 212, and D.A. Carson (1991) 496.

[32] R.E. Brown (1966) 2.633 notes the similarity between Mt. 21.21 and Jn. 14.12 but makes nothing of it.

[33] Which may run on from v. 12 without a break. The semi-colon in the Nestle-Aland text at the end of 14.12 may not, of course, have been in the original manuscript.

all the types of literature we have been surveying in this appendix. Moreover, we have seen that the terminology of 'doing the works of God' as the means of expressing this idea may be used in Jer. 48.10 and 1 Cor. 16.10, though in both cases there was an element of doubt. Nevertheless, the Johannine material we have considered strongly suggests that this terminology carries this meaning in 10.37f.

5 General Conclusions

Our survey of the Jewish, New Testament and Johannine backgrounds to the phrase 'doing the works of God' has revealed that it can mean any or all of the ideas mentioned in section 1 above and that in 10.37f. it probably means all. This conclusion is confirmed by the context of 10.37f. itself, which comes at the very climax of Jesus' public ministry in Jerusalem prior to passion week itself, and by the fact that this phrase is associated with an expression of the intimately close relationship between the Father and the Son in v. 38 ('the Father is in me and I am in the Father'). We would expect the phrase 'doing the works of God', therefore, to carry its fullest possible christological meaning, i.e. not simply that Jesus was obedient to the Father's commands, nor simply that he imitated his Father's example, but also that the Father himself was acting in and through him to do his own works, such that the actions of Jesus and the actions of the Father were the same.

Just how full this christological meaning might be, however, has yet to be fully spelt out. It was mentioned in section 1 above that the phrase the 'works of God' is one which occurs very frequently in Jewish and christian literature, and is used at least in part to refer to God's very wide-ranging activities such as those of creating, providing, ruling, delivering, judging and so on. In view of this background, it is easy to see how the idea of Jesus doing the works of God (which, as has been argued in chapters 4-9, probably goes back ultimately to Jesus himself) might have come to be understood to refer not simply to Jesus' acts of healing the sick, forgiving sinners, preaching good news etc., but to the full range of divine activities without exception, and moreover understood to refer not simply to those activities exercised during a short life on earth but also to those same activities exercised throughout eternity. If so, it is not difficult to see why the author should have wanted to weave this motif into the christological structure of his Gospel and make it serve his presentation of Jesus as the divine Son of God. Perhaps he was given the perception to see that a claim Jesus made was susceptible of a christological understanding of infinite height, and that Jesus' activities on earth were not incidental to his being, but were the external evidence of a total and eternal unity with God.

Bibliography

Abbott, E.A., *Johannine Vocabulary*, 1905, London, A. and C. Black.
Abbott-Smith, G., *A Manual Greek Lexicon of the New Testament*, 1936³, Edinburgh, T. & T. Clark.
Abrahams, I., *Studies in Pharisaism and the Gospels*, 1917, CUP.
Albrecht, E., *Zeugnis durch Wort und Verhalten. Untersucht an ausgewählten Texten des Neuen Testaments*, 1977, Basel, F. Reinhardt.
Allison, D.C., 'Two Notes on a Key Text Mt. 11.25-30' in *JTS*, 39, 1988, 477-485.
Anderson, H., *The Gospel of Mark*, 1976, London, Oliphants.
Appold, M.L., *The Oneness Motif in the Fourth Gospel*, 1976, Tübingen, J.C.B. Mohr.
Ashton, J., *Understanding the Fourth Gospel*, 1991, Oxford, Clarendon.
Bacchiochi, S., 'John 5.17: Negation or Clarification of the Sabbath?' in *Andrews University Seminary Studies*, 19.1, 1981, 3-19.
Banks, R., *Jesus and the Law in the Synoptic Tradition*, 1975, CUP.
Barbour, R.S., *Traditio-Historical Criticism of the Gospels*, 1972, London, SPCK.
Barclay, W., *The Gospel of John*, 1956, Edinburgh.
Barr, J., 'Abba Isn't "Daddy"' in *JTS*, n.s. 39, 1988, 28-47.
Barr, J., '"Abba, Father" and the Familiarity of Jesus' Speech' in *Theology*, 91, 1988, 173-179.
Barrett, C.K., 'The Old Testament in the Fourth Gospel' in *JTS*, 48, 1947, 155-169.
Barrett, C.K., Review of W. Wilkens' *Die Entstehungsgeschichte des vierten Evangeliums* in *TLZ*, 84, 1959, 828f.
Barrett, C.K., Review of R.T. Fortna's *The Gospel of Signs* in *JTS*, n.s. 22, 1971, 571-574.
Barrett, C.K., '"The Father is Greater than I" (Jn. 14.28). Subordinationist Christology in the New Testament' in J. Gnilka, ed., *Neues Testament und Kirche*, 1974, Freiburg, Basel, Wien, Herder, 144-159.
Barrett, C.K., *The Gospel According to St. John*, 1955, 1978², London, SPCK.
Bauckham, R., 'The Sonship of the Historical Jesus in Christology', 1978, *SJT*, 31, 245-260.
Beare, F.W., *The Gospel According to Matthew. A Commentary*, 1981, Oxford, Blackwell.
Beasley-Murray, G.R., *John*, 1987, Waco, Texas, Word Books.
Becker, J., 'Wunder und Christologie' in *NTS*, 16, 1969-70, 130-148.
Becker, J., *Das Evangelium nach Johannes*, Kapitel 1-10, 1979, Kapitel 11-21, 1981, Würzburg, Gütersloher Verlaghaus, Gerd Mohn.
Bergmeier, R., 'Glaube als Werk? Die "Werke Gottes" in Damaskusschrift 2.14-15 und Johannes 6.28-29' in *Revue de Qumran*, 6, 1967, 253-260.

Bernard, J., 'La guérison de Bethesda un jour de sabbat. Harmoniques judéo-hellénistiques d'un récit de miracle un jour de sabbat' in *MSR*, 34, 1977, 13-44.
Bernard, J., 'Témoinage pour Jésus-Christ: Jean 5.31-47' in *MSR*, 36, 1979, 3-55.
Bernard, J.H., *A Critical and Exegetical Commentary on the Gospel According to St.John*, 2 vols., 1928, Edinburgh, T. & T. Clark.
Best, E., 'Mark 3.20, 21, 31-35' in *NTS*, 22, 1976, 309-319.
Black, M., *An Aramaic Approach to the Gospels and Acts*, 1946, 1967[3], Oxford, Clarendon.
Bligh, J., 'Jesus in Samaria' in *HJ*, 3, 1962, 329-346.
Bligh, J., 'Jesus in Jerusalem' in *HJ*, 4, 1963, 115-134.
Bligh, J., 'Four Studies in St. John, 1: The Man Born Blind' in *HJ*, 7, 1966, 129-144.
Blinzler, J., *Johannes und die Synoptiker. Ein Forschungsbericht*, 1965, Stuttgart, Verlag Katholisches Bibelwerk.
Blomberg, C.L., *The Historical Reliability of the Gospels*, 1987, Leicester and Downers Grove, Illinois, IVP.
Blomberg, C.L., *Interpreting the Parables*, 1990, Leicester, Apollos.
Boismard, M.- É., and Lamouille, A., edd., *L'Évangile de Jean. Synopse des quatre Évangiles en Français*, vol. 3, 1977, Paris, Éditions de Cerf.
Borg, M., *Conflict, Holiness, and Politics in the Teachings of Jesus*, 1984, New York, E. Mellen.
Borgen, P., 'John and the Synoptics in the Passion Narrative' in *NTS*, 5, 1959, 246-259.
Borgen, P., *Bread from Heaven: An Exegetical Study of the Concept of Manna in the Gospel of John and the Writings of Philo*, 1965, Leiden, E.J. Brill, Nov. Test. Suppl. vol. 10.
Borgen, P., *Logos Was the True Light and Other Essays on the Gospel of John*, 1983, Trondheim, Tapir Publishers.
Bornkamm, G., *Jesus of Nazareth*, ET 1973, London, Sydney, Auckland and Toronto, Hodder and Stoughton.
Bostock, D.G., 'Jesus as the New Elisha' in *Exp.T.*, 92, 1980-1, 39-41.
Bovon, F., *Das Evangelium nach Lukas. 1 Teilband Lk. 1.1-9.50*, 1989, Zürich, Benziger Verlag & Neukirchener Verlag.
Brederek, E., 'Konkordanz zum Targum Onkelos' in *Beihefte zur Zeitschrift für die alttestamentliche Wissenschaft*, vol. 9, 1906, Giessen, A. Töpelmann.
Bridges, L.M., 'Gems of Illumination. Jesus' Aphorisms in the Gospel of John' in *Westar Magazine*, 1, 1987, 10-13.
Brown, C., *Miracles and the Critical Mind*, 1984, Grand Rapids, Eerdmans, and Exeter, Paternoster.
Brown, F., Driver, S.R., and Briggs, C.A., *A Hebrew and English Lexicon of the Old Testament*, 1974[9], Oxford, Clarendon Press.
Brown, R.E., *The Gospel According to John*, 1966, Garden City, New York, Doubleday and Co. Inc.
Brown, R.E., Review of M.- É. Boismard and A. Lamouille's *L'Évangile de Jean. Synopse des Quatre Évangiles en Français* in *CBQ*, 40, 1978, 624-628.
Brown, R.E., *The Community of the Beloved Disciple. The Life, Loves, and Hates of an Individual Church in New Testament Times*, 1979, London, G. Chapman.
Brown, R.E., *The Epistles of John*, 1982, London, G. Chapman.

Brown, R.E., Review of W.J. Bittner's *Jesu Zeichen im Johannesevangelium* in *CBQ*, 51, 1989, 147f.
Bruce, F.F., *The Gospel of John*, 1983, Grand Rapids, Michigan, Eerdmans.
Bultmann, R., *Jesus and the Word*, ET 1935, London, Ivor Nicholson and Watson.
Bultmann, R., *The History of the Synoptic Tradition*, ET 1968^2, Oxford, Blackwell.
Bultmann, R., *The Gospel of John. A Commentary*, ET 1971, Oxford, Blackwell.
Burge, G.M., *Interpreting the Fourth Gospel*, 1992, Grand Rapids, Baker Book House.
Burney, C.F., *The Aramaic Origin of the Fourth Gospel*, 1922, Oxford, Clarendon.
Burney, C.F., *The Poetry of Our Lord*, 1925, Oxford, Clarendon.
Caird, G.B., *Saint Luke*, 1963, Middlesex, Penguin.
Calvert, D.G.A., 'An Examination of the Criteria for Distinguishing the Authentic Words of Jesus' in *NTS*, 18, 1971-2, 209-219.
Calvin, J., *The Gospel According to St. John*, chs. 1-10, ET 1959, Edinburgh and London, Oliver and Boyd.
Carson, D.A., 'Current Source Criticism of the Fourth Gospel: Some Methodological Questions' in *JBL*, 97, 1978, 411-429.
Carson, D.A., 'Historical Tradition in the Fourth Gospel: After Dodd, What?' in R.T. France and D. Wenham, edd., *Gospel Perspectives. Studies of History and Tradition in the Four Gospels*, vol. 2, 1981, Sheffield, JSOT Press.
Carson, D.A., 'Understanding Misunderstandings in the Fourth Gospel' in *TB*, 33, 1982, 59-91.
Carson, D.A., 'Historical Tradition in the Fourth Gospel: A Response to J.S. King' in *JSNT*, 23, 1985, 73-81.
Carson, D.A., 'John and the Johannine Epistles' in D.A. Carson and H.G.M. Williamson, edd., *It is Written: Scripture Citing Scripture. Essays in Honour of Barnabas Lindars, SSF*, 1988, CUP, 245-264.
Carson, D.A., *The Gospel According to John*, 1991, Leicester, IVP.
Carrington, P., *According to Mark. A Running Commentary on the Oldest Gospel*, 1960, CUP.
Casey, P.M., *From Jewish Prophet to Gentile God. The Origins and Development of New Testament Christology*, 1991, Cambridge, James Clark and Co.
Catchpole, D., 'Tradition History' in I.H.Marshall, ed., *New Testament Interpretation*, 1977, Exeter, Paternoster, 165-180.
Cerfaux, L., 'Les miracles, signes messianiques de Jésus et oeuvres de Dieu selon l'Évangile de Jean' in *RechBib*, vol.1, 1958, 131-138.
Cerfaux, L., *Jésus aux Origines de la Tradition*, 1968, Paris, Desclee de Brouwer.
Charlesworth, J.H., ed., *John and Qumran*, 1972, London, G. Chapman.
Charlesworth, J.H., *Jesus within Judaism. New Light from Exciting Archaeological Discoveries*, 1989, London, SPCK.
Christ, F., *Jesus Sophia. Die Sophia-Christologie bei den Synoptikern*, 1970, Zürich, Zwingli-Verlag.
Collins, R.F., 'Proverbial Sayings in St. John's Gospel' in *Melita Theologica*, 37, 1986, 42-58.
Conzelmann, H., *The Theology of St. Luke*, ET 1960, London, Faber and Faber.
Cranfield, C.E.B., *The Gospel According to Mark*, 1959, CUP.
Creed, J.M., *The Gospel According to St.Luke*, 1950, London, Macmillan.
Crossan, J.D., 'Mark and the Relatives of Jesus' in *NT*, 15, 1973, 81-113.

Cullmann, O., 'Sabbat und Sonntag nach dem Johannesevangelium (Joh. 5.17)', 1951, in K. Fröhlich, ed., *Oscar Cullmann Vorträge und Aufsätze 1925-1962*, 1966, Tübingen, J.C.B. Mohr.
Cullmann, O., *The Christology of the New Testament*, ET 1959, London, SCM.
Cullmann, O., *Salvation in History*, ET 1967, London, SCM.
Cullmann, O., *The Johannine Circle*, ET 1976, London, SCM.
Culpepper, R.A., *Anatomy of the Fourth Gospel: A Study in Literary Design*, 1983, Philadelphia, Fortress Press.
Dalman, G., *The Words of Jesus*, ET 1902, Edinburgh, T.& T. Clark.
Dalman, G., *Grammatik des Jüdisch-Palästinischen Aramäisch und Aramäische Dialektproben*, 1960, Darmstadt, Wissenschaftliche Buchgesellschaft.
Davey, J.E., *The Jesus of St. John. Historical and Christological Studies in the Fourth Gospel*, 1958, London, Lutterworth Press.
Davies, W.D., and Allison, D.C., *A Critical and Exegetical Commentary on the Gospel According to St. Matthew*, vol.2, 1991, Edinburgh, T. & T. Clark.
Delling, G., *Wort und Werk Jesu im Johannes-Evangelium*, 1966, Berlin, Evangelische Verlaganstalt.
Dewey, K.E., 'Paroimiai in the Gospel of John' in *Semeia*, 17, 1980, 81-99.
Dibelius, M., *From Tradition to Gospel*, ET 1971, Cambridge and London, James Clarke and Co. Ltd.
Dodd, C.H., *The Parables of the Kingdom*, 1935, London, Nisbet.
Dodd, C.H., *According to the Scriptures. The Sub-Structure of New Testament Theology*, 1952, London, Nisbet.
Dodd, C.H., *The Interpretation of the Fourth Gospel*, 1953, CUP.
Dodd, C.H., 'Note on John 21.24' in *JTS*, n.s. 4, 1953, 212f.
Dodd, C.H., 'À l'arrière-plan d'un dialogue Johannique' in *RHPR*, 37, 1957, 5-17.
Dodd, C.H., 'Une parabole cachée dans le quatrieme Évangile' in *RHPR*, 42, 1962, 107-115, reprinted in English as 'A Hidden Parable in the Fourth Gospel' in C.H.Dodd, *More New Testament Studies*, 1968, Manchester University Press, 30-40.
Dodd, C.H., *Historical Tradition in the Fourth Gospel*, 1963, CUP.
Dodd, C.H., 'The Portrait of Jesus in John and in the Synoptics' in W.R. Farmer, C.F.D. Moule, R.R. Niebuhr, edd., *Christian History and Interpretation: Studies Presented to John Knox*, 1967, CUP, pp. 183-198.
Downing, F.G., *The Church and Jesus*, 1968, London, SCM.
Drummond, J., *An Inquiry into the Character and Authorship of the Fourth Gospel*, 1903, London, Williams and Norgate.
Dunn, J.D.G., *Jesus and the Spirit. A Study of the Religious and Charismatic Experience of Jesus and the First Christians as Reflected in the New Testament*, 1975, London, SCM.
Dunn, J.D.G., 'Mt. 12.28/ Lk. 11.20 - A Word of Jesus?' in W.H. Gloer, ed., *Eschatology and the New Testament*, 1988, Peabody, Massachusetts, Hendrickson Pub., ch. 3, 29-49.
Dunn, J.D.G., *Christology in the Making. An Inquiry into the Origins of the Doctrine of the Incarnation*, 1989[2], London, SCM.
Dunstone, A.S., 'Ipsissima Verba Christi' in F.L. Cross, ed., *Studia Evangelica*, vol. 2, 1964, Berlin, Akademie-Verlag, 57-64.
Ellis, E., *The Gospel of Luke*, 1966, London etc., Nelson.

Evans, C.F., *Saint Luke*, 1990, London, SCM.
Filson, F.V., 'Who was the Beloved Disciple?' in *JBL*, 68, 1949, 83-88.
Fitzmyer, J.A., 'Methodology in the Study of the Aramaic Substratum of Jesus' Sayings in the New Testament' in J. Dupont, ed., *Jésus aux origines de la christologie*, 1975, Leuven, at the University Press, 73-102.
Fitzmyer, J.A., *The Gospel According to Luke*, chs.1-9, 1981, chs. 10-24, 1985, New York etc., Doubleday.
Fletcher, B., *The Aramaic Sayings of Jesus*, 1967, London, Hodder and Stoughton.
Fortna, R.T., *The Gospel of Signs. A Reconstruction of the Narrative Source Underlying the Fourth Gospel*, 1970, CUP.
Fortna, R.T., *The Fourth Gospel and its Predecessor*, 1988, Edinburgh, T. & T. Clark.
France, R.T., *Jesus and the Old Testament*, 1971, London, Tyndale Press.
France, R.T., 'The Authenticity of the Sayings of Jesus' in C. Brown, ed., *History, Criticism and Faith*, 1976, Leicester, IVP.
Freed, E.D., *Old Testament Quotations in the Gospel of John*, 1965, Leiden, E.J. Brill.
Friend, H.S., 'Like Father, Like Son. A Discussion of the Concept of Agency in Halakah and John' in *Ashland Theological Journal*, 21, 1990, 18-28.
Fuller, R.H., *A Critical Introduction to the New Testament*, 1966, London, Duckworth.
Funk, R.W., Scott, B.B., and Butts, J.R., *The Parables of Jesus. Red Letter Edition. A Report of the Jesus Seminar*, 1988, Sonoma, California, Polebridge Press.
Gaechter, P., 'Zur Form von Joh. 5.19-30' in J. Blinzler, O. Kuss, F. Mussner, edd., *Neutestamentliche Aufsätze*, 1963, Regensburg, Verlag Friedrich Pustet.
Gardner-Smith, P., *Saint John and the Synoptics*, 1938, CUP.
Garrison, R., *Mt. 11.25-27 = Lk. 10.21f. A Bridge between the Synoptic and Johannine Traditions*, 1979, Oxford, unpublished D.Phil. thesis.
Gerhardsson, B., *The Origins of the Gospel Traditions*, 1979, London, SCM.
Giblet, J.,'Le témoinage du Père' in *Bible et Vie Chrétienne*, vol. 12, 1955, 49-59.
Giblet, J., 'La sainte Trinité selon l'Évangile de saint Jean' in *Lumière et Vie*, 29, 1956, 95-126.
Giblet, J., 'Et il y eut la dedicace. Jean 10.22-39' in *Bible et Vie Chrétienne*, vol. 66, 1965, 17-25.
Gnilka, J., *Das Evangelium nach Markus. 1 Teilband. Mk. 1-8.26*, 1978, Zürich, Benziger Verlag.
Goguel, M., *L'Église Primitive*, 1947, Paris, Payot.
Goodwin, C., 'How Did John Treat His Sources?' in *JBL*, 73, 1954, 61-75.
Gordon, C.H., '"In" of Predication or Equivalence' in *JBL*, 100, 1981, 612f.
Grant, F.C., 'The Authenticity of Jesus' Sayings' in W. Eltester, ed., *Neutestamentliche Studien für Rudolf Bultmann*, 1954, Berlin, Topelmann.
Greig, J.C.G., 'Abba and Amen. Their Relevance to Christology' in F.L. Cross, ed., *Studia Evangelica*, vol. 5, part 2, 1968, Berlin, Akademie-Verlag.
Grigsby, B., 'Washing in the Pool of Siloam - A Thematic Anticipation of the Johannine Cross' in *NT*, 27.3, 1985, 227-235.
Grob, F., *Faire l'Oeuvre de Dieu. Christologie et Éthique dans L'Évangile de Jean*, 1986, Paris, Presses Universitaires de France.
Gruenler, R.G., *New Approaches to Jesus and the Gospels*, 1982, Grand Rapids, Baker.
Grundmann, W., 'Mt. 11.27 und die johanneischen "Der Vater - Der Sohn" - Stellen' in *NTS*, 12, 1965-6, 42-49.

Gryglewicz, F., 'Die Aussagen Jesu und ihre Rolle in Joh. 5.16-30' in *Studien N.T. Umwelt*, 5, 1980, 5-17.
Guelich, R.A., *Mark 1-8.26*, 1989, Dallas, Word Books.
Guilding, A., *The Fourth Gospel and Jewish Worship. A Study of the Relation of John's Gospel to the Ancient Jewish Lectionary System*, 1960, Oxford, Clarendon.
Gunther, J.J., 'Early Identifications of Authorship of the Johannine Writings' in *JEH*, 31, 1980, 407-427.
Gunther, J.J., 'The Relation of the Beloved Disciple to the Twelve' in *TZ*, 37, 1981, 127-148.
Guthrie, D., *New Testament Introduction: The Gospels and Acts*, 1965, London, Tyndale Press.
Haenchen, E., 'Johanneische Probleme' in *ZTK*, 56, 1959, 19-54.
Haenchen, E., 'Der Vater, der mich Gesandt hat' in *NTS*, 9, 1962-3, 208-216.
Haenchen, E., *Johannes Evangelium. Ein Kommentar*, 1980, Tübingen, J.C.B. Mohr.
Hahn, F., 'Methodologische Überlegungen zur Rückfrage nach Jesus' in K. Kertelge, *Rückfrage nach Jesu*, 1974, Freiburg, Herder, 11-77.
Hanson, A.T., *The Living Utterances of God. The New Testament Exegesis of the Old*, 1983, London, Darton, Longman and Todd Ltd.
Hanson, A.T., *The Prophetic Gospel. A Study of John and the Old Testament*, 1991, Edinburgh, T. & T.Clark.
Harrison, E.F., 'The Discourses of the Fourth Gospel' in *Bibliotheca Sacra*, 117, 1960, 23-31.
Harvey, A.E., *Jesus and the Constraints of History*, 1982, London, Duckworth.
Harvey, A.E., 'Christ as Agent' in L.D. Hurst and N.T. Wright, edd., *The Glory of Christ in the New Testament. Studies in Christology*, 1987, Oxford, Clarendon, 239-250.
Hatch, E., Redpath, H.A., et al., *A Concordance to the Septuagint and the Other Greek Versions of the Old Testament (including the Apocryphal Books)*, 1897, Oxford, Clarendon.
Headlam, A.C., *The Fourth Gospel as History*, 1948, Oxford, Blackwell.
Heiligenthal, R., *Werke als Zeichen. Untersuchungen zur Bedeutung der menschlichen Taten im Frühjudentum, Neuen Testament und Frühchristentum*, 1983, Tübingen, J.C.B. Mohr.
Hengel, M., *Judaism and Hellenism. Studies in their Encounter in Palestine during the Early Hellenistic Period*, ET 1974, London, SCM.
Hengel, M., *The Son of God*, 1976, London, SCM.
Hengel, M., *The Charismatic Leader and His Followers*, ET 1981, Edinburgh, T. & T. Clark.
Hengel, M., *Studies in the Gospel of Mark*, 1985, London, SCM.
Hengel, M., *The Johannine Question*, 1989, London, SCM.
Hengel, M., *The 'Hellenization' of Judaea in the First Century after Christ*, ET 1989, London, SCM.
Hengel, M., 'The Old Testament in the Fourth Gospel' in *Horizons in Biblical Theology*, 12, 1990, 19-41.
Higgins, A.J.B., *The Historicity of the Fourth Gospel*, 1960, London, Lutterworth Press.
Higgins, A.J.B., 'The Words of Jesus According to St. John' in *BJRL*, 49, 1966-7, 363-386.
Hill, D., *The Gospel of Matthew*, 1972, London, Marshall, Morgan, and Scott.

Hooker, M., 'Christology and Methodology' in *NTS*, 17, 1971, 480-487.
Hooker, M.D., 'On Using the Wrong Tool' in *Theology*, 75, 1972, 570-581.
Hooker, M.D., *A Commentary on the Gospel According to St. Mark*, 1991, London, A. and C. Black.
Hoskyns, E.C., *The Fourth Gospel*, 2 vols., 1940, London, Faber and Faber.
Howard, W.F., *The Fourth Gospel in Recent Criticism*, 1955[4], London, Epworth.
Hultgren, A.J., 'The Formation of the Sabbath Pericope in Mark 2.23-28' in *JBL*, 91, 1972, 38-43.
Hunter, A.M., 'Crux Criticorum - Mt. 11.25-30 - a Re-Appraisal' in *NTS*, 8, 1961-2, 241-249.
Hunter, A.M., *According to John*, 1968, London, SCM.
Jastrow, M., *A Dictionary of the Targumim, the Talmud Babli and Yerushalmi, and the Midrashic Literature*, 1903, London, Luzac and Co.
Jeremias, J., *The Parables of Jesus*, ET 1954, London, SCM.
Jeremias, J., *Abba. Studien zur Neutestamentlichen Theologie und Zeitgeschichte*, 1966, Göttingen, Vandenhoeck & Ruprecht.
Jeremias, J., *The Prayers of Jesus*, ET 1967, London, SCM.
Jeremias, J., *New Testament Theology*, ET 1971, London, SCM.
Jeremias, J., 'Die Drei-Tage-Worte der Evangelien' in G. Jeremias, H.-W. Kuhn, and H. Stegemann, edd., *Tradition und Glaube. Das frühe Christentum in seiner Umwelt*, 1971, Göttingen, Vandenhoeck & Ruprecht, 221-229.
Jeremias, J., 'Zum nicht-responsischen Amen' in *ZNW*, 64, 1973, 122f.
Jeremias, J., *Die Sprache des Lukasevangeliums. Redaktion und Tradition im Nicht-Markusstoff des dritten Evangeliums*, 1980, Göttingen, Vandenhoeck & Ruprecht.
Johnson, L., 'Who Was the Beloved Disciple?' in *Exp.T.*, 77, 1965-6, 157f.
Johnson, L., 'The Beloved Disciple - A Reply' in *Exp.T.*, 77, 1965-6, 380.
Jonge, M. de, 'Signs and Works in the Fourth Gospel' in T. Baarda, A.F.J. Klijn and W.C. van Unnik, edd., *Miscellanea Neotestamentica*, 1978, Leiden, E.J. Brill.
Jülicher, A., *Die Gleichnisreden Jesu*, 1899, Freiburg, Mohr.
Käsemann, E., *Essays on New Testament Themes*, ET 1964, London, SCM.
Käsemann, E., *The Testament of Jesus*, ET 1968, London, SCM.
King, J.S., 'Has D.A. Carson been Fair to C.H. Dodd?' in *JSNT*, 17, 1983, 97-102.
Knox, J., *Criticism and Faith*, 1953, London, Hodder and Stoughton.
Knox, J., *The Church and the Reality of Christ*, 1962, New York and Evanston, Harper and Row.
Kragerud, A., *Der Lieblingsjünger im Johannesevangelium*, 1959, Oslo, Osloer Universitätsverlag.
Kümmel, W.G., *Promise and Fulfilment. The Eschatological Message of Jesus*, ET 1957, London, SCM.
Kümmel, W.G., *The Theology of the New Testament*, ET 1974, London, SCM.
Kümmel, W.G., *Introduction to the New Testament*, ET 1975, London, SCM.
Kysar, R., 'The Source Analysis of the Fourth Gospel. A Growing Consensus?' in *NT*, 15, 1973, 134-152.
Kysar, R., Review of H.M. Teeple's *The Literary Origin of the Gospel of John* in *JBL*, 93, 1974, 308-312.
Kysar, R., *The Fourth Evangelist and His Gospel: An Examination of Contemporary Scholarship*, 1975, Minneapolis, Augsburg Publishing House.

Kysar, R., 'The Fourth Gospel. A Report on Recent Research' in W. Haase, ed., *Aufstieg und Niedergang der Romischen Welt*, 2.25.3, 1985, 2389-2480, Berlin and New York, Walter de Gruyter.
Kysar, R., *John*, 1986, Minneapolis, Augsburg Publishing House.
Ladd, G.E., *A Theology of the New Tesatament*, 1974, Grand Rapids, Eerdmans.
Lambrecht, J., 'The Relatives of Jesus in Mark' in *NT*, 16, 1974, 241-258.
Lane, W.L., *The Gospel According to Mark*, 1974, London, Marshall, Morgan and Scott.
Latourelle, R., *Finding Jesus through the Gospels*, 1978, New York, Alba House.
Leaney, A.R.C., *A Commentary on the Gospel According to St. Luke*, 1958, London, Adam and Charles Black.
Lee, E.K., 'The Historicity of the Fourth Gospel' in *CQR*, 167, 1966, 292-302.
Leivestad, R., *Jesus in his own Perspective. An Examination of his Sayings, Actions, and Eschatological Titles*, ET 1987, Minneapolis, Augsburg Publishing House.
Lemcio, E.E., 'External Evidence for the Structure and Function of Mk. 4.1-20, 7.14-23, and 8.14-21' in *JTS*, n.s. 29, 1978, 323-338.
Lenski, R.C.H., *The Interpretation of St. John's Gospel*, 1943, Minneapolis, Augsburg Publishing House.
Levy, J., *Neuhebraisches und Chaldaisches Wörterbuch über die Talmudim und Midrashim*, vol.1, 1876, Leipzig, F.A. Brockhaus.
Liddell, H.G., and Scott, R., *A Greek-English Lexicon*, 1940^9, Oxford, Clarendon.
Lightfoot, J.B., *Biblical Essays*, 1893, London, Macmillan and Co.
Lightfoot, R.H., *St. John's Gospel. A Commentary*, 1956, Oxford, Clarendon.
Lindars, B., *New Testament Apologetic. The Doctrinal Significance of Old Testament Quotations*, 1961, London, SCM.
Lindars, B., *Behind the Fourth Gospel*, 1971, London, SPCK.
Lindars, B., *The Gospel of John*, 1972, London, Oliphants.
Lindars, B., 'Traditions behind the Fourth Gospel' in M. de Jonge, ed., *L'Évangile de Jean. Sources, Rédaction, Théologie*, 1977, Leuven, at the University Press.
Lindars, B., 'The Persecution of Christians in Jn. 15.18-16.4a' in W. Horbury and B. McNeil, edd., *Suffering and Martyrdom in the New Testament*, 1981, CUP.
Lindars, B., 'Discourse and Tradition: the Use of the Sayings of Jesus in the Discourses of the Fourth Gospel' in *JSNT*, 13, 1981, 83-101.
Lindars, B., *John*, 1990, Sheffield, JSOT Press.
Loader, W., *The Christology of the Fourth Gospel: Structure and Issues*, 1989, Frankfurt am Main, Berne, New York, Paris, Verlag Peter Lang.
Lohmeyer, E., 'Probleme Paulinische Theologie. 2. "Gesetzeswerke"' in *ZNW*, 28, 1929, 177-207.
Lohse, E., 'Jesu Worte über den Sabbat' in E. Lohse, *Die Einheit des Neuen Testaments*, 1973, Göttingen, Vandenhoeck & Ruprecht, 62-72.
Longenecker, R.N., 'Literary Criteria in Life of Jesus Research: An Evaluation and Proposal' in G.F. Hawthorne, ed., *Current Issues in Biblical and Patristic Interpretation*, 1975, Grand Rapids, Eerdmans.
Malatesta, E., *Interiority and Covenant*, 1978, Rome, Biblical Institute Press.
Manson, T.W., *The Sayings of Jesus*, 1949, London, SCM.
Manson, W., *The Gospel of Luke*, 1930, London, Hodder and Stoughton.
Marsh, J., *Saint John*, 1968, London, SCM.
Marshall, I.H., 'The Divine Sonship of Jesus' in *Interpretation*, 21, 1967, 87-103.
Marshall, I.H., 'The Problem of New Testament Exegesis' in *JETS*, 1974, 17.2, 67-73.

Marshall, I.H., *The Origins of New Testament Christology*, 1976, Leicester, IVP.
Marshall, I.H., *I Believe in the Historical Jesus*, 1977, London, Sydney, Auckland, and Toronto, Hodder and Stoughton.
Marshall, I.H., *The Gospel of Luke. A Commentary on the Greek Text*, 1978, Exeter, Paternoster Press.
Marshall, I.H., *Jesus the Saviour. Studies in New Testament Theology*, 1990, London, SPCK.
Marshall, J.T., *Manual of the Aramaic Language of the Palestinian Talmud, Grammar, Vocalised Text, Translation, and Vocabulary*, 1929, Leiden, E.J. Brill.
Martin, R.A., *Syntax Criticism of Johannine Literature, the Catholic and the Gospel Passion Accounts*, 1989, Lewiston, Lampeter, Queenstown, E. Mellen.
Martin, R.P., *New Testament Foundations. A Guide for Christian Students. vol.1, the Four Gospels*, 1975, Exeter, Paternoster.
Martyn, J.L., *History and Theology in the Fourth Gospel*, 1968, 1979², Nashville, Abingdon.
Maurer, C., 'Steckt hinter Joh.5.17 ein Übersetzungsfehler?' in *Wort und Dienst*, 5, 1957, 130-140.
McArthur, H.K., *In Search of the Historical Jesus*, 1969, London, SPCK.
McArthur, H.K., 'The Burden of Proof in Historical Jesus Research' in *Exp.T.*, 82, 1970-1, 116-119.
McEleney, N.J., 'Authenticity Criteria and Mark 7.1-23' in *CBQ*, 34, 1972, 431-460.
McNamara, M., *Targum and Testament*, 1972, Shannon, Ireland, Irish University Press.
McNeile, A.H., *The Gospel According to St. Matthew*, 1915, London, Macmillan.
Mealand, D.L., 'The Dissimilarity Test' in *SJT*, 31, 1978, 41-50.
Meeks, W.A., 'The Divine Agent and his Counterfeit in Philo and the Fourth Gospel' in E.S. Fiorenza, ed., *Aspects of Religious Propaganda in Judaism and Early Christianity*, 1976, Notre Dame and London, University of Notre Dame Press.
Menken, M.J.J., 'The Quotation from Isa.40.3 in John 1.23' in *Biblica*, 66, 1985, 190-205.
Menken, M.J.J., 'The Provenance and Meaning of the Old Testament Quotation in John 6.31' in *NT*, 30, 1988, 39-56.
Menken, M.J.J., 'Die Form des Zitates aus Jes. 6.10 in Joh. 12.40. Ein Beitrag zum Schriftgebrauch des vierten Evangelisten' in *BZ*, 32, 1988, 189-209.
Menken, M.J.J., 'The Old Testament Quotation in John 6.45. Source and Redaction' in *ETL*, 64, 1988, 164-172.
Menken, M.J.J., 'The Translation of Psalm 41.10 in John 13.18' in *JSNT*, 40, 1990, 61-79.
Metzger, B.M., *A Textual Commentary on the Greek New Testament*, 1971, London and New York, United Bible Societies.
Meyer, B., *The Aims of Jesus*, 1979, London, SCM.
Michaels, J.R., *John*, 1983, San Francisco, Harper and Row.
Mitton, C.L., *Jesus: the Fact behind the Faith*, 1975, London, Mowbray.
Miyoshi, M., *Der Anfang des Reiseberichts. Lk. 9.51-10.24. Eine redaktionsgeschichtliche Untersuchung*, 1974, Rome, Biblical Institute Press.
Morris, L., *Studies in the Fourth Gospel*, 1969, Exeter, Paternoster.
Morris, L., *The Gospel According to John*, 1971, London, Marshall, Morgan, and Scott.
Morris, L., 'The Composition of the Fourth Gospel' in W.W. Gasque and W.S. Lasor, edd., *Scripture, Tradition and Interpretation*, 1978, Grand Rapids, Eerdmans.

Moule, C.F.D., *The Phenomenon of the New Testament*, 1967, London, SCM.
Moule, C.F.D., *The Origin of Christology*, 1977, CUP.
Müller, P.- G., *Der Traditionprozess im Neuen Testament - Kommunikationsanalytische Studien zur Versprachlichung des Jesusphänomens*, 1982, Herder, Freiburg.
Mussner, F., *The Historical Jesus in the Gospel of St. John*, ET 1967, London, Burns and Oates.
Neirynck, F., 'Jesus and the Sabbath. Some Observations on Mk. 2.27' in J. Dupont, ed., *Jésus aux origines de la christologie*, 1975, Leuven, at the University Press.
Neirynck, F., 'John and the Synoptics' in M. de Jonge, ed., *L'Évangile de Jean. Sources, Rédaction, Théologie*, 1977, Leuven, at the University Press.
Neirynck, F., *Jean et les Synoptiques. Examen Critique de l'Exégèse de M.-É. Boismard*, 1979, Leuven, at the University Press.
Nicol, W., *The Semeia in the Fourth Gospel: Tradition and Redaction*, 1972, Leiden, E.J. Brill.
Noack, B., *Zur johanneischen Tradition: Beiträge zur Kritik an der literarkritischen Analyse des vierten Evangeliums*, 1954, Copenhagen, Rosenkilde og Bagger.
Nunn, H.P.V., *The Authorship of the Fourth Gospel*, 1952, Eton, Alden and Blackwell Ltd.
Odeberg, H., *The Fourth Gospel*, ET 1968, Chicago, Argonaut Inc. Publishers.
Painter, J., *John - Witness and Theologian*, 1975, London, SPCK.
Painter, J., *The Quest for the Messiah. The History, Literature, and Theology of the Johannine Community*, 1991, Edinburgh, T. & T. Clark.
Pancaro, S., *The Law in the Fourth Gospel*, 1975, Leiden, E.J. Brill.
Parker, P., 'Two Editions of John' in *JBL*, 75, 1956, 303-314.
Parker, P., 'John and John Mark' in *JBL*, 79, 1960, 97-110.
Parker, P., 'John the Son of Zebedee and the Fourth Gospel' in *JBL*, 81, 1962, 35-43.
Parker, P., 'Luke and the Fourth Evangelist' in *NTS*, 9, 1963, 317-336.
Paul, G.J., *St. John's Gospel. A Commentary*, 1965, Madras.
Perrin, N., *Rediscovering the Teaching of Jesus*, 1967, London, SCM.
Perrin, N., *What is Redaction Criticism?*, 1970, London, SPCK.
Pesch, R., and Kratz, R., *So liest man Synoptisch: Anleitung und Kommentar zum Studium der Synoptischen Evangelien*, vol. 2, 1976, Frankfurt am Main, J. Knecht.
Plummer, A., *The Gospel According to St. John*, 1882, reprinted 1981, Grand Rapids, Michigan, Baker Book House.
Pollard, T.E., *Johannine Christology and the Early Church*, 1970, CUP.
Potter, R.D., 'Topography and Archaeology in the Fourth Gospel' in K. Aland, F.L. Cross, J. Danielou, H. Riesenfeld, and W.C. van Unnik, edd., *Studia Evangelica. Papers Presented to the International Congress on "the Four Gospels in 1957" held at Christ Church, Oxford, 1957*, 1959, Berlin, Akademie-Verlag, 329-337.
Quast, K., *Peter and the Beloved Disciple. Figures for a Community in Crisis*, JSNT Supplement Series 32, 1989, Sheffield, JSOT Press.
Reim, G., *Studien zum Alttestamentlichen Hintergrund des Johannesevangeliums*, 1974, CUP.
Reynolds, H.R., *The Gospel of St. John*, 1888, London, Kegan Paul, Trench, and Co.
Richard, E., 'Expressions of Double Meaning and their Function in the Gospel of John' in *NTS*, 31, 1985, 96-112.

Riedl, J., *Das Heilswerk Jesu nach Johannes*, 1973, Freiburg, Basel, Wien, Herder.
Riesenfeld, H., *The Gospel Tradition and its Beginnings. A Study in the Limits of 'Formgeschichte'*, 1957, London, Mowbray.
Riesner, R., *Jesus als Lehrer. Eine Untersuchung zum Ursprung der Evangelien-Überlieferung*, 1988³, Tübingen, J.C.B. Mohr.
Robinson, J.A.T., 'The Destination and Purpose of St. John's Gospel' in *NTS*, 6, 1959-60, 117-131.
Robinson, J.A.T., 'The Place of the Fourth Gospel' in P. Gardner- Smith, ed., *The Roads Converge*, 1963, London, Edward Arnold Ltd.
Robinson, J.A.T., *Redating the New Testament*, 1975, London, SCM.
Robinson, J.A.T., *The Priority of John*, 1985, London, SCM.
Robinson, J.M., *A New Quest for the Historical Jesus*, 1959, London, SCM.
Rodd, C.S., 'Spirit or Finger' in *Exp.T.*, 72, 1961, 157f.
Rogers, D., 'Who was the Beloved Disciple?' in *Exp.T.*, 77, 1965-6, 214.
Roloff, J., *Das Kerygma und der irdische Jesus. Historische Motive in den Jesus-Erzählungen der Evangelien*, 1970, Göttingen, Vandenhoeck & Ruprecht.
Ruckstuhl, E., *Die Literarische Einheit des Johannesevangeliums*, 1951, 1987², Freiburg in der Schweiz, Paulusverlag.
Ruckstuhl, E., 'Johannine Language and Style. The Question of their Unity' in M. de Jonge, ed., *L'Évangile de Jean. Sources, Rédaction, Théologie*, 1977, Leuven, at the University Press.
Sanders, E.P., *Jesus and Judaism*, 1985, London, SCM.
Sanders, J.N., *The Fourth Gospel in the Early Church. Its Origin and Influence on Christian Theology up to Irenaeus*, 1943, CUP.
Sanders, J.N., 'Those Whom Jesus Loved (Jn. 11.5)' in *NTS*, 1, 1954-5, 29-41.
Sanders, J.N., and Mastin, B.A., *A Commentary on the Gospel According to St. John*, 1968, London, A. and C. Black.
Schlatter, D.A., *Die Sprache und Heimat des vierten Evangelisten*, 1902, Gütersloh, G. Bertelsmann.
Schlier, H., *Essais sur le Nouveau Testament*, 1968, Paris, Les Editions du Cerf.
Schnackenburg, R., *The Gospel According to St. John*, vol.1, ET 1968, vol. 2, ET 1980, vol. 3, ET 1982, London, Burns and Oates.
Schulz, S., *Komposition und Herkunft der Johanneischen Reden*, 1960, Stuttgart, W. Kohlhammer Verlag.
Schulz, S, *Das Evangelium nach Johannes*, 1972, Göttingen, Vandenhoeck & Ruprecht.
Schulz, S., *Q. Die Spruchquelle der Evangelisten*, 1972, Zürich, Theologischer Verlag.
Schürmann, H., *Traditionsgeschichtliche Untersuchungen zu den synoptischen Evangelien*, 1968, Düsseldorf, Patmos-Verlag.
Schweitzer, A., *The Quest of the Historical Jesus. A Critical Study of its Progress from Reimarus to Wrede*, ET 1954³, London, SCM.
Schweizer, E., *Ego Eimi: Die religionsgeschichtliche Herkunft und theologische Bedeutung der johanneischen Bildreden, zugleich ein Beitrag zur Quellenfrage des vierten Evangeliums*, 1939, Göttingen, Vandenhoeck & Ruprecht.
Schweizer, E., *The Good News According to Mark*, ET 1971, London, SPCK.
Schweizer, E., *The Good News According to Matthew*, ET 1976, London, SPCK.
Selby, G.R., *Jesus, Aramaic, and Greek*, 1989, Doncaster, Brynmill Press.
Sevenster, J.N., *Do You Know Greek? How Much Greek Could the First Jewish Christians Have Known?*, 1968, Leiden, E.J. Brill.

Sidebottom, E.M., *The Christ of the Fourth Gospel in the Light of First-Century Thought*, 1961, London, SPCK.
Smalley, S.S., *John: Evangelist and Interpreter*, 1978, Exeter, Paternoster.
Smith, D.M., 'John 12.12ff. and the Question of John's Use of the Synoptics' in *JBL*, 82, 1963, 58-64.
Smith, D.M., 'The Sources of the Gospel of John: An Assessment of the State of the Problem' in *NTS*, 10, 1964, 336-351.
Smith, D.M., *The Composition and Order of the Fourth Gospel: Bultmann's Literary Theory*, 1965, New Haven, Yale University Press.
Smith, D.M., *Johannine Christianity: Essays on its Setting, Sources, and Theology*, 1984, University of South Carolina Press.
Sperber, A., 'New Testament and Septuagint' in *JBL*, 59, 1940, 193-293.
Sproston, W.E., 'Witness to what was ἀπ' ἀρχῆς: 1 John's Contribution to our Knowledge of Tradition in the Fourth Gospel' in *JSNT*, 48, 1992, 43-65.
Stanton, V.H., *The Gospels as Historical Documents. Part 3: The Fourth Gospel*, 1920, CUP.
Stein, R.H., 'The "Criteria" for Authenticity' in R.T. France and D. Wenham, edd., *Gospel Perspectives*, vol. 1, 1980, Sheffield, JSOT Press.
Stevenson, W.B., *A Grammar of Palestinian Jewish Aramaic*, 1962, OUP.
Strachan, R.H., *The Fourth Gospel: Its Significance and Environment*, 1941[3], London, SCM.
Streeter, B.H., *The Four Gospels. A Study of Origins*, 1924, London, Macmillan and Co. Ltd.
Suggs, M.J., *Wisdom, Christology and Law in Matthew's Gospel*, 1970, Cambridge, Massachusetts, Harvard University Press.
Sundberg, A.C., 'Isos to Theo Christology in John 5.17-30' in *Biblical Research*, 15, 1970, 19-31.
Tarrelli, C.C., 'Johannine Synonyms' in *JTS*, 47, 1946, 175-177.
Taylor, V., *Jesus and His Sacrifice. A Study of the Passion-Sayings in the Gospels*, 1939, London, Macmillan and Co. Ltd.
Taylor, V., *The Names of Jesus*, 1959, London, Macmillan and Co. Ltd.
Taylor, V., *The Gospel According to St. Mark*, 1966[2], London and Basingstoke, Macmillan Press Ltd.
Teeple, H.M., 'Methodology in Source Analysis of the Fourth Gospel' in *JBL*, 81, 1962, 279-286.
Teeple, H.M., *The Literary Origin of the Gospel of John*, 1974, Evanston, Religion and Ethics Institute.
Temple, S., 'A Key to the Composition of the Fourth Gospel' in *JBL*, 80, 1961, 220-232.
Temple, S., *The Core of the Fourth Gospel*, 1975, London and Oxford, Mowbrays.
Thackeray, H.St.J., *A Grammar of the Old Testament in Greek According to the Septuagint*, vol. 1, 1909, CUP.
Thornecroft, J.K., 'The Redactor and the "Beloved" in John' in *Exp.T.*, 98, 1986-7, 135-139.
Thüsing, W., *Die Erhöhung und Verherrlichung Jesu im Johannesevangelium*, 1970, Münster, Verlag Aschendorff.
Toy, C.H., *Quotations in the New Testament*, 1884, New York, C. Scribner's Sons.
Trites, A.A., *The New Testament Concept of Witness*, 1977, CUP.
Trocmé, E., *Jesus and his Contemporaries*, ET 1973, London, SCM.

Turner, H.E.W., *Historicity and the Gospels*, 1963, London, Mowbray.
Turner, N., *Grammatical Insights into the New Testament*, 1965, Edinburgh, T. & T. Clark.
Unnik, W.C. van, 'The Quotation from the Old Testament in John 12.23' in *NT*, 3, 1959, 174-179.
Unnik, W.C. van, *The New Testament, its History and Message*, 1964, London, Collins.
Vanhoye, A., 'L'Oeuvre du Christ, don du Père' in *RSR*, 48, 1960, 377-419.
Vermes, G., *Jesus the Jew*, 1983², London, SCM.
Wahlde, U.C. von, 'Faith and Works in John 6. 28-29. Exegesis or Eisegesis?' in *NT*, 22.4, 1980, 304-315.
Wahlde, U.C. von, 'The Witnesses to Jesus in John 5.31-40 and Belief in the Fourth Gospel' in *CBQ*, 43, 1981, 385-404.
Wahlde, U.C. von, *The Earliest Version of John's Gospel*, 1989, Wilmington, Delaware, Michael Glazier.
Wahlde, U.C. von, *The Johannine Commandments: 1 John and the Struggle for the Johannine Tradition*, 1990, New York, Paulist Press.
Weiss, H., 'The Sabbath in the Fourth Gospel' in *JBL*, 110, 1991, 311-321.
Wendt, H.H., *The Gospel According to St. John. An Inquiry into its Genesis and Historical Value*, ET 1902, Edinburgh, T. & T. Clark.
Westcott, B.F., *The Gospel According to St. John. The Greek Text with Introduction and Notes*, 2 vols., 1908, London, J. Murray.
Westerholm, S., *Jesus and Scribal Authority*, 1978, Lund, CWK Gleerup.
Whiteacre, R.A., *Johannine Polemic. The Role of Tradition and Theology*, SBL Dissertation Series 67, 1982, Chico, California, Scholars Press.
Wilkens, W., *Die Entstehungsgeschichte des vierten Evangeliums*, 1958, Zollikon, Evangelische Verlag.
Wilkens, W., *Zeichen und Werke: Ein Beitrag zur Theologie des 4. Evangeliums in Erzählungs- und Redestoff*, 1969, Zürich, Zwingli Verlag.
Wise, M.O., 'Languages of Palestine' in J.B. Green, S. McKnight, and I.H. Marshall, edd., *Dictionary of Jesus and the Gospels*, 1992, Leicester and Downers Grove, Illinois, IVP.
Witherington, B., *The Christology of Jesus*, 1990, Minneapolis, Fortress Press.
Witkamp, L.Th., 'The Use of Traditions in John 5.1-18' in *JSNT*, 25, 1985, 19-47.
Yamauchi, E., *Pre-Christian Gnosticism*, 1973, London, Tyndale Press.

Index of Sources

I. Old Testament

Genesis

1.1–2.3	126
2.2f.	173, 182, 183, 186
2.2	137
2.3	170
2.6f.	102, 126
3	284
4	284

Exodus

4.1-9	231
4.1	282
4.3	282
4.12	238
4.16	197
5.13	137
7.1	197
8.19	122, 122
12.10	66, 67
12.46	66, 67
14.13	204
16.2	71
16.4	71, 72
16.15	71, 72
17.6	74
19.4	204
20.5	104
20.9-11	173
20.9	173
20.10	173
23.12	173
24.9-11	239
25.9	204
25.40	204
26.30	204
31.14-17	173
31.14	173
31.15	173
31.18	122
33.18	239
34.7	104
34.10	204
34.21	173
35.2	173
40.33	137

Leviticus

4	242
18.5	179
24.16	235

Numbers

3-8	279
4.3	279
4.23	279
4.30	280
4.31	279
4.33	279
4.35	279
4.39	279
4.43	279
4.47	279
7.1	233
7.5	280
8.11	279f.
8.19	280
9.12	66
14.18	104
14.22	204
15.27-31	242

16.28	206, 219	5	249
20.7-11	74	5.10	102
23.3	204		
35.30	77	*1 Chronicles*	
		28.10	137
Deuteronomy			
3.21	204	*2 Chronicles*	
3.24	204	4.11	137
4.3	204	5.1	137
4.5	204	29.34	137
5.9	104		
5.13	173	*Nehemiah*	
5.14	173		
8.3	137, 139, 148	6.16	137
9.10	122	9.15	71f., 74
11.7	204	9.19f.	74
13.1-5	231	13.19	189
17.7	77		
18.18	250	*Psalms*	
19.15	77	2.7	210
29.2f.	204	8.3	122
30.15f.	138	18.50	77
32.39	179	19.12f.	242
32.46f.	138	22	66
33.9	142	22.1	202
		22.15	80
1 Samuel		22.18	65
2.30	159	31.20	187
17.15	77	34	67
20.6	77	34.21	66f.
21.1-6	175	35.19	79
		40.8	137
2 Samuel		41.9	76
7.12-16	77	41.10	299
7.16	77	42.2	80
12.13	199	42.7	145
18.28	76	46.4	75
18.33	202	61.6f.	77
19.4	202	63.1	80
		63.5	137, 148
1 Kings		69	61, 80
7.22	137	69.2	145
7.40	137	69.3	80
		69.4	79
2 Kings		69.9	61
2.12	202	69.15	145
		69.21	80, 82

Index of Sources

72.5	77	26.12	285
78.1-8	72	26.19	249
78.16	75	29.15-21	252
78.24	71f.	29.18f.	249
79.8	104	29.18	101, 124
82.6	75, 197	33.1	252
89.3f.	77	35.4	62
89.35-37	77	35.5f.	249
89.36	77	35.5	101, 124
90.17	285	35.6f.	75
103.21	137	38.19	202
104.23	115	40.3	69f., 299
105.40	71	40.9	62
105.41	75	41.10	62
109.3	79	41.13	62
109.14	104	41.18	75
110.4	77	42–43	124
114.8	75	42.7	101, 124
118.25f.	78	42.19	124
118.25	78	43.1	62, 124
118.26	78	43.5	62
119.161	79	43.7	124
124.1f.	202	43.9-13	228
132.11	77	43.10	124
143.10	137	43.12	124
		43.19f.	75
Proverbs		44.2	62
		44.3	75
8.22	258	44.7-11	228
9.5	137, 148	44.18	65
18.4	75	44.28	137
		48.14	137
Song of Solomon		49.10	75
4.15	75	51.7	62
		53.1	63
Isaiah		54.4	62
		54.13	71-73, 82, 211
5.11-17	252	54.15	73, 82
6.1	239	55.1f.	137, 148
6.3	186	55.1	75
6.8	250	58.11	75
6.10	64f., 299	61.1	123, 246, 249-250
9.6f.	77	65.6f.	104
11.1	77		
11.9	211	*Jeremiah*	
11.10	77		
12.3	75	1.5-7	123
14.13-15	252	1.6	250
21.4	145	2.13	75

17.13	75	*Joel*	
17.21	189	3.18	75
23.5	77		
23.24	186	*Amos*	
24.1	204	7.1	204
31.3	73	7.4	204
31.31	73	7.7	204
31.33	73		
31.34	73, 211	*Obadiah*	
46.27f.	62	18	282
48	285		
48.10	282, 285, 289	*Micah*	
50.25	187, 285	2.1-5	252
		5.2	77
Ezekiel			
3.5	250	*Habakkuk*	
11.25	204	2.9-11	252
18.4	179	2.14	211
18.9	179		
18.20	279	*Zephaniah*	
18.27f.	179	3.14f.	62
18.27	179	3.15	78
20.11	179	3.16	62
34.1ff	232		
37.16ff	232	*Zechariah*	
37.25	77	1.9	204
40.4	204	9.9	62, 78
47.1-12	75	12.10	67
		13.1	75
Daniel		14.8	75
5.23	159		
7.14	77		

Hosea

2.20   211

II. New Testament

Matthew

3.3	69
3.9	217
3.11	247
3.17	210
4.1-11	245
4.3f.	139
4.4	116
4.19	92
5–7	36f.
5	189
5.3	246, 249f.
5.11	241
5.15	203
5.16	91, 158, 255
5.45	172
6.2	158
6.9	156
6.10	139, 143
6.13	156
6.26	172
6.30	172
7.3-5	140
7.16-20	255
7.21f.	202
7.21	139, 143
7.22	93
7.23	92
8.21f.	142
8.27	216
9.1-8	199
9.2	199
9.3	199
9.15	245
9.27-31	101
9.27	101
9.28	92
9.33	216, 261
9.37f.	53, 120
9.37	92
9.38	92
10	49, 113
10.5f.	131
10.10	92
10.15	253
10.17-22	241
10.17f.	54
10.19f.	54
10.23-39	241
10.24	53
10.26	106, 209
10.34-37	142
10.40	53, 109f., 144, 245
11.1-19	251
11.2-6	176, 246, 255
11.2	92, 124, 246, 251
11.3	246
11.4-6	248
11.4f.	124, 250, 256
11.4	246-249
11.5f.	120, 246f.
11.5	124, 248
11.6	248
11.11	120
11.12	120, 187
11.19	91, 251
11.20-24	251, 255
11.20	94
11.21-23	253
11.21f.	252f.
11.21	93f., 251f.
11.22	253
11.23f.	252, 253
11.23	93f., 251, 252
11.25-30	291, 297
11.25-27	106, 295
11.25f.	208
11.25	156, 207, 209
11.27	56, 205, 207-212, 219, 245, 264, 295
11.28	190
12.3f.	173f.
12.5	174
12.9-14	199
12.11	174, 179
12.12	92, 173, 177
12.14	199
12.18	122
12.22-30	118
12.22f.	101
12.26	122
12.27f.	118, 140

12.27	119f.	21.21	288
12.28	107, 118f., 122, 125, 246, 254, 294	21.24	92
		21.27	92
12.31f.	122	21.28	92
12.33-35	255	21.31	139
12.39	93	21.33-46	207, 245
12.41f.	120	21.37	210, 245
12.43	203	21.42	175
12.46-50	139, 245	22.22	216
12.50	143	22.23-33	175
13	35-37	22.29	93
13.11	210	22.41-46	175f.
13.16f.	120, 249	23.1-12	255
13.55	203	23.3	91
13.58	94	23.5	91
15.1-8	175	23.24	203
15.10-20	255	23.37	109, 144, 233, 245
15.24	109, 131, 144, 245	24.24	90, 93
15.30f.	101	24.29	93
15.31	216	24.30	93
16.3	93	24.36	207, 210, 245
16.4	93	25.15	93
16.8-12	254	25.16	92
16.12	133	25.40	142
16.16	210	25.46	53
16.17	106, 209	26.10	91f.
16.21	245	26.18	92
16.24f.	241	26.24	245
17.22f.	245	26.28	211
17.27	113	26.31	245
18.12-14	53	26.39	245
18.14	139, 143	26.42	139, 143
18.18	54	26.54	115, 144, 245
18.35	93	26.62-67	200
19.4	93	26.63	200
19.12	101	26.64	93
19.26	246	27.14	216
20.1	92	27.34	61
20.2	92	27.48	61
20.8	92	28.19	30f., 210
20.18f.	245		
20.28	245	*Mark*	
20.30	101	1.2	69
20.32	92	1.7	247
21.5	62	1.11	210
21.9	77	1.16	101
21.14	101	1.17	55, 92
21.20	216	1.35	156

Index of Sources

1.38	109	8.17-21	211, 254
2.1-12	166, 199	8.22-26	101
2.5	104, 166, 168, 199	8.29	210
2.7	199	8.31	115f., 144, 245
2.9	166	8.34f.	241
2.14	101	8.34	143
2.18	177	8.38	143
2.20	245	9.1	93
2.23-3.6	167	9.23	116, 246
2.23-28	169, 189, 297	9.31	116, 245
2.23f.	174f.	9.37	53, 109f., 144, 245
2.25f.	173f., 177	9.39	92f.
2.27	300	9.40	113
2.28	178	10.6	93
3.1-6	103, 125, 166, 169, 177, 199	10.15	53
		10.18	140
3.4	92, 173, 177	10.27	246
3.6	190, 199	10.29f.	55, 142
3.20	292	10.33f.	116, 245
3.21	140, 292	10.36	92
3.22-27	118	10.38f.	146
3.27	203	10.38	144-146
3.31-35	139f., 245, 292	10.45	116, 245
3.33f.	140	10.46-52	101
3.34f.	141	10.51	92
3.35	116, 139, 141-143	11.3	233
4.1-20	133, 298	11.9f.	77
4.11	210	11.17	140
4.20	143	11.29	92
4.21	203	11.33	92
4.22	106	12.1-12	207, 245
4.30	113	12.10f.	175
5.19	93	12.17	216
5.20	216	12.18-27	175
5.30	94	12.24	93
6.3	203	12.35-37	175f.
6.4	53	12.37-40	255
6.5	94	13.9-13	241
6.46	156	13.9	54
7.1-23	299	13.11	54
7.1-13	175	13.22	90, 92f.
7.5	177	13.25f.	93
7.14-23	133, 255, 298	13.32	56, 207, 210, 245
7.33	101	13.34	91
7.37	216	14.6	91f.
8.12	93, 140	14.13-15	233
8.14-21	133, 298	14.18	76
8.15	133, 138	14.21	116, 245

14.24	211	7.18-23	246, 255
14.27	54, 116, 245	7.18f.	246
14.32-42	155	7.18	246
14.35f.	53	7.19	246
14.36	116, 158, 245	7.21f.	101
14.49	106	7.21	246
14.58	119	7.22f.	120, 246f.
14.60-65	200	7.22	124, 246-249, 250, 256
14.61	200	7.23	248
14.62	93	7.28	120
14.64	200	8.10	210
15.5	216	8.16	203
15.34	202	8.19-21	139, 245
15.39	6	8.24	202
16.17	93	8.25	216
		8.39	93
Luke		8.46	93
		9.1	94
2.35	210	9.18	156
2.49	115, 144, 245	9.20	211
3.4	69	9.22	245
3.8	217	9.23f.	241
3.16	144, 247	9.28	156
3.20	246	9.43	216
3.21	156	9.44	245
3.22	210	9.48	245
4.1-13	245	9.51–10.24	299
4.14	94	9.51-56	131
4.18-21	246, 249f.	9.51	156
4.18	109, 144, 245	10	113
4.21	109, 144, 245	10.1-16	251
4.22	216	10.2	92, 120
4.43	109, 115, 144, 245	10.7	92
5.16	156	10.12-15	251, 255
5.17-26	199	10.12	253
5.17	94	10.13-15	253
5.20	199	10.13f.	252
5.21	199	10.13	93f., 252
5.35	245	10.15	252
6.6-11	199	10.16	53, 109f., 245
6.3f.	173f.	10.17-20	251
6.9	173, 177	10.19	93
6.12	156	10.21f.	210, 295
6.19	94	10.21	207f., 210
6.20	246, 249f.	10.22	205, 207, 219, 245
6.22	241	10.23f.	120, 249
6.40	54, 203	10.41	202
6.43-45	255	11.1	156
7.11-17	103, 166		

11.2	185	18.31-33	245
11.14-23	118	18.41	92
11.14	216	19.37	94
11.19f.	118	19.38	77
11.19	119f.	20.8	92
11.20	107, 118f., 122, 125, 246, 254, 294	20.9-19	207, 245
		20.13	210, 245
11.21f.	203	20.17	175
11.29	93	20.26	216
11.30	93	20.27-40	175
11.31f.	120	20.41-44	175f.
11.38	216	20.42	122
11.40	93	20.45-47	255
11.48	91	21.11	93
12.2-9	241	21.12-17	241
12.2	106, 210	21.25	93
12.47f.	203, 255	21.26f.	93
12.47	139	22.20	211
12.49-53	146f.	22.22	245
12.49-51	147	22.24-27	53
12.49	144	22.27	140
12.50	144, 146, 245	22.31	202
12.51-53	241	22.32	156
12.51	140	22.37	115, 144, 245
12.58	92	22.42	156, 245
13.1-5	104	22.67-70	200
13.10-17	103, 125, 166f., 169	22.69	93
13.13	173	22.70	200
13.14	92	23.25	139
13.15	174	23.34	156
13.24	55	23.46	156
13.27	92	24.7	115, 144, 245
13.32	144, 245	24.19	92
13.33	115, 144, 245	24.26	115, 144, 245
13.34	202, 245	24.41	216
14.1-6	103, 125, 166f., 169, 179	24.44	115, 144, 245
14.5	174, 179	24.49	93
14.25-27	241		
15.3-7	53	*John*	
16.16	120		
17.11-19	102	1–20	7
17.20f.	120	1.1-18	126
17.25	115, 144, 245	1.1-3	126
17.30	106, 210	1.1	59, 83, 191, 198, 269
17.33	241	1.3	191, 270
18.7	93	1.4	104
18.8	93	1.5	104
18.27	246	1.6	123, 250
		1.7f.	228

1.7	104	3.14f.	59
1.8	104, 106	3.16-21	89, 96
1.9	12, 104	3.16	213
1.14	5f., 150, 158, 160	3.17	108, 126, 213
1.15	228	3.18-21	126, 222
1.18	213, 269	3.18	213
1.19-28	69	3.19-21	2, 4, 278
1.19	228, 275	3.19	89, 104, 287
1.20	60	3.20f.	287
1.23	59, 69, 81f., 299	3.20	89, 104, 287
1.24	274	3.21	89, 104, 106, 286f.
1.27	247	3.25	273
1.29	66, 75, 153, 214	3.26	228
1.31	106	3.28	6, 60, 123, 250
1.32	60, 228	3.29	203
1.33	123, 250	3.30	6
1.34	60, 228	3.32	214, 221, 228
1.35-50	17	3.34	221
1.35-40	22	3.35	160, 213
1.36	66, 75	3.36	213
1.41	197	4	17, 131, 150, 152f.
1.49	276	4.1-42	130, 134, 151
1.50	60	4.1-26	131
1.51	59	4.1-9	132
2.4	59	4.1	132, 274
2.5	59	4.3	130, 132
2.6	125, 168	4.4-7	132
2.10	187	4.5-9	132
2.11	90, 106, 158, 274	4.5-7	132
2.12	160	4.5	132
2.13-22	60	4.6f.	150
2.13	130	4.6	130, 132
2.16	234	4.7-26	130, 133
2.17	59-61, 68, 79f.	4.7	132
2.18	90, 214, 273f., 276	4.8	130f.
2.19	234	4.9-18	132
2.20	274	4.9	130, 132
2.21	75	4.10-21	132
2.22	60	4.10-14	148
2.23-25	90	4.14	80
2.23	17, 90, 273f.	4.16-19	132
3	104	4.17	60
3.1f.	273f.	4.18	153
3.2	90, 118, 238	4.19-29	152
3.3	53	4.19	130
3.11	60, 113, 202, 214, 221, 228	4.20-26	132
		4.20	60
3.13	126, 221	4.23	132

4.24-26	132	5.1	165
4.25-30	132	5.2-15	167, 169f.
4.25f.	132	5.2-9	167-169
4.26	234	5.2-4	165
4.27-30	132	5.2	165
4.27	132, 134	5.3	165
4.28-35	132	5.4	165
4.28-30	132	5.5	165
4.28f.	131	5.6	165
4.29	130	5.7	165
4.30	152	5.8	165, 173
4.31-38	130, 132	5.9-18	164, 169
4.31-34	130, 132-136, 140, 149, 151f., 163	5.9-16	166
		5.9-15	168
4.31	135	5.9-14	167
4.32f.	134	5.9	165f., 168
4.32	135	5.10-20	274
4.33	132, 135	5.10-18	274
4.34	2, 85, 89, 97, 108, 116, 130, 134-136, 138f., 144, 147-149, 151-153, 159-163, 195, 221, 229, 236, 245, 266f., 269, 275, 278, 281f.	5.10-13	167
		5.10ff.	189
		5.12	167
		5.14	104, 166-169
		5.15	60, 167, 170
		5.16-30	296
4.35-38	113, 152	5.16-18	125
4.35	53, 60, 140	5.16	167-169, 173, 189f., 196
4.36-38	152	5.17-30	302
4.37	60	5.17-23	236
4.39-42	132	5.17	2, 4, 87, 89, 97, 138, 164, 167, 169f., 172f., 182-184, 186-188, 190-198, 221, 222-224, 236, 245, 266f., 269, 278, 291, 294, 299
4.39	60, 132, 228		
4.40-42	132		
4.40	132		
4.42	60, 130-132		
4.44	53, 60, 197,		
4.45	17	5.18	173, 186, 189f., 196-200, 219-20
4.48	90, 274		
4.50	164	5.19-47	196, 257
4.51	60, 164	5.19-30	55, 164, 186, 191, 228, 295
4.52	60		
4.53	164	5.19-29	169
4.54	17, 90, 274	5.19ff.	154, 198
5	23, 49, 125, 128, 153, 164, 169, 191, 193, 228, 230, 234, 244, 270	5.19f.	2, 4, 97, 164, 183, 191, 195f., 201-207, 212, 214-221, 222, 224f., 229, 236, 245, 266f., 269, 278, 284
5.1-18	190, 303		
5.1-17	196	5.19	118, 169, 196f., 206, 222-225
5.1-15	196		
5.1-9	164f., 169, 221, 228	5.20-29	218

5.20-22	229	6.27	89, 149, 281
5.20ff.	220	6.28f.	291, 303
5.20	89, 195, 203, 214-216, 222, 225	6.28	89, 281
		6.29	89, 108, 130, 281
5.21-25	216	6.30	89f., 274
5.21ff.	215f., 221f.	6.31f.	71
5.21f.	215	6.31	59, 71f., 81f., 299
5.21	203, 213	6.32	71f., 202
5.22-30	126	6.35-58	148
5.22	160, 203, 213	6.36	60, 243
5.23	108, 203, 213, 243	6.38-40	153
5.24	60, 108, 237	6.38f.	126
5.25	60	6.38	108, 195, 198, 221
5.26-29	216	6.39	108, 160
5.26	160, 203, 213	6.40	213
5.27	160, 195	6.41	71, 274
5.28	222	6.42	60
5.29	53	6.43	71
5.30	108, 118, 195, 198, 216, 218, 221	6.44	73, 108
		6.45	59, 71-73, 81f.
5.31-47	164, 228, 292	6.46	214
5.31-40	257, 303	6.47	202
5.31-33	11	6.51	153
5.31	20, 228f.	6.52	274
5.32	228f.	6.53	202
5.33-35	229	6.55	149
5.33	228	6.57	108
5.34	229	6.59	125, 168
5.35	104	6.62	126
5.36-38	109	6.65	60
5.36	2, 4, 60, 89, 97, 108, 116, 160, 195, 227-232, 234, 236, 240, 244f., 250, 256-258, 261, 269	6.67	9
		6.70	9
		7-10	232
		7	98
5.37f.	229	7.1-21	274
5.37	108, 228	7.1ff.	98
5.38	108, 237	7.3f.	229
5.39f.	229	7.3	2, 89, 103, 239
5.39	228, 234	7.4	106
5.43	197	7.5	89, 140
5.45	220	7.7	2, 60, 89, 278
6	12, 23, 49, 149, 152, 164	7.11	6
6.1-21	17	7.12	60
6.1-14	49	7.14-24	164
6.2	90, 274	7.16-18	213
6.14	60, 90, 236, 274	7.16f.	83
6.26	90, 93, 274	7.16	221
6.27-30	2	7.17f.	221

Index of Sources 317

7.18	11, 108, 160, 197	8.38	214, 221
7.21	89, 130, 222, 229, 239	8.39-41	236
7.22f.	174	8.39	2, 89, 278, 283
7.23	167, 170, 189	8.40	11, 283f.
7.24	59	8.41	2, 89, 278, 283f.
7.25-27	273	8.42	108, 213, 221
7.28	108, 204, 213, 221	8.44-46	11
7.29	108	8.44	283f.
7.31f.	273-275	8.45f.	284
7.31	90, 236, 242, 255	8.48	60, 274
7.32	275	8.52	274
7.33-39	275	8.54	60, 160
7.33f.	117	8.55	60
7.33	108, 275	8.56	234, 283
7.35	274f.	8.57	274
7.37-39	80, 148	8.58	126, 234
7.37	74, 99	8.59	98f.
7.38	59, 73, 81f.	9	98-100, 103, 105, 123, 153, 167, 270
7.39	158, 160		
7.42	60, 77, 79, 81	9.1-10.21	98, 100
7.45	274	9.1-12	113
7.47	274	9.1-7	98, 100f.
7.48	274	9.1-3	100
7.51	236	9.1ff.	98
8	98f.	9.1	99-101, 103
8.12	104, 115, 125	9.2-5	98
8.13-20	164	9.2f.	100, 103f., 168
8.13f.	11	9.2	100, 104, 107
8.13	274	9.3f.	2, 85, 97f., 100, 103, 105-108, 116, 118, 122f., 125, 126-129, 154, 245, 275, 278
8.14	20, 228		
8.15	20		
8.16	20, 108, 126		
8.17	60, 77, 79, 81, 228	9.3	89, 100, 104, 106f., 114, 118, 127f.
8.18	108, 228		
8.21	117	9.4f.	115, 117, 126
8.22	274	9.4	89, 104-108, 110f., 114-118, 123f., 126-129, 136, 138, 150, 162, 187f., 195, 221, 229, 236, 245, 266, 269, 282
8.24	60, 234		
8.26	11, 108, 221		
8.28f.	195, 198		
8.28	83, 204, 213, 221, 239		
8.29	108, 116	9.5	101, 104f., 115, 123, 125
8.31	274	9.6-21	100
8.32	11	9.6-17	100
8.33	60	9.6	100-103, 125f.
8.34	60	9.7	99-101, 103, 214
8.35	203	9.8-41	101
8.36	213	9.8	99f.
8.37	283f.	9.9	60

9.11	60, 99	10.30	198, 232, 235
9.13-16	274	10.32-38	258
9.14	99f., 125	10.32f.	233
9.15	214	10.32	2, 89, 97, 116, 130, 154, 214, 227, 232-236, 238, 240, 244f., 258, 261
9.16f.	100		
9.16	90, 118		
9.17	60	10.33	89, 232, 235
9.18	274	10.34-36	232f., 236
9.19	60, 214	10.34	59f., 75, 81
9.21	214	10.36	60, 108, 232f.
9.22	100, 274	10.37f.	2, 97, 116, 195, 227, 232-234, 236, 238-240, 244f., 259, 261f., 278f., 281, 284, 288, 289
9.23	60		
9.24-34	100		
9.24-28	100		
9.25	214, 236	10.37	89, 154, 240, 244, 261
9.28	6, 220	10.38	89, 237, 240, 242, 244, 257, 259, 270, 287, 289
9.31-38	100		
9.32	242, 255, 261	10.40-42	90
9.33	118	10.41	11, 60, 90, 274
9.35-41	125	11.1-16	113
9.35-38	100	11.4	107, 160
9.35-37	234	11.5	301
9.39-41	126, 222	11.8	274
9.39	59, 101, 214	11.9	104, 214
9.40	274	11.10	104
9.41	60, 214, 243	11.11-14	275
10	99, 244	11.19	273
10.1-18	233	11.22	116
10.1-16	53	11.25	55
10.1-5	203	11.31	273
10.7	60, 202	11.33	273
10.9	55	11.36	273
10.11	153	11.40	60, 160
10.15	153	11.41f.	116
10.16	59, 288	11.42	108
10.17	214	11.45	236, 273
10.18	221	11.46f.	274
10.19	274	11.47	90
10.21	99, 118, 236	11.49	274
10.22-39	98, 232, 295	11.50-52	153
10.23ff.	232	11.50	65
10.24-38	274	11.51	60, 274
10.24	232-234	11.52	106
10.25-39	231	11.54	273
10.25	2, 89, 97, 116, 195, 227f., 232-234, 236, 238, 240, 244f., 258, 261	11.57	274
		12.1-8	91
		12.9	273
10.27-29	232f.	12.10	274

12.11	236, 273	13.23	155
12.12ff.	302	13.30	125, 154, 168
12.13	59, 77f., 81f.	13.31-38	154
12.14	62	13.31	118, 154, 160
12.15	59, 61, 68-70, 78, 82	13.32	118
12.16	60, 77f., 158, 160	13.33	60, 117, 274
12.17	228	14	154, 238, 244
12.18f.	274	14.2	60
12.18	90	14.5	154
12.20-22	273	14.6	11, 55
12.23	118, 160	14.7	212
12.27	53, 59	14.8-11	231
12.28	118, 160	14.8	154, 214, 238
12.34	60, 77, 79, 81	14.9	214, 239, 243
12.35f.	115, 117, 125	14.10f.	2, 97, 227, 236, 239-241, 259, 261f., 270, 288
12.35	104, 203		
12.36-50	63	14.10	83, 89, 106, 116, 154, 195, 198, 204, 213, 221, 230, 235, 238-241, 244f., 260, 270
12.36	104		
12.37-43	90, 274		
12.37	64, 90		
12.38	59, 63, 66, 68f., 75	14.11	89, 239f., 242, 244f., 257, 275
12.40	59, 63, 68-70, 82, 243, 299		
		14.12-14	195, 287
12.41	158	14.12	2, 89, 117, 275, 288
12.43	60, 158	14.13f.	221, 270, 288
12.44f.	53	14.13	213
12.44	108	14.16f.	154, 288
12.45	108	14.19	117
12.46	104, 115, 125	14.22	9, 154
12.47f.	222	14.24	83, 108, 221
12.47	126	14.26	54, 288
12.48	126	14.31	106, 154, 160, 195, 198, 221
12.49f.	83		
12.49	108, 160, 198, 204, 213, 221	15-17	154f.
		15-16	154
12.50	221	15.4f.	237
13-17	154	15.5	288
13.1-31	154	15.8	160
13.3	160	15.9	214
13.4f.	53	15.10	221
13.11	60	15.13	153
13.12-17	53	15.14	141
13.16	53, 108	15.18-16.4	241, 256, 298
13.18	59, 75, 81f., 106, 299	15.18-25	78
13.20	108, 110, 243	15.18-21	256
13.21	60	15.21	108, 243
13.22	214	15.22-25	241, 256
13.23-26	8	15.22	239, 241f., 244

15.23	241, 243	17.22	160
15.24	2, 89, 97, 195, 227, 231, 239, 241f., 244, 254f., 260, 275	17.23	108, 214, 237
		17.24	156, 160, 214, 221
		17.25	108, 156
15.25	60, 78, 80f., 106, 241	17.26	156, 214, 237
15.26-16.2	256	18	275
15.26f.	288	18.1-3	275
15.26	54, 228, 270	18.1ff.	154
15.27	228	18.1	154
16.1-4	54	18.3	274
16.3	243	18.7	275
16.5	108	18.8	60, 275
16.7-15	288	18.9	60
16.7	11, 288	18.10	274f.
16.8	242	18.11	80, 149, 275
16.14	160	18.12	274
16.15	60	18.13	274
16.16	117	18.14	60, 65, 153, 274
16.20	60	18.15	274
16.22	59	18.16	274
16.24	187	18.19-24	275
16.26	60	18.19	274
16.32	54	18.22	274
17	154-156, 159	18.24	274
17.1-6	191	18.26	274
17.1-5	155-157	18.28-35	275
17.1	156f., 160, 213	18.28f.	273
17.2-4	157	18.28	66, 125, 168
17.2	157, 160	18.29	276
17.3f.	162	18.30-32	275
17.3	108, 152, 157, 212, 221	18.30ff.	275
17.4	2, 4, 89, 97, 116, 130, 150, 152, 154, 157-163, 195, 229-231, 236, 275	18.30f.	275
		18.31	274f.
		18.32	275
17.5	118, 126, 156, 160	18.33-19.6	276
17.6-26	155	18.33-35	273, 275
17.6	106, 156	18.33	275f.
17.7f.	116	18.35	274-276
17.8	83, 108	18.36-38	276
17.10	160	18.36	274, 276
17.11	156, 160	18.37	11, 60
17.12	156	18.38	274, 276
17.15	156	19.1	276
17.17	11	19.4	276
17.18	108f.	19.6-12	276
17.19	11, 155	19.6	274, 276
17.21f.	260	19.7	274, 276
17.21	108, 156, 237	19.9	276

19.12	274, 276	21.20-24	155
19.13	276	21.20-23	7f.
19.14f.	276	21.20-22	7
19.14	66, 125, 168, 274, 276	21.20	214
19.15	274, 276	21.22	7
19.19	8	21.23	60
19.21	60, 274	21.24	6-9, 11, 24, 228, 294
19.22	8		
19.24	59, 65, 67-69, 75	*Acts*	
19.26f.	8		
19.27	6, 197	1.6	211
19.28	59, 67, 79-82	1.14	140
19.29	66, 80	1.20	61
19.30	79, 153, 231	3.2	99, 101
19.31-34	66	4.13	222
19.31	274	7.58	235
19.34	6, 67	8.4-25	131
19.35	6, 11, 228	8.7	120
19.36f.	66	9.4	202
19.36	59, 66-68, 82	12.17	140
19.37	59, 67-69	14.8	101
19.38	274	15.13-21	140
20-21	17	16.16-18	120
20.1	214	21.18	140
20.2-10	8		
20.5	214	*Romans*	
20.9	60		
20.14	125, 168	6.3f.	146
20.18	60	8.15	185
20.19	274	8.29	143
20.20	214	11.9f.	61
20.21-23	288	15.3	61
20.21	90, 108f.	15.15	8
20.23	54	15.18	286
20.28	83, 191, 198, 269		
20.30f.	7, 90, 277	*1 Corinthians*	
20.30	18f., 90, 274		
20.31f.	17	4.13	187
20.31	126, 276	8.7	187
21	7	10.4	75
21.1-22	7	12.6	286
21.1-14	17	12.11	286
21.1	106	15.6	187
21.7	8	15.10	286
21.9	214	15.58	280, 285
21.14	106	16.10	285, 289
21.15-22	7		
21.19	158		

2 Corinthians

5.16	212
9.13	159

Galatians

1.19	140
2.8	286
2.9	140
2.12	140
3.5	286
4.6	185

Ephesians

1.11	286
1.20	286
3.20	286

Philippians

2.12f.	286
3.10	212

Colossians

1.29	286
2.12	146

2 Thessalonians

2.4	198

2 Timothy

1.12	212
4.5	283

Hebrews

2.11	143

1 John

1.1-3	6
1.2	106
1.5	104
1.7	104
2.3	212
2.6	6
2.8	104
2.9	187
2.19	106
2.25	157
2.28	106
3.2	106
3.3	6
3.5	6, 106
3.7	6
3.8	89, 106
3.12	89
3.16	6
3.18	89
3.24	237
4.9	106
4.15f.	237
5.20	157

2 John

8	89
11	89

3 John

5	89
10	89

Revelation

1.7	68
2.26	280
11.5	61
12.4	61
20.9	61

III. Apocrypha and Pseudepigrapha

1 Baruch

2.9	280

2 Baruch

57.2	280

Ecclesiasticus

2.6	70
7.25	137
24.21	137, 148
37.15	70
38.8	137
38.27	137
49.9	70
50.19	137

1 Enoch

49.1	77
62.14	77

3 Enoch

8.1	148

1 Esdras

8.16	137
9.9	137, 159
7.9	280
7.15	280

4 Esdras

7.24	280

Judith

8.34	137

1 Maccabees

2.32ff.	178
4.7	73
4.51	137

2 Maccabees

1.3	137
9.12	198
9.28	198

4 Maccabees

18.16	137

Psalms of Solomon

6.3	285
7.1	79
16.9	285
17.4	77

Sibylline Oracles

3.49f.	77
3.767	77

Testament of Levi

19.1	280

Wisdom

7.25f.	223
16.20	71

IV. Qumran Writings

CD

1.1	87
2.14f.	291
2.14	87
13.7	87

1QH

5.36	87

1QS

1-9	142
4.4	87
8.14	69
9.13	137
9.20	69
9.23	137

V. Hellenistic-Jewish Literature

Josephus
Jewish War
2.120-158   142

Philo
Cher.
87   186
Leg. Alleg.
1.5f.   186

1.49   198
1.97   137, 148
Opif.
158   137, 147
Sacr. Abel et Cain
86   137, 147
Vita Mosis
2.69   137, 147

VI. Rabbinic Literature

Aboth

1.6	135
5.19	282

A.Z.

10b	282

p.Bik.

3.65d.22	282

Cant.R.

1.4	148

Ex.R.

3 (69d)	282
30.9	186

Gen.R.

11.10	187

54.1	148
70.5	148

Kethuboth

2.9	228

Qoh.R.

2.24	137, 148

TB Sabb.

120a	148

Sanh.

7.5	199

Shab.

10.5	189

S.Nu.

5.15.8 (4a)	282

VII. Early Christian and Patristic Authors

Alexander of Alexandria

Catholic Epistle
    259

Ambrose

Duties of the Clergy
1.31.162   161

Of the Christian Faith
1.2.13   224
1.3.22   260
1.3.25   260
2.8.69   224
4.4.44f.   224
4.5.59f.   224
4.6.67   224
4.10.136   162
5.11.132   260

Of the Holy Spirit
2.12.134f.   224

Archelaus

Disputation with Manes
31   192

Athanasius

Ad Afros
7   224

Contra Gentes
3.46.7   224

De Decretis
5.21   260

De Incarnatione
18.2-6   260

De Synodis
3.49   224

Festal letters
1.5   161

On Lk. 10.22
1   192

Orations against the Arians
2.15.12   260
2.16.21   192, 224
2.17.29   192
2.21.66   258
3.23   260
3.23.3   260
3.25.16   260
3.25.23   161, 260
3.26.32   260
3.27.37   260

Augustine

Harmony of the Gospels
1.4.7   260
1.47   224
4.10.14   193

Holy Virginity
28   161

On the Creed
5   224

On Ps. 86
20   260

On Ps. 110
8   260

On the Trinity
2.1.3   224
2.4.6   162

Sermons
2.14   260
21.25f.   260
75.6   193
76.5   224
76.9   224
76.10   224
76.13-15   224
85.4f.   128
86.1   127

Tractates on John's Gospel
17.16   193
18.5   224
18.6f.   224

20.8	224f.
21.2	224
21.4	224
23.11	224
43.14	162
44.6	127
48.10	260
71.2	260
91.1	261
91.3f.	261
105.3	161
105.4	162
105.5	161

Basil

Letters

8.9	224
38.8	260

On the Spirit

8.19	224
18.46	162

Cassian

Institutes

12.8	259
12.17	259

Chrysostom

Homilies on John's Gospel

3.4	260
20.3	161
36.2	192
38.2	193
38.3f.	224
38.4	224
39.1	193
40.3	258, 260
49.2	223
56.2	128
61.2f.	260
64.1	224, 260
74.2	260
77	261
80.2	162

Homily on Matthew's Gospel

40.1	193

Homily on the Paralytic let down through the Roof

6	193

On the Priesthood

4.1	260

2 Clement

9.11	140f.

Clement of Alexandria

Eclog. Proph.

20	141

Paidogogos

1.6	161

Stromata

1.1	192, 222

Cyprian

Test. against the Jews

3.60	161

Cyril of Jerusalem

Catechetical Lectures

11.16	259f.
11.23	193

Dionysius of Rome

Against the Sabellians

2	259

Eusebius of Caesarea

Eccl. Hist.

3.39.3f.	9
6.14.7	13
10.4.25	222

De Eccl. Theol.

3.19.4	260

Index of Sources

Gospel of Thomas
99   141

Gregory of Nazianzus
Theol. Or.
3.17   161, 223
4.10   224
4.11   193

Gregory of Nyssa
Against Eunomius
1.39   260
2.4   260
2.9   260
2.15   192
4.8   260
6.3   260
8.5   260
9.4   260
10.4   260
On the Holy Spirit
     162

Hilary
De Synodis
19   224
75   224
On the Trinity
3.1ff.   260
3.15f.   161
3.23   260
6.27   258
7.12   260
7.17   224
7.18   224
7.21   128, 224
7.26   260
7.38-41   260
7.41   260
8.4   260
8.52   260
9.20   258
9.43-47   224
9.44f.   193
9.52   260
9.69f.   260
9.72   224
11.12   224, 260

Hippolytus
Refutation of all Heresies
7.22.4   12

Irenaeus
Against the Heresies
15.2   127

Jerome
Letter to Castrutius
68.1   127
126.1   192
Letter to Pammachius
22   192
132.6   192

John of Damascus
Exposition of the Orthodox Faith
8   224, 260
18   224, 260

Justin Martyr
Apology   12

Methodius
Concerning Chastity
2.1   191

Novatian
Treatise Concerning the Trinity
14   223
15   258
21   223
26   162
28   192

Origen

Commentary on John
| ad 4.34 | 161 |
| 10.21 | 223 |

De Principia
| 1.2.12 | 224 |

Against Celsus
| 12 | 259 |

Pseudo-Athanasius

Orations against the Arians
| 4.16 | 259 |

Tertullian

Against Praxeas
8	259
15	223
21	161, 192, 223, 258
22	258f.
24	259

On Fasting
| 15 | 161 |

Author Index

Abbott, E.A. 109
Abbott-Smith, G. 5, 106
Abrahams, I. 174
Albrecht, E. 3, 231, 233
Allison, D.C. 119-121, 140-142, 175-177, 180f., 208-210, 246-248, 250f., 252
Anderson, H. 140, 175, 177
Anderson, N. 30
Appold, M.L. 198, 236f.
Ashton, J. 23, 50, 219

Bacchiochi, S. 171, 184, 188
Banks, R. 177f., 189f.
Barbour, R.S. 40-43
Barclay, W. 10
Barr, J. 170, 185
Barrett, C.K. 3, 6f., 10, 14f., 18, 20f., 23, 48, 52, 59, 61, 63f., 67-70, 72, 74, 76, 78-80, 90, 99, 101-103, 109, 111, 131, 133, 139, 150f., 154-158, 166, 197f., 203, 220, 222, 228-230, 232-235, 238, 242, 281, 287
Bauckham, R. 185, 205, 218
Beare, F.W. 121, 207, 248, 251
Beasley-Murray, G.R. 6-9, 61, 65, 67, 72, 74, 79f., 99, 103f., 111, 113, 148, 151, 154, 157f., 165, 198, 203, 222, 228, 233f., 235, 239, 243, 281, 283, 288
Becker, J. 7, 14, 16f., 19, 62, 74, 76, 99-101, 103, 107, 113, 125, 132, 135, 167, 198, 202, 215, 228f., 231f., 241, 283
Berger, K. 201
Bergmeier, R. 280f., 285
Bernard, J. 4, 203f., 220, 228-231
Bernard, J.H. 6-8, 12, 61, 63f., 67, 74, 76, 79f., 99, 101f., 104f., 109, 111f., 131, 133, 135f., 150, 152, 154, 156f., 166, 169, 197, 202, 222, 232-234, 239, 243, 280f., 283, 285, 287
Bertram, G. 3, 88, 170, 187, 278
Best, E. 140, 143
Black, M. 33, 58, 141, 170f., 179f.
Bligh, J. 4, 106, 110, 117, 135, 151-153, 169, 197, 228f.
Blinzler, J. 13-15
Blomberg, C.L. 29, 39, 41-44, 49, 53-55, 218
Bock, D.L. 32
Boismard, M.-É. 21, 23f., 238
Borg, M. 28, 41-44, 169, 174-176, 180, 182
Borgen, P. 14, 58f., 71
Bornkamm, G. 32, 120, 185, 199f., 208
Bostock, D.G. 102
Bovon, F. 246, 248, 250
Brederek, E. 88, 92
Bridges, L.M. 115
Briggs, C.A. 142, 145, 238, 252
Brown, C. 231
Brown, F. 142, 145, 238, 252
Brown, R.E. 1, 3, 6-9, 14, 19, 21-24, 53, 56, 60-62, 64f., 67, 74, 76, 78, 80, 89, 99-101, 103, 105, 107, 111, 113, 124, 131, 150, 154, 156, 159, 161, 166, 168f., 197, 204, 215f., 220, 228f., 232-234, 239, 242f., 255, 281, 283, 288
Bruce, F.F. 7
Bultmann, R. 5-8, 16, 21, 39, 50, 52, 61, 64, 67, 71, 74, 78, 80, 99-104, 107, 110, 112, 114, 117, 119f., 125, 132f., 136, 140, 145, 148f., 152, 154-156, 165, 167, 169, 175, 177, 197f., 202, 207, 210, 215, 229-231, 233, 236, 239, 242f., 247f., 251, 280f., 283, 285,

287f.
Burge, G.M.   9, 14, 53, 58, 85
Burney, C.F.   33, 53, 110, 113, 138, 144, 171, 206, 209
Butts, J.R.   31

Caird, G.B.   146f., 247
Calvert, D.G.A.   28, 40-45
Calvin, J.   105, 117, 150-152, 158
Carrington, P.   141
Carson, D.A.   6-9, 12, 18-20, 52f., 55f., 58-61, 64, 74-76, 79f., 85, 99, 105, 111, 113, 133, 135, 139, 151, 154-158, 198, 204, 222, 229, 233-234, 239, 255, 281, 283, 288
Casey, P.M.   50, 159, 198
Catchpole, D.   40-44
Cerfaux, L.   4, 31, 239
Charlesworth, J.H.   29f., 53
Christ, F.   208f.
Collins, R.F.   206
Conzelmann, H.   144
Cranfield, C.E.B.   94, 95, 140, 177, 199f., 232
Creed, J.M.   179, 247
Crossan, J.D.   140
Cuthmann, O.   4, 8f., 45, 53, 170f., 187f., 208, 219
Culpepper, R.A.   133, 148f.

Dalman, G.   28, 33, 58, 94, 170
Davey, J.E.   183
Davies, W.D.   119-121, 140-142, 175-177, 179-181, 208-210, 246-248, 250f., 252
Delling, G.   5, 53, 153
Dewey, K.E.   110, 183, 206, 221
Dibelius, M.   140, 207
Dodd, C.H.   4, 6f. 14, 25, 35-38, 52, 54-56, 58, 62, 69, 79f., 85, 99, 101-105, 107, 113, 115, 134, 139, 148, 150f., 155f., 159, 191, 197, 203f., 215f., 218, 228f., 233, 238, 241, 283
Donaldson, J.   127
Downing, F.G.   39, 41-44
Driver, S.R.   142, 145, 238, 252
Drummond, J.   54f., 115, 138, 172
Dunn, J.D.G.   50, 110, 119-123, 126, 185, 207-210, 219, 247-251, 252f.
Dunstone, A.S.   39

Ellis, E.   120f., 176, 247, 254
Evans, C.F.   120, 122, 144, 181, 207, 209, 246, 251

Filson, F.V.   9
Findley, J.A.   131
Fitzmyer, J.A.   28, 33, 120f., 140, 144f., 147, 174, 180f., 208, 246, 248, 250f., 253
Fletcher, B.   28
Fortna, R.T.   14, 16-19, 48, 100, 103-105, 107, 132, 165, 167-169
France, R.T.   30f., 39, 40, 42-44
Freed, E.D.   61f., 67, 70, 72-77, 80, 83
Friend, H.S.   219
Fuller, R,H.   40-44
Funk, R.W.   31

Gaechter, P.   203, 215
Gardner - Smith, P.   14
Garrison, R.   28, 54, 207f., 210
Gerhardsson, B.   58
Giblet, J.   4, 221, 232, 250
Gnilka, J.   140, 142
Godet, F.L.   184
Goguel, M.   287
Goodwin, C.   59, 61, 64f., 72, 76f., 80
Gordon, C.H.   237
Grant, F.C.   31
Greig, J.C.G.   201
Grigsby, B.   99
Grob, F.   2, 105, 118, 124, 126, 150-152, 203f., 213, 228f., 286
Gruenler, R.G.   55
Grundmann, W.   94, 207, 215
Gryglewicz, F.   4, 87, 184, 201, 204
Guelich, R.A.   175-177
Guilding, A.   232
Gunther, J.J.   8f., 12
Guthrie, D.   6f., 9, 49, 53

Haenchen, E.   7, 9, 14, 71, 73f. 101, 104, 123, 132, 151f., 168, 228f., 231f., 239, 281
Hahn, F.   30

Author Index

Hanson, A.T. 50, 58f., 67, 71, 73f., 76, 79f., 241
Harnack, A. 210
Harrison, E.F. 55f.
Harvey, A.E. 43f., 102, 123, 199, 208, 219, 233, 247f.
Hasler, V. 201
Hatch, E. 87
Headlam, A.C. 55
Heiligenthal, R. 3, 148, 206, 229, 231, 235, 236, 281f., 287
Hengel, M. 6, 9, 11f., 24, 28, 42, 52f., 59, 142, 219
Higgins, A.J.B. 14, 53f., 183
Hill, D. 120-122, 175, 210, 251, 254
Hooker, M.D. 28, 39-45, 141, 175
Hoskyns, E.C. 6, 64, 74, 99, 105, 111, 113, 124, 169, 229, 232-234, 237, 239, 255, 281, 283f., 287
Howard, W.F. 20, 54, 115, 138, 172, 183, 197, 238
Hultgren, A.J. 174f.
Hunter, A.M. 53, 58, 135, 147, 183, 208-210

Jastrow, M. 88, 94
Jeremias, J. 28f., 32, 34-39, 41, 43, 50, 110, 119-122, 138, 145, 169-171, 184f., 199, 201, 204-210, 217f., 238, 246, 249, 252f.
Johnson, L. 9
Jonge, M. de 4
Jülicher, A. 218

Käsemann, E. 27, 39f., 43, 49f., 150, 155
King, J.S. 56
Knox, J. 31
Köster, H. 144, 146
Kragerud, A. 8
Kratz, R. 107
Kuhn, H.-W. 201
Kümmel, W.G. 6-8, 14f., 20, 41, 43f., 119-121, 146, 246-250, 255
Kysar, R. 8, 16, 19, 23, 102, 105, 111, 161, 198

Ladd, G.E. 49, 53

Lambrecht, J. 140
Lamouille, A. 21
Lane, W.L. 199
Latourelle, R. 39, 40, 42-44
Leaney, A.R.C. 247, 251
Lee, E.K. 9, 53
Leivestad, R. 247-250
Lemcio, E.E. 54, 133
Lenski, R.C.H. 6-8, 99, 105, 111, 113, 151f.
Leroy, H. 135
Levy, J. 238
Liddell, H.G. 5, 86
Lightfoot, J.B. 10, 12
Lightfoot, R.H. 6, 105, 113, 124f.
Lindars, B. 6-9, 13, 18, 20-23, 50, 58, 62-64, 67, 71-76, 79f., 99-103, 110f., 131, 139, 154-157, 166-168, 197f., 204f., 215, 220, 222, 228f., 233f., 236, 238, 241, 283f., 287
Loader, W. 58, 150, 153f., 198, 204, 214, 220, 230, 236, 238, 288
Lohmeyer, E. 280, 285
Lohse, E. 135, 169, 175, 177, 181, 188
Loisy, A. 166
Longenecker, R.N. 28, 40, 42, 43, 45

Malatesta, E. 238
Manson, T.W. 109, 121, 144, 176, 208, 246, 252f.
Manson, W. 247, 254
Marsh, J. 6, 8f., 222
Marshall, I.H. 39, 40-45, 109, 119-122, 132, 144f., 175-177, 179-181, 199-201, 207f., 210, 217, 219, 246-250, 252
Marshall, J.T. 113
Martin, R.A. 53, 113, 157, 169
Martin, R.P. 14
Martyn, J.L. 1, 100f., 107, 111, 113, 117, 167f., 191, 198
Mastin, B.A. 9, 14, 99, 112-114, 196, 198, 222
Maurer, C. 4, 187f.
McArthur, H.K. 39-42
McEleney, N.J. 30, 39, 41f.
McNamara, M. 58
McNeile, A.H. 119, 121

Mealand, D.L. 40, 42-44
Meeks, W.A. 219
Menken, M.J.J. 64f., 70, 72f., 76
Metzger, B.M. 111
Meyer, B. 39, 40, 42, 44, 140, 200, 208, 210, 247, 252
Michaels, J.R. 6
Mitton, C.L. 40, 42f., 45
Miyoshi, M. 207f., 211
Morris, L. 3, 6-12, 14, 19, 53, 57, 62, 65, 67, 70f., 74, 76, 78, 105, 109, 111, 113, 123f., 131, 135, 150-152, 155-158, 169, 188, 196, 198, 204, 217, 222, 229, 234, 236f., 239, 240, 242f., 281, 283, 287
Moule, C.F.D. 45, 69, 219
Müller, P.-G. 30
Mussner, F. 58, 253
Neirynck, F. 15, 175, 177
Nicol, W. 4, 16f., 19, 86, 100-102, 104, 107, 113, 132-134, 167, 214, 272
Noack, B. 14, 59, 61, 67, 69, 71, 76, 79
Nunn, H.P.V. 9, 12

Odeberg, H. 117, 137, 148, 197, 229, 231, 281, 284
Oepke, A. 145

Painter, J. 9, 14, 53, 100-103, 107, 124, 133, 183, 191, 198, 203, 220, 228, 232, 234, 237, 281
Pancaro, S. 3, 88, 137, 139, 150, 152, 168, 170, 182, 195, 228-230, 233, 235, 237, 278, 280f., 283, 285
Parker, P. 9, 14, 19
Paul, G.J. 9
Perrin, N. 28, 39-44
Pesch, R. 107
Plummer, A. 133, 150, 154
Pollard, T.E. 260
Potter, R.D. 10

Quast, K. 8

Redpath, H.A. 87
Reim, G. 15, 59, 61-64, 69-71, 73-76, 80
Rengstorf, K.H. 108
Reynolds, H.R. 57

Richard, E. 133
Riedl, J. 2, 106, 125, 149-153, 159-61, 188, 195, 204, 221f., 228, 229-231, 234, 236-239, 240, 242f., 281, 283, 287f.
Riesenfeld, H. 14, 57f.
Riesner, R. 30, 39, 41-45, 109, 205, 207-210, 247-249, 253
Roberts, A. 127
Robinson, J.A.T. 7-10, 14, 20, 53-56, 85, 98f., 102, 109, 116, 126, 151, 156, 197, 204, 208, 232f., 234, 238
Robinson, J.M. 27, 32, 39
Rodd, C.S. 121
Rogers, D. 9
Roloff, J. 175-177, 188
Ruckstuhl, E. 16, 18-20, 58, 133f.

Sanders, E.P. 28f., 39, 41, 44, 103, 119, 165, 173f., 181, 199f., 251
Sanders, J.N. 9, 12, 14, 99, 111, 113-114, 196, 198, 222
Schaff, P. 127
Schlatter, D.A. 206, 217
Schlier, H. 5, 217
Schnackenburg, R. 3, 6-10, 14, 16, 18f., 50, 58, 61f., 65, 70f., 74, 76, 79f., 99, 102, 104, 107, 111, 113, 125, 131, 136, 138, 148, 150f., 154-158, 166f., 196-198, 204, 229, 232f., 236-238, 239f., 243, 281, 283
Schrenk, G. 8
Schulz, S. 52, 167, 209
Schürmann, H. 144
Schweitzer, A. 49
Schweizer, E. 16, 58, 121, 140, 174, 199, 207, 211, 247, 251, 253
Scott, B.B. 31
Scott, R. 5, 86
Selby, G.R. 28
Sevenster, J.N. 28
Sidebottom, E.M. 52, 58
Smalley, S.S. 9, 14, 48, 51, 53, 138
Smith, D.M. 14, 16, 23, 25, 53
Sperber, A. 68
Stanton, V.H. 54, 135
Stein, R.H. 29f., 39-45
Stevenson, W.D. 205

Strachan, R.H. 152
Strathmann, H. 50
Streeter, B.H. 23
Suggs, M.J. 209
Sundberg, A.C. 4, 197

Tarrelli, C.C. 6, 109
Taylor, V. 109, 140, 144, 199f., 207f.
Teeple, H.M. 16-21, 167
Temple, S. 4, 14, 16, 18f., 53, 132, 215, 272
Thackeray, H.St.J. 242
Thornecroft, J.K. 9
Thüsing, W. 113, 150, 160, 229
Torrey, C.C. 67
Toy, C.H. 61, 72, 76
Trites, A.A. 228f.
Trocmé, E. 41
Turner, H.E.W. 39
Turner, N. 28

Unnik, W.C. van 10

Vanhoye, A. 4, 150, 160, 221, 230, 235f.
Vermes, G. 173, 185, 208, 247

Wace, H. 127
Wahlde, U.C. von 4, 17, 86, 100, 103, 132f., 149, 152f., 167, 229, 272-277, 280f., 285
Weiss, H. 188, 191
Wendt, H.H. 4, 54, 277
Westcott, B.F. 6-8, 10, 12, 65, 73, 76, 78, 80, 99, 102, 105, 108, 117, 131, 155f., 196-198, 222, 230, 232-234, 239, 240, 242f., 281, 284, 287
Westerholm, S. 29, 42-45, 169, 174, 176f.
Whiteacre, R.A. 1
Wilkens, W. 3, 21-24, 102, 107, 153, 239
Wise, M.O. 33
Witherington, B. 41-44, 119f., 121-123, 175-177, 185, 189, 205, 207-210, 247-249, 251f., 255
Witkamp, L.Th. 4, 85, 168, 183
Wright, C.J. 131

Yamauchi, E. 52

Zahn, T. 152

Subject Index

Abba 171, 184-186, 193, 210
Amen 171, 201f., 204, 215, 216f., 225, 266
Apocryphal Gospels 10-12
Aporia 17f., 20, 22, 24, 154, 272f., 275
Apprenticeship Imagery 203-207, 213-216, 218-221, 224-226, 269, 284
Aramaic Sayings of Jesus (postulated retroversions) 114, 120, 137, 141, 145, 170f., 177, 180, 205, 209, 248, 252
Authenticity
—burden of proof for 27, 38-40, 47
—concept of 1, 5, 26-48, 264f.
—criteria for 27, 32f., 40-48
—of Jesus' Johannine sayings 1, 2, 4f., 13, 21, 24-26, 38, 49-51, 57f., 83-98, 105-122, 128-130, 135-149, 155-159, 162, 164, 170-184, 190f., 193, 196, 201-216, 221, 225, 227, 245-256, 261-268
—of Jesus' non-Johannine sayings 1, 2, 5, 27-48, 83f., 106, 110, 116, 119f., 139-147, 174-181, 184, 207-212, 246-253
Authorship 1, 5-13, 20, 24, 51, 263

Beloved Disciple 6-9, 22-24
Blasphemy 3, 197, 199f., 232, 235, 238

Christology 22, 55, 65, 68, 82, 84, 95, 102, 126-129, 143, 151, 161-163, 167f., 177f., 182f., 189-200, 203f., 206-208, 214, 217-221, 223-226, 248, 257, 258-262, 267, 269-272, 278, 289f.
Creation 102, 122, 126-129, 182, 186f., 191-194, 221, 224
Crucifixion of Christ 61, 65f., 80, 116, 118, 124, 144-147, 151, 153, 155-161, 163, 187f., 248

Dead Sea Scrolls 52, 56, 69, 87, 137, 264, 280

Exorcisms 118-122, 125, 249, 254

Feasts
—Dedication 98f., 232f.
—Passover 66, 130, 158, 165
—Pentecost 165, 210-212
—Tabernacles 73-75, 98-100, 102, 232

Gnosticism 51f., 56, 127, 145, 202, 207-209, 239

Hellenism 51f., 207-209, 264
Hermetic Literature 51f., 203
Herodians 199

Johannine Community 1, 100, 135, 191, 194, 198, 200, 222, 228, 241
Johannine Style 16-20, 22, 24, 48-53, 56-58, 65, 83, 89-91, 96, 101, 105-107, 109f., 115, 117f., 132-134, 155, 157f., 169, 184, 195, 202, 208, 214-216, 237, 240, 256f., 264, 266, 268, 272f., 281
John's Gospel
—development theories 1, 21-25, 51, 154, 263
—relationship/coherence with the synoptic gospels 1, 13-16, 22-25, 48f., 51, 53-57, 62, 69, 77, 80, 91-96, 98, 101-104, 106f., 109, 115f., 118, 128, 131, 133f., 136, 138-147, 155f., 158f., 162, 164, 166f., 169, 171-184, 189, 191, 193, 199f., 203, 205-212, 216,

225, 229, 231, 233, 241, 245-258, 263f., 267
—source theories 1, 4, 10f., 16-21, 25, 51, 83, 100, 103, 132, 167, 263, 268, 272-277
—use of Old Testament quotations 2, 51, 58-84, 256, 265, 268
John the Apostle 9-11, 22f., 146, 277
John the Baptist 69f., 124, 145, 228f., 246-251, 273, 275
John the Elder 9, 23
Judgement 23, 53, 55, 64f., 101, 122, 126, 129, 182, 186f., 191, 194, 216, 218-222, 225, 228-230, 248, 251-254, 257, 262, 269f., 289

Last Supper / Lord's Supper 53, 76, 152, 154, 156, 163,
Law, the 55, 70-72, 125, 129, 148, 152, 163, 179, 189
Life-Giving 151, 153, 157, 163f., 191, 194, 214-216, 219-222, 225, 228-230, 257, 262, 269f.

Mandaean Literature 51f., 203
Messiahship 124-126, 129f., 188, 193, 211, 234f., 244, 248-250, 254-257, 261, 272
Miracles 3, 17-19, 21, 23, 92-94, 96, 101, 103, 106, 116, 124, 126, 130, 160, 169, 172, 174, 176, 179, 184, 188-190, 193, 196, 199, 216, 221f., 229-231, 233-235, 239, 242-244, 247, 251-254, 255, 260f., 269, 272-274, 281, 286-289
Misunderstandings 132f., 135, 191, 275
Moses 71, 206, 209, 219-20, 225
Mystery Religions 51, 239

Parable and Allegory 205, 218f., 220

Patristic Exegesis of the Johannine 'Works' Sayings 1f., 5, 84, 98, 127-130, 161-163, 191-194, 196, 223-227, 237, 258-262, 270f.
Pharisees 101, 129, 133, 173-175, 177-180, 182, 189, 199, 272-276
Pre-existence 23, 126, 129, 160, 202, 231, 269

Rabbinic Judaism 53, 104, 113, 115f., 125, 135, 137, 148, 170, 175f., 178, 180f., 186-190, 197, 206, 228, 233, 235, 242, 280, 282
Revelation 55, 122, 153, 158, 160, 162f., 191, 194, 202, 207, 210, 214f., 220f., 225, 243, 255, 269-271

Sabbath 3, 99f., 102, 106, 125, 129, 153, 166-170, 172-184, 186-191, 193f., 196, 199, 216, 221
Sadducees 133
Sanhedrin 200
Signs 3f., 17f., 21, 25, 86, 90, 93, 96, 235, 272-277
Son (of God) 23, 94, 126-128, 161-164, 184-186, 192-194, 200, 203-207, 210-212, 213, 218-226, 232, 234, 236, 240, 245, 256f., 258-262, 266, 269f., 276, 289
Son of Man 94, 200

θεῖος ἀνήρ 17, 272

Use of ὅτι 59f., 77, 79

Vaticinia ex Eventu 146

Witness 3, 97, 188, 228f., 231f., 233-235, 237, 240-246, 250, 253-257, 261, 268

Wissenschaftliche Untersuchungen zum Neuen Testament

Alphabetical Index of the First and Second Series

Anderson, Paul N.: The Christology of the Fourth Gospel. 1996. *Volume II/78.*
Appold, Mark L.: The Oneness Motif in the Fourth Gospel. 1976. *Volume II/1.*
Arnold, Clinton E.: The Colossian Syncretism. 1995. *Volume II/77.*
Bachmann, Michael: Sünder oder Übertreter. 1992. *Volume 59.*
Baker, William R.: Personal Speech-Ethics in the Epistle of James. 1995. *Volume II/68.*
Bammel, Ernst: Judaica. Volume I 1986. Volume 37 - Volume II 1996. *Volume 91.*
Bauernfeind, Otto: Kommentar und Studien zur Apostelgeschichte. 1980. *Volume 22.*
Bayer, Hans Friedrich: Jesus' Predictions of Vindication and Resurrection. 1986. *Volume II/20.*
Bell, Richard H.: Provoked to Jealousy. 1994. *Volume II/63.*
Betz, Otto: Jesus, der Messias Israels. 1987. *Volume 42.*
– Jesus, der Herr der Kirche. 1990. Volume 52.
Beyschlag, Karlmann: Simon Magus und die christliche Gnosis. 1974. *Volume 16.*
Bittner, Wolfgang J.: Jesu Zeichen im Johannesevangelium. 1987. *Volume II/26.*
Bjerkelund, Carl J.: Tauta Egeneto. 1987. *Volume 40.*
Blackburn, Barry Lee: Theios Aner and the Markan Miracle Traditions. 1991. *Volume II/40.*
Bockmuehl, Markus N.A.: Revelation and Mystery in Ancient Judaism and Pauline Christianity. 1990. *Volume II/36.*
Böhlig, Alexander: Gnosis und Synkretismus. Teil 1 1989. *Volume 47* – Teil 2 1989. *Volume 48.*
Böttrich, Christfried: Weltweisheit – Menschheitsethik – Urkult. 1992. *Volume II/50.*
Büchli, Jörg: Der Poimandres – ein paganisiertes Evangelium. 1987. *Volume II/27.*
Bühner, Jan A.: Der Gesandte und sein Weg im 4.Evangelium. 1977. *Volume II/2.*
Burchard, Christoph: Untersuchungen zu Joseph und Aseneth. 1965. *Volume 8.*
Cancik, Hubert (Ed.): Markus-Philologie. 1984. *Volume 33.*
Capes, David B.: Old Testament Yaweh Texts in Paul's Christology. 1992. *Volume II/47.*
Caragounis, Chrys C.: The Son of Man. 1986. *Volume 38.*
– see *Fridrichsen, Anton.*
Carleton Paget, James: The Epistle of Barnabas. 1994. *Volume II/64.*
Crump, David: Jesus the Intercessor. 1992. *Volume II/49.*
Deines, Roland: Jüdische Steingefäße und pharisäische Frömmigkeit. 1993. *Volume II/52.*
Dobbeler, Axel von: Glaube als Teilhabe. 1987. *Volume II/22.*
Dunn, James D.G. (Ed.): Jews and Christians. 1992. *Volume 66.*
Ebertz, Michael N.: Das Charisma des Gekreuzigten. 1987. *Volume 45.*
Eckstein, Hans-Joachim: Der Begriff Syneidesis bei Paulus. 1983. *Volume II/10.*
– Verheißung und Gesetz. 1996. *Volume 86.*
Ego, Beate: Im Himmel wie auf Erden. 1989. *Volume II/34.*
Ellis, E. Earle: Prophecy and Hermeneutic in Early Christianity. 1978. *Volume 18.*
– The Old Testament in Early Christianity. 1991. *Volume 54.*
Ennulat, Andreas: Die 'Minor Agreements'. 1994. *Volume II/62.*
Ensor, Peter W.: Paul and His 'Work'. 1996. *Volume II/85.*
Feldmeier, Reinhard: Die Krisis des Gottessohnes. 1987. *Volume II/21.*
– Die Christen als Fremde. 1992. *Volume 64.*
Feldmeier, Reinhard and *Ulrich Heckel* (Ed.): Die Heiden. 1994. *Volume 70.*
Forbes, Christopher Brian: Prophecy and Inspired Speech in Early Christianity and its Hellenistic Environment. 1995. *Volume II/75.*
Fornberg, Tord: see *Fridrichsen, Anton.*
Fossum, Jarl E.: The Name of God and the Angel of the Lord. 1985. *Volume 36.*
Frenschkowski, Marco: Offenbarung und Epiphanie. Volume 1 1995. *Volume II/79* – Volume 2 1996. *Volume II/80.*

Frey, Jörg: Eugen Drewermann und die biblische Exegese. 1995. *Volume II/71.*
Fridrichsen, Anton: Exegetical Writings. Ed. by C.C. Caragounis and T. Fornberg. 1994. *Volume 76.*
Garlington, Don B.: 'The Obedience of Faith'. 1991. *Volume II/38.*
– Faith, Obedience, and Perseverance. 1994. *Volume 79.*
Garnet, Paul: Salvation and Atonement in the Qumran Scrolls. 1977. *Volume II/3.*
Gräßer, Erich: Der Alte Bund im Neuen. 1985. *Volume 35.*
Green, Joel B.: The Death of Jesus. 1988. *Volume II/33.*
Gundry Volf, Judith M.: Paul and Perseverance. 1990. *Volume II/37.*
Hafemann, Scott J.: Suffering and the Spirit. 1986. *Volume II/19.*
– Paul, Moses, and the History of Israel. 1995. *Volume 81.*
Heckel, Theo K.: Der Innere Mensch. 1993. *Volume II/53.*
Heckel, Ulrich: Kraft in Schwachheit. 1993. *Volume II/56.*
– see *Feldmeier, Reinhard.*
– see *Hengel, Martin.*
Heiligenthal, Roman: Werke als Zeichen. 1983. *Volume II/9.*
Hemer, Colin J.: The Book of Acts in the Setting of Hellenistic History. 1989. *Volume 49.*
Hengel, Martin: Judentum und Hellenismus. 1969, ³1988. *Volume 10.*
– Die johanneische Frage. 1993. *Volume 67.*
Hengel, Martin and *Ulrich Heckel* (Ed.): Paulus und das antike Judentum. 1991. *Volume 58.*
Hengel, Martin and *Hermut Löhr* (Ed.): Schriftauslegung im antiken Judentum und im Urchristentum. 1994. *Volume 73.*
Hengel, Martin and *Anna Maria Schwemer* (Ed.): Königsherrschaft Gottes und himmlischer Kult. 1991. *Volume 55.*
– Die Septuaginta. 1994. *Volume 72.*
Herrenbrück, Fritz: Jesus und die Zöllner. 1990. *Volume II/41.*
Hoegen-Rohls, Christina: Der nachösterliche Johannes. 1996. *Volume II/84.*
Hofius, Otfried: Katapausis. 1970. *Volume 11.*
– Der Vorhang vor dem Thron Gottes. 1972. *Volume 14.*
– Der Christushymnus Philipper 2,6-11. 1976, ²1991. *Volume 17.*
– Paulusstudien. 1989, 21994. *Volume 51.*
Holtz, Traugott: Geschichte und Theologie des Urchristentums. 1991. *Volume 57.*
Hommel, Hildebrecht: Sebasmata. Volume 1 1983. *Volume 31* – Volume 2 1984. *Volume 32.*
Hvlavik, Reidar: The Struggle of Scripture and Convenant. 1996. *Volume II/82.*
Kähler, Christoph: Jesu Gleichnisse als Poesie und Therapie. 1995. *Volume 78.*
Kamlah, Ehrhard: Die Form der katalogischen Paränese im Neuen Testament. 1964. *Volume 7.*
Kim, Seyoon: The Origin of Paul's Gospel. 1981, ²1984. *Volume II/4.*
– "The 'Son of Man'" as the Son of God. 1983. *Volume 30.*
Kleinknecht, Karl Th.: Der leidende Gerechtfertigte. 1984, ²1988. *Volume II/13.*
Klinghardt, Matthias: Gesetz und Volk Gottes. 1988. *Volume II/32.*
Köhler, Wolf-Dietrich: Rezeption des Matthäusevangeliums in der Zeit vor Irenäus. 1987. *Volume II/24.*
Korn, Manfred: Die Geschichte Jesu in veränderter Zeit. 1993. *Volume II/51.*
Koskenniemi, Erkki: Apollonios von Tyana in der neutestamentlichen Exegese. 1994. *Volume II/61.*
Kraus, Wolfgang: Das Volk Gottes. 1995. *Volume 85.*
Kuhn, Karl G.: Achtzehngebet und Vaterunser und der Reim. 1950. *Volume 1.*
Lampe, Peter: Die stadtrömischen Christen in den ersten beiden Jahrhunderten. 1987, ²1989. *Volume II/18.*
Lieu, Samuel N.C.: Manichaeism in the Later Roman Empire and Medieval China. ²1992. *Volume 63.*
Löhr, Hermut: see *Hengel, Martin.*
Löhr, Winrich Alfried: Basilides und seine Schule. 1995. *Volume 83.*
Maier, Gerhard: Mensch und freier Wille. 1971. *Volume 12.*
– Die Johannesoffenbarung und die Kirche. 1981. *Volume 25.*
Markschies, Christoph: Valentinus Gnosticus? 1992. *Volume 65.*

Marshall, Peter: Enmity in Corinth: Social Conventions in Paul's Relations with the Corinthians. 1987. *Volume II/23.*
Meade, David G.: Pseudonymity and Canon. 1986. *Volume 39.*
Meadors, Edward P.: Jesus the Messianic Herald of Salvation. 1995. *Volume II/72.*
Mell, Ulrich: Die „anderen" Winzer. 1994. *Volume 77.*
Mengel, Berthold: Studien zum Philipperbrief. 1982. *Volume II/8.*
Merkel, Helmut: Die Widersprüche zwischen den Evangelien. 1971. *Volume 13.*
Merklein, Helmut: Studien zu Jesus und Paulus. 1987. *Volume 43.*
Metzler, Karin: Der griechische Begriff des Verzeihens. 1991. *Volume II/44.*
Metzner, Rainer: Die Rezeption des Matthäusevangeliums im 1. Petrusbrief. 1995. *Volume II/74.*
Niebuhr, Karl-Wilhelm: Gesetz und Paränese. 1987. *Volume II/28.*
– Heidenapostel aus Israel. 1992. *Volume 62.*
Nissen, Andreas: Gott und der Nächste im antiken Judentum. 1974. *Volume 15.*
Noormann, Rolf: Irenäus als Paulusinterpret. 1994. *Volume II/66.*
Obermann, Andreas: Die christologische Erfüllung der Schrift im Johannesevangelium. 1996. *Volume II/83.*
Okure, Teresa: The Johannine Approach to Mission. 1988. *Volume II/31.*
Park, Eung Chun: The Mission Discourse in Matthew's Interpretation. 1995. *Volume II/81.*
Philonenko, Marc (Ed.): Le Trône de Dieu. 1993. *Volume 69.*
Pilhofer, Peter: Presbyteron Kreitton. 1990. *Volume II/39.*
– Philippi. Volume 1 1995. *Volume 87.*
Pöhlmann, Wolfgang: Der Verlorene Sohn und das Haus. 1993. *Volume 68.*
Probst, Hermann: Paulus und der Brief. 1991. *Volume II/45.*
Räisänen, Heikki: Paul and the Law. 1983, ²1987. *Volume 29.*
Rehkopf, Friedrich: Die lukanische Sonderquelle. 1959. *Volume 5.*
Rein, Matthias: Die Heilung des Blindgeborenen (Joh 9). 1995. *Volume II/73.*
Reinmuth, Eckart: Pseudo-Philo und Lukas. 1994. *Volume 74.*
Reiser, Marius: Syntax und Stil des Markusevangeliums. 1984. *Volume II/11.*
Richards, E. Randolph: The Secretary in the Letters of Paul. 1991. *Volume II/42.*
Riesner, Rainer: Jesus als Lehrer. 1981, ³1988. *Volume II/7.*
– Die Frühzeit des Apostels Paulus. 1994. *Volume 71.*
Rissi, Mathias: Die Theologie des Hebräerbriefs. 1987. *Volume 41.*
Röhser, Günter: Metaphorik und Personifikation der Sünde. 1987. *Volume II/25.*
Rose, Christian: Die Wolke der Zeugen. 1994. *Volume II/60.*
Rüger, Hans Peter: Die Weisheitsschrift aus der Kairoer Geniza. 1991. *Volume 53.*
Sänger, Dieter: Antikes Judentum und die Mysterien. 1980. *Volume II/5.*
– Die Verkündigung des Gekreuzigten und Israel. 1994. *Volume 75.*
Salzmann, Jorg Christian: Lehren und Ermahnen. 1994. *Volume II/59.*
Sandnes, Karl Olav: Paul - One of the Prophets? 1991. *Volume II/43.*
Sato, Migaku: Q und Prophetie. 1988. *Volume II/29.*
Schaper, Joachim: Eschatology in the Greek Psalter. 1995. *Volume II/76.*
Schimanowski, Gottfried: Weisheit und Messias. 1985. *Volume II/17.*
Schlichting, Günter: Ein jüdisches Leben Jesu. 1982. *Volume 24.*
Schnabel, Eckhard J.: Law and Wisdom from Ben Sira to Paul. 1985. *Volume II/16.*
Schutter, William L.: Hermeneutic and Composition in I Peter. 1989. *Volume II/30.*
Schwartz, Daniel R.: Studies in the Jewish Background of Christianity. 1992. *Volume 60.*
Schwemer, Anna Maria: see *Hengel, Martin*
Scott, James M.: Adoption as Sons of God. 1992. *Volume II/48.*
– Paul and the Nations. 1995. *Volume 84.*
Siegert, Folker: Drei hellenistisch-jüdische Predigten. Teil I 1980. *Volume 20* – Teil II 1992. *Volume 61.*
– Nag-Hammadi-Register. 1982. *Volume 26.*
– Argumentation bei Paulus. 1985. *Volume 34.*
– Philon von Alexandrien. 1988. *Volume 46.*
Simon, Marcel: Le christianisme antique et son contexte religieux I/II. 1981. *Volume 23.*
Snodgrass, Klyne: The Parable of the Wicked Tenants. 1983. *Volume 27.*

Wissenschaftliche Untersuchungen zum Neuen Testament

Söding, Thomas: see *Thüsing, Wilhelm.*
Sommer, Urs: Die Passionsgeschichte des Markusevangeliums. 1993. *Volume II/58.*
Spangenberg, Volker: Herrlichkeit des Neuen Bundes. 1993. *Volume II/55.*
Speyer, Wolfgang: Frühes Christentum im antiken Strahlungsfeld. 1989. *Volume 50.*
Stadelmann, Helge: Ben Sira als Schriftgelehrter. 1980. *Volume II/6.*
Strobel, August: Die Stunde der Wahrheit. 1980. *Volume 21.*
Stuckenbruck, Loren T.: Angel Veneration and Christology. 1995. *Volume II/70.*
Stuhlmacher, Peter (Ed.): Das Evangelium und die Evangelien. 1983. *Volume 28.*
Sung, Chong-Hyon: Vergebung der Sünden. 1993. *Volume II/57.*
Tajra, Harry W.: The Trial of St. Paul. 1989. *Volume II/35.*
– The Martyrdom of St.Paul. 1994. *Volume II/67.*
Theißen, Gerd: Studien zur Soziologie des Urchristentums. 1979, ³1989. *Volume 19.*
Thornton, Claus-Jürgen: Der Zeuge des Zeugen. 1991. *Volume 56.*
Thüsing, Wilhelm: Studien zur neutestamentlichen Theologie. Ed. by Thomas Söding. 1995. *Volume 82.*
Twelftree, Graham H.: Jesus the Exorcist. 1993. *Volume II/54.*
Visotzky, Burton L.: Fathers of the World. 1995. *Volume 80.*
Wagener, Ulrike: Die Ordnung des „Hauses Gottes". 1994. *Volume II/65.*
Wedderburn, A.J.M.: Baptism and Resurrection. 1987. *Volume 44.*
Wegner, Uwe: Der Hauptmann von Kafarnaum. 1985. *Volume II/14.*
Welck, Christian: Erzählte ‚Zeichen'. 1994. *Volume II/69.*
Wilson, Walter T.: Love without Pretense. 1991. *Volume II/46.*
Zimmermann, Alfred E.: Die urchristlichen Lehrer. 1984, ²1988. *Volume II/12.*

For a complete catalogue please write to
J.C.B. Mohr (Paul Siebeck), Postfach 2040, D-72010 Tübingen.

GENERAL THEOLOGICAL SEMINARY
NEW YORK